EXPLORING INTERPERSONAL DYNAMICS

RESEARCH IN OCCUPATIONAL STRESS AND WELL BEING

Series Editors: Pamela L. Perrewé and Daniel C. Ganster

RESEARCH IN OCCUPATIONAL STRESS AND WELL BEING
VOLUME 4

EXPLORING INTERPERSONAL DYNAMICS

EDITED BY

PAMELA L. PERREWÉ

Florida State University, USA

DANIEL C. GANSTER

University of Arkansas, USA

2005

ELSEVIER
JAI

Amsterdam – Boston – Heidelberg – London – New York – Oxford
Paris – San Diego – San Francisco – Singapore – Sydney – Tokyo

ELSEVIER B.V.
Radarweg 29
P.O. Box 211
1000 AE Amsterdam
The Netherlands

ELSEVIER Inc.
525 B Street, Suite 1900
San Diego
CA 92101-4495
USA

ELSEVIER Ltd
The Boulevard, Langford
Lane, Kidlington
Oxford OX5 1GB
UK

ELSEVIER Ltd
84 Theobalds Road
London
WC1X 8RR
UK

First edition 2005

British Library Cataloguing in Publication Data
A catalogue record is available from the British Library.

ISBN: 0-7623-1153-3
ISSN: 1479-3555 (Series)

⊗ The paper used in this publication meets the requirements of ANSI/NISO Z39.48-1992 (Permanence of Paper). Printed in The Netherlands.

Working together to grow
libraries in developing countries

www.elsevier.com | www.bookaid.org | www.sabre.org

ELSEVIER   BOOK AID
            International   Sabre Foundation

CONTENTS

OVERVIEW

The field of work stress continues to stimulate exciting and path-breaking research that examines how our work lives affect our health, happiness, and well being. Regardless of the specific discipline, we have the common goal of trying to understand how the workplace affects our mental and physical health. In spite of the diversity of questions, theories, and methodologies that characterize our research programs, we share the desire to explain and understand the dynamics of occupational stress and well being.

In our fourth volume of the annual series *Research in Occupational Stress and Well Being*, we offer a selection of papers that reflects the diversity of the field in regard to interpersonal relationships in organizations and its association with health and well being. The theme for this volume is *Exploring interpersonal dynamics*. Two of the chapters examine the central role that interpersonal relationships play in workplace aggression and violence. Several of the chapters in this volume reflect the opposite concern – namely, processes that promote happiness, positive experiences and mental and physical well being. Finally, several chapters examine strategies for improving workplace interpersonal dynamics and reducing job strain within an organization.

In the first chapter, Lori Anderson Snyder, Peter Chen, Paula Grubb, Rashaun Robets, Steven Sauter, and Naomi Swanson examine workplace aggression and violence in the workplace. They propose a conceptual model that examines the psychological and organizational mechanisms underlying aggression and violence. Finally, based on prior theoretical and empirical work, they offer a set of research propositions aimed at furthering our research in workplace aggression and violence. Michelle Duffy, Kristin Scott, and Anne O'Leary-Kelly continue with the workplace violence theme in their chapter on intimate partner violence. Using both ecological and work-family models, they argue that the effects of intimate partner violence negatively impact worker health and organizational well being.

The third chapter by Mark Tausig, Rudy Fenwick, Steven Sauter, Lawrence Murphy and Corina Graif examines the changing nature of work and quality of work life in the American labor force over the past 30 years. They discuss interesting trends as well as how these trends impact workers differentially. The fourth chapter by Toon Taris and Michiel Kompier is a review of employee learning behavior as a function of work characteristics. They use Demand–Control Theory and German Action Theory as the theoretical backdrop to their review.

The fifth chapter written by Mina Westman, Stevan Hobfoll, Shoshi Chen, Oranit Davidson, and Shavit Laski examine a number of occupational stress issues using Conservation of Resources (COR) Theory. Applications of COR theory to burnout, respite, and preventive intervention are emphasized in this work. Thomas Wright is the author of the next chapter on the role of happiness in organizational research. He examines the positive psychology movement and argues that the broaden-and-build theory of positive emotions is well suited for research to better understand happy and productive workers.

The next chapter, by Alicia Grandey and Glenda Fisk, examines the popular topic of emotional labor and display rules as they relate to occupational stress. They extend prior thinking by incorporating organizational justice research and develop a new individual variable they call service emotion rule fairness (SERF). The final chapter, by Angela Young, focuses on the role of mentoring in occupational stress and employee well being. She develops a conceptual model that specifies stress points to each aspect of the mentoring process. We believe volume four brings forth a wealth of new conceptual models and theoretical ideas that should inspire exciting new programs of research. The focus of these chapters is on the dynamics of interpersonal relationships in the diverse and growing field of work stress and well being. We look forward to continuing this series on occupational stress and well being with the goal of moving this important field of study forward.

Pamela L. Perrewé and Daniel C. Ganster
Series Editors

WORKPLACE AGGRESSION AND VIOLENCE AGAINST INDIVIDUALS AND ORGANIZATIONS: CAUSES, CONSEQUENCES, AND INTERVENTIONS

Lori Anderson Snyder, Peter Y. Chen, Paula L. Grubb, Rashaun K. Roberts, Steven L. Sauter and Naomi G. Swanson

ABSTRACT

This chapter examines aggression at work perpetrated by individual insiders by bringing together streams of research that have often been examined separately. A comparison of the similarities and differences of aggression toward individuals, such as verbal abuse or physical attack, and aggression toward organizations, such as embezzlement or work slowdowns, is shown to provide important insights about the causes and consequences of workplace aggression. We propose a comprehensive model based on the integration of prior theoretical treatments and empirical findings. The model attempts to offer a framework to systematically examine psychological and organizational mechanisms underlying workplace aggression, and to explain the reasons why workplace violence policies and procedures sometimes fail.

Exploring Interpersonal Dynamics
Research in Occupational Stress and Well Being, Volume 4, 1–65
Copyright © 2005 by Elsevier Ltd.
ISSN: 1479-3555/doi:10.1016/S1479-3555(04)04001-6

A set of research propositions is also suggested to assist in achieving this end in future research.

INTRODUCTION

Workplace aggression is a disturbingly prevalent problem in organizations. Studies in the realm of workplace aggression report that the majority of workers may experience an aggressive event that is mild in form, such as being talked to in an angry tone of voice or being given a dirty look (Glomb, 2002). In addition, approximately 8–10% of workers may experience more persistent bullying at work (Zapf et al., 2003) and 4% may experience physical attacks (Chappell & Di Martino, 1998). Incidents of aggression at work have severe and direct impacts on the victims, such as depression, anxiety, and psychosomatic symptoms (Einarsen & Mikkelsen, 2003; Mikkelsen & Einarsen, 2001). In addition, such incidents may have serious implications for the organization, in terms of lowered productivity, turnover, or litigation (Hoel et al., 2001; Rayner et al., 2002). Additional influences are likely observed on victims' co-workers, families, friends, communities, and society. Empirical evidence has shown that even those present in the environment who are not victims, but fear aggression, can be affected (Rogers & Kelloway, 1997; VandenBos & Bulatao, 1996). The purpose of this chapter is to review and summarize previous empirical findings in the framework of an integrated model of workplace aggression developed from diverse literature. A set of research propositions is also presented to highlight potential directions for future investigation. Specifically, we will first contrast diverse definitions of workplace aggression proposed in the literature, describe various models of workplace aggression and propose an integrated model which will guide the remaining reviews, classify different forms of aggressive behaviors, review the process of workplace aggression including possible antecedents, cognitive appraisal, emotions, and consequences of aggressive behaviors, and present a variety of preventive and reactive strategies.

DEFINITION OF WORKPLACE AGGRESSION

The definition of workplace aggression is a complex issue, which has been noted in numerous reviews (e.g. Keashley & Jagatic, 2003; Neuman & Baron, 1998; Robinson & Greenberg, 1998). Indeed, research under a variety of categorizations, such as delinquency (Hogan & Hogan, 1989), bullying/mobbing (Zapf et al., 2003), retaliatory behavior (Skarlicki & Folger, 1997), workplace incivility

(Andersson & Pearson, 1999), deviant behaviors (Robinson & Bennett, 1995), antisocial work behavior (Giacalone & Greenberg, 1997; O'Leary-Kelly et al., 2000), harassment (Brodsky, 1976), abuse (Richman et al., 1997), mistreatment (Tepper, 2000), sabotage (Giacalone & Rosenfeld, 1987), counterproductive behavior (Chen & Spector, 1992; Sackett & DeVore, 2003), and workplace aggression (Neuman & Baron, 1998), are relevant to understanding the causes and consequences of aggressive behavior in the workplace. Table 1 presents a spectrum of definitions used in previous research.

As seen in Table 1, definitions relevant to workplace aggression differ along several dimensions, including perpetrators, intended targets, actions, intentionality, and consequences (O'Leary-Kelly et al., 2000; Robinson & Greenberg, 1998). With regard to the range of perpetrators, some definitions such as Brodsky (1976) and O'Leary-Kelly et al. (1996) include both organizational insiders (individuals or groups employed by the organization e.g. employees, teams) and outsiders (e.g. customers, suppliers) as potential perpetrators, while many other definitions (e.g. Baron & Neuman, 1996; Giacalone & Rosenfeld, 1987) specify that only organizational insiders be included. Because the factors predicting aggression by organizational outsiders (e.g. working alone and/or late at night or handling money) are likely to be different from those related to aggression from insiders (e.g. injustice or interpersonal conflict), it is essential to examine them separately. In addition, it is possible for the perpetrator of aggression to be a work team, unit or entire organization, rather than an individual.[1] However, research on such incidents is rare and little understanding has been gained of such events. Thus, in the present chapter, we focus on acts perpetrated by individuals within an organization given that this phenomenon occurs daily across all organizations.

A second dimension on which definitions have differed is the focus on the intention of the action. The majority of definitions listed either implicitly (e.g. Brodsky, 1976; Keashley et al., 1994) or explicitly (e.g. Baron & Neuman, 1996; Namie & Namie, 2000; Spector & Fox, 2002; Vardi & Wiener, 1996) refer to the perpetrator's intention of harming others or the organization. However, a few definitions either do not mention intention (e.g. Dubois, 1979; Puffer, 1987) or specify that intention may be ambiguous (Andersson & Pearson, 1999). Our conception of workplace aggression includes only intentional actions, because although we believe unintentional actions may have important consequences, they are likely to occur through a different mechanism than intentional behaviors.

Definitions used in previous research have also varied as to the intended targets of the aggression. Of the definitions listed in Table 1, only O'Leary-Kelly et al. (1996) include targets outside the organization, such as customers or clients. Other definitions include only behaviors directed toward organizational insiders or the organization itself. Some definitions include only behaviors against

Table 1.   Sample of Construct Definitions Relevant to Workplace Aggression.

Harassment (Brodsky, 1976)	Repeated and persistent attempts by one person to torment, wear down, frustrate, or get a reaction from another. It is treatment that persistently provokes, pressures, frightens, intimidates, or otherwise discomforts another person
Abusive behavior (Keashley et al., 1994)	Hostile verbal and nonverbal behaviors (excluding physical contact) directed by one or more persons towards another that are aimed at undermining the other to ensure compliance
Workplace deviance (Robinson & Bennett, 1995)	Voluntary behavior that violates significant organizational norms and, in so doing, threatens the well being of the organization or its members, or both
Generalised workplace abuse (Richman et al., 1997)	Violations of workers' physical, psychological and/or professional integrities . . . nonsexual yet psychologically demeaning or discriminatory relationships
Workplace incivility (Andersson & Pearson, 1999)	Low-intensity deviant behavior with ambiguous intent to harm the target, in violation of workplace norms for mutual respect. Uncivil behaviors are characteristically rude and discourteous, displaying a lack of regard for others
Organizational misbehavior (Vardi & Wiener, 1996)	An intentional action by members of organizations that violates core organizational and/or social norms
Abusive supervision (Tepper, 2000)	Subordinates' perceptions of the extent to which supervisors engage in the sustained display of hostile verbal and nonverbal behaviors, excluding physical contact
Ethnic harassment (Schneider et al., 2000)	Threatening verbal conduct of exclusionary behavior that has an ethnic component and is directed at a target because of his or her ethnicity . . . behaviors that may be encountered on a daily basis and may contribute to a hostile environment, particularly for ethnic minorities
Workplace bullying (Namie & Namie, 2000)	The deliberate, hurtful and repeated mistreatment of a Target (the recipient) by a bully (the perpetrator) that is driven by the bully's desire to control the Target . . . encompasses all types of mistreatment at work . . . as long as the actions have the effect, intended or not, of hurting the Target, if felt by the Target
Bullying at work (Einarsen et al., 2003)	Harassing, offending, socially excluding someone or negatively affecting someone's work tasks. . . Has to occur repeatedly and regularly (e.g. weekly) and over a period of time (e.g. about six months) . . . A conflict cannot be called bullying if the incident is an isolated event or if two parties of approximately equal "strength" are in conflict

Table 1. (*Continued*)

Emotional abuse at work (Keashley, 2001)	Interactions between organizational members that are characterized by repeated hostile verbal and nonverbal, often nonphysical behaviors directed at a person(s) such that the target's sense of him/herself as a competent worker and person is negatively affected
Workplace violence (Jenkins, 1996)	Violent acts, including physical assaults and threat of assault, directed toward persons at work or on duty
Counterproductive behavior (Spector & Fox, 2002)	Voluntary, potentially destructive or detrimental acts that hurt colleagues or organizations
Organizational deliquency (Hogan & Hogan, 1989)	A syndrome, including counterproductive acts, such as theft, drug and alcohol abuse, lying, insubordination, vandalism, sabotage, absenteeism, and assaultive actions
Antisocial behavior (Giacalone & Greenberg, 1997)	Any behavior that brings harm, or is intended to bring harm to the organization, its employees, or its stakeholders
Workplace aggression (Baron & Neuman, 1996)	Efforts by individuals to harm others with whom they work, or have worked, or the organization in which they are currently, or were previously, employed. This harm-doing is intentional and includes psychological as well as physical injury
Workplace aggression (Geddes & Baron, 1997)	Intentional harm-doing (physical, emotional, and/or job related) directed toward other organizational members and/or the organization itself
Sabotage (Giacalone & Rosenfeld, 1987)	When people currently employed in an organization engage in intentional behaviors that effectively damage that organization's property, reputation, product, or service
Sabotage (Dubois, 1979)	Any act done by workers, individually or collectively, to the manufactured product or the machinery of production, that results in lowering the quantity or quality of production, whether temporarily or permanently
Organization-motivated aggression (O'Leary-Kelly et al., 1996)	Attempted injurious or destructive behavior initiated by either an organizational insider or outsider that is instigated by some factor in the organizational context
Organizational retaliation behaviors (Skarlicki & Folger, 1997)	Adverse reactions to perceived unfairness by disgruntled employees toward their employer

Table 1.   (*Continued*)

Employee deviance (Hollinger & Clark, 1983)	Acts by employees against the property of the organization ad the violations of norms regulating acceptable levels of production
Non-compliant behavior (Puffer, 1987)	Non-task behaviors that have negative organizational implications
Counterproductive workplace behaviors (Sackett & DeVore, 2003)	Any intentional behavior on the part of an organization member viewed by the organization as contrary to its legitimate interests

other individuals inside the organization (e.g. Andersson & Pearson, 1999; Einarsen et al., 2003; Keashley et al., 1994), while others focus on acts against the organization (e.g. Giacalone & Rosenfeld, 1987; Sackett & DeVore, 2003; Skarlicki & Folger, 1997). Another group of studies have proposed definitions including both aggression against individuals and organizations (e.g. Baron & Neuman, 1996; Geddes & Baron, 1997; Giacalone & Greenberg, 1997; Spector & Fox, 2002). It is also possible that aggressive acts are committed against bystanders or friends or family of the organizational insiders. Because these targets are not officially related to organizations and are relatively rare, we do not include them in our examination. Paralleling the reality observed in organizational behaviors, we endorse the inclusion of both aggression toward individuals and organizations, which may provide useful insights by comparing and contrasting the correlates and interventions relevant to each.

Several characteristics of aggressive actions have been delineated in previous definitions. These include the frequency or duration of the behavior (e.g. Einarsen et al., 2003), or a requirement that the action violates norms (e.g. Hollinger & Clark, 1983; Vardi & Wiener, 1996). In addition, some definitions specify particular types of actions, such as those including only verbal and nonverbal behaviors (e.g. Keashley, 2001; Keashley et al., 1994; Tepper, 2000). However, most definitions include both physical and nonphysical behaviors (e.g. Baron & Neuman, 1996; Jenkins, 1996; Richman et al., 1997). While the definition of aggression proposed by this chapter will not specify the frequency or duration of the behavior, or the norm-violating properties of the action, actions that are either physical or nonphysical will be considered.

Traditionally, most definitions have focused on negative outcomes of aggressive behaviors for the individuals or organizations who are targeted (e.g. Baron & Neuman, 1996; Giacalone & Rosenfeld, 1987; Namie & Namie, 2000;

Puffer, 1987; Sackett & DeVore, 2003). However, several researchers have recently proposed that the consequences of deviant or aggressive acts may have beneficial consequences to some parties in addition to or instead of harmful effects (Vardi & Wiener, 1996). Such actions may provide benefits for the perpetrator, such as stealing supplies, or for others, including the organization, such as overcharging customers (Robinson & Greenberg, 1998; Vardi & Wiener, 1996). Because of the small number of studies published in this area, and the greater need for organizations to address those actions with negative consequences, we have maintained the conventional focus on aggressive behaviors that result in potential negative outcomes for the target.

In sum, we follow the conceptualization formulated by Baron and Neuman (1998) and view workplace aggression as "efforts by individuals to harm others with whom they work, or have worked, or the organization in which they are currently, or were previously, employed" (Baron & Neuman, 1998, p. 395). This conception of workplace aggression is supported by O'Leary-Kelly et al.'s (2000) analysis of construct confusion in the realm of antisocial work behavior. Their analysis concludes that the construct of workplace aggression consists of those behaviors perpetrated by organizational insiders, directed toward organizational insiders or the organization itself, and caused by either organizational or non-organizational factors. In contrast, other constructs, such as organizational-motivated aggression, organizational retaliatory behavior, and employee deviance differ in their inclusion of perpetrators outside the organization or targets outside the organization.

MODELS OF WORKPLACE AGGRESSION

Several workplace aggression models have been proposed over past decades. In this section, we will briefly review these models, followed by an integrated model of workplace aggression, which will guide us in the subsequent reviews. The earliest workplace aggression model was proposed by Spector (1978), which is based on the frustration-aggression hypothesis (Dollard et al., 1939). Dollard et al. defined a frustration as "an interference with the occurrence of an instigated goal-response at its proper time in the behavior sequence" (p. 7). More specifically, frustration can be thought of as an impediment preventing the attainment of an expected achievement (Berkowitz, 1993). Based on the above views, strength of frustration is likely to be affected as a function of the importance of interfered goals to an individual, and the intensity and frequency of interference. If the interfered goals are not viewed as important and the hindrance is minor and occurs infrequently, an individual will experience little frustration or arousal. However, if the hindered goals are deemed important, or the interference occurs frequently or strongly, the individual will feel frustrated, which may trigger various types of aggressive behaviors.

Integrating Dollard et al.'s hypothesis with other empirical research (e.g. Buss, 1963; Spector et al., 1975), Spector proposed a model of organizational frustration that contains four main components: sources of organizational frustration that prevent people from achieving their goals (i.e. frustrators), which lead to emotional reactions varying from subtle to severe emotions such as irritation, frustration, and rage, followed by behavioral reactions ranging from withdrawal to workplace aggression. In his model, types of behavioral reactions are suggested to vary as a function of intensity of anger arousal and frustration as well as expected punishment.

The organization frustration model was subsequently expanded and revised (Spector, 1997) by integrating Lazarus' (1995) view pertaining to the role of cognitive appraisal in interpreting the external environment. As seen in Fig. 1, the model consists of six components: sources of frustration (i.e. frustrators), cognitive appraisal, frustrated emotions, behavioral reactions, factors moderating the relationships between frustrators and cognitive appraisal, and factors moderating the relationships between frustrated emotions and behavioral reactions. According to Spector, sources of frustration lead to frustrated emotions via cognitive appraisal, and frustrated emotion leads to various behavioral reactions.

Spector (1997) also suggested that there are important factors that affect how frustrators are interpreted and what behaviors persons would engage in. People interpret the sources of frustration at work differently contingent upon how important the blocked goals are to them, how frequent and severe the frustrators are, and the intention of the agents responsible for the frustrators. If the blocked goals

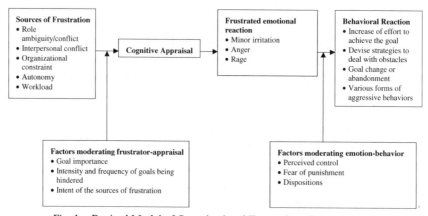

Fig. 1.   Revised Model of Organizational Frustration (Spector, 1997).

are perceived to be important, frustrators occur very frequently or are intense, or aggression agents intentionally create frustrators at work, people may have stronger emotional and behavioral reactions. However, frustrated emotion does not necessarily lead to various forms of aggressive behaviors. The types of behaviors people engage in may depend upon dispositions (Hogan & Hogan, 1989), goal changes or abandonment (Adams, 1963), consequence of behaviors (Skinner, 1953; Trevino & Youngblood, 1990), and degree of control over the environment (Allen & Greenberger, 1980; Seligman, 1975).

In addition to Spector's (1978, 1997) model of organizational frustration, O'Leary-Kelly et al. (1996) proposed a model of organization-motivated aggression, depicted in Fig. 2. The model consists of six elements: individual characteristics, organizational environment characteristics, organization-motivated aggression, organization-motivated violence, organizational action toward organization-motivated aggression, and organizational response toward organization-motivated violence and antecedent factors (i.e. individual, organizational, and environment characteristics). The model distinguishes attempted behaviors from negative outcome of the behaviors (conceptualized as organization-motivated violence). It also focuses on relatively severe behaviors that may have physical or verbal forms which can harm a person (physically or psychologically) or property.

O'Leary-Kelly et al.'s (1996) model is based on social learning theory (Bandura, 1973), which suggests that aggressive behaviors are learned via ways such as direct experience, observation, and imitation. If one observes, experiences, or imitates these behaviors (either verbal or physical form), and is reinforced by

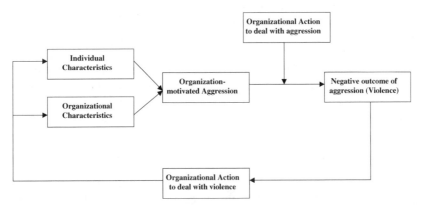

Fig. 2. Simplified Model of Organization-Motivated Aggression (O'Leary-Kelly et al., 1996).

positive outcomes (i.e. any forms of reward), this individual is more likely to engage in aggressive behaviors. These behaviors can also be regulated by the environmental cues. For instance, an organization with a contentious culture would encourage employees to engage in ruthless arguments and competition. As suggested in the model, destructive behaviors are instigated by individual and organizational characteristics, which may lead to negative outcomes. However, the presumed effects of aggressive behaviors are regulated by organizational actions, which may include providing incentives for constructive behaviors at work, changing individual characteristics (e.g. employee screening), or altering organizational characteristics (e.g. increasing security control system to prevent violent outcomes). The model further suggests that violent outcomes trigger organizations to take either reactive (set up security barriers) and/or proactive actions in altering individual and organization characteristics such as improvement of performance evaluation process, revision of personnel selection strategies, or alteration of termination policies.

Organization-motivated aggression in the above model is referred to as "*attempted* injurious or destructive behavior initiated by either an organizational insider or outsider that is instigated by some factor in the organizational context" (O'Leary-Kelly et al., 1996, p. 229; italics emphasized). The attempt explicitly implies one's motivation and intention to engage in aggressive behaviors. Hence, O'Leary-Kelly and her colleagues (O'Leary-Kelly et al., 2000) subsequently included these two factors in their antisocial behavior model.

Neuman and Baron (1998) also presented a model of workplace aggression, which overall is constituted of six components: social determinants, situational determinants, personal determinants, internal states, cognitive appraisal, and behaviors. Social determinants include unfair treatment, frustration-inducing events, diversity of workforce, and social norms; while situational determinants contain various changes in workplaces such as downsizing, layoffs, electronic monitoring, environmental conditions such as temperature, noise, etc. According to their model both social determinants and situational determinants would impact individuals' propensity to aggress, contingent upon dispositional factors, termed as personal determinants. The model further suggests that personal determinants will influence people's internal states (i.e. unpleasant feelings and hostile/aggressive thoughts), which in turn lead them to identify possible reasons of the internal states. The results of cognitive appraisal, then, lead people to consider various options to react.

Based on the above models as well as the bullying model, which emphasizes the victim's reaction (Einarsen et al., 2003), we propose an integrated model of workplace aggression as shown in Fig. 3. Similar to the models reviewed earlier, the model is built upon the interaction paradigm, which consists of the

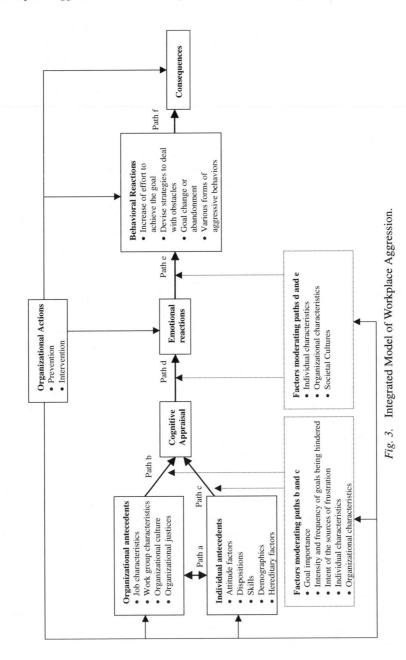

Fig. 3. Integrated Model of Workplace Aggression.

following nine components: organizational antecedents, individual antecedents, cognitive appraisal, emotional reactions, behavioral reactions, consequences toward individuals and organizations, organizational actions, factors moderating the relationships of cognitive appraisals with organizational and individual characteristics, and factors moderating the relationships between cognitive appraisal and emotional reactions as well as the relationship between emotional reactions and behavioral reactions.

Organizational antecedents are aspects of the work environment that can interfere with goal attainment. Antecedents relevant to the organization may include undesirable job characteristics (e.g. situational constraints), work-group characteristics (e.g. diversity), organizational culture (e.g. formal/informal rules or policies), and organizational justices (e.g. leadership styles). Individual antecedents include those factors specific to the perpetrator that increase the likelihood of aggressive acts. They may include attitudinal factors (e.g. job satisfaction or attitudes toward violence), dispositions, skills, personal background, and hereditary factors.

We further propose that both types of antecedents likely influence how one evaluates goal interference (as shown in paths B and C). In addition, the appraisal process varies for individuals, contingent upon factors such as the nature of the blocked goal, how and why the goals are hindered, and individual (e.g. hostility-attribution bias) and organizational (e.g. normative attitude toward sources of frustration) characteristics.

The model further suggests that results of cognitive appraisal may lead to frustrated emotions (path D), which may lead to various behaviors (path E) including aggressive behaviors. The strength of paths E and F may vary to a great degree, contingent upon individual and organizational characteristics, as well as societal cultures or norms. Although there are various behavioral options, we primarily focus on aggressive behaviors, which may affect other individuals and organizations (path F).

Aggressive behaviors generate consequences for both individuals and organizations. Individual consequences are the negative outcomes to the victim, which may be psychological (e.g. depression or suicide), physical (e.g. pain), or behavioral (e.g. performance decrement). Organizational consequences are the negative results that influence the organization. As a result of workplace aggression, organizations may suffer lowered production rates, turnover, or absenteeism. Finally, the model points out at which stages organizational preventions and interventions can be implemented. In the next few sections, we will review each component of the integrated model in detail. We will begin by discussing the central topic of this chapter, aggressive behavior, and then examine various antecedents, mechanisms, and consequences.

TAXONOMY OF AGGRESSIVE BEHAVIORS AT WORK

As proposed in the integrated model, frustrated emotions may lead to different behaviors, which may or may not be related to aggressive behaviors. Frustrated emotions may increase cognitive arousal so that individuals can display effort and develop strategies to accomplish the hindered goals under the existing constraints or to remove the hindering obstacles. Individuals may also change their expectations by changing or abandoning their goals. Furthermore, individuals can exhibit various forms of aggressive behaviors with different intensity. In this chapter, we focus only on forms of aggressive behaviors.

Several researchers have proposed taxonomies of aggressive workplace behavior in an effort to help categorize the myriad actions that may be observed (see Table 2). The most commonly used of these taxonomies is from Buss (1961), who proposed that aggressive behaviors may vary on three dimensions, physical-verbal, active-passive, and direct-indirect. Physical aggression includes pushing, attack, or hitting, while verbal aggression includes name calling, making threats, and cursing. Active actions require conducting some intentional behavior, such as making threats, while passive behaviors are marked by the absence of a behavior, such as failure to return a phone call. Direct actions are aimed specifically at the intended target, such as assault, while indirect actions are conducted through an intermediary or focus on a something the target values, such as harming one's reputation by spreading rumors (Neuman & Baron, 1997). While Buss's taxonomy has proven useful, it focuses only on interpersonal aggression, not aggression toward the organization. In contrast, several other categorization schemes have included behaviors that intend harm to the organization.

Robinson and Bennett's (1995) study proposed two dimensions on which deviant behaviors may vary: harming individuals to harming the organization and minor to serious. Results of a multidimensional scaling analysis place behaviors into one of four quadrants: *production deviance*, minor behaviors that harm the organization, such as leaving work early or wasting resources, *property deviance*, serious acts that harm the organization, such as sabotaging equipment or theft, *political deviance*, minor acts that cause interpersonal harm, such as gossiping or blaming others, and *personal aggression*, seriously harmful interpersonal acts, such as verbal abuse or physical threats. This conceptualization is useful in confirming that acts against the organization may be distinct from acts perpetrated against others.

The taxonomy proposed by Griffin et al. (1998) focuses on behaviors that harm the self, others, or the organization. Their scheme proposes two broader dimensions, behaviors injurious to human welfare and behaviors injurious to the organization, each with two sub-categories, behaviors that harm others and

Table 2.   Taxonomies of Workplace Aggression Proposed in Previous Research.

Buss (1961)	Focuses on interpersonal aggression Includes three dimensions: physical-verbal, active-passive, and direct-indirect Results in eight categories of aggression
Robinson and Bennett (1995)	Focuses on aggression toward others or the organization Composed of two continuous dimensions: harming individuals to harming the organization, minor to serious Results in four quadrants: *Production deviance*, minor behaviors that harm the organization, such as leaving work early or wasting resources; *Property deviance*, serious acts that harm the organization, such as sabotaging equipment or theft; *Political deviance*, minor acts that cause interpersonal harm, such as gossiping or blaming others; *Personal aggression*, seriously harmful interpersonal acts, such as verbal abuse or physical threats.
Griffin et al. (1998)	Focuses on aggression toward self, others, or the organization Includes two broad categories, each with two sub-categories Behaviors injurious to human welfare Behaviors that harm others, such as violence or harassment; Behaviors that harm self, such as smoking or unsafe actions. Behaviors injurious to the organization Behaviors that have specific costs, such as absenteeism or theft; Behaviors that have general costs, such as breach of confidentiality or sustained low performance.
O'Leary-Kelly et al. (1996)	Focuses on aggression against organization Includes three dimensions Perpetrator: organizational insider or outsider; Target: Within or outside organization; Target Specificity: Specific or nonspecific.
Dubois (1979)	Focuses on aggression against organization Includes three categories Destroying machinery or goods Stopping production Reducing amount of work done
Giacalone and Rosenfeld (1987)	Focuses on sabotage against organization Includes four dimensions Slowdowns Destructiveness Dishonesty Causing chaos

behaviors that harm self, and behaviors that have specific costs and behaviors that have general costs, respectively.

O'Leary-Kelly et al.'s (1996) taxonomy is relevant to organization-motivated aggression, and focuses on the perpetrator (organizational insider or outsider), target (within or outside organization), and specificity of target (specific or nonspecific). As discussed above, this categorization scheme is broader than the definition used by this chapter, because we will not examine actions perpetrated by organizational outsiders or those directed outside the organization. O'Leary-Kelly et al.'s conception of specificity of target can be seen as somewhat related to Buss's (1961) dimension of direct-indirect. However, these dimensions are not synonymous. The indirect-direct dimension assumes that the perpetrator will have a particular target in mind, and will act against that target using either direct or indirect means. In contrast, O'Leary-Kelly et al.'s dimension supposes that perpetrators have a particular target, and that their behavior may be directed specifically toward that target, or may be generalized to a broader target due to individual differences or due to the difficulty of direct attack on the target.

A scheme proposed by Dubois (1979) focuses only on aggression toward the organization, which includes: destroying machinery or goods, stopping production, and reducing amount of work done. This typology appears to be most relevant to manufacturing-type organizations, and may not include other acts against the organization, such as theft, deviant whistle-blowing, or misuse of employee benefits that may be present in other organizations. Giacalone and Rosenfeld's (1987) typology, which also focuses only on actions toward the organization, is somewhat more inclusive, covering slowdowns, destructiveness, dishonesty, and causing chaos. While these categorization schemes are helpful in organizing the specific behaviors against the organization, they are less useful in understanding the antecedents and correlates of actions against the organization, because behaviors within different categories may have similar antecedents and consequences.

In developing a taxonomy for use in this chapter, we sought to synthesize the previously proposed categorization schemes to develop one applicable to both aggression against individuals and against the organization. We conceptualize aggressive behaviors via three dimensions: acts against individuals-acts against the organization, direct-indirect, and active-passive (see Table 3). This typology results in eight categories, which we believe clearly combine the spectrum of aggressive acts and allow for examination of antecedents and correlates of behaviors within the same category.

For both aggressive acts against individuals and against the organization, the active-passive dimension represents the extent to which the perpetrator takes intentional action versus a lack of appropriate action. However, the meaning of the direct-indirect dimension is not as clear when applied to aggressive behavior

Table 3. Proposed Taxonomy of Workplace Aggression.

	Aggression Against Individual	Aggression Against Organization
Direct		
Active	Threats	Theft
	Assault	Destruction of property
	Glaring/dirty looks	Pull fire alarm
	Obscene gestures	Call in bomb threats
	Verbal abuse	Falsify timecard
	Insulting jokes	Altruistic deviance
	Criticize in front of others	Wasting resources
	Interrupt when speaking	Arson
	Belittle opinion	Embezzlement
Passive	Silent treatment	Work slowdowns
	Failure to return calls	Absenteeism
	Leave work area when target arrives	Leaving work early
		Taking excessive breaks
	Refuse work-related requests from the target	Pass on defective work
Indirect		
Active	Spread rumors	Deviant whistle-blowing
	Remove or hide needed resources	Breach of confidentiality
	Talk behind target's back	Alter company records
	Steal from others	Insult customers
	Assign work overload	Harm relationships with other organizations
	Assign unreasonable deadlines	Poison products
Passive	Failure to communicate information	Failure to deny false claims made against organization
	Failure to defend	
	Show up late for meetings	
	Failure to protect target's welfare	
	Failure to warn of impending danger	
	Deliberately exclude target	
	Cause others to delay on matters of importance to target	

against the organization. Because the organization is a collection of physical space and property, members, and ideas, it is not clear what would constitute a direct attack. Thus, we refer to O'Leary-Kelly et al.'s (1996) taxonomy, which includes behaviors that have specific costs and behaviors that have general costs to the organization. We believe that this distinction may be used to clarify the meaning of direct versus indirect actions against the organization. Those behaviors that result in costs that can be objectively measured can be considered more directly damaging to the organization than those actions that generate more ambiguous outcomes and thus whose costs cannot be accurately calculated.

Research on bullying, or mobbing as it is sometimes labeled in Europe, can be viewed as a pattern of aggressive behaviors against individuals. The types of incidents included in definitions of bullying are likely to cross the categories of behaviors we have identified for use in this chapter. For example, Zapf (1999, cited in Einarsen et al., 2003) identified five types of bullying: work-related bullying, social isolation, personal attacks, verbal threats, and spreading rumors. Because we prefer to examine the aggressive actions in the context of our taxonomy, we have identified studies that look at more specific bullying behaviors and will review the findings for each category.

While either individual or organizational antecedents may lead to aggression perpetrated against other individuals or the organization, there is reason to believe that perpetrators generally target aggressive behavior at the perceived cause of the situation (Spector & Fox, 2002). Thus, if organizational injustice or high workload create a stressful and frustrating situation, employees may be more likely to respond with aggression toward the organization. This line of thought leads to our first proposition:

Proposition 1. Organizational antecedents are more highly related to aggression against the organization than individual antecedents, while individual antecedents are more strongly related to aggression against individuals than organizational antecedents.

Aggressive Behaviors Against Individuals

In the next section we will review previous research on types of aggressive behaviors against individuals using two dimensions: direct-indirect and active-passive. Our discussion will include an examination of the various behaviors that fall into each category and frequency rates of each behavior.

Direct-Active
Direct-active actions against individuals include interpersonal actions perpetrated overtly toward the target, such as verbal harassment, dirty looks, criticism, threats, or physical attacks. Significant proportions of employees have experienced direct-active aggression via verbal methods. Glomb's (2002) study of a sample of

workers at manufacturing plants found that 25–82% of targets reported being talked to in angry tone of voice, sworn at, interrupted or cut off, threatened, etc. Mikkelsen and Einarsen's (2001) study of hospital and manufacturing workers in Denmark also showed that 11–32% of workers experienced verbal aggression in the form of insulting teasing, verbal abuse, ridicule, offensive remarks, etc. Salin's (2001) study of business professionals in Finland found that 3–19% reported being shouted at, persistently criticized, insulted, etc. Fox and Spector (1999) examined aggressive behaviors from the perpetrator's perspective using a sample composed of workers in a variety of jobs and found that 44% reported being nasty to a coworker and 14% admitted verbally abusing a coworker.

Targets may also experience nonverbal types of direct-active aggression. For example, workers in Glomb's (2002) study were asked to report on several nonverbal types of aggression. Dirty looks or angry facial expressions were reported by 66% of respondents, angry gestures by 32%, and hostile body language by 23%.

Many of the most severe acts of direct, active aggression are physical. Glomb's (2002) study found that 11% of respondents had an object thrown at them. In her study, no participants reported physical assault, but this behavior has been reported as more frequent in other studies. Of respondents in Mikkelsen and Einarsen's (2001) study, approximately 10% reported physical abuse or threats of physical abuse. A much smaller proportion (1%) reported physical abuse or threats in Salin (2001), and 2% experienced intimidating behavior.

Direct-active acts of aggression may also be directed toward targets' work efforts. Mikkelsen and Einarsen (2001) found that 7% of respondents reported threats of being fired or made redundant, 12% reported signals from others that they should quit, and 33% reported experiencing devaluation of work and efforts. Similarly, Salin (2001) found that 7% reported being transferred or moved against their will, 3% experienced threats of making work life difficult, and 3% reported signals from others that they should quit. Of respondents in Fox and Spector's (1999) study, 10–12% admitted purposefully interfering with someone else doing their job or blaming someone else for errors they had made themselves.

Direct-Passive

Direct-passive actions against individuals include behaviors perpetrated by one organizational insider against another through failure to act. Such actions include giving the target the silent treatment or leaving the work area when the target arrives.

Behaviors within the direct-passive category have been less studied than more active actions. This may be due to the difficulty of determining the intention of the behaviors. For example, when someone fails to return a phone call, this may be caused by aggressive intent or by simple forgetfulness. In Glomb's (2002) study, 39% of participants reported the experience of others avoiding him or her. Mikkelsen and Einarsen's (2001) study found that 27% of respondents reported silence or hostility in response to attempts to make conversation and 49% reported neglect of opinions by others. Of participants in Salin's (2001) study, 74% reported their opinions being ignored at least now and then. Other behaviors that would fall into the direct-passive category have not been specifically researched, including failure to return phone calls and refusal of work-related requests from the target.

Indirect-Active
Indirect-active behaviors against individuals are defined as overt behaviors manifested by an insider toward an individual target either through an intermediary or by attacking something that the target values. Such actions including stealing the target's belongings, spreading rumors, or assigning a work overload.

A sizable proportion of participants in Glomb's (2002) study reported experiencing indirect-active behaviors via verbal communication. Forty-six percent reported others making them look bad, 33% reported others talking behind their back, and 12% reported others telling superiors about their negative behavior. Of respondents in Mikkelsen and Einarsen's (2001) study, 45% experienced slander or rumors. Salin (2001) reported that 22% or participants indicated rumors or gossip had been spread about them. Of respondents in Fox and Spector's (1999) study, 17% indicated they had started or continued a harmful rumor about another person at work.

Indirect-active aggression may also be communicated through attacks on things that the target values. In Glomb (2002), 7% of workers reported someone sabotaging their work, and 7% reported someone damaging their property. Of participants in Salin (2001), 4% reported sabotage of work, and 1% reported economic or material damages. Fox and Spector's (1999) study found that 1% of respondents admitted stealing something from a coworker.

Acts of indirect-active aggression against individuals may also be directed at work tasks. In Mikkelsen and Einarsen's (2001) study, 10–36% of respondents reported being ordered to do work below their level of competence, being deprived of work responsibilities and tasks, or suffering exploitation. In Salin's (2001) study of business professionals, 17–69% reported being given impossible deadlines, ordered to do work below their level of competence, excessively monitored, etc. In addition, 13% reported pressure not to claim something to which they were entitled, such as holiday pay.

Indirect-Passive

Indirect-passive actions against individuals include those in which the perpetrator attacks the target through failure to protect something that the target values, such as excluding the target or failing to warn of impending danger. Similar to the direct-passive category, a lack of research has been conducted on indirect-passive behaviors. This is despite the fact that studies have indicated that indirect aggressive actions occur more frequently than direct actions (Baron & Neuman, 1998; Baron et al., 1999; Bjorkqvist et al., 1994).

Of respondents in Mikkelsen and Einarsen's (2001) study, 50% reported that someone had withheld information that affected their performance, and 25% reported social exclusion. Salin's (2001) study found that 62% reported others withholding information necessary for performance at least now and then, 22% reported being ignored or excluded at work, and 13% reported exclusion from social events. Fox and Spector (1999) found that 35% of respondents reported failing to help a coworker and 22% reported withholding information from a coworker. Several other behaviors that fall into the category of indirect-passive aggression have not been directly studied. These include failure to defend the target or their welfare, failure to warn of impending danger, showing up late for meetings, and causing others to delay on matters of importance to target.

Aggressive Behaviors Against the Organization

Aggressive actions toward the organization can take a variety of forms. We chose not to include the use of alcohol or drugs on the job as an act of organizational aggression. This is because it is often very difficult to determine the intent of this action. We believe that in many cases, such behavior is generated by addiction or attempts to reduce stress, with little thought for the ramification on the organization, thus bringing into question the intentionality of the action. We also will not focus on sexual harassment behavior, due to the adequate coverage of this topic in other research and the complexity of factors related to this behavior (e.g. Pryor & Fitzgerald, 2003).

Direct-Active

Direct-active actions against organizations are those behaviors perpetrated covertly against the organization that have costs that can be objectively calculated, including theft, arson, and wasting resources. Kamp and Brooks (1991) examined a sample of retail employees and a sample of student employees. Each sample included a considerable number who admitted stealing from their organization. In the retail sample, 30% admitted taking merchandise or property and 9% admitted taking money in the past six months. In the college sample, 44% admitted taking merchandise or property and 11% cash. Hollinger et al. (1992) examined a variety of counterproductive actions in the fast-food industry, and found that about 60% admitted involvement in theft of merchandise, supplies, food, or money over the past six months. Of respondents in Fox and Spector's (1999) study, 20% admitted stealing something from work and 7% reported trying to cheat their employer.

In Kamp and Brooks' (1991) study, 29% of retail workers and 30% of student workers reported giving unauthorized discounts. In a study of the fast-food industry, approximately 36% reported involvement in altruistic deviance such as using an employee discount for friends or selling merchandise at a reduced cost (Hollinger et al., 1992).

Fox and Spector (1999) found that 30% of respondents admitted to purposefully wasting materials or supplies at work. Of respondents in Fox and Spector's study, none admitted purposefully damaging a valuable piece of property or equipment, but 2% admitted purposefully dirtying the workplace or organizational property.

While direct-active acts against the organization are likely the most researched type of aggression against the organization, there are numerous behaviors that have not been specifically examined. These include destruction of property, pulling the fire alarm or calling in bomb threats, falsifying timecards, and arson.

Direct-Passive

Direct-passive actions against organizations are those that are perpetrated overtly against the organization, but whose costs are more difficult to assess. Such behaviors include absenteeism and passing on defective products. The intentionality of such behaviors may be debatable. However, it is clear that employees may use tactics such as coming in late and taking long breaks as retribution against the organization. A pattern of such behaviors is likely to at least express lack of consideration about the organization's well being, and at most represent a blatant attempt to harm the organization.

In general, there has been little research on direct-passive forms of aggression against the organization. Hollinger et al. (1992) combined several direct-passive actions (coming to work late, absenteeism, or intentionally sloppy work) into a composite measure titled production deviance, which was reported by approximately 82% of respondents in the fast-food industry. A large proportion of workers in Fox and Spector's (1999) study reported withdrawal behaviors in the form of coming to work late or coming back from lunch late (55%) and falsely calling in sick (51%). Using a sample from several industries, Hollinger and Clark (1983) found that between 56 and 72% took long lunches or breaks at least once during the course of a year. Between 20 and 42% of respondents took long lunch or breaks once a week or more frequently. Between 29 and 44% of respondents came to work late or left early during the course of a year. Between 4 and 11% came to work late or left early once a week or more frequently.

Direct-passive actions against the organization may also take the form of reduced production. Respondents in Fox and Spector's (1999) study also reported daydreaming rather than conducting work (82%), purposefully ignoring the boss (53%), and purposefully failing to work hard when there were tasks to be done (44%). Hollinger and Clark's (1983) study found that 1–2% did slow or sloppy work once per week or more frequently, and between 11 and 16% reported this behavior at least once during a year.

Indirect-Active

Indirect-active actions against organizations also cause measurable costs, but are perpetrated covertly. Actions within this category include deviant whistle-blowing, filing false legal claims, breach of confidentiality, altering company records, insulting customers, harming relationships with other organizations, and poisoning products. In general, indirect-active forms of organizational aggression have also been neglected in research. While case studies and examples of such behaviors have been described (Lind, 1997; Miceli & Near, 1997), there is not much empirical evidence on the frequency of such acts or the antecedents and correlates of the behavior. However, Fox and Spector (1999) found that a sizable proportion of respondents told others that their organization was an undesirable place to work (49%) and complained about insignificant things at work (82%).

Indirect-Passive

Indirect-passive actions against organizations are covertly perpetrated against the organization through failure to act, such as failure to defend the organization or failure to pass on important information to the organization. It is likely that indirect-passive methods of attack on the organization are rare. Examples of such actions have not been described in the literature, and it is difficult to generate potential behavioral examples. Acts in this category would include those that cause general costs to the organization and are caused by lack of action. One such behavior may be failure to deny false claims made against organization, such as ignoring rumors being spread in the community or refusing to testify in court about false allegations. A second example may be failure to communicate important information to the organization, such as warning of the development of a competitor's product or bringing attention to illegal acts by coworkers. Clearly, researchers have not adequately explored this category of aggressive behavior.

In the following sections, we will examine the organizational and individual antecedents that may play critical roles in triggering aggression. We propose that the antecedents of aggression toward individuals are likely quite different than aggression against organizations and hope that a comparison of the similarities and differences between the two may provide important insights about potentially overlooked causes and consequences.

ORGANIZATIONAL ANTECEDENTS

Previous research has examined several organizational antecedents that are presumed to prevent workers from accomplishing their goals, which inevitably increases frustration at work (Chen & Spector, 1992), which may in turn lead to various levels of aggression (Fox et al., 2001).

Job Characteristics

Meta-analytic results have revealed that organizational constraints and workload (Spector & Jex, 1998), and role ambiguity and conflict (Jackson & Schuler, 1985) relate with a variety of psychological strains (e.g. anxiety, frustration, anger) and physical symptoms. Arguably, these job characteristics are thus likely to be related to aggressive behaviors.

Organizational Constraints
Organizational constraints represent job circumstances that prevent employees from performing their work or achieving goals. These constraints include faulty equipment, incomplete or poor information, and interruptions by others. Empirically, organizational constraints have been related to poor performance, frustration, and job dissatisfaction (Peters & O'Connor, 1988). Storms and Spector (1987) and Chen and Spector (1992) reported a correlation with increased rates of aggressive behaviors including sabotage, and theft, as well as interpersonal aggression and hostility and complaints. Similar results were reported by Fox and Spector (1999), who found that constraints are related to organizational aggression, particularly acts of minor severity.

Role Ambiguity and Role Conflict
According to Kahn et al. (1964), a role is a set of potential expected work behaviors within a job. Role ambiguity refers to the degree to which required job information is unclear and unavailable to a worker. It could occur as a result of a simple miscommunication between a supervisor and a worker about the expected behaviors or goals. Similarly, role conflict refers to two or more competing job pressures for workers such that compliance with one pressure (e.g. increase

production rate) makes compliance with the other pressure (e.g. reduce stocks of raw materials) more difficult. Role conflict can also occur when two supervisors put pressure on a worker to complete two assignments that are in conflict with one another. Here, conflict emerges when both requests cannot be satisfactorily completed within a reasonable time frame. Mean correlations with frustration at work based on a meta-analysis (Spector, 1997) are 0.33 and 0.43 for role ambiguity and role conflict, respectively. Empirical findings also revealed that role conflict and ambiguity are associated with workplace aggression (Chen & Spector, 1992).

Workload

Workload refers to the amount and complexity of the work that employees are required to perform. This definition can be operationalized as the number of hours worked, the amount of time provided to complete work tasks (i.e. time pressure), or even the mental demands (i.e. role overload) of the work being performed (Spector & Jex, 1998). Spector (1997) reported the mean correlation between workload and experienced frustration as 0.49. Chen and Spector (1992) also found a positive relationship between workload and hostility and complaining.

Sense of Control

Sense of control refers to one's perception of how much he or she can control the outcomes of the work environment or the work environment itself and is regarded as a key determinant of an individual's effectiveness at work (Karasek, 1979; Karasek & Theorell, 1990). The proposal that lack of control may be related to aggression has been supported by Rentsch and Steel's (1998) study, which found job autonomy (a surrogate of sense of control) to be negatively correlated with absence from work. In addition, Klein et al. (1996) reported a relationship between lack of autonomy and self-reported sabotage.

> **Proposition 2.** High levels of frustrating job characteristics, including organizational constraints, role ambiguity and conflict, workload, and sense of control, are likely to be related to increased frustrated emotion, which may in turn trigger aggressive behaviors at work.

Organizational Justice

In addition to job characteristics, a second source of increased frustration and potential aggression may be the experience of injustice in the workplace. Organizational justice refers to perceptions of fairness in the workplace, which have been shown to play critical roles in triggering deviant or aggressive behaviors.

Research has consistently shown that judgments about what is fair, deserved, should have been, or just, are central to the attitudes individuals form on the job and behaviors they subsequently display. Justice researchers have typically distinguished between three types of justice: distributive justice, procedural justice, and interactional justice.

Distributive justice refers to the perceived fairness of the outcomes that one receives (Deutsch, 1985). For example, an annual bonus can be distributively fair or unfair. Distributive justice is an important predictor of reactions to particular outcomes, such as pay satisfaction (Folger & Konovsky, 1989; Sweeney et al., 1990). Procedural justice refers to the fairness of the process by which an allocation decision is determined (Lind & Tyler, 1988; Tyler & Lind, 1992). Research has shown that procedural fairness tends to be high when employees receive voice (Folger & Lewis, 1993), are treated consistently (VandenBos et al., 1996), and when decisions are based on accurate information (Greenberg, 1990).

Interactional justice comprises the third type of workplace fairness (Bies, 2001; Malatesta & Byrne, 1997; Sitkin & Bies, 1993; Skarlicki & Folger, 1997), which is generally viewed as having two related components (Brockner & Wiesenfeld, 1996; Tyler & Bies, 1990). The social component refers to the amount of dignity and respect that an individual receives (Bies & Moag, 1986). The informational component refers to the provision of adequate justifications for workplace decisions (Bobocel et al., 1997). Interactional justice tends to be a good predictor of how workers respond to their supervisors (e.g. Masterson et al., 2000). Recent meta-analyses further supported demonstrating differential relationships among the above forms of justice with various organizational outcomes (e.g. Colquitt et al., 2001).

Numerous situations in the workplace may lead to perceptions of injustice, including pay and promotion decisions, and performance appraisal. For example, Geddes and Baron (1997) examined managers' experience of aggression as a result of negative performance appraisals to subordinate. Nearly all managers (98%) reported experiencing some form of aggression as a response to providing negative performance feedback. Many of the actions verbally, passively, and/or indirectly targeted the supervisor, although behaviors relevant to lowered productivity or absenteeism also were reported.

Perceptions of unfair treatment may lead to aggression or violence through retaliation (Navran, 1991). Empirical research has shown that that reactions to the lack of justice (i.e. injustice) include workplace deviance (Fisher & Baron, 1982; Greenberg & Scott, 1996; Neuman & Baron, 1998) or retaliatory behaviors (Skarlicki & Folger, 1997). For instance, Bennett and Robinson (2000) found that deviant behaviors (e.g. playing a mean prank on someone at work, or littering the work environment) were negatively correlated with both procedural and interactional justice. Hollinger et al. (1992) found injustice to predict production deviance (e.g. coming to work late or doing intentionally sloppy work). Lehman and Simpson (1992) demonstrated that supervisory injustice predicted antagonistic work behaviors such as arguing with coworkers, disobeying supervisors, or spreading rumors. Baron et al. (1999) reported that unjust treatment from the supervisor was related to tendency to aggress both toward the supervisor and the organization. Greenberg (1990) found that pay inequity led to high theft levels because insufficient explanations were given for pay cuts.

Additional research has shown that procedural justice is negatively correlated with aggression against coworkers, subordinates, and supervisors, while distributive justice is negatively correlated with aggression against supervisors (Greenberg & Barling, 1999). Skarlicki and Folger (1997) found an interactive relationship between the types of justice and retaliatory behaviors. They detected a three-way interaction between distributive, procedural, and interactional justice such that an interaction between distributive and procedural justice occurred under conditions of low interactional justice and an interaction between distributive and interactional justice occurred under conditions of low procedural justice.

While justice has consistently been found to relate to aggressive behavior at work, it is not clear how the distributive, procedural, and interactional injustice may differentially lead to various types of aggressive actions against different targets. For instance, it is possible that distributive injustice, such as inequity in pay, tends to be related to retributive actions against the organization such as theft, while procedural or interactional injustice from the supervisor may be more highly correlated with interpersonal aggression against the supervisor. The likely underlying pattern of such behavior may be the direction of aggressive behavior toward those who are perceived as the cause of the injustice. This notion is supported by Spector and Fox (2002), who proposed that perpetrators generally target aggressive behavior at the perceived cause of the situation. However, because supervisors are seen both as individuals and as representatives of the organization (Levinson, 1965) injustice from supervisors may lead to aggressive behaviors against the supervisor personally or against the organization.

The lack of clear understanding about the relationship between types of justice and aggressive behavior may be due to the various measures used to assess justice and the focus of these measures. For instance, procedural justice may be assessed by asking about formal company policies, supervisor work assignments, or work group decision making, or by conducting various manipulations. The differing context in which justice is assessed is likely to affect the extent to which procedural justice is found to be related to behaviors such as theft, work slowdowns, and interpersonal aggression against coworkers or the supervisor.

Proposition 3. Based on previous research, it is expected that perceived injustice is related to frustrated emotions and perpetration of workplace aggression. The strength of correlation between types of justice and types of aggressive behaviors may differ depending on the magnitude of the injustice and the perceived cause of the situation. Interactions between the types of justice are likely in predicting frustrated emotions and aggressions, but the particular nature of this interaction may differ.

Workgroup Characteristics

The experience of frustration is often triggered by interaction with others, and workgroup characteristics provide several potential factors that may relate to increased levels of frustration and aggression. We will discuss three such factors, interpersonal conflict, demographic characteristics, and coworker attitudes and behaviors.

Interpersonal Conflict

Interpersonal conflict occurs daily in the workplace, ranging from disagreements to physical assaults between coworkers or with a supervisor. The conflict can be exhibited as overt behaviors such as making rude remarks or covert behaviors such as spreading rumors (Chen & Spector, 1992). Keenan and Newton (1984) have shown that interpersonal conflict in the workplace is one of the most frequently reported job stressors accompanied with frequent anger and annoyance. Mean correlation with experienced frustration was reported to be 0.37 (Spector, 1997). Cole et al. (1997) also found that work group harmony negatively predicted outcomes such as threats, harassment, and fear of becoming a victim of violence. Stress resulting from conflict with others at work is also related to sabotage, theft, interpersonal aggression, hostility and complaining (Chen & Spector, 1992).

Demographic Characteristics

It may be expected that diversity of the workgroup on characteristics such as gender and race or ethnicity would relate to aggression through conflict that may arise as a result of different norms or expectations of each group (Neuman & Baron, 1998). Nevertheless, Rogers (1983) notes that the hypothesis that prejudiced individuals will aggress toward the target of their prejudice has not been supported. Instead, individuals possessing greater prejudice are seen to express greater aggression than those who possess less prejudice, but against any available target, rather than against a particular group. Glomb (2002) also reported that 80% of victims of aggression indicated that the perpetrator was of the same ethnic group. However, these figures may reflect the ethnic composition of the workforce more than tendencies against interracial aggression.

In contrast to Glomb (2002) and Rogers (1983), Baron and Neuman (1996) reported a relationship between perceptions of increasing diversity and both experienced and witnessed aggression. In addition, Baron and Neuman (1998) reported a relationship between changes in the social environment of organizations (e.g. increased diversity or new affirmative action policies) and verbal aggression, obstructionism, and workplace aggression.

Coworker Attitudes and Behaviors

Deducing from four different theories, attraction-selection-attrition theory, social information processing theory, social learning theory, and social bonding theory, Sackett and DeVore (2003) predict how attitudes and behaviors of others at work would affect employees' behaviors. Attraction-selection-attrition theory (Schneider, 1987) proposes that elements of the organization, including culture and policies toward aggressive behaviors, may attract and choose certain applicants. Those who do not match the prevailing attitude about aggression will either not be hired or will eventually leave. Social information processing theory (Salancik & Pfeffer, 1978) predicts that employees will look to others in the work environment for information. The attitudes and behaviors expressed by others will then be integrated into the individual's beliefs about aggression and his or her likelihood of engaging in such behavior. In social learning theory (Bandura, 1973), it is expected that individuals will view the behavior of others and the resulting consequences as information to guide their own actions. Finally, Hirschi's social bonding theory (Hollinger, 1986), proposes that connection to non-deviant individuals in the organization will promote a low level of engagement in aggression due to attachment, commitment, and involvement.

Kamp and Brooks (1991) found support that coworker attitudes and behaviors relating to theft were related to respondent's level of abuse of employee discount, merchandise theft, and cash theft in both a retail and student employee sample. Hollinger and Clark (1983) also found support that the severity of coworker sanctions against deviant behavior significantly related to both production and property deviance, to a greater extent than formal sanctions. Robinson and O'Leary-Kelly (1998) examined existing workgroups to determine the effect of a group aggregate measure of counterproductivity on counterproductivity of target individuals. They reported a significant effect of the group aggregate on individual behavior, indicating that high levels of deviant behavior of the workgroup were related to increased counterproductive behavior by the target individual, implying that coworker behavior has a significant effect on individuals. However, the results of this study have been questioned by Sackett and DeVore (2003), who were unable to replicate Robinson and O-Leary-Kelly's results using the correlation matrix provided in the article.

The above review leads to our next proposition:

Proposition 4. Workgroup characteristics, in particular interpersonal conflict, high workgroup diversity, and lenient coworker attitudes and behaviors toward aggression, are related to higher prevalence of workplace aggression.

Organizational Culture

Several researchers (e.g. Tobin, 2001) have theorized that organizational structure, policies, and procedures may be related to aggressive behavior. Elements of organizational culture may lead to frustration through increased conflict, alienation, or routinization (Tobin, 2001).

Policies against Deviance

Hollinger and Clark (1983) reported that perceptions of the severity of formal sanctions against deviant behavior were significantly related to both production and property deviance. Cherrington and Cherrington (1985) reported that several aspects of organizational climate related to shrinkage (loss of goods of monetary value): lack of well-defined ethics code, lack of internal accounting controls, and punitive system of punishment with regard to theft. Fox and Spector (1999) found that perceptions about the risk of punishment were related to both minor and serious acts of organizational aggression. Kamp and Brooks (1991) similarly reported that perceptions of the severity of company theft policies were related to misuse of employee discount, merchandise theft, and cash theft in both a retail and student employee sample.

Organizational Changes

Few studies have examined the impact of changes in company policies and procedures on counterproductive behavior. Baron and Neuman (1998) examined relationships between workplace aggression and four types of organizational changes: cost cutting (e.g. downsizing and layoffs), organizational change (e.g. restructuring), social change (e.g. increased diversity), and job insecurity (e.g. increased use of part time help). They reported such changes tend to be related to verbal aggression, obstructionism, and workplace violence (e.g. physical attack and theft). Workplace violence was related to social changes and job insecurity, but not cost cutting or organizational change. In contrast, verbal aggression and obstructionism were related to all four types of change.

Proposition 5. Policies against deviance that are communicated and enforced are negatively related to acts of aggression at work. Organizational changes are positively related to frustrated emotions and acts of aggression at work.

INDIVIDUAL ANTECEDENTS

A variety of individual characteristics have been related to perpetration of aggression (e.g. Baron et al., 1999; Douglas & Martinko, 2001; Fox & Spector, 1999; Greenberg & Barling, 1999; Kamp & Brooks, 1991). These characteristics may be related to the experience or interpretation of frustration or the ability to cope with frustration, and thus be related to aggressive behaviors in the workplace.

Attitude Variables

Job Satisfaction
Research has consistently indicated that the level of job satisfaction is related to aggressive outcomes (e.g. Fox et al., 2001; Hollinger & Clark, 1979; Kamp & Brooks, 1991; Mangione & Quinn, 1975). Fox and Spector (1999) found that job satisfaction was related to both minor and serious acts of organizational aggression, with satisfaction being more closely correlated to less serious behaviors. Keashley et al. (1994) found that several types of satisfaction, including job satisfaction, coworker satisfaction, and supervisor satisfaction, were related to the number, impact, and frequency of abusive events at work. Hollinger and Clark (1983) reported that several dimensions of satisfaction were related to both property deviance and production deviance in retail, manufacturing, and hospital samples. It should be noted that the causal mechanism between job satisfaction and aggressive behaviors is not conceptually clear.

Attitudes toward Violence and Dishonesty
Several studies have indicated that accepting attitudes toward antisocial notions such as violence and dishonesty are related to negative organizational outcomes. It is expected that such attitudes allow perpetrators to justify their actions against the organization or individuals. Moretti (1986) found that condoning attitudes toward violence were related to frequency and dollar amount of damage to merchandise and property, dollar amount of supplies and material wasted, and counterproductive behaviors. In addition, condoning attitudes toward dishonesty were related to frequency and dollar amount of damage to merchandise

and property, counterproductive behaviors, and on-the-job waste. Kamp and Brooks (1991) also revealed that lenient personal attitudes toward theft were positively correlated with abuse of employee discount, merchandise theft, and cash theft in both a retail and student employee sample.

Proposition 6. Low job satisfaction and lenient attitudes toward violence and dishonesty are related to workplace aggression, particularly against supervisors or the organization.

Demographics

Empirical research has shown that some demographic variables are associated with aggression at work. Researchers (e.g. Hollinger & Clark, 1983) have proposed that deviance is most likely to be perpetrated by those who are "marginalized," meaning those who are most often young, temporary workers that are treated without appropriate fairness. Hollinger et al. (1992) supported the above speculation by revealing the relationship between age and deviance behaviors such as theft and altruistic deviance (e.g. using discounts inappropriately for friends, selling merchandise at a reduced price) among fast-food workers. Hollinger and Clark (1983) also found a significant relationship between age and theft, with younger workers committing greater levels of theft. A similar finding was reported by Baron et al. (1999), who found younger workers to report engaging in workplace aggression more frequently than older participants.

In addition to age, general findings suggest men tend to behave more aggressively than women (Eagly & Steffen, 1986). Hence, it would be expected that this would be true in the workplace as well. Perlow and Latham (1993) indeed found male workers were more likely to exhibit abusive behaviors against clients than female counterparts. Baron et al. (1999) also reported that male workers admitted engaging in workplace aggression more frequently than females.

The mechanisms explaining why aggressive behaviors are associated with young or male workers are not easy to pinpoint (Geen, 1998). Possible explanations may be attributed to physiological, psychological, organizational, or cultural factors. The type of job, structure of organizations, masculine culture in the workplace, length of tenure, status of positions, perceived fairness, sense of job and career security may be the underlying reasons why personal characteristics are associated with workplace aggression. For example, one empirical study has shown that tenure interacts with age and justice in predicting theft such that unfairness has a greater effect on both young and older workers with longer tenure (Hollinger et al., 1992).

Proposition 7. Young, male, and temporary workers are more likely to exhibit aggressive behaviors than their counterparts. These demographic factors may also interact in predicting aggression such that tenure interacts with other demographic variables.

Hereditary Factors

Roles of hereditary factors in predicting workplace aggression in particular have received little or no discussion, although the behavioral genetics literature has provided some affirmative evidence. A comparison of similarity between monozygotic twins and dizygotic twins has shown that the former pairs are more similar on self-report aggression than the latter pairs (Rushton et al., 1986). Affirmative findings about the role of heritability in aggression have also been reported over the past two decades by Tellegen et al. (1988), McGue et al. (1993), Rowe et al. (1999), as well as Eley et al. (2003). However, the conclusion of the amount of role heritability plays in aggression is not without challenge (Carmelli et al., 1988; Carmelli et al., 1990), which led Geen (1998) to propose that sufficient evidence to draw a strong conclusion has not yet emerged. Nevertheless, two recent meta-analytic studies (Beatty et al., 2002; Miles & Carey, 1997) estimated that up to 50% of variance in aggression may be attributed to hereditary factors, and the variance tends to vary as a function of the age of sample, aggression measures used, or self-reports vs. behavior observation. While the research cited does not relate specifically to workplace aggression, we believe that the findings of these studies imply that hereditary factors may be an important factor in aggressive behavior, and should be examined systematically in future research.

Individual Characteristics

Factorial structures about aggressive personality and delinquent personality have been proposed by Carpara and his colleagues (Caprara, 1986; Caprara et al., 1994, 1985) and Hogan and Hogan (1988). Hogan and Hogan suggested that four personality factors are related to aggressive behaviors, including hostility to rules, impulsiveness, sense of alienation, and social insensitivity. Similarly, Carpara and his colleagues outlined three aggressive dispositions based on factor analytic results: irritability, emotional susceptibility, and dissipation-rumination. In contrast to the above approaches to outlining aggression disposition or delinquent personality, we focus on individual characteristics that are not specifically constructed by factor analysis as aggression dispositions.

Negative Affectivity

Negative affectivity (NA) or neuroticism, one of the five factors that cluster personality traits (Big Five, Costa & McCrae, 1992a), refers to a pervasive disposition experiencing negative emotion states (Watson & Clark, 1984). NA tends to be associated with stress, distress, or health problems (Chen & Spector, 1991; Spector et al., 2000). A positive relationship between NA and self-reported incidence of workplace aggression either toward individuals or organizations has been documented in the literature (e.g. Aquino et al., 1999; Berkowitz, 1993; Douglas & Martinko, 2001; Fox & Spector, 1999; Fox et al., 2001; Skarlicki et al., 1999). However, Salgado's (2000) meta-analytic results reveal only a minuscule association with counterproductive behaviors operationalized as theft and disciplinary problems. This result may suggest that individual characteristics may be more strongly related to aggression toward individuals than toward organizations. In addition to the bivariate relationship between NA and workplace aggression, NA also functions as a moderator. Skarlicki et al. reported that the relationship between organizational justice and workplace aggression was stronger for people with high NA.

Based on diverse literature, there are five possible reasons why people with high NA might engage in frequent aggressive behaviors.

(1) People with high NA are hyper-responsive to the job environment so that they may have an exaggerated reaction to the environment, which may lead to confrontation or conflict (Spector et al., 2000).

(2) People high in NA tend to interpret the world in a negative view. As a result, they may be frustrated and react aggressively outward (Berkowitz, 1993; Geen, 1995).

(3) High NA individuals may have a tendency toward exhibiting hostile attribution styles (Martinko & Zellars, 1998), which may trigger aggressive incidents at work. It has been found that the NA disposition is generally positively related to various forms of anger expression (described below) with the size of correlations ranging from 0.34 to 0.50 in absolute values (Deffenbacher et al., 1996b).

(4) Preliminary studies have revealed that people high in NA are likely found in jobs with low autonomy (Spector et al., 1995) or low complexity (Spector et al., 1999). Although it is not clear why high NA workers are found in jobs with low autonomy, one available study has reported a significant relationship between

low autonomy and frequent aggressive behaviors toward organizations (Fox et al., 2001).

(5) Depue and Monroe (1986) suggested that high NA individuals may create or enact adverse circumstances. Consequently, they may frequently develop poor interpersonal relationships with colleagues at work (George, 1992).

Based on the above review, we present our next proposition:

Proposition 8. It is expected that NA is positively related to frustrated emotions and attempted aggressive behaviors.

Trait Anger

Individuals with high trait anger, a disposition of anger proneness, tend to experience anger frequently and intensely. They are angered easily while being provoked (Deffenbacher et al., 1996b), and experience anger for longer durations (Spielberger et al., 1988). Furthermore, high trait anger people lack the ability to control anger as well as express anger outward in constructive ways (Deffenbacher & Shepard, 1991). As a result, they often experience negative anger-related consequences such as physical symptoms or verbal or physical antagonism (Deffenbacher et al., 1996b) and instigate aggressive behavior (Berkowitz, 1993). Positive relationships between trait anger and workplace aggression were also recently reported (Douglas & Martinko, 2001; Penney & Spector, 2002).

Trait anger is related to how anger is expressed. However, the ways in which anger is expressed may be quite different even among people with high trait anger under different or the same circumstances (Deffenbacher et al., 1996a; Spielberger, 1988). As suggested by Deffenbacher et al., among three people high in trait anger, one may be calm, another may suppress angry feelings and withdraw into a bitter silence, and yet the third person may become agitated. Deffenbacher et al. have empirically shown that trait anger consistently predicts various aggressive behaviors. However, different tendencies to express anger (e.g. often slam door when one is angry) predict different aggressive behaviors (e.g. physical fights).

Proposition 9. It is expected that trait anger is positively related to frustrated emotions and aggressive behaviors.

Agreeableness

Agreeableness, one of the Big Five personality characteristics, is defined as expressing cooperative, sociable, and empathetic behaviors while interacting with people. Individuals high on agreeableness tend to avoid arguments and are less likely to show extreme emotion. In contrast, people with low agreeableness have a tendency to be antagonistic, temperamental, argumentative, and emotional.

Laursen et al. (2002) reported that, based on a prospective study, respondents rated as highly agreeable by teacher and peer at the age of 8 reported high compliance, constructivensss, and self-control as well as low aggression at the age of 33. Furthermore, they reported low alcoholism and high aggression inhibition at the age of 36. Costa et al. (1989) also found that agreeableness was related to low hostility and anger. Similar results were found that agreeableness was related to low antisocial personality disorder symptoms as well as aggression (Miller et al., 2003). Factor analysis evidence based on NEO Personality Inventory (Costa & McCrae, 1992b), Eysenck Personality Questionnaire (Eysenck & Eysenck, 1985), and Zuckerman–Kuhlman Personality Questionnaire further suggested that agreeableness and aggression-hostility should be formed into the same factor (Zuckerman et al., 1993).

There has been little research in the workplace context examining the relationship between agreeableness and various aggressive behaviors, with a few exceptions (Salgado, 2000; Skarlicki et al., 1999). Skarlicki et al. found no significant relationship between agreeableness and self-reported retaliatory behavior against the organization (e.g. intentional sabotage or damaging equipment). However, they did find evidence to support their hypothesis that a combination of low interactional and distributive justice predicts retaliatory behaviors for people with low agreeableness. Salgado reported a small mean correlation of 0.13 with counterproductive behaviors (operationalized as theft and disciplinary actions). The above results again may suggest that agreeableness is more related to aggression toward individuals, rather than organizations.

Proposition 10. A significant negative relationship exists between agreeableness and aggressive actions.

Conscientiousness
Conscientiousness, a disposition in the Big Five Model, refers to the extent to which individuals control their impulses and are self disciplined. People high in conscientiousness tend to be reliable and persevering (Costa & McCrae, 1992a). Lynam et al. (2003) presented post-prediction (10–12 years apart) and concurrent prediction evidence pertaining to the relationship between conscientiousness and antisocial behaviors in a group of young adults.

Past research has shown positive relationships between conscientiousness and job performance criteria (Barrick & Mount, 1991). However, little evidence has supported its relationships with aggressive behaviors. Similar to the findings about agreeableness and NA with aggression, Salgado (2000) also reported a small relationship between conscientiousness and counterproductive behaviors at work (operationalized as theft and disciplinary actions).

Proposition 11. People with high conscientiousness exhibit fewer aggressive behaviors.

Type A Behavior Pattern

Type A behavior pattern is viewed as "an action-emotion complex that can be observed in any person who is aggressively involved in a chronic, incessant struggle to achieve more and more in less and less time, and if required to do so, against the opposing efforts of other things or persons" (Friedman & Rosenman, 1974, p. 67). Type A people tend to react to stressors easily, and are characterized as challenged, competitive, uncontrollable, as well as ambitious, time urgent, impatient, and aggressive or hostile (Baron et al., 1985; Spence et al., 1987). Compared to Type B people, Type A people tend to have greater heart rate, diastolic blood pressure, and systolic blood pressure responses (Lyness, 1993). Lyness further revealed that Type A people exhibit greater cardiovascular reactivity in situations characterized as having socially aversive elements such as verbal harassment or criticism. Traditional Type A research has focused on health problems, job stress, and performance (Conte et al., 1998; Landy et al., 1991; Spence et al., 1989). Little research has examined its role in workplace aggression with one exception (i.e. Baron et al., 1999). Baron et al. found that Type A people tended to report greater frequency of committing hostility, obstructionism, and overt aggression, particularly against the supervisor.

In the past decades, researchers have proposed components of Type A Behavior Patterns, and predicted the components to have differential relationships with various outcomes. The components proposed have varied based on the researchers involved (Edwards et al., 1990; Ganster et al., 1991; Landy et al., 1991; Spence et al., 1987). Among the components of Type A behavior pattern, the component of hostility/anger or impatience-irritability (II), a behavioral tendency to express anger and hostility, is expected be a stronger predictor of workplace aggression than other components such as achievement striving, a tendency to take one's work seriously.

Proposition 12. Based on the above review, it is reasonable to expect that Type A people generally will react more strongly to experienced frustration, leading to stronger frustrated emotions and aggressive reactions compared to Type B people. In addition, people who exhibit the Type A behavior pattern with high hostility/anger or impatience-irritability will react more strongly than Type A with high achievement striving.

Locus of Control

Locus of control (LOC) is viewed as a generalized expectancy (Rotter, 1966) that an individual's behavior will lead to attainment of rewards or avoidance of punishment. People with a high degree of perceived control (i.e. an internal locus of control) believe that the consequences of their actions are mainly controlled by their own actions, and tend to use active or problem-focus coping strategies (Carver et al., 1989). Conversely, people with a low degree of perceived control (i.e. an external locus of control) believe that outcomes of their behaviors are primarily determined by outside forces, such as luck or timing. If one perceives the source of frustration and problems at work to be external, reactions are more likely to be in the form of acting out than expending effort to make changes to alter the circumstance.

Recent empirical findings have demonstrated the role of locus of control in predicting counterproductive behaviors at work (Storms & Spector, 1987), organizational aggression of both minor and serious severity (Fox & Spector, 1999), vandalistic activities on campus (DeMore et al., 1988), and client abuse incidents (Perlow & Latham, 1993). Specifically, people with high external locus of control tend to engage in more aggressive behaviors. Storms and Spector also reported a moderating role of locus of control, such that those with external locus of control are more likely to respond to organizational frustration with counterproductive behaviors, such as aggression, sabotage, withdrawal, and hostility and complaining.

The above review leads us to predict:

Proposition 13. Individuals with internal LOC experience fewer frustrated emotions and attempt fewer aggressive behaviors than those with external LOC. Specifically, externals will report higher frustrated emotions and aggressive behaviors than internals when experiencing goal interference, but the difference between them may not be observed when their goals are not hindered.

Narcissism
Narcissism is marked by inflated, grandiose, or unjustified favorable views of the self with a tendency to behave aggressively when one's ego is threatened. Narcissists tend to have an exaggerated or unstable high self-esteem, and extreme emotional investment to demonstrate or establish their superiority, even in the absence of superiority (Bushman & Baumeister, 1998). Furthermore, they tend to be preoccupied with fantasies of unlimited success, power, brilliance, beauty or ideal love. Narcissim can be viewed as a defense mechanism that inflates self-worth to protect oneself from unfavorable self-image, and accompanied negative emotions. As a result, they are sensitive to injury from criticism or defeat (Papps & O'Carroll, 1998), and tend to be hostile (Kernis et al., 1989), angry (McCann & Biaggio, 1989), engage aggressive behaviors (Bushman & Baumeister, 1998), counterproductive behaviors (Penney & Spector, 2002), and react to negative feedback with increasing hostility (Smalley & Stake, 1996).

Self-Esteem

Self-esteem is a value evaluation (positive or negative orientation) about oneself. It reflects an overall evaluation of one's worth or value. People with high self-esteem tend to possess positive self-regard, but not egotism (Rosenberg, 1986). Research relating self-esteem and aggression has revealed conflicting results (Papps & O'Carroll, 1998). Some researchers found low self-esteem people tend to be involved in aggression (Kirschner, 1992; Oates & Forrest, 1985), while others showed high self-esteem people tended to exhibit aggressive behaviors (Baumeister et al., 1993, 1996). Baumeister et al. (1996) pointed out that threatened egotism (an inflated self-esteem or narcissism) is a major contributor to violence in general.

The conflicting results may be largely attributed to the failure to distinguish between true high self-esteem and inflated high self-esteem reported in early literature. Papps and O'Carroll (1998) revealed that individuals high on both self-esteem and narcissism generally express more anger outwards than people high on self-esteem but low on narcissism. Bushman and Baumeister (1998) gave participants an opportunity to aggress against someone who had insulted them. It was found that the combination of narcissism and insult led to exceptionally high levels of aggression toward the source of the insult, while self-esteem did not seem play any role in aggression. This result further complicates the role of self-esteem, and supports the need for further investigation.

Proposition 14. An interaction between narcissism, self-esteem, and sources of frustration is expected in the prediction of frustrated emotions and aggressive behaviors. More specifically, while encountering sources of frustration, individuals high on both self-esteem and narcissism would express more frustrated emotions and engage more aggressive behaviors than those either high in self-esteem and low in narcissism, or low in self-esteem and high in narcissism.

Tolerance for Ambiguity

Tolerance for ambiguity refers to "the way an individual perceives and processes information about ambiguous situations or stimuli when confronted by an array of unfamiliar, complex, or incongruent clues" (Furnham & Ribchester, 1995, p. 179). People with low tolerance for ambiguity tend to hold a rigid, black-white view of life (Frenkel-Brunswik, 1948), are authoritative, dogmatic, and aggressive (Bochner, 1965), and sensitive to stress (Frone, 1990). Based on a meta-analytic study, Frone (1990) reported a positive relationship between role ambiguity and indices of strain that was substantially stronger among employees with low than high tolerance for ambiguity. O'Driscoll and Beehr (2000) also reported that need for clarity (i.e. intolerance for ambiguity) moderated the relationship of role ambiguity and conflict to both satisfaction and strain. Although Furnham and Ribchester concluded that this construct has been proven to be a highly predictive individual difference variable, no research has specifically examined the relationship between tolerance for ambiguity and aggression in the organizational setting, nor studied the moderating role of tolerance for ambiguity on the relationship between organizational risk factors and workplace aggression.

Proposition 15. High tolerance for ambiguity is negatively related to frustrated emotions and aggressive behaviors. In addition, we expect an interaction between sources of frustration and tolerance for ambiguity on emotions and aggressive behaviors. Specifically, the relationships of sources of frustration with emotion and aggressive behaviors are expected to be stronger among those with low tolerance for ambiguity than those with high tolerance for ambiguity.

Optimism

Similar to locus of control, dispositional optimism may also be viewed as a generalized expectancy. However, while the focus in locus of control is on whether individual actions are responsible for rewards or consequences, the emphasis in dispositional optimism is on whether people expect things to go their way, or not. It has been shown that optimism is a relatively stable disposition across time and settings (Scheier & Carver, 1992). Compared to pessimists, optimists tend to expect good things will happen to them (Scheier et al., 1994), adjust favorably to life transitions (Aspinwall & Taylor, 1992) or failure (Litt et al., 1992), engage in stressful events actively with problem-focused coping strategies (Hart & Hittner, 1995), and believe in prospects for future reemployment (Leana & Feldman, 1995). When encountering frustrating conditions that interfere with goal attainment, people with different expectations about favorable outcomes will undertake goal-related activities differently (Scheier & Carver, 1986). The optimists' expectation of successful outcomes likely energizes their efforts to attain the obstructed goals by utilizing problem-focused coping strategies such as quickly acting before things get out of hand. However, the unfavorable expectancies of a pessimist would lead to effort withdrawal, and may even result in disengagement from obtaining the disrupted goals (Scheier et al., 1986).

Proposition 16. Based on the above review, we expect that optimism is negatively related to frustrated emotions and aggressive behaviors. Furthermore, we expect that optimism moderates the relationship of organizational antecedents (e.g. downsizing) with frustrated emotions, as well as aggressive behaviors. Specifically, optimistic people react with less frustrated emotions and aggressive behaviors than their counterparts when sources of frustration appear.

Cognitive Moral Development

Theorists such as Kohlberg (1969) have proposed hierarchical stages of moral development. Kohlberg argued that people's moral capacity in judging selves and world progresses gradually while they gain more life experience and wisdom. At each stage of moral development, people have a particular approach to judge the external and internal world. For instance, at the stage of "preconventional" moral reasoning people are concerned more about obedience and external reward and punishment. While moving to the stage of "postconventional" moral reasoning, they will less be influenced by external environment and use more universal principles to make judgments. Kohlberg contended that only about 25% of people grow into the latter stage of postconventional moral reasoning, with the majority of adults staying at the stage of conventional moral reasoning. Empirical evidence has shown the relationship between moral development and both ethical decision-making behavior (Trevino, 1986; Trevino & Youngblood, 1990) and cheating (Malinowski & Smith, 1985). Few empirical studies about the relationship between moral development and aggression in the workplace exist, although the developmental (Hawley, 2003) and educational literature (e.g. Meyer et al., 2004) suggests its potential role in predicting workplace aggression

Proposition 17. A negative relationship between the stage of cognitive moral development and aggressive behaviors is expected. Furthermore, people high in moral development experience fewer frustrated emotions and engage in fewer aggressive behaviors than people low in moral development when their goals are hindered by the environment.

Communication Skills

It has been estimated that employees spend 60–80% of time engaging in some form of communication (Brownell, 1990), which may cause interpersonal conflict in work relationships. In a survey on MBA students, Reinshch and Shelby (1996) reported that 64% of MBA students felt challenged while interacting with people at work, 78% felt challenged when they engaged in face to face communication, and 47% felt challenged when two people were involved in communication. As pointed out earlier (Chen & Spector, 1992; Keenan & Newton, 1985), interpersonal conflict has been associated with anger and workplace aggression. Based on communication theories (e.g. Jablin & Sias, 2001) and conflict management theories (e.g. Thomas, 1992), individual differences in communication skill likely increase or minimize possible confrontations among people. Furthermore, emotional reactions toward conflict sources such as bursts of anger may also exacerbate the problem.

Examining various negotiation tactics such as convincing others, asking questions, giving information, summarizing, presenting alternatives, or using humor (Thomas, 1992), we expect that competent communication skills (e.g. listening skills, Cooper, 1997; or oral communication skills, Maes et al., 1997) could play critical roles in understanding workplace aggression between perpetrators and victims. Jablin and Sias conceptualized competence as it refers to the extent of abilities or resources that a communicator has available for use in the communication process. These abilities and resources include strategic communication knowledge about rules and norms, and communication capacities (e.g. put one self into others' shoes, listening, comprehending, etc.). Aquino (2000) has shown that people who employ avoiding styles tended to be victimized at work. According to Rahim (1983), people who utilize the avoiding style to deal with conflict generally have a low concern for their and others' interest and tend to ignore conflict.

Proposition 18. Deducing from the above review, we propose that competent communication skills are associated with a decrease of frustrated emotions and aggressive behaviors.

INTERACTION BETWEEN ORGANIZATIONAL AND INDIVIDUAL ANTECEDENTS

Based on the literature of job stress (e.g. self-selection, Spector et al., 2000) and climate (theory of Attraction-Selection-Attrition, Schneider, 1987), it is likely that these individual and organizational antecedents influence each other (as shown in path A in Fig. 3) and interact in predicting aggressive actions. We thus predict:

Proposition 19. Individual characteristics (e.g. trait anger, locus of control, agreeableness) interact with organizational frustrators (e.g. job characteristics, organizational injustice) in predicting experience of frustrated goals as well as perpetration of workplace aggression.

COGNITIVE APPRAISAL

Given our examination of individual and organizational antecedents of aggressive behavior, this section will explore the cognitive mechanisms by which such factors lead to exhibition of aggressive behavior. When individuals' goals are interfered with by organizational factors, the implications are interpreted or appraised by the individuals. Results of the cognitive appraisal play a critical role in forming one's view about the sources of frustration, which may in turn lead to different emotional and behavioral reactions (Lazarus, 1995; Lazarus & Folkman, 1984; Perrewé & Zellars, 1999). As pointed out by Lazarus and his colleagues, emotional reactions are likely the result of evaluating the environment, which is jointly affected by individual and organizational characteristics (path b and path c in Fig. 3). Geen (1998) and Zillmann (1988) suggested that emotional arousal is contingent upon both provocative objects as well as the interpretation of provocation, which leads to several potential mechanisms of cognitive appraisal.

(1) While encountering sources of frustration such as lack of resources to complete tasks, employees evaluate the significance of these factors. The evaluation of the interference may vary as a function of whether: (a) interfered goals have little or no personal significance; (b) the goals are infrequently blocked; (c) the interference is trivial; and (d) the interference is intentionally created (Spector, 1997).

(2) Appraisal process can also be influenced by one's subculture and past experience. The culture in which one is raised provides a frame of reference and values to interpret how and why goals are hindered, and personal past experience formulates one's beliefs and attitudes in the appraisal process.

(3) Peer group attitude may play an important role in interpreting the external world. Social information processing theory (Salancik & Pfeffer, 1978) further suggests that an individual's judgment about environment can be affected by peers' comments. For instance, if coworkers in the accounting department comment that meeting the pressing deadline to file taxes is part of the nature of the job and everyone should have the ability to cope with the challenge, this comment may likely influence whether one interprets the time pressure as "normal."

(4) Finally, some individual characteristics such as locus of control or narcissism may also influence how people interpret the sources of frustration. People who believe that they have personal control (internals), for instance, may view the interference of goals as less threatening than externals (Storms & Spector, 1987). In one study, Nasby et al. (1979) observed that institutionalized aggressive boys tended to attribute peers' benign intentions as hostile. This hostile-attribution bias may be the result of deficiency in cognitive skills while interpreting environmental cues (Geen, 1998).

EMOTIONAL REACTIONS

As suggested in the integrated model, different frustrated emotions may be elicited after people evaluate the sources of frustration. In general, the interfered goals that are deemed important may lead people to experience from "little or no anger through mild to moderate emotions such as irritation, annoyance, and frustration to highly emotionally charged states such as fury and rage" (Deffenbacher et al., 1996b; p. 131). Spector and colleagues (Chen & Spector, 1992; Fox & Spector, 1999; Spector, 1975, 1997; Spector & Jex, 1998; Storms & Spector, 1989) as well as Peters and O'Conner (1980) have consistently demonstrated the relationship between experienced frustration and sources of frustration. Furthermore, some of the above studies further revealed that frustration predicts aggressive behaviors at work including interpersonal aggression, sabotage, withdrawal, and hostility and complaining. Results of a meta-analysis by Spector (1997) revealed experienced frustration to be related to aggression, hostility, and sabotage with the uncorrected mean correlations of 0.25, 0.49, and 0.20, respectively.

POTENTIAL FACTORS INFLUENCING PATHS D AND E

As we earlier reviewed, cognitive appraisal may likely shape one's view about the sources of frustration. If the blocked goals are essential, or the interference occurs frequently or intensely, one would very likely feel frustrated emotions such as annoyance or anger. While experiencing the same source of frustration or threat (e.g. unfair treatment or layoff), people may express different levels of frustrated emotions or behavioral reactions. As depicted in Fig. 3, the variation of intensity of emotions or types of behaviors while experiencing the same provoking incidents can be attributed to individual and organizational characteristics, as well as societal cultures.

For instance, formal or informal reward (or punishment) policies or norms in organizations about appropriate emotional expression or behaviors can influence how individuals express their emotions or react while encountering obstacles. This hypothesis has been supported by recent empirical findings. Fox and Spector (1999) found that perceived risk of being punished while engaging in counterproductive behaviors was negatively related to both minor and serious acts of organizational aggression. Hollinger and Clark (1983) also reported that perceived formal sanctions against deviant behaviors were related to a decrease in both production and property deviance. Kamp and Brooks (1991) similarly showed that perception of company theft policies was related to decreased misuse of employee discount, merchandise theft, and cash theft in both a retail and student employee sample.

Ways of expressing emotions or judging others' emotions can also be affected by cultures, subcultures, or norms (Archer & McDaniel, 1995; Bagozzi et al., 1999; Eagly & Steffen, 1986; Matsumoto et al., 1999). Similarly, individual characteristics such as past experience (e.g. vicarious learning, Bandura, 1973) or dispositions (e.g. locus of control, Storms & Spector, 1987; Type A, Baron et al., 1999; Narcissism, Bushman & Baumeister, 1998) could likely influence emotional or behavioral reactions.

Although frustrated emotion may lead to various behaviors including aggression, the frustrated emotion such as anger does not a necesarily result in aggressive behavior (Averill, 1982). Averill revealed that angered people would react to instigators in both aggressive and nonaggressive forms of behavior. In our view, it is important to differentiate between various levels of frustrated emotions (e.g. frustration vs. rage) and various ways emotions are expressed behaviorally. Specifically, people with the same level anger or frustrated emotions may or may not express the same behavioral reactions. For instance, a person who feels annoyed because of her coworker's comment on her performance may suppress her anger and direct the frustrated emotions inward to herself. However, another individual who experiences the same annoyance may direct her anger outward to her coworker. The above example suggests the importance of understanding ways of expressing anger, which is an important but neglected topic in understanding and predicting aggressive behaviors. Hence, we will focus on the concept of anger expression in detail below.

In the anger literature, the concept of anger expression has received intensive attention (Deffenbacher et al., 1996a; Funkenstein et al., 1954; Gentry et al., 1972; Spielberger, 1988). Based on factor analytical findings, Spielberger (1988) described three forms of anger expression tendency: Anger-Out, Anger-In, and Anger-Control. Anger-Out is observed when people overtly express anger, typically in negative, aggressive ways (e.g. often make sarcastic remarks to others when one feels angry); Anger-In (anger suppression) is seen when people suppress their overt expression of anger (e.g. often keep things in when one is angry); and Anger-Control is shown when people are patient and calm when they are provoked (e.g. often control the temper when one is angry) (Deffenbacher et al., 1996a). According to Deffenbacher (personal communication, January 30, 2004), anger expression can be viewed as an individual tendency to express anger. Anger expression can be specific in certain contexts such as driving or work.

The main difference between Anger-In and Anger-Control is that the former inhibits aggressive responses, but maintains cognitive and emotional arousal, and the latter lessens aggressive tendency by lowering cognitive and emotional arousal. Empirical evidence demonstrates that Anger-Control and Anger-Out are strongly related to each other in the negative direction (e.g. -0.60 in Deffenbacher et al., 1996a). Both are strongly related to trait anger, with correlations ranging between absolute value of 0.5 and 0.6 (Defffenbacher et al., 1996a, b). However, the relationships of Anger-In with Anger-Control, Anger-Out, and trait anger are relatively small. Interestingly, suppression of one's anger is more strongly related to negative affectivity (or trait anxiety) than to trait anger. One of the striking findings about anger expression tendency is that only Anger-Out, instead of Anger-In and Anger-Control, predicts aggressive behaviors such as physical/verbal fights and property damage (Deffenbacher et al., 1996b). In contrast, Anger-In and Anger-Control only are associated with negative emotions (e.g. shame, embarrassment).

Based on the above review, trait anger is positively related to Anger-In and Anger-Out, and inversely related to anger control, and Anger-In is more strongly related to trait anxiety than trait anger. However, it is not clear why people have different ways to express their anger even though they experience similar frustrated emotions. There has been little research done to explore the underlying mechanisms of why people may have different anger expression under certain circumstance. It is our contention that the exploration should go beyond finding the correlates with individual dispositions. Norms and regulations in organizations and culture, as well as past experiences (reward or punishment, consequences of behaviors) and learned skills (e.g. communication skills, negotiations skills, conflict resolution skills) can also play important roles in anger expression following provocation.

CONSEQUENCES

Workplace aggression has been traditionally viewed as consequence of sources of frustration. Recently, some researchers have viewed aggression as a job stressor (e.g. Rogers & Kelloway, 1997), and applied job stress models (Beehr & Newman, 1978) to examine its relationships with psychological, physical, and behavioral outcomes.

Individual Outcomes

Psychological Outcomes
Several studies have looked at the relationship between experience of aggression and psychological well being. For instance, Kelloway and his colleagues (Rogers & Kelloway, 1997; Schat & Kelloway, 2000) reported a significant relationship of experience of violence with psychological well being and emotional well being. In a study of geriatric nurses, experience of psychological and physical aggression from the patients was related to emotional exhaustion and depersonalization

(Evers et al., 2001). Correlates with related variables such as anxiety and depression were also documented by Tepper (2000), Quine (2001), and Mikkelsen and Einarsen (2001).

The experience of workplace aggression has been related to job dissatisfaction of victims. Keashley et al. (1994) found the number of abusive events, and the frequency and impact of such events to be related to a decrease of job satisfaction, coworker satisfaction, supervision satisfaction, and satisfaction with work on the job. Furthermore, Tepper (2000) reported that abusive supervision was related to a decrease in job satisfaction and organizational commitment. Interestingly, the abusive supervision was positively related to continuance commitment (intention to remain with the organization due to need or costs of leaving), but negatively related to both normative commitment (dedication to the organization because of obligation) and affective commitment (emotional attachment to the organization). Quine (2001) also reported a similar finding that people had experienced bulling reported lower levels of job satisfaction than those who had not. In a study of teachers and school administrators, Sinclair et al. (2002) found that perceptions of property crimes and criminal activity by students were negatively related to job satisfaction, although student aggression was positively related to job satisfaction. The above unexpected findings coincided with the recent finding by Glomb (2002) that reported that most victims reported their level of satisfaction with the job, coworkers, or supervisor did not change due to the experience of aggression.

Correlates with post-traumatic stress disorder (PTSD) have also been revealed in several studies. PTSD includes reliving the traumatic event as well as related psychological or physical reactions, avoidance of the stimuli and numbing of emotions or interest, and high levels of arousal. A series of studies by European researchers have indicated that approximately 65–75% of victims of serious long-term bullying experience PTSD (Derogatis et al., 1974; Leymann & Gustafsson, 1996).

Physical Outcomes

Researchers across a variety of industries have found relationships between the experience of aggression and physical symptoms. Mikkelsen and Einarsen (2001) reported correlations between experience of aggression and psychosomatic symptoms ranging from 0.21 to 0.39 across three industries: hospital, manufacturing, and retail. Kelloway and his colleagues (Rogers & Kelloway, 1997; Schat & Kelloway, 2000) also revealed significant correlations between experience of violence and physical symptoms, although these relationships were not substantiated in a recent study by Schat and Kelloway (2003).

Organizational Outcomes

While a significant amount of research has examined the effects of workplace aggression on victims, the result for organizations has not been extensively investigated. Several implications for the organization are likely, however.

Job Performance
Fear of workplace violence is likely to cause cognitive distraction, which may result in negative effects on job performance (Barling, 1995; Barling & Boswell, 1995). A study by the Northwestern National Life cited in VandenBos and Bulatao (1996) supports this proposal. This study found that of those who experienced violence or harassment, 20% reported a lowering of productivity as compared to 1% of those who had not experienced aggression. Similarly, Glomb (2002) reported that 23% of aggression targets reported decreased job performance.

Absenteeism
Theoretically, it has been expected that the experience of workplace aggression would be related to increased levels of absence from work. It is anticipated that those witnessing or personally experiencing will experience higher levels of absenteeism because of the fear of aggression (Barling, 1996). Empirical results have provided weak support to this prediction, however. It appears that in most cases, bullying and aggression only explain 1–2% of absences (Kivimaki et al., 2000; Price Spratlan, 1995), although there is a significant cost to organizations (Hoel et al., 2001). With regard to actual sick leave, victims of bullying have been found to take significantly more sick days (Quine, 2001).

Turnover
Workplace aggression has also been linked with turnover intentions (Barling, 1996; Quine, 2001; Rogers & Kelloway, 1997; Sinclair et al., 2002). The Northwestern National Life study (VandenBos & Bulatao, 1996) supported the notion that experience of aggression is related to actual turnover. The study reported that 39% of those who experienced violence or harassment changed jobs over the course of a year, while 4% of those who had not experienced aggression changed jobs.

Organizational Actions

Over the past decade, numerous workplace aggression prevention or intervention strategies have been suggested in scientific reviews (e.g. Cabral, 1996; Collins &

Griffin, 1998; D'Addario, 1996; Hoel et al., 1999; Leymann, 1996; McClure, 1999; Neuman & Baron, 1997, 1998; O'Leary-Kelly et al., 1996; Pearson et al., 2000) and task force reports (e.g. United States Postal Service, Anfuso, 1994). As pointed out by Hoel et al. (1999), the prevention and intervention literature still primarily relies on propositions inferred from correlational findings and field experience. Specifically, there is a general paucity of empirical evidence on the effectiveness of various interventions and preventions for decreasing rates of workplace aggression.

It should be emphasized that there have been positive empirical findings about intervention or prevention programs developed with aims unrelated to workplace aggression. For instance, numerous personnel selection strategies were developed to select candidates who would exhibit desired job performance (Sackett & DeVore, 2003), organizational changes developed to increase self-efficacy (Parker, 1998), stress management interventions developed to cope with job stressors (Bellarosa, & Chen, 1997), electronic performance monitoring programs developed to prevent theft (Hovorka-Mead et al., 2002), leadership training generated to increase safety records (Zohar, 2002), or interventions to increase participation or control developed to improve justice perceptions (Spector, 1997). Hence, research findings about these programs would shed light on the organizational actions in aggression prevention and intervention.

Nevertheless, three main challenges arise when integrating past intervention findings to develop an effective organizational action plan. First, it is paramount to identify what types of interventions or preventive strategies should be implemented at a particular stage of the antecedent-behavior-consequence process. Certain strategies may only be effective under particular organizational climates or work situations. Second, "one-size-fits-all" approach has traditionally been the preferred choice in interventions (Bellarosa & Chen, 1997) due to practicality. However, this view tends to be overly simplistic and likely ignores the intricate interactions between person attributes and environmental characteristics. Third, we still lack of conclusive evidence pertaining to the causes of workplace aggression. Without having affirmative understanding, the current strategies tend to be reactive rather than preventive. We do not attempt to reiterate an exhaustive list of thoughtful strategies proposed by scholars and practitioners in this chapter, and readers can refer to the above references. Instead, in the remaining section we will focus on problems/challenges that might be encountered when using typically proposed strategies.

The most often suggested organization action plan is to implement organizational policies of workplace aggression. As shown in Fig. 3, the policies provide guidelines to handle or react to observed aggressive behaviors. The policies may contain termination or reprimand procedures (Anfuso, 1994), security monitoring (Stanton, 2000), or track aggressive incidents (Giacalone et al., 1997).

Parilla et al. (1988) reported that an anti-theft policy was strongly negatively correlated with lower theft rates. In the safety realm, corporate policies about safety seem to be associated with an increase of safety (Huang et al., in press).

In general, the enforcement of the policy is used to handle aggression occurrences, with the intention to reduce future occurrence, or even to change organizational norms or cultures. However, the policy pays relatively less attention to the possible causes or moderators described in Fig. 3. Furthermore, policies may be useless unless they are consistently applied (Boye & Jones, 1997).

Another suggested plan is to implement various intervention/prevention programs aimed at the organization and its agents (i.e. management), as well as individual employees. For instance, individual employees may receive training to improve social skill, conflict management, communication, emotion control, and stress management. The organization may implement training programs for their agents to improve leadership skills, administrative skills, organizational cultures, and perception of justice.

Selection of programs to prevent workplace aggression assumes that individual and organizational needs have already been identified. From a practical viewpoint, the program should be generated based on the needs of the organization. In reality, however, needs assessments are rarely practiced, at least in the U.S. (Bellarosa & Chen, 1997; Kraiger, 2003; Saari et al., 1988). The process of selecting a prevention/intervention program also assumes that one can ascertain the causes of workplace aggression, allowing a specific training program to be developed to minimize occurrence of the causes. However, these programs tend to be one-size-fits-all, and are almost never tailored to individual employees or organizations mainly for reasons of practicality. The problems associated with such programs are depicted in Fig. 3, which points out the complex interaction between organizational and individual antecedents as well as interaction with other factors, that effective prevention/intervention programs would need to address.

The third often suggested strategy focuses on personnel selection or screening. The evidence indicating that individual characteristics are related to workplace aggression implies the potential for reducing aggressive acts by preventing hiring of employees with extreme levels of certain characteristics. The most commonly proposed method of screening is pre-employment testing of characteristics such as integrity (Spector, 1997), hostile attributions, and negative affectivity (Neuman & Baron, 1997). Sackett et al. (1989) categorized such tests into two types: overt integrity tests and personality based tests. Research has shown that efforts to use personality testing to identify problematic employees may be effective (Hogan & Hogan, 1989; Ones et al., 1993). Neuman and Baron (1997) have also proposed that background checks may be useful in assessing applicant characteristics predictive of aggression.

Empirical findings indeed have supported the utility of selection approaches to effectively "filter" out people with high aggression tendency from the workforce. This approach is primarily developed based on choosing candidates with characteristics preferred by organizational values (Binning & Barrett, 1989). As outlined by the Schneider's (1987) attraction-selection-attrition model, the personality of employees in any organization is similar to that of the organization because they are attracted to, chosen by, and choose to stay in the organization. Accordingly, this approach may select candidates who tend to be aggressive or deviant under certain circumstances.

CONCLUSION

Generating effective interventions to address the pervasiveness of workplace aggression requires an understanding of the antecedents, cognitive appraisals, emotions, aggressive behaviors, consequences, and factors that may moderate the relationships among prior factors at both an individual and organizational level. Our review reveals that there are many types of aggressive behaviors that have not received much attention in previous research. In particular, very little examination of indirect actions (both active and passive) has occurred, despite the fact that such covert actions are more likely than more direct actions in work contexts (Baron & Neuman, 1998; Baron et al., 1999; Bjorkqvist et al., 1994). These behaviors may be affected by different mechanisms, and may have differential impacts on victimized individuals and organizations. However, this line of research requires innovative research paradigms in order to observe indirect behaviors.

The propositions in Table 4 summarize potential research questions that may provide fruitful directions for further research. In addition to hypotheses about particular variables, we propose that differential relationships between individual and organizational antecedents and behaviors against individuals and organizations may exist such that individual antecedents tend to be more strongly related to behaviors against individuals than organizational antecedents. Similarly, organizational antecedents may be more strongly related to aggression toward the organization than individual antecedents. We also propose that individual and organizational antecedents are likely to interact in predicting experienced frustration and perpetration of aggressive actions. If indeed, these hypotheses are supported, development of interventions may have clearer direction as to the antecedents that should be targeted to minimize aggressive actions.

Fig. 3 also presents a number of research hypotheses. First, the importance of the goal, frequency of frustration, and intent of agents who are responsible for

Table 4. Summary Listing of Research Propositions.

Proposition 1	Organizational antecedents are more highly related to aggression against the organization than individual antecedents, while individual antecedents are more strongly related to aggression against individuals than organizational antecedents.
Proposition 2	High levels of frustrating job characteristics, including organizational constraints, role ambiguity and conflict, workload, and sense of control, are likely to be related to increased frustrated emotion, which may in turn trigger aggressive behaviors at work.
Proposition 3	Based on previous research, it is expected that perceived injustice is related to frustrated emotions and perpetration of workplace aggression. The strength of correlation between types of justice and types of aggressive behaviors may differ depending on the magnitude of the injustice and the perceived cause of the situation. Interactions between the types of justice are likely in predicting frustrated emotions and aggressions, but the particular nature of this interaction may differ.
Proposition 4	Workgroup characteristics, in particular interpersonal conflict, high workgroup diversity, and lenient coworker attitudes and behaviors toward aggression, are related to higher prevalence of workplace aggression.
Proposition 5	Policies against deviance that are communicated and enforced are negatively related to acts of aggression at work. Organizational changes are positively related to frustrated emotions and acts of aggression at work.
Proposition 6	Low job satisfaction and lenient attitudes toward violence and dishonesty are related to workplace aggression, particularly against supervisors or the organization.
Proposition 7	Young, male, and temporary workers are more likely to exhibit aggressive behaviors than their counterparts. These demographic factors may also interact in predicting aggression such that tenure interacts with other demographic variables.
Proposition 8	It is expected that NA is positively related to frustrated emotions and attempted aggressive behaviors.
Proposition 9	It is expected that trait anger is positively related to frustrated emotions and attempted aggressive behaviors.
Proposition 10	A significant negative relationship exists between agreeableness and aggressive actions.
Proposition 11	People with high conscientiousness exhibit fewer aggressive behaviors.
Proposition 12	Based on the above review, it is reasonable to expect that Type A people generally will react more strongly to experienced frustration, leading to stronger frustrated emotions and aggressive reactions compared to Type B people. In addition, people who exhibit the Type A behavior pattern with high hostility/anger or impatience-irritability will react more strongly than Type A with high achievement striving.
Proposition 13	Individuals with internal LOC experience fewer frustrated emotions and attempt fewer aggressive behaviors than those with external LOC. Specifically, externals will report higher frustrated emotions and aggressive behaviors than internals when experiencing goal interference, but the difference between them may not be observed when their goals are not hindered.

Table 4.   (*Continued*)

Proposition 14	An interaction between narcissism, self-esteem, and sources of frustration is expected in the prediction of frustrated emotions and aggressive behaviors. More specifically, while encountering sources of frustration, individuals high on both self-esteem and narcissism would express more frustrated emotions and engage more aggressive behaviors than those either high in self-esteem and low in narcissism, or low in self-esteem and high in narcissism.
Proposition 15	High tolerance for ambiguity is negatively related to frustrated emotions and aggressive behaviors. In addition, we expect an interaction between sources of frustration and tolerance for ambiguity on emotions and aggressive behaviors. Specifically, the relationships of sources of frustration with emotion and aggressive behaviors are expected to be stronger among those with low tolerance for ambiguity than those with high tolerance for ambiguity.
Proposition 16	Optimism is negatively related to frustrated emotions and aggressive behaviors. Furthermore, we expect that optimism moderates the relationship of organizational antecedents (e.g. downsizing) with frustrated emotions, as well as aggressive behaviors. Specifically, optimistic people react with less frustrated emotions and aggressive behaviors than their counterparts when sources of frustration appear.
Proposition 17	A negative relationship between the stage of cognitive moral development and aggressive behaviors is expected. Furthermore, people high in moral development experience fewer frustrated emotions and engage in fewer aggressive behaviors than people low in moral development when their goals are hindered by the environment.
Proposition 18	Competent communication skills are associated with a decrease of frustrated emotions and aggressive behaviors.
Proposition 19	Individual characteristics (e.g. trait anger, locus of control, agreeableness) interact with organizational frustrators (e.g. job characteristics, organizational injustice) in predicting experience of frustrated goals as well as perpetration of workplace aggression, such that individual characteristics have a greater effect when frustrators are high than when they are low.

blocked goals interact with individual and organizational antecedents in predicting cognitive appraisal. Second, individual and organizational characteristics as well as other factors such as past experience would also likely interact with cognitive appraisal in predicting emotional reactions. Third, we also propose that these factors would interact with emotional reactions in predicting behavioral reactions. Each of these propositions may provide additional understanding of the process by which aggressive behaviors result and generate potentially effective methods of prevention or intervention strategies. Additional research and examination is clearly warranted for the mental process that results in aggressive actions. It is not clear why individuals express their anger differently when they experience similar frustration and emotions.

Because the factors resulting in aggressive behavior are not conclusive, organizations face many challenges in implementing effective organizational action to prevent workplace aggression. The effectiveness of selection procedures such as using integrity tests has received some support in predicting certain behaviors such as theft or disciplinary actions. However, these procedures have not proven the ability to predict indirect aggressive behaviors, which occur often in the work setting. In addition, job applicants may react negatively to such procedures because of their intrusive or covert nature. Furthermore, the characteristics viewed as predictive of aggression may reflect undesirable organizational values (i.e. contentious culture in sale department).

Policies against aggressive behavior may be useful in reacting to counterproductive behavior, but are not likely to prevent such actions because they do not alter the antecedent factors. Training programs intended to address workplace aggression must address the myriad of potential individual and organizational antecedents and their interactions. In addition, such programs should consider the particular circumstances of individual organizations.

We view workplace aggression policies and procedures as similar to traffic regulations. While clear guidelines regarding stopping at red lights have been communicated to society, some people still choose to run through the red lights occasionally or on a regular basis. This chapter is not meant to suggest that the establishment of workplace aggression policies is not necessary. Instead, we argue that the establishment of policies should not be viewed as a panacea for preventing and intervening workplace aggression. In our opinion, researchers and practitioners must address the need to investigate the mechanisms of why some individuals perpetrate aggression at work despite such policies and organizational efforts.

NOTE

1. We appreciate that Vaughan Bowie (University of Western Sydney) pointed out these possibilities.

ACKNOWLEDGMENTS

We like to express our appreciation to Vaughan Bowie, Bonnie Fisher, Lynn Jenkins, Steve Jex, and Pamela Perrewé (in an alphabetic order) for their comments in the early revisions. This chapter is prepared under the contract HHS-CDC #236983.

REFERENCES

Adams, J. S. (1963). Toward an understanding of inequity. *Journal of Abnormal and Social Psychology*, *67*, 422–436.

Allen, V. L., & Greenberger, D. B. (1980). Destruction and perceived control. In: A. Baum & J. E. Singer (Eds), *Applications of Personal Control* (Vol. 2, pp. 85–109). Hillsdale, NJ: Lawrence Erlbaum.

Andersson, L. M., & Pearson, C. M. (1999). Tit for tat? The spiraling effect of incivility in the workplace. *Academy of Management Review*, *24*, 452–471.

Anfuso, D. (1994). Deflecting workplace violence. *Personnel Journal*, *73*, 66–77.

Aquino, K. (2000). Structural and individual determinants of workplace victimization: The effects of hierarchical status and conflict management style. *Journal of Management*, *26*, 171–193.

Aquino, K., Grover, S. L., Bradfield, M. A., & David, G. (1999). The effects of negative affectivity, hierarchical status, and self-determination on workplace victimization. *Academy of Management Journal*, *42*, 260–272.

Archer, D., & McDaniel, P. (1995). Violence and gender: Differences and similarities across societies. In: R. B., Ruback & N. W. Weiner (Eds), *Interpersonal Violent Behaviors: Social and Cultural Aspects* (pp. 63–87). New York: Springer.

Aspinwall, L. G., & Taylor, S. E. (1992). Modeling cognitive adaptation: A longitudinal investigation of the impact of individual differences and coping on college adjustment and performance. *Journal of Personality & Social Psychology*, *63*, 989–1003.

Averill, J. R. (1982). *Aggression: A social learning analysis*. Englewood Cliffs, NJ: Prentice-Hall.

Bagozzi, R. P., Wong, N., & Yi, Y. (1999). The role of culture and gender in the relationship between positive and negative affect. *Cognition & Emotion*, *13*, 641–672.

Bandura, A. (1973). *Aggression: A social learning analysis*. Englewood Cliffs, NJ: Prentice-Hall.

Barling, J. (1995). The prediction, experience, and consequences of workplace violence. In: G. R. VandenBos & E. Q. Bulatao (Eds), *Violence on the Job*. Washington, DC: American Psychological Association.

Barling, J., & Boswell, R. (1995). Work performance and the achievement-strivings and impatience-irritability dimensions of Type A behavior. *Applied Psychology: An International Journal*, *44*, 143–153.

Baron, R. A., & Neuman, J. H. (1996). Workplace violence and workplace aggression: Evidence on their relative frequency and potential causes. *Aggressive Behavior*, *22*, 161–173.

Baron, R. A., & Neuman, J. H. (1998). Workplace aggression – The iceberg beneath the tip of workplace violence: Evidence on its forms, frequency, and targets. *Public Administration Quarterly*, *21*, 446–464.

Baron, R. A., Neuman, J. H., & Geddes, D. (1999). Social and personal determinants of workplace aggression: Evidence for the impact of perceived injustice and the Type A behavior pattern. *Aggressive Behavior*, *25*, 281–296.

Baron, R. A., Russell, G. W., & Arms, R. L. (1985). Negative ions and behavior: Impact on mood, memory, and aggression among Type A and Type B persons. *Journal of Personality & Social Psychology*, *48*, 746–754.

Barrick, M. R., & Mount, M. K. (1991). The Big Five personality dimensions and job performance: A meta-analysis. *Personnel Psychology*, *44*, 1–26.

Baumeister, R. F., Heatherton, T. F., & Tice, D. M. (1993). When ego threats lead to self-regulation failure: Negative consequences of high self-esteem. *Journal of Personality and Social Psychology*, *64*, 141–156.

Baumeister, R. F., Smart, L., & Boden, J. M. (1996). Relation of threatened egotism to violence and aggression: The dark side of high self-esteem. *Psychological Review, 103*, 5–33.

Beatty, M. J., Heisel, A. D., Hall, A. E., Levine, T. R., & La France, B. H. (2002). What can we learn from the study of twins about genetic and environmental influences on interpersonal affiliation, aggressiveness, and social anxiety?: A meta-analytic study. *Communication Monographs, 69*, 1–18.

Beehr, T. A., & Newman, J. E. (1978). Job stress, employee health, and organizational effectiveness: A facet analysis, model, and literature review. *Personnel Psychology, 31*, 665–699.

Bellarosa, C., & Chen, P. Y. (1997). The Effectiveness and practicality of occupational stress management interventions: A survey of subject matter expert opinions. *Journal of Occupational Health Psychology, 2*, 247–262.

Berkowitz, L. (1993). *Aggression: Its causes, consequences, and control.* Philadelphia: Temple University Press.

Bies, R. J. (2001). Interactional (in)justice: The sacred and the profane. In: J. Greenberg & R. Cropanzano (Eds), *Advance in Organizational Justice* (pp. 89–118). Lexington, MA: New Lexington Press.

Bies, R. J., & Moag, J. S. (1986). Interactional justice: Communication criteria of fairness. In: R. J. Lewicki, B. H. Sheppard & M. H. Bazerman (Eds), *Research on Negotiation in Organizations* (Vol. 1, pp. 43–55). Greenwich, CT: JAI Press.

Binning, J. F., & Barrett, G. V. (1989). Validity of personnel decisions: A conceptual analysis of the inferential and evidential bases. *Journal of Applied Psychology, 74*, 478–494.

Bjorkqvist, K. K., Osterman, K., & Lagerspetz, K. M. J. (1994). Sex differences in covert aggression among adults. *Aggressive Behavior, 20*, 27–33.

Bobocel, D. R., McCline, R. L., & Folger, R. (1997). Letting them down gently: Conceptual advances in explaining controversial organizational policies. In: C. L. Cooper & D. M. Rousseau (Eds), *Trends in Organizational Behavior* (Vol. 4, pp. 73–88). Sussex, England: Wiley.

Boye, M. W., & Jones, J. W. (1997). Organizational culture and employee counterproductivity. In: R. A. Giacalone & J. Greenberg (Eds), *Antisocial Behavior in Organizations* (pp. 172–184). Thousand Oaks, CA: Sage.

Brockner, J., & Wiesenfeld, B. M. (1996). An integrative framework for explaining reactions to decisions: Interactive effects of outcomes and procedures. *Psychological Bulletin, 120*, 189–208.

Brodsky, C. M. (1976). *The harassed worker.* Lexington, MA: D.C. Heath & Company.

Brownell, J. (1990). Perceptions of effective listeners: A management study. *Journal of Business Communication, 27*, 401–415.

Bushman, B. J., & Baumeister, R. F. (1998). Threatened egotism, narcissism, self-esteem, and direct and displaced aggression: Does self-love or self-hate lead to violence? *Journal of Personality & Social Psychology, 75*, 219–229.

Buss, A. H. (1961). *The psychology of aggression.* New York: Wiley.

Buss, A. H. (1963). Physical aggression in relation to different frustrations. *Journal of Abnormal and Social Psychology, 67*, 1–7.

Cabral, R. (1996). Policies for developing workplace violence prevention strategies. *Occupational Medicine, 11*, 303–314.

Caprara, G. V. (1986). Indicators of aggression: The Dissipation-Rumination Scale. *Personality and Individual Differences, 7*, 763–769.

Caprara, G. V., Barbaranelli, C., Pastorelli, C., & Perugini, M. (1994). Individual differences in the study of aggression. *Aggressive Behavior, 20*, 291–303.

Caprara, G. V., Cinanni, V., D'Imperio, G., Passerini, S., Renzi, P., & Travaglia, G. (1985). Indicators of impulsive aggression: Present status of research on irritability and emotional susceptibility Scales. *Personality and Individual Differences, 8*, 885–893.

Carmelli, D., Rosenman, R. H., & Swan, G. E. (1988). The Cook and Medley Hostility Scale: A heritability analysis in adult male twins. *Psychosomatic Medicine, 50*, 165–174.

Carmelli, D., Swan, G. E., & Rosenman, R. H. (1990). The Cook and Medley Hostility Scale revisited. *Journal of Social Behavior and Personality, 5*, 165–174.

Carver, Scheier, & Weintraub (1989). Assessing coping strategies: A theoretically based approach. *Journal of Personality & Social Psychology, 56*, 267–283.

Chappell, D., & Di Martino, V. (1998). *Violence at work.* Geneva: International Labour Office.

Chen, P. Y., & Spector, P. E. (1992). Relationships of work stressors with aggression, withdrawal, theft and substance use: An exploratory study. *Journal of Occupational and Organizational Psychology, 65*, 177–184.

Cherrington, D. J., & Cherrington, J. O. (1985). The climate of honesty in retail stores. In: W. Terris (Ed.), *Employee Theft: Research, Theory, and Applications* (pp. 51–65). Chicago: London House.

Cole, L. L., Grubb, P. L., Sauter, S. L., Swanson, N. G., & Lawless, P. (1997). Psychosocial correlates of harassment, threats and fear of violence in the workplace. *Scandinavian Journal of Work, Environment & Health, 23*, 450–457.

Collins, J. M., & Griffin, R. (1998). The psychology underlying counterproductive job performance, and practical tools for prediction. In: R. Griffin, A. O'Leary-Kelly & J. M. Collins (Eds), *Dysfunctional Work Behavior* (Vol. 1. pp. 219–242). JAI Press.

Colquitt, J. A., Conlon, D. E., Wesson, M. J., Porter, O. L. H., & Ng, K. Y. (2001). Justice at the millenium: A meta-analytic review of 25 years of organizational justice research. *Journal of Applied Psychology, 86*, 425–445.

Conte, J. M., Mathieu, J. E., & Landy, F. J. (1998). The nomological and predictive validity of time urgency. *Journal of Organizational Behavior, 19*, 1–13.

Cooper, L. O. (1997). Listening competency in the workplace: A model for training. *Business Communication Quarterly, 60*, 75–84.

Costa, P. T., & McCrae, R. R. (1992a). Four ways five factors are basic. *Personality and Individual Differences, 13*, 653–665.

Costa, P. T., & McCrae, R. R. (1992b). *NEO-PI-R: Revised NEO Personality Inventory (NEO-PI-R).* Odessa, FL: Psychological Assessment Resources.

Costa, P. T., Jr., McCrae, R. R., & Dembroski, T. M. (1989). Agreeableness versus antagonism: Explication of a potential risk factor for CHD. In: A. Siegman & T. M. Dembroski (Eds), *In Search of Coronary-Prone Behavior* (pp. 41–63). Hillsdale, NJ: Erlbaum.

D'Addario, F. J. (1996). Improving workplace security. *Occupational Medicine, 11*, 349–361.

Deffenbacher, J. L., Oetting, E. R., Lynch, R. S., & Morris, C. D. (1996a). The expression of anger and its consequences. *Behaviour Research and Therapy, 34*, 575–590.

Deffenbacher, J. L., Oetting, E. R., Thwaites, G. A., Lynch, R. S., Baker, D. A., Stark, R. S., Thacker, S., & Eiswerth-Cox, L. (1996b). State-trait anger theory and the utility of the Trait Anger Scale. *Journal of Counseling Psychology, 43*, 131–148.

Deffenbacher, J. L., & Shepard, J. (1991, April). Relationship of trait anger to anger expression style and trait anxiety. Paper presented at Rocky Mountain Psychological Association, Denver, Colorado.

DeMore, S. W., Fisher, J. D., & Baron, R. M. (1988). The equity-control model as a predictor of vandalism among college students. *Journal of Applied Social Psychology, 18*, 80–91.

Depue, R. A., & Monroe, S. M. (1986). Conceptualization and measurement of human disorder in life stress research: The problem of chronic disturbance. *Psychological Bulletin, 99*, 36–51.

Derogatis, L. R., Lipman, R. S., Rickels, K., Uhlenhuth, E. H., & Covi, L. (1974). The Hopkins Symptom Checklist (HSCL): A self-report symptom inventory. *Behavioral Science, 19*, 1–15.

Deutsch, M. (1985). *Distributive justice: A social-psychological perspective.* New Haven: Yale University Press.

Dollard, J., Doob, L. W., Miller, N. E., Mowrer, O. H., & Sears, R. R. (1939). *Frustration and aggression.* New Haven, CT: Yale University Press.

Douglas, S. C., & Martinko, M. J. (2001). Exploring the role of individual differences in the prediction of workplace aggression. *Journal of Applied Psychology, 86*, 547–559.

Dubois, P. (1979). *Sabotage in industry.* New York, NY: Penguin.

Eagly, A. H., & Steffen, V. J. (1986). Gender and aggressive behavior: A meta-analytic review of the social psychology literature. *Psychological Bulletin, 100*, 309–330.

Einarsen, S., Hoel, H., Zapf, D., & Cooper, C. L. (2003). The concept of bullying at work: The European tradition. In: S. Einarsen, H. Hoel, D. Zapf & C. L. Cooper (Eds), *Bullying and Emotional Abuse in the Workplace.* New York: Taylor & Francis.

Einarsen, S., & Mikkelsen, E. G. (2003). Individual effects of exposure to bullying at work. In: S. Einarsen, H. Hoel, D. Zapf & C. L. Cooper (Eds), *Bullying and Emotional Abuse in the Workplace.* New York: Taylor & Francis.

Eley, T. C., Lichtenstein, P., & Moffitt, T. E. (2003). A longitudinal behavioral genetic analysis of the etiology of aggressive and nonaggressive antisocial behavior. *Development & Psychopathology, 15*, 383–402.

Evers, W., Tomic, W., & Brouwers, A. (2001). Effects of aggressive behavior and perceived self-efficacy on burnout among staff of homes for the elderly. *Issues in Mental Health Nursing, 22*, 439–454.

Edwards, J. R., Baglioni, A. J., & Cooper, C. L. (1990). Examining the relationships among self-report measures of Type A behavior pattern: The effects of dimensionality, measurement error, and differences in underlying constructs. *Journal of Applied Psychology, 75*, 440–454.

Eysenck, H. J., & Eysenck, M. W. (1985). *Personality and individual differences: A natural science approach.* New York: Plenum Press.

Fisher, J. D., & Baron, R. M. (1982). An equity-based model of vandalism [Journal Article]. *Population & Environment: Behavioral & Social Issues, 5*, 182–200.

Folger, R., & Konovsky, M. A. (1989). Effects of procedural and distributive justice on reactions to pay raise decisions. *Academy of Management Journal, 32*, 115–130.

Folger, R., & Lewis, D. (1993). Self-appraisal and fairness in evaluations. In: R. Cropanzano (Ed.), *Justice in the Workplace: Approaching Fairness in Human Resource Management. Series in Applied Psychology* (pp. 107–131). Mahwah, NJ: Lawrence Erlbaum.

Fox, S., & Spector, P. E. (1999). A model of work frustration-aggression. *Journal of Organizational Behavior, 20*, 915–931.

Fox, S., Spector, P. E., & Miles, D. (2001). Counterproductive work behavior (CWB) in response to job stressors and organizational justice: Some mediator and moderator tests for autonomy and emotions. *Journal of Vocational Behavior, 59*, 291–309.

Frenkel-Brunswik, E. (1948). Tolerance towards ambiguity as a personality variable. *American Psychologist, 3*, 268.

Friedman, M., & Rosenman, R. (1974). *Type A behavior and your heart.* New York: Knopf.

Frone, M. R. (1990). Intolerance of ambiguity as a moderator of the occupational role stress-strain relationship: A meta-analysis. *Journal of Organizational Behavior, 11*, 309–320.

Funkenstein, D. H., King, S. H., & Droletter, M. E. (1954). The direction of anger during a laboratory stress-inducing situation. *Psychosomatic Medicine, 16*, 404–413.

Furnham, A., & Ribchester, T. (1995). Tolerance of ambiguity: A review of the concept, its measurement and applications. *Current Psychology: Developmental, Learning, Personality, Social, 14*, 179–199.

Geddes, D., & Baron, R. A. (1997). Workplace aggression as a consequence on negative performance feedback. *Management Communication Quarterly, 10*, 433–454.

Geen, R. G. (1995). Human aggression. In: A. Tesser (Ed.), *Advanced Social Psychology* (pp. 282–417). New York: McGraw-Hill.

Geen, R. G. (1998). Aggression and antisocial behavior. In: D. T. Gilbert, S. T. Fiske & G. Lindzey (Eds), *The Handbook of Social Psychology* (Vol. 2, pp. 317–356). New York, NY: McGraw-Hill.

Gentry, W. D., Chesney, A. P., Gary, H. G., Hall, R. P., & Harburg, E. (1972). Habitual anger coping styles: Effect on mean blood pressure and risk for essential hypertension. *Psychosomatic Medicine, 34*, 195–202.

George, J. M. (1992). The role of personality in organizational life: Issues and evidence. *Journal of Management, 18*, 185–213.

Giacalone, R. A., & Greenberg, J. (1997). *Antisocial Behavior in Organizations*. Thousand Oaks, CA: Sage.

Giacalone, R. A., Riordan, C. A., & Rosenfeld, P. (1997). Employee sabotage: Toward a practitioner-scholar understanding. In: R. A. Giacalone & J. Greenberg (Eds), *Antisocial Behavior in Organizations*. Thousand Oaks, CA: Sage.

Giacalone, R. A., & Rosenfeld, P. (1987). Reasons for employee sabotage in the workplace. *Journal of Business and Psychology, 1*, 367–378.

Glomb, T. M. (2002). Workplace anger and aggression: Informing conceptual models with data from specific encounters. *Journal of Occupational Health Psychology, 7*, 20–36.

Greenberg, J. (1990). Employee theft as a reaction to underpayment inequity: The hidden cost of pay cuts. *Journal of Applied Psychology, 75*, 561–568.

Greenberg, J., & Scott, K. S. (1996). Why do workers bite the hands that feed them? Employee theft as a social exchange process. In: B. M. Staw & L. L. Cummings (Eds), *Research in Organizational Behavior: An Annual Series of Analytical Essays and Critical Reviews* (Vol. 18, pp. 111–156).

Greenberg, L., & Barling, J. (1999). Predicting employee aggression against coworkers, subordinates and supervisors: The roles of person behaviors and perceived workplace factors. *Journal of Organizational Behavior, 20*, 897–913.

Griffin, R. W., O'Leary-Kelly, A., & Collins, J. (1998). Dysfunctional work behaviors in organizations. In: C. L. Cooper & D. M. Rousseau (Eds), *Trends in Organizational Behavior* (Vol. 5, pp. 65–82).

Hart, K. E., & Hittner, J. B. (1995). Optimism and pessimism: Associations to coping and anger-reactivity. *Personality and Individual Differences, 19*, 827–839.

Hawley, P. H. (2003). Strategies of control, aggression and morality in preschoolers: An evolutionary perspectives. *Journal of Experimental Child Psychology, 85*, 213–235.

Hoel, H., Einarsen, S., & Cooper, C. L. (2001). Organisational effects of bullying. In: S. Einarsen, H. Hoel, D. Zapf & C. L. Cooper (Eds), *Bullying and Emotional Abuse in the Workplace*. New York: Taylor & Francis.

Hoel, H., Rayner, C., & Cooper, C. L. (1999). Workplace bullying. In: C. L. Cooper & I. T. Robertson (Eds), *International Review of Industrial and Organizational Psychology* (Vol. 14, pp. 195–230). New York, NY: Wiley.

Hogan, J., & Hogan, R. (1989). How to measure employee reliability. *Journal of Applied Psychology, 74*, 273–279.

Hollinger, R. C. (1986). Acts against the workplace: Social bonding and employee deviance. *Deviant Behavior, 7*, 53–75.

Hollinger, R. D., & Clark, J. P. (1979). *Theft by employees*. Lexington, MA: Lexington Books.

Hollinger, R. C., Slora, K. B., & Terris, W. (1992). Deviance in the fast-food restaurant: Correlates of employee theft, altruism, and counterproductivity. *Deviant Behavior: An Interdisciplinary Journal, 13*, 155–184.

Hovorka-Mead, A. D., Ross, W. H., Jr., Whipple, T., & Renchin, M. B. (2002). Watching the detectives: Seasonal student employee reactions to electronic monitoring with and without advance notification. *Personnel Psychology, 55*, 329–362.

Huang, Y. E., Chen, P. Y., Krauss, A. D., & Rogers, D. A. (in press). Quality of the execution of corporate safety policies and employee safety outcomes: Assessing the moderating role of supervisor support and the mediating role of employee safety control. *Journal of Business and Psychology*.

Jackson, S. E., & Schuler, R. S. (1985). A meta-analysis and conceptual critique of research on role ambiguity and role conflict in work settings. *Organizational Behavior & Human Decision Processes, 36*, 16–78.

Jenkins, E. L. (1996). *Violence in the workplace: Risk factors and prevention strategies* (DHHS, NIOSH publication 96–100). Washington, DC: Government Printing Office.

Jablin, F. M., & Sias, P. M. (2001). Communication competency. In: F. M. Jablin & L. L. Putnam (Eds), *The New Handbook of Organizational Communication* (pp. 819–864). Newbury, CA: Sage.

Kahn, R. L., Wolfe, D. M., Quinn, R. P., Snoek, J. D., & Rosenthal, R. A. (1964). *Organizational stress: Studies in role conflict and ambiguity*. New York, NY: Wiley.

Kamp, J., & Brooks, P. (1991). Perceived organizational climate and employee counterpoductivity. *Journal of Business and Psychology, 5*, 447–458.

Karasek, R. A. (1979). Job demands, job decision latitude, and mental strain: Implications for job design. *Administrative Science Quarterly, 24*, 285–306.

Karasek, R. A., & Theorell, T. (1990). *Healthy work: Stress, productivity, and the reconstruction of working life*. New York: Basic Books.

Keashley, L. (2001). Interpersonal and systemic aspects of emotional abuse at work: The target's perspective. *Violence and Victims, 16*, 233–268.

Keashley, L., & Jagatic, K. (2003). By any other name: American perspective on workplace bullying. In: S. Einarsen, H. Hoel, D. Zapf, & C. L. Cooper (Eds), *Bullying and Emotional Abuse in the Workplace*. New York: Taylor & Francis.

Keashley, L., Trott, V., & MacLean, L. M. (1994). Abusive behavior in the workplace: A preliminary investigation. *Violence and Victims, 9*, 341–357.

Keenan, A., & Newton, T. J. (1984). Frustration in organizations: Relationships to role stress, climate, & psychological strain. *Journal of Occupational Psychology, 57*, 57–65.

Kernis, M. H., Grannemann, B. D., & Barclay, L. C. (1989). Stability and level of self-esteem as predictors of anger arousal and hostility. *Journal of Personality and Social Psychology, 56*, 1013–1022.

Kirschner, D. (1992). Understanding adoptees who kill: Dissociation, patricide, and the psychodynamics of adoption. *International Journal of Offender Therapy and Comparative Criminology, 36*, 323–333.

Kivimaki, K., Elovainio, M., & Vathera, J. (2000). Workplace bullying and sickness absence in hospital staff. *Occupational and Environmental Medicine, 57*, 600–656.

Klein, R. L., Leong, G. B., & Silvia, J. A. (1996). Employee sabotage in the workplace: A biopsychosocial model. *Journal of Forensic Sciences, 41*, 52–55.

Kohlberg, L. (1969). Stage and sequence: The cognitive–developmental approach to socialization. In: D. A. Goslin (Ed.), *Handbook of Socialization Theory and Research* (pp. 347–480). Chicago: Rand McNally.

Kraiger, K. (2003). Perspectives on training and development. In: W. C. Borman, D. R. Ilgen & R. J. Klimoski (Eds), *Handbook of Psychology: Vol. 12. Industrial and Organizational Psychology.* Hoboken, NJ: Wiley.

Landy, F. J., Rastegary, H., Thayer, J., & Colvin, C. (1991). Time urgency: The construct and its measurement. *Journal of Applied Psychology, 76*, 644–657.

Laursen, B., Pulkkinen, L., & Adams, R. (2002). The antecedents and correlates of agreeableness in adulthood. *Developmental Psychology, 38*, 591–603.

Lazarus, R. S. (1995). Psychological stress in the workplace. In: R. Crandall & P. L. Perrewé (Eds), *Occupational Stress* (pp. 3–14). Washington, DC: Taylor & Francis.

Lazarus, R. S., & Folkman, S. (1984). *Stress, appraisal, and coping.* New York, NY: Springer.

Lehman, W. E. K., & Simpson, D. D. (1992). Employee substance use and on-the-job behaviors. *Journal of Applied Psychology, 77*, 309–321.

Levinson, H. (1965). Reciprocation: The relationship between man and the organization. *Administrative Science Quarterly, 9*, 370–390.

Leymann, H. (1996). The content and development of mobbing at work. *European Journal of Work and Organizational Psychology, 5*, 165–184.

Leymann, H., & Gustafsson, A. (1996). Mobbing at work and the development of post-traumatic stress disorders. *European Journal of Work and Organizational Psychology, 5*, 251–275.

Lind, E. A. (1997). Litigation and claiming in organizations. In: R. A. Giacalone & J.Greenberg (Eds), *Antisocial Behavior in Organizations.* Thousand Oaks, CA: Sage.

Lind, E. A., & Tyler, T. R. (1988). *The social psychology of procedural justice.* New York, NY: Plenum Press.

Lynam, D. R., Leukefeld, C., & Clayton, R. R. (2003). The contribution of personality to the overlap between antisocial behavior and substance use/misuse. *Aggressive Behavior, 29*, 316–331.

Lyness, . S. A. (1993). Predictors of differences between Type A and B individuals in heart rate and blood pressure reactivity. *Psychological Bulletin, 114*, 266–295.

Maes, J. D., Weldy, T. G., & Icenogle, M. L. (1997). A managerial perspective: Oral communication competency is most important for business students in the workplace. *Journal of Business Communication, 34*, 67–80.

Malatesta, R. M., & Byrne, Z. S. (1997). The impact of formal and interactional procedures on organizational outcomes. Paper presented at the 12th annual conference of the Society for Industrial and Organizational Psychology, St. Lois, MO.

Malinowski, C. I., & Smith, C. P. (1985). Moral reasoning and moral conduct: An investigation prompted by Kohlberg's theory. *Journal of Personality and Social Psychology, 49*, 1016–1027.

Mangione, T. W., & Quinn, R. P. (1975). Job satisfaction, counterproductive behavior, and drug use at work. *Journal of Applied Psychology, 60*, 114–116.

Martinko, M. J., & Zellars, K. L. (1998). Toward a theory of workplace violence: A cognitive appraisal perspective. In: R. W. Griffin, A. O'Leary-Kelly & J. M. Collins (Eds), *Dysfunctional Behavior in Organizations: Violent and Deviant Behavior* (pp. 1–42). Stamford, CT: JAI Press.

Masterson, S. S., Lewis, K., Goldman, B. M., & Taylor, M. S. (2000). Integrating justice and social exchange: The differing effects of fair procedures and treatment on work relationships. *Academy of Management Journal, 43*, 738–748.

Matsumoto, D., Kasri, F., & Kooken, K. (1999). American-Japanese cultural differences in judgements of expression intensity and subjective experience. *Cognition & Emotion, 13*, 201–218.

McCann, J. T., & Biaggio, M. K. (1989). Narcissistic personality features and self reported anger. *Psychological Reports, 64*, 55–58.

McClure, L. F. (1999). Origins and incidence of workplace violence in North America. In: T. P. Gullotta & S. J. McElhaney (Eds), *Violence in Homes and Communities: Prevention, Intervention and Treatment* (pp. 71–99). Thousand Oaks, CA: Sage.

McGue, M., Bacon, S., & Lykken, D. T. (1993). Personality stability and change in early adulthood: A behavioral genetic analysis. *Developmental Psychology, 29*, 96–109.

Meyer, H. A., Astor, R. A., & Behre, W. J. (2004). Teachers' reasoning about school fights, contexts, and gender: An expanded cognitive developmental domain approach. *Aggression & Violent Behavior, 9*, 45–74.

Miceli, M. P., & Near, J. P. (1997). Whistle-blowing as antisocial behavior. In: R. A. Giacalone & J.Greenberg (Eds), *Antisocial Behavior in Organizations*. Thousand Oaks, CA: Sage.

Mikkelsen, E. G., & Einarsen, S. (2001). Bullying in danish work-life: Prevalence and health correlates. *European Journal of Work and Organiational Psychology, 10*, 393–413.

Miles, D. R., & Carey, G. (1997). Genetic and environmental architecture on human aggression. *Journal of Personality & Social Psychology, 72*, 207–217.

Miller, J. D., Lynam, D., & Leukefeld, C. (2003). Examining antisocial behavior through the lens of the five factor model of personality. *Aggressive Behavior, 29*, 497–514.

Moretti, D. M. (1986). The prediction of employee counterproductivity through attitude assessment. *Journal of Business and Psychology, 1*, 134–147.

Namie, G., & Namie, R. (2000). *The bully at work: What you can do to stop the hurt and reclaim your dignity on the job*. Naperville, IL: Sourcebooks.

Nasby, W., Hayden, B., & DePaulo, B. M. (1979). Attributional bias among aggressive boys to interpret unambiguous social stimuli as displays of hostility. *Journal of Abnormal Psychology, 89*, 459–468.

Navran, F. J. (1991). Silent saboteurs. *Executive Excellence, 8*, 11–13.

Neuman, J. H., & Baron, R. A. (1997). Aggression in the workplace. In: R. A. Giacalone & J. Greenberg (Eds), *Antisocial Behavior in Organizations* (pp. 37–65). Thousand Oaks, CA: Sage.

Neuman, J. H., & Baron, R. A. (1998). Workplace violence and workplace aggression: Evidence concerning specific forms, potential causes, and preferred targets. *Journal of Management, 24*, 391–419.

O'Driscoll, M. P., & Beehr, T. A. (2000). Moderating effects of perceived control and need for clarity on the relationship between role stressors and employee affective reactions. *Journal of Social Psychology, 140*, 151–159.

O'Leary-Kelly, A. M., Duffy, M. K., & Griffin, R. W. (2000). Construct confusion in the study of antisocial work behavior. *Research in Personnel and Human Resources Management* (Vol. 18, pp. 275–303). JAI Press.

O'Leary-Kelly, A. M., Griffin, R. W., & Glew, D. J. (1996). Organization-motivated aggression: A research framework. *Academy of Management Review, 21*, 225–253.

Oates, R. K., & Forrest, D. (1985). Self-esteem and early background of abusive mothers. *Child Abuse and Neglect, 9*, 89–93.

Ones, D. S., Viswesvararan, C., & Schmidt, F. (1993). Comprehensive meta-analysis of integrity test validities: Findings and implications for personnel selection and theories of job performance. *Journal of Applied Psychology Monograph, 78*, 679–703.

Papps, B. P., & O'Carroll, R. E. (1998). Extremes of self-esteem and narcissism and the experience and expression of anger and aggression. *Aggressive Behavior, 24*, 421–438.

Parker, S. K. (1998). Enhancing role breadth self-efficacy: The roles of job enrichment and other organizational interventions. *Journal of Applied Psychology, 83*, 835–852.

Parilla, P. F., Hollinger, R. C., & Clark, J. P. (1988). Organizational control of deviant behavior: The case of employee theft. *Social Science Quarterly, 69*, 261–280.

Pearson, C. M., Andersson, L. M., & Porath, C. L. (2000). Assessing and attacking workplace incivility. *Organizational Dynamics, 29*, 123–137.

Penney, L. M., & Spector, P. E. (2002). Narcissism and counterproductive work behavior: Do bigger egos mean bigger problems? *International Journal of Selection and Assessment, 10*, 59–67.

Perlow, R., & Latham, L. L. (1993). Relationship of client abuse with locus of control and gender: A longitudinal study in mental retardation facilities. *Journal of Applied Psychology, 78*, 831–834.

Perrewé, P. L., & Zellars, K. L. (1999). An examination of attributions and emotions in the transactional approach to the organizational process. *Journal of Organizational Behavior, 20*, 739–752.

Peters, L. H., & O'Connor, E. J. (1988). Measuring work obstacles: Procedures, issues, and implications. In: F. D. Schoorman & B. Schneider (Eds), *Facilitating Work Effectiveness* (pp. 105–123). Lexington, MA: Lexington Books.

Price Spratlan, L. (1995). Interpersonal conflict which includes mistreatment in a university workplace. *Violence and Victims, 10*, 285–297.

Pryor, J. B., & Fitzgerald, L. F. (2003). Sexual harassment research in the United States. In: S. Einarsen, H. Hoel, D. Zapf & C. L. Cooper (Eds), *Bullying and Emotional Abuse in the Workplace*. New York: Taylor & Francis.

Puffer, S. M. (1987). Prosocial behavior, noncompliant behavior, and work performance among commission sales people. *Journal of Applied Psychology, 72*, 615–621.

Quine, L. (2001). Workplace bullying in nurses. *Journal of Health Psychology, 6*, 73–84.

Rayner, C., Hoel, H., & Cooper, C. L. (2002). *Workplace bullying: What we know, who is to blame, and what can we do?* New York: Taylor & Francis.

Reinshch, L., Jr., & Shelby, A. N. (1996). Communication challenges and needs: Perceptions of MBA students. *Business Communication Quarterly, 59*, 36–53.

Rentsch, J. R., & Steel, R. P. (1998). Testing the durability of job characteristics as predictors of absenteeism over a six-year period. *Personnel Psychology, 51*, 165–189.

Richman, J. A., Rospenda, K. M., Nawyn, S. J., & Flaherty, J. A. (1997). Workplace harassment and the self-medication of distress: A conceptual model and case illustrations. *Contemporary Drug Problems, 24*, 179–199.

Robinson, S. L., & Bennett, R. J. (1995). A typology of deviant workplace behaviors: A multidimensional scaling study. *Academy of Management Journal, 38*, 555–572.

Robinson, S. L., & Greenberg, J. (1998). Employees behaving badly: Dimension, determinants and dilemmas in the study of workplace deviance. In: C. L. Cooper & D. M. Rousseau (Eds), *Trends in Organizational Behavior* (Vol. 5, pp. 1–30). New York, NY: Wiley.

Robinson, S. L., & O'Leary-Kelly, A. M. (1998). Monkey see, monkey do: The influence of work groups on the antisocial behavior of employees. *Academy of Management Journal, 41*, 658–672.

Rogers, R. W. (1983). Race variables in aggression. In: R. G. Geen & E. I. Donnerstein (Eds), *Aggression: Theoretical and Empirical Reviews* (Vol. 2, pp. 27–50). New York: Academic Press.

Rogers, K. A., & Kelloway, E. K. (1997). Violence at work: Personal and organizational outcomes. *Journal of Occupational Health Psychology, 2*, 63–71.

Rosenberg, M. (1986). *Conceiving the Self*. Krieger: Malabar, FL.

Rotter, J. B. (1966). Generalized expectancies for internal versus external control of reinforcement. *Psychological Monographs, 80* (Whole No. 609).

Rowe, D. C., Almeida, D. M., & Jacobson, K. C. (1999). School context and genetic influences on aggression in adolescence. *Psychological Science, 10*, 277–280.

Rushton, J. P., Fulker, D. W., Neale, M. C., Nias, D. K. B., & Eysenck, H. J. (1986). Altruism and aggression: The heritability of individual difference. *Journal of Personality and Social Psychology, 50*, 1192–1198.

Sackett, P. R., Burris, L. R., & Callahan, C. (1989). Integrity testing for personnel selection: An update. *Personnel Psychology, 42*, 491–529.

Sackett, P. R., & DeVore, C. J. (2003). Counterproductive behaviors at work. *Handbook of Industrial, Work and Organizational Psychology*, 145–164.

Saari, L. M., Johnson, T. R., McLaughlin, S. D., & Zimmerle, D. M. (1988). A survey of management training and education practices in U.S. companies. *Personnel Psychology, 41*, 731–743.

Salancik, G. J., & Pfeffer, J. (1978). A social information processing approach to job attitudes and task design. *Administrative Science Quarterly, 23*, 224–253.

Salgado, J. F. (2000). The big five personality dimensions as predictors of alternative criteria. Paper presented a the 15th Annual Conference of the Society for Industrial and Organizational Psychology, New Orleans, LA.

Salancik, G. J., & Pfeffer, J. (1978). A social information processing approach to job attitudes and task design. *Administrative Science Quarterly, 23*, 224–253.

Salin, D. (2001). Prevalence and forms of bullying among business professionals: A comparison of two different strategies for measuring bullying. *European Journal of Work and Organizational Psychology, 10*, 425–441.

Schat, A. C. H., & Kelloway, E. K. (2000). Effects of perceived control on the outcomes of workplace aggression and violence. *Journal of Occupational Health Psychology, 5*, 386–402.

Schat, A. C. H., & Kelloway, E. K. (2003). Reducing the adverse consequences of workplace aggression and violence: The buffering effects of organizational support. *Journal of Occupational Health Psychology, 8*, 110–122.

Scheier, M. F., & Carver, C. S. (1992). Effects of optimism on psychological and physical well being: Theoretical overview and empirical update. *Cognitive Therapy & Research, 16*, 201–228.

Scheier, M. F., Carver, C. S., & Bridges, M. W. (1994). Distinguishing optimism from neuroticism (and trait anxiety, self-mastery, and self-esteem): A reevaluation of the Life Orientation Test. *Journal of Personality & Social Psychology, 67*, 1063–1078.

Scheier, M. F., Weintraub, & Carver, C. S. (1986). Coping with stress: Divergent strategies of optimists and pessimists. *Journal of Personality & Social Psychology, 51*, 1257–1264.

Schneider, B. (1987). The people make the place. *Personnel Psychology, 40*, 437–454.

Schneider, K. T., Hitlan, R. T., & Radhakrishnan, P. (2000). An examination of the nature and correlates of ethnic harassment experiences in multiple contexts. *Journal of Applied Psychology, 85*, 3–12.

Seligman, M. E. P. (1975). *Helplessness: ON depression, development, and death.* San Francisco: W. H. Freeman.

Sinclair, R. R., Martin, J. E., & Croll, L. W. (2002). A threat-appraisal perspective on employees' fear about antisocial workplace behavior. *Journal of Occupational Health Psychology, 7*, 37–56.

Sitkin, S. B., & Bies, R. J. (1993). The legalistic organization: Definitions, dimensions, and dilemmas. *Organization Science, 4*, 345–351.

Skarlicki, D. P., & Folger, R. (1997). Retaliation in the workplace: The roles of distributive, procedural, and interactional justice. *Journal of Applied Psychology, 82*, 434–443.

Skarlicki, D. P., Folger, R., & Tesluk, P. (1999). Personality as a moderator in the relationship between fairness and retaliation. *Academy of Management Journal, 42*, 100–108.

Skinner, B. F. (1953). *Science and Human Behavior.* New York: Free Press.

Smalley, R. L., & Stake, J. E. (1996). Evaluating sources of ego-threatening feedback: Self-esteem and narcissism effects. *Journal of Research in Personality, 30*, 483–495.

Spector, P. E. (1975). Relationships of organizational frustrations with reported behavioral reactions of employees. *Journal of Applied Psychology, 60*, 635–637.

Spector, P. E. (1978). Organizational Frustration: A model and review of the literature. *Personnel Psychology, 31*, 815–829.

Spector, P. E. (1997). The role of frustration in antisocial behavior at work. In: R. A. Giacalone & J. Greenberg (Eds), *Anti-Social Behavior in Organizations* (pp 1–17). Thousand Oaks, CA: Sage.

Spector, P. E., Chen, P. Y., & O'Connell, B. J. (2000). A Longitudinal study of relations between job stressors and job strains while controlling for prior negative affectivity and strains. *Journal of Applied Psychology, 85*, 211–218.

Spector, P. E., & Fox, S. (2002). An emotion-centered model of voluntary work behavior: Some parallels between counterproductive work behavior (CWB) and organizational citizenship behavior (OCB). *Human Resources Management Review, 12*, 269–292.

Spector, P. E., Fox, S., & Van Katwyk, P. T. (1999). The role of negative affectivity in employee reactions to job characteristics: Bias effect or substantive effect. *Journal of Occupational and Organizational Psychology, 72*, 205–218.

Spector, P. E., & Jex, S. M. (1998). Development of Four Self-Report Measures of Job Stressors and Strain: Interpersonal Conflict at Work Scale, Organizational Constraints Scale, Quantitative Workload Inventory, and Physical Symptoms Inventory. *Journal of Occupational Health Psychology, 3*, 356–367.

Spector, P. E., Jex, S. M., & Chen, P. Y. (1995). Relations of incumbent affect-related personality traits with incumbent and objective measures of characteristics of jobs. *Journal of Organizational Behavior, 16*, 59–65.

Spector, P. E., Pennder, L. A., & Hawkins, H. L. (1975). The effect of the thwarting of aggression on subsequent aggression. *Social Behavior and Personality, 3*, 233–241.

Spector, P. E., Zapf, D., Chen, P. Y., & Frese, M. (2000). Why negative affectivity should not be controlled in job stress research: Don't throw out the baby with the bath water. *Journal of Organizational Behavior, 21*, 79–95.

Spence, J. T., Helmreich, R. L., & Pred, R. S. (1987). Impatience versus achievement strivings in the Type A pattern: Differential effects on students' health and academic achievement. *Journal of Applied Psychology, 72*, 522–528.

Spence, J. T., Pred, R. S., & Helmreich, R. L. (1989). Achievement strivings, scholastic aptitude, and academic performance: A follow-up to "Impatience versus achievement strivings in the Type A pattern". *Journal of Applied Psychology, 74*, 176–178.

Spielberger, C. D. (1988). *State–Trait Anger Expression Inventory*. Odessa, FL: Psychological Assessment Resources.

Stanton, J. M. (2000). Reactions to employee performance monitoring: Framework, review, and research directions. *Human Performance, 13*, 85–113.

Storms, P. L., & Spector, P. E. (1987). Relationships of frustration with reported behavioural reactions: The moderating effect of locus of control. *Journal of Occupational Psychology, 60*, 227–234.

Sweeney, P. D., McFarlin, D. B., & Inderrieden, E. J. (1990). Using relative deprivation theory to explain satisfaction with income and pay level: A multistudy examination. *Academy of Management Journal, 33*, 423–436.

Tellegen, A., Lykken, D. T., Bouchard, T. J., Wilcox, K., Segal, N., & Rich, S. (1988). Personality similarity in twins reared apart and together. *Journal of Personality and Social Psychology, 54*, 1031–1039.

Tepper, B. J. (2000). Consequences of abusive supervision. *Academy of Management Journal, 43*, 178–190.

Thomas, K. W. (1992). Conflict and negotiation processes. In: M. Dunnette & L. Hough (Eds), *Handbook of Industrial and Organizational Psychology* (2nd ed., Vol. 3, pp 651–717). Chicago, IL: Rand McNally.

Tobin, T. J. (2001). Organizational determinants of violence in the workplace. *Aggression and Violent Behavior, 6*, 91–102.

Trevino, L. K. (1986). Ethical decision making in organizations: A person–situation interactionist model. *Academy of Management Review, 11*, 601–617.

Trevino, L. K., & Youngblood, S. A. (1990). Bad apples in bad barrels: A causal analysis of ethical decision-making behavior. *Journal of Applied Psychology, 75*, 378–385.

Tyler, T. R., & Bies, R. J. (1990). Beyond formal procedures: The interpersonal context of procedural justice. In: J. S. Carroll (Ed.), *Applied Social Psychology and Organizational Settings* (pp. 77–98). Hillsdale, NJ: Lawrence Erlbaum.

Tyler, T. R., & Lind, E. A. (1992). A relational model of authority in groups. In: M. Zanna (Ed.), *Advances in Experimental Social Psychology* (Vol. 25, pp. 115–192). New York: Academic Press.

VandenBos, G. R., & Bulatao, E. Q. (1996). *Violence on the job: Identifying risks and developing solutions.* Washington, DC: American Psychological Association.

VandenBos, K., Vermunt, R., & Wilke, H. A. M. (1996). The consistency rule and the voice effect: The influence of expectations on procedural fairness judgments and performance. *European Journal of Social Psychology, 26*, 411–428.

Vardi, Y., & Wiener, Y. (1996). Misbehavior in organizations: A motivational framework. *Organizational Science, 7*, 151–165.

Watson, D., & Clark, L. A. (1984). Negative affectivity: The disposition to experience aversive emotional states. *Psychological Bulletin, 96*, 465–490.

Zapf, D., Einarsen, S., Hoel, H., & Vartia, M. (2003). Individual effects of exposure to bullying at work. In: S. Einarsen, H. Hoel, D. Zapf & C. L. Cooper (Eds), *Bullying and Emotional Abuse in the Workplace.* New York: Taylor & Francis.

Zillmann, D. (1988). Cognitive-excitation interdependencies in aggressive behavior. *Aggressive Behavior, 14*, 51–64.

Zohar, D. (2002). Modifying supervisory practices to improve subunit safety: A leadership-based intervention model. *Journal of Applied Psychology, 87*, 156–163.

Zuckerman, M., Kuhlman, D. M., Joireman, J., Teta, P., & Kraft, M. (1993). A comparison of three structural models for personality: The Big Three, the Big Five, and the Alternative Five. *Journal of Personality & Social Psychology, 65*, 757–768.

THE RADIATING EFFECTS OF INTIMATE PARTNER VIOLENCE ON OCCUPATIONAL STRESS AND WELL BEING

Michelle K. Duffy, Kristin L. Scott and Anne M. O'Leary-Kelly

ABSTRACT

The impact of workplace violence on occupational stress and well being is garnering increasing attention. Despite the fact that workplace violence has been identified as a critical organizational safety and health issue, there has been limited scholarly focus on the problem of domestic or intimate partner violence in the workplace. This paper examines intimate partner violence from both ecological and work family spillover modes of theorizing. Within this framework, we propose that the effects of intimate partner violence are reciprocal and spillover into the workplace, impacting employee and organizational well being. We conclude by discussing the implications of the integrated framework and by offering suggestions for future research in this area.

INTRODUCTION

The devastating effects of workplace violence on employee and organizational well being have received considerable attention in recent years (e.g. Mack et al.,

Exploring Interpersonal Dynamics
Research in Occupational Stress and Well Being, Volume 4, 67–92
© 2005 Published by Elsevier Ltd.
ISSN: 1479-3555/doi:10.1016/S1479-3555(04)04002-8

1998; Paetzold, 1998). Between the years 1993 and 1999, 1.7 million workers were victimized annually while at work (Bureau of Justice Statistics, 2001). Such incidents affect organizational and employee well being through decreased morale, health, and productivity, and cost organizations billions of dollars each year (e.g. AMA, 1994; Flannery, 1995). In fact, violence at work is such a serious problem that the National Institute for Occupational Safety and Health, with funding from Congress, started a workplace violence initiative in 2002 designed to develop a prevention research program targeting all aspects of violence at work.

One form of violence, intimate partner violence (IPV), has received very little research attention despite its substantial presence at work (Scalora et al., 2003). Statistics indicate that employees are equally as likely to be assaulted (while at work) by an intimate partner as by a colleague (Warchol, 1998), that between 16 and 20% of all women who are fatally injured in the workplace are attacked by a partner, and that 15,000 women are assaulted at work each year by a partner (Bell et al., 2002; NIOSH, 2004). Although these statistics are attention-getting on their own, even they do not fully capture the workplace-related impact of partner violence. In addition to the direct harm experienced by victims, employers also must consider the potential for spillover of partner violence to targets' workplace colleagues (Riger et al., 2002). This suggests that the effects of IPV on the workplace are highly significant.

Interestingly, initial research indicates that although many managers and executives recognize IPV as a critical organizational concern, most do not see that their organization can play a critical role in addressing IPV (RoperASW, 2003). For example, two studies commissioned by Liz Claiborne and conducted by RoperASW (1994, 2002) found that 66% of executives believed that IPV was a serious problem that affected their bottom-line. These same executives overwhelmingly believed that IPV spilled over into organizational life. Nonetheless, only 12% of these executives believed organizations should have a major role in developing a framework and strategy for dealing with the effects of IPV.

Academic researchers are similarly remiss in their attention given to IPV, despite its clear place as an organizational safety and health issue (Bell et al., 2002). Therefore, we suggest that a more profound understanding of the radiating impact of IPV on occupational well being is imperative. Further, we believe that research attention must recognize the multifaceted nature of IPV (i.e. that it has effects beyond psychological and physical effects for targets) and its multidimensional effects (e.g. employee morale, organizational productivity). To this end, researchers must utilize a focused and systematic research agenda in this area. With this goal in mind, we suggest an ecological approach as a potential framework for understanding the impact of IPV on occupational well being.

THE ECOLOGICAL MODEL

Grounded in both the biological and social sciences, ecological theory argues that the interrelationships among components in an environment are complex and interactive (Kelly, 1966). An ecological approach to IPV recognizes the interdependence of individuals and "interconnectedness among people and other elements" in settings such as work organizations, thereby allowing an examination of the reciprocal nature of IPV (Riger et al., 2002, p. 185). Such a framework highlights the notion that IPV is indeed an organizational, and not just a "family" problem. Given that IPV and its spillover into the workplace are complex and multi-determined, we believe an ecological approach offers an ideal framework to evaluate IPV and its relationship with occupational stress and well being.

Moreover, such a framework is in line with the growing body of theory and research examining the interface between family and work (Perrewé et al., 2003). A recent growth in the amount of research examining the linkages between work and family indicates that work and family are "closely interconnected domains" (Eckenrode & Gore, 1990; Edwards & Rothbard, 2000; Zedeck, 1992). According to spillover theory, the stressors and strains experienced in one domain are likely to have an effect on experiences in the other domain (Aldous, 1969; Caliguiri et al., 1998; Leiter & Durup, 1996) through a reciprocal influence process. For example, recent research in the work-stress arena clearly suggests that adjustment and performance at work are influenced by factors that occur outside the work domain (e.g. Williams & Alliger, 1994). Likewise, demands experienced by one spouse in the workplace may cross over to affect the other spouse's well being (Hoobler, 2004; Rook et al., 1991). As Perrewé and her colleagues (2003) note, "the line of demarcation separating work and family domains is blurred by the fact that situations at work spill over into the family and vice versa" (p. 287). Therefore, incorporating these spillover effects into our understanding of the IPV phenomenon is a major goal of this chapter.

Before presenting a detailed discussion of our ecological model, we wish to reiterate a few points regarding the use of ecology theory to explain IPV and the workplace. First, an ecological perspective allows for the integration of individual, family and contextual factors (Shinn, 1996) that we believe more thoroughly depict the pervasive nature of IPV effects on the work environment. This line of reasoning is further supported by the National Research Council which advocates the use of the ecological approach to study IPV as it takes into account the multiple factors that influence this phenomenon (U.S. Department of Health and Human Services, 1997). Ecology theory has also been utilized, for these reasons, to study community violence (Cicchetti & Lynch, 1993; Salzinger et al., 2002). Second, an ecological approach further suggests that these relationships are reciprocal such that the existence of IPV at home not only has deleterious effects for an individual at work, but also that factors inherent to the work place can further exacerbate IPV and IPV-related problems at home. Third, the implications of IPV extend beyond the physical abuse of the target to include the target's ability to function at work as well as the negative implications for the individual's co-workers and entire organization (what will be described later as first, second, third, and fourth order effects).

This chapter is divided into five major sections intended to develop this ecological approach to describing IPV and workplace well being. We begin by defining IPV and briefly reviewing the scope of the IPV problem in general and in the workplace. We then introduce the ecological model, presenting the multiple effects of IPV (e.g. first order effects, second order effects) and highlighting the reciprocal nature of these relationships. Next we discuss the role of the organizational context in terms of its influence on IPV. Finally, this chapter concludes by posing several areas of future research related to the various components of the ecological model.

INTIMATE PARTNER VIOLENCE

IPV is defined as a "pattern of assaultive and coercive behaviors including physical, psychological, and sexual attacks as well as economic coercion, that adults use against intimate partners" (Ganley & Warshaw, 1995). Frequency statistics for IPV are, simply stated, astonishing. Research by the Centers for Disease Control and Prevention and the National Institute of Justice (authored by Tjaden & Thoennes, 2000) indicates that over 25% of American women report having been physically assaulted, raped, or stalked by an intimate partner in their lifetime. Further, IPV is the *leading* cause of injury to women in the United States (American Institute on Domestic Violence, 2001). Although a review of the general research on IPV is too extensive to include here, it clearly establishes that IPV has serious negative consequences. For example, research indicates that targets of IPV generally have lower levels of self-esteem, greater substance abuse, and more frequent problems with interpersonal and work relationships (Riger et al., 2002). In addition to immediate injury, victimization can cause chronic physical and mental health problems that result in significant IPV-related health care costs (exact costs are difficult to ascertain, but they are estimated to be as high as $4.1 billion (National Center for Injury Prevention and Control, 2003)). It is important to note that although partner violence can be experienced by either men or women, it is more likely to be experienced by women (Reeves et al., 2001; Tjaden & Thoennes, 2000).

INTIMATE PARTNER VIOLENCE AND WORK

Unfortunately, the workplace is no sanctuary for IPV victims. Initial research indicates that there is significant spillover of family violence into the work domain (Reeves, 2004). According to the American Institute on Domestic Violence (2001), 96% of IPV victims who are working, experience some work-related problems caused by the IPV. For example, 74% are harassed by their intimate partner while at work, 56% are late to work, 28% leave work early, and 54% miss entire days of work. Other research indicates that IPV spillover to work is a more profound problem for female than male victims in that women are five times more likely to be attacked at work by a partner than are men (Johnson & Indvik, 1999).

When IPV enters the workplace, there are significant costs not only for victims, but also for employers. The total employer-related costs associated with IPV are difficult to assess, but several prominent agencies have provided estimates. For example, a 1995 National Violence Against Women study sponsored by the National Institute of Justice and the Center for Disease Control and Prevention suggested that IPV costs organizations approximately $5.8 billion per year in terms of absenteeism and health-care costs. The Centers for Disease Control estimates that employers lose about $900 million annually to nonfatal IPV incidents. Other estimates suggest that over 1,750,000 workdays and $100 million in wages (Partnership for Prevention, 2002) are lost due to domestic violence, and that IPV in the United States costs employers an estimated $67 billion annually (American Institute on Domestic Violence, 2003).

These estimates regarding the employer-related costs of IPV are noteworthy in two ways. First, they are alarming because of their significant size. Second, they create frustration because it is difficult to harmonize these varied estimates from multiple sources (e.g. one estimate will suggest $3.5 billion in lost productivity while another will suggest $100 million in lost wages and other expenses). Much of the problem related to this latter point comes from the fact that different estimates appear to quantify IPV-related costs in different ways. For example, one agency may assess health care costs for victims, while others include health care and lost work days. Essentially, then, the costs related to IPV can be quantified differentially depending on how broadly IPV-related effects are defined. This suggests the benefits of an ecological framework for understanding IPV. In the next section; we elaborate on this framework and further explain how the ecological approach recognizes the differing forms and cumulating effects of IPV.

AN ECOLOGICAL VIEW OF WORK-RELATED IPV

An ecological approach to understanding IPV recognizes that the effects (and, thereby, the costs) of IPV will depend on how broadly the phenomenon is considered. As noted above, an ecological approach to social systems acknowledges that components in a system are interrelated (Kelly, 1996). As Fig. 1 shows, this framework expands the focus of attention to consider the system-wide consequences of IPV, beyond the target's home. Through this framework, we can see that an IPV event will "ripple" throughout the social system to affect other interrelated components (Kelly, 1971). Seen in this light, it is clear that IPV has not only first order or direct effects on the target, in the form of physical and

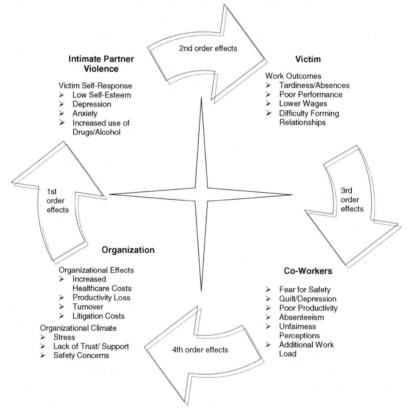

Fig. 1. The Ecological Model of the Effects of Intimate Partner Violence on Occupational Stress and Well being.

mental well being, but also second-, third-, and even fourth-order consequences. More specifically, second order effects involve outcomes for the target beyond the immediate physical and psychological consequences of the abuse; third order effects include consequences of the IPV for people other than the target; and fourth order effects include the aggregate consequences for the social system (i.e. work organization) that are associated with the IPV.

For example, a target who has experienced IPV may suffer the first order effects of psychological trauma (depression and anxiety). These first order effects (if untreated) then may make it difficult for the target to perform well or to establish necessary relationships with coworkers, thereby creating second-order effects. The target's lower performance then may lead to additional responsibilities for coworkers who must compensate for the target's lower performance, resulting in third order effects. Finally, as target and coworker productivity suffers, the organization as a whole suffers financially, creating fourth order effects. This series of events demonstrates the *radiating impact* of IPV that is evident when this phenomenon is considered from an ecological perspective. In the following sections we report more specifically on current evidence that suggests the radiating impact of IPV.

First-Order Effects

As noted above, first order effects of IPV include the direct effects on the target such as physical and emotional health issues. These first order effects are well documented (e.g. Riger et al., 2002) and therefore we will review those consequences only briefly. In addition to the physical trauma of the violence itself, targets of IPV are more likely than their non-abused counterparts to experience chronic pain, ulcers, vision and auditory impairment (Wilson, 1997). Emotionally, targets are at increased risk for lower levels of self-esteem (Mitchell & Hodson, 1983; Perilla et al., 1994), increased anxiety and inability to concentrate (Partnership for Prevention, 2002), post-traumatic stress disorder, shame, and eating disorders (Bell et al., 2002; Laffaye et al., 2003a, b). IPV targets are also more likely to self-medicate through the use of drugs and alcohol (Johnson & Gardner, 1999; Kilpatrick, 1990).

Second Order Effects of IPV

Second order effects of IPV hinder the target's ability to function in the social world and, for purposes of the present paper, the workplace in particular. These effects would include the target's ability to be productive and to maintain a job, as well as to maintain important interpersonal work relationships. Given that targets are more likely to be employed than non-abused individuals (Farmer & Tiefenthaler, 2003a), the ramifications of IPV for women in the workplace are significant (Reeves, 2004). Although studies on this topic are limited, existing research suggests numerous forms of negative work-related effects. First, targets are often absent, late, or leave work early; a study by Ruckelshaus (1996) indicates that 54% of targets missed at least three days of work per month and 56% were late for work five times per month. Second, when targets are at work, they may experience "presenteism" and find it difficult to concentrate and perform to expected or desired standards (Johnson & Gardner, 1999; Laszlo & Rinehart, 2002). While at work, targets may spend company time calling support personnel and agencies (e.g. doctors, attorneys, and shelters) instead of concentrating on work-related tasks (Ruckelshaus, 1996). Many targets report being afraid to go to work because they know the perpetrator can find them there (Bell et al., 2002). Other studies have found similar rates of absence, tardiness, and poor work performance among targets of IPV (e.g. Farmer & Tiefenthaler, 2003a).

Not surprisingly, targets of IPV often receive lower wages as a result of their declining productivity (e.g. Farmer & Tiefenthaler, 2003a). Likewise, targets of IPV may not be protected from losing their jobs when their employer is aware of the IPV (Reeves et al., 2001). It is not uncommon for targets of IPV to be suspended or terminated from work, clearly making it difficult for them to function well in their workplace environment as they deal with the stressors of IPV. Reports indicate that about 25–50% of IPV targets lose their jobs as a consequence of IPV (Chicago National Organization for Women, 2004). Beyond the financial consequences of reduced wages or terminations, targets also may have to cope with damage to their identities as successful employees. Given that work roles can be a significant part of an individual's identity (e.g. Frone, 2000), the loss of the work-related identity is likely to decrease target well being even further.

On an interpersonal level, IPV may affect targets' relationships with their colleagues. Although we are not aware of research that has directly examined IPV and workplace relationships, research does indicate that IPV affects targets' relationships with family and friends (Riger et al., 2002). Given that targets of abuse are unsure about who they can trust with their "secret" (i.e. they cannot always predict how coworkers will react if they learn of their abusive situation), they are likely to be reluctant to form close relationships at work. Research suggests that individuals are often uncomfortable sharing what is perceived as negative information about themselves because of impression management concerns (e.g. Gardner, 1992). Sadly, the more severely a target is physically abused, the less likely she is to disclose the abuse to others and the more likely she is to withdraw from social relationships (Yoshinko et al., 2003). Research suggests that both the lack of disclosure of stressful life events and social withdrawal can cause additional physical and mental health problems beyond the initial trauma (Bolton et al., 2003). Moreover, if targets do not disclose the IPV, they can miss out on potentially valuable sources of social support.

In terms of the ecological framework presented here, it is important to emphasize the connection (radiating impact) between first and second order effects. First order effects seem very likely to be causally related to many second order effects; for example, higher levels of depression and anxiety (first order) may make it difficult for IPV targets to concentrate on work and perform well or to create beneficial work relationships (second order).

Third Order Effects of IPV

Third order effects refer to the effects of IPV on the targets' social contacts, in this case her coworkers. The first and second order effects of IPV radiate into the workplace in part because the workplace is an easy place for abusive partners to seek out their targets (i.e. they know that the target will be there). As Farmer and Tiefenthaler (1997) note, perpetrators often are eager to have their targets fired so that the target will become more dependent on them. Consequently, harassing, stalking, and threatening the targets is likely to occur at work (Reeves et al., 2001). Indeed, perpetrators of abuse commit 13,000 acts of violence against women in the workplace every year (American Institute on Domestic Violence, 2001) with abusive partners harassing 74% of targets at work (Johnson & Indvik, 1999). As a result, the workplace is dangerous not only for targets, but also for the target's colleagues (Johnson & Gardner, 1999).

Although there is a very limited body of work regarding the third order effects of IPV, research indicates that when abusers attempt to stalk, harass, threaten, or injure targets at work, their violence not only harms the target but also creates a dangerous environment for co-workers, clients, customers, and the general public (American Bar Association Commission on Domestic Violence, 2003). According to recent studies, in as many as 66% of the cases of workplace IPV, someone other than the target is harmed (Nevonen, 2001; Reeves et al., 2001). In addition to the risks of actual physical harm to the colleagues of targets, the psychological fear of perpetrator attacks in the workplace can lead to personal safety concerns and increase the stress levels of a target's co-workers (Mack et al., 1998). These third order effects can include emotional and health effects on colleagues similar to those of targets (Bell et al., 2002). Although relatively little work has examined the effects of workplace IPV on witnesses, the stressful impact of violent events in general on witnesses has been well documented (e.g. Allcorn, 1994; Mack et al., 1998). Coworkers who witness an act of violence may need psychological assistance and time away from work (Zachary, 2000). Feelings of guilt, depression, vulnerability, and post-traumatic stress symptoms may fester and, if left untreated, can result in serious mental health problems (e.g. Pynoos et al., 1993). It is important to note that such effects last well beyond the initial violent act and, in addition to the emotional implications, there are attitudinal and behavioral effects on witnesses of workplace violence (Mack et al., 1998). Witnesses of workplace violence have reported increased levels of job stress, job turnover, and a greater tendency to bring guns and other weapons into the workplace (Budd et al., 1996; Pynoos et al., 1993). As Mack and his colleagues point out, it is possible and "even likely that these negative effects may lead to other acts of violence" (p. 131).

The work of targets' colleagues may be affected as well, especially in the form of lowered productivity (Zachary, 2000). Some Employee Assistance Programs recommend that coworkers screen calls for targets, an action which can have an unintended effect on productivity (Bell et al., 2002). In addition, the target's co-workers may perceive themselves as being treated unfairly when they have to pick up additional responsibilities resulting from the target's absenteeism or poor performance. Studies have shown that perceptions of unfair treatment often lead to negative behavior directed towards the organization (Bies & Tripp, 1998; Greenberg, 1997) and, thus, add to the already significant costs associated with IPV.

Again, it is important to reiterate the causal relationships that are expected between first, second, and third order effects. As argued in this section, coworkers may be negatively influenced (third order effects) when family violence is brought into the workplace in the form of second order effects (e.g. through increased absenteeism, decreased productivity, less significant work relationships). It should be noted that although our discussion has focused primarily on spillover that occurs with IPV targets in the workplace, it also seems certain that there will be spillover when perpetrators are at work (e.g. they may miss work due to legal proceedings, which will have implications for coworkers). However, the effects on the workplace of perpetrator (versus victim) employment has received even less research attention to date.

Fourth-Order Effects

Fourth order effects include those that influence the well being of the organization such as losses in productivity, higher levels of turnover and absence, increased medical and litigation costs, and undesirable workplace climate. As mentioned earlier, it is difficult to harmonize across the numerous and varied cost estimates that have been provided by different authors and government agencies (Reeves, 2004) because they appear to differ in both their estimation methods and in the cost dimensions that are included. In addition, it appears that most estimates have not included all possible costs of IPV, such as the effects on coworkers (described here as third-order effects). Clearly, there is a need for more precise and standardized research on this topic. It should be noted, however, that all existing estimates present IPV as having a significant financial effect on businesses. The significance of these costs is further supported by survey data from executives which indicates that they regard IPV as having seriously negative effects on their organization's bottom line (RoperASW, 1994, 2003).

Despite the lack of research on the specific degree and nature of IPV-related effects for the organization, the ecological model provides some insights into how these effects might reveal themselves. The fourth order (organizational) effects are likely linked to first order effects (e.g. target physical and emotional health issues), second order effects (e.g. decreased target productivity), and third order effects (e.g. lost productivity from coworkers fearing harm, liability for coworkers harmed). For example, the consequences for IPV on target health (first order) leads to higher company medical and benefit costs, increased insurance premiums, and sick leave costs (Bell et al., 2002). More specifically, evidence suggests that women who are targeted for IPV incur $24 million in medical expenses alone annually (Greenfeld, 1998).

As the second and third order effects of lowered quality and quantity of productivity for targets and their colleagues spread, organizational productivity as a whole may be significantly diminished. If there is a violent episode at work, the work site may have to be closed which clearly has implications for organizational productivity (Bell et al., 2002). Likewise, if targets of IPV lose their jobs (second order), organizations must incur training costs because of this turnover (Popham, 1998).

In addition, organizational liability for IPV may be higher than that for random acts of violence (Bell et al., 2002; Johnson & Indvik, 1999). Organizations can be held legally accountable for IPV-related issues especially when the employer was aware the employee was at risk but failed to take preventive action (Perin, 1999; Reeves et al., 2001). Likewise, organizations may incur costs if the co-worker of a target is harmed in an IPV-related incident at work (Johnson & Gardner, 1999). Finally, if the perpetrator of an IPV incident at work is an employee, organizations can be held liable for negligent hiring (Zachary, 2000). As mentioned earlier, in this paper we do not address directly the issues related to IPV perpetrators, but it should be noted that organizations are likely to suffer significant costs related to perpetrators as well. For example, Rothman (2002) found that organizations lost money due to the absence of perpetrators as a result of time in court, counseling, jail, and meeting with probation officers.

In summary, IPV generates numerous costs not only to organizations but also to the employees who are both directly and indirectly affected. Consequently, developing a better understanding of how IPV affects organizations and employees should lead to more effective organizational interventions that will minimize these costs and contribute to the overall efforts directed at reducing IPVs devastating consequences.

EXTENSIONS WITHIN AN ECOLOGICAL FRAMEWORK: REVERSE CAUSALITY AND ORGANIZATIONAL ANTECDENTS OF IPV

The ecological perspective outlined in the preceding sections details the likely consequences of IPV in terms of the targets' self-response, the targets' work-related behaviors, the behaviors and attitudes of coworkers, and the effects on aggregate outcomes at the organizational level. To this point, we have assumed that the causal sequence in the ecological model proceeds from IPV through each of the levels (or through multiple levels), but have not considered the likely possibility that reverse causality is present in the model. Moreover, although the organizational literature increasingly emphasizes the linkages between employees' work and family lives (e.g. Burke & Greenglass, 1987; Eckenrode & Gore, 1990; Edwards & Rothbard, 2000; Zedeck, 1992), the empirical IPV literature is essentially silent on the organizational factors that may lead to the perpetration of IPV at home. Therefore, in the following section we draw on the broader organizational literature and outline a sample of ideas that pertain to issues of reverse causality in the ecological model or relate to organizational factors that may be antecedent to IPV. We note here that these ideas are intended to be logical points of departure for theoretical and empirical extensions within the ecological framework. First, we draw on the broader sociological and social psychological literature on stigmatization and suggest that coworker reactions to IPV may exacerbate the negative outcomes associated with being the target of IPV. Next, we highlight occupational stress and injustice in the workplace as potential spillover antecedents of IPV at home.

Stigmatization of Targets

One organizational factor that is expected to influence IPV outcomes is the extent to which coworkers stigmatize targets of IPV. Stigma is defined as a negative perception of an individual based on actual or inferred attributes that deviate from normal or commonly held social expectations (Goffman, 1963). Given that targets of IPV exhibit greater absenteeism, tardiness and poorer work performance (Farmer & Tiefenthaler, 2003a), organizational members often may stigmatize IPV targets. It is not clear, however, which types of attitudinal and behavioral reactions will result from stigmatization. The literature on disability-based stigmas shows a negative relationship between stronger coworker perceptions of stigmatic characteristics and the target's work performance. Perceptions of stigmatic characteristics also influence whether or not colleagues will accept the stigmatized person (McLaughlin et al., 2004). In other words, extrapolating from the person's with disability literature, it may be that stigmatizing by coworkers will have a negative effect on the target's work performance. This represents a reciprocal relationship in the ecological model (see Fig. 1) between coworkers and victims, emphasizing that not only will the actions of the IPV target influence coworkers, but coworker responses may influence the target's behavior, attitudes, and even self perceptions.

Further, research on disability-based stigma (Collela, 2001) suggests that coworkers tend to be less accepting of the target and less willing to make accommodations if the situation (e.g. the disability) is perceived to be self-caused. In terms of self-caused disabilities, Collela (2001) uses the example of a person disabled in a crash while he or she was intoxicated. With respect to IPV, a frequently-held belief is that targets of IPV simply could leave the abusive home situation and, by extension, that victims cause the IPV by staying. If this perception is the norm, it seems likely that coworkers will be less accepting of the target, especially when the target's work performance is affected by the abuse.

Other research indicates that third party reactions to stigmatized individuals depend on the perceived degree of peril, or the extent to which these individuals may pose a threat to others (Jones et al., 1984). In regard to IPV, this research would imply that when coworkers feel threatened by the IPV perpetration (i.e. third order effects), coworkers are more likely to stigmatize the target and less likely to be tolerant of the target. It is interesting to consider whether such perceived threats must be physical in order to have these negative effects. For example, if an IPV target is absent or tardy and assignments are transferred to coworkers, this transfer may become a threat to the well being of coworkers and/or to their own level of productivity. This, in turn, may reinforce the stigmatization of targets and any detrimental outcomes associated with it.

In addition to general reactions (i.e. level of acceptance) of IPV targets, another facet of this phenomenon is the response of organizational members to policies or procedures designed to protect or assist the targets of IPV. Turning again to the literature on disability-based stigma, previous research utilized equity theory to predict reactions of coworkers to accommodation practices aimed at employees with stigmatized disabilities. The findings of such studies demonstrate that coworkers are more accepting of accommodation practices (perceived as additional outcomes granted to the employee) when it they believe that the individual with the disability was deserving of them (McLaughlin et al., 2004). In line with this, we would argue that coworkers will be tolerant of IPV targets and the accommodations made for them, so long as they perceive that the IPV was not "self-caused" and so long as their own status is not threatened.

The findings of McLaughlin et al. (2004) clearly demonstrate that coworkers accepted workers with disabilities and any accommodations when no stigma of poor performance existed. Colleagues appear to hold the expectation that if accommodations are being made to help an individual overcome a negative situation, then that person should ultimately display adequate performance levels, or at least performance equal to that of coworkers. This holds interesting implications for IPV targets. If an organization maintains policies or practices designed to assist the targets of IPV, according to equity theory, coworkers will expect IPV targets to make use of the accommodations to overcome their situation and minimize the impact of IPV on their performance. Thus, if an employee is granted leniency to accommodate absences, tardiness or poor performance due to IPV, this may contribute to stigmatization and lack of acceptance for the target, especially if the situation does not improve over time. This suggests that organizations will need to carefully devise policies and programs designed to manage IPV in the workplace so as not to exacerbate existing stigmas or intolerance that may exist.

Considering all of these factors together, it is probable that targets of IPV are more likely to be stigmatized and less accepted by coworkers, thus resulting in an organizational climate which may exacerbate negative consequences. Here, we return to the notion of spillover effects. Given that the IPV target encounters further stress in the workplace due to stigmatization, spillover theory posits that these stressors and strains experienced in the work domain are likely to have an effect on experiences in the home domain (Perrewé et al., 2003). In terms of reverse causation, IPV-target stigmatization, negative perceptions, and lack of acceptance may cause dissatisfaction (McLaughlin et al., 2004), which foreseeably contributes to absenteeism, tardiness, poor performance and overall increased costs for the organization and ultimately other self-response outcomes that diminish well being (Bolger et al., 1989).

Antecedents to the Perpetration of IPV

A number of theories have been proposed to explain the causal relationship between occupational stress and IPV (see Holtzworth-Munroe et al., 1997 for a review). Explanations for this relationship run from theories suggesting that IPV perpetrators experience extreme frustration due to life stress and act out violently as a way to reduce their negative affect, to those that suggest social norms encourage and reinforce the relationships among stress, frustration, and interpersonal violence (Farrington, 1986). Despite the rich theoretical foundation for understanding the stress-violence relationship, research examining the association between occupational stressors and IPV is very limited (Cano & Vivian, 2001; but see Barling & Rosenbaum, 1986 for an exception). There is both theoretical and limited empirical evidence, however, that links work-related stress to spillover into family life in the form of IPV.

First, empirical research suggests a significant and direct association between life stress and family violence (e.g. Farrington, 1986; Jasinski et al., 1997; Margolin et al., 1998). Second, in terms of occupational stress, there is evidence that perpetrators of IPV report more occupational stress and occupational loss-related stress (e.g. demotion, suspension), than non-perpetrators (Barnett & Fagan, 1993; Barnett et al., 1991; Cano & Vivian, 2003) and this is true for both male and female perpetrators of IPV. For example, Barling and Rosenbaum (1986) found that occurrence of both objective and subjective stressful work events was related to IPV. Brinkerhoff and Lupri (1988) found work-related stressors to be moderately, but significantly associated with IPV.

In addition to occupational stressors, the broader justice literature can be used to predict that workplace injustice will be a consequential antecedent of IPV at home. For example, research suggests that sources of interactional injustice and stress such as psychological contract breach, abusive supervision, undermining, and incivility tend to invoke strong emotional responses such as resentment, powerlessness, and antagonism (Ashforth, 1997; Bies, 1987; Duffy et al., 2002; Pearson & Porath, 2004; Tepper, 2000). The threat to self-esteem and sense of injustice from these events has been linked to frustration, aggression, revenge and deviant behavior (Bies & Trip, 1999; Duffy et al., 2004; Skarlicki & Folger, 1997). However, research indicates that individuals rarely aggress against targets who are more powerful than themselves (e.g. supervisors), so it is unlikely that targets of supervisor undermining and abuse will reciprocate by abusing their supervisors (American Medical Association, 1994; Lord, 1998; Tepper et al., 1998). Therefore, employees who perceive they are targets of negative supervisory acts or perceive that their psychological contracts have been violated at work may attempt to restore their feelings of self-worth and power through aggressing on people in their family life.

While there is no direct evidence that injustice at work leads to IPV at home, there is indirect evidence that this may be the case. For example, Hoobler (2003) found that family members of employees who believed they were the targets of supervisor abuse reported a higher incidence of family undermining in the home (e.g. expressions of dislike, negative affect). According to Hoobler (2003), employees targeted less powerful others at whose expense they restored their self-worth and self-esteem. Although undermining behavior is a much more mild form of aggression than IPV, this finding is in line with empirical evidence which indicates that perpetrators of IPV generally report higher levels of state anger and hostility. Likewise, there is some evidence suggesting that IPV perpetrators have lower levels of self-esteem and self-efficacy and greater perceptions of powerlessness than non-perpetrators (Holtzworth-Munroe et al., 1997).

AN AGENDA FOR FUTURE RESEARCH ON THE ECOLOGICAL MODEL OF IPV

We have illustrated that the workplace effects of IPV pose numerous costs and negative consequences not only for its targets but also for the target's employers and co-workers. Moreover, we have begun the process of addressing the possible reciprocal effects within the ecological framework as well as taking some initial steps toward developing a work-related spillover etiology of IPV. Although the initial research in this area is promising, there is a scarcity of scholarly work concerning the impact of IPV on organizations. Bell and her colleagues argue (2002), "that management researchers have yet to investigate the relationship between PVA (IPV) and organizations presents researchers with unique advantages" (p. 5). First, there is an opportunity to start a systematic research program on IPV which is theoretically grounded. Second, management researchers have the unique opportunity to provide organizations with useful research-driven answers that should significantly enhance employee and organizational well being and in turn lower the incidence of IPV in the long run (Bell et al., 2002; Reeves et al., 2001). Given the scope of the problem of IPV, there are numerous avenues for future research in this area. In the following section we present a sample of ideas for how research on IPV might proceed.

First and Second Order Effects

Although researchers in other social science disciplines have investigated the direct or first order effects of IPV on targets, many questions remain unanswered regarding the second order effects outlined above. Building on the ecological model, it will be important for researchers to examine the links among these interrelated and reciprocal effects. As a starting point, we encourage investigators to systematically examine the "spillover" of IPV into the workplace in terms of the following research questions:

IPV and Workplace Functioning
- What is the impact of IPV on target work productivity?
- What is the impact of IPV on target wages?
- What are the physical and psychological effects of the necessity of thought and emotion suppression regarding the IPV on targets while at work?
- What is the impact of IPV on target antisocial behavior at work?

IPV and Workplace Relationships and Identity
- What is the impact of IPV on target workplace relationships (e.g. withdrawal from workplace relationships. increased emotional intensity in workplace relationships)?
- What is the impact of IPV on targets' work-related role identity?
- What is the impact of IPV on targets' organizational citizenship behavior and deviant work behavior?
- Does social support from coworkers mitigate the effects of IPV on targets' mental and physical distress?
- How does being stigmatized by co-workers affect the target's workplace behavior, productivity and well being?
- What organizational factors moderate the deleterious impact of IPV on target workplace productivity?
- How are target perceptions of supervisor relationships affected by IPV?

IPV Disclosure
As noted earlier in this paper, whether a target discloses the IPV can have a significant impact on her well being. A critical next step then is to determine when, how and why targets of IPV choose to disclose to their employer that they are being abused. Likewise, we would be interested in the consequences of disclosure for both the targets and coworkers of the targets. More specifically, we suggest the following research questions regarding IPV disclosure.

- What is the impact of IPV disclosure to coworkers on the mental and physical health of targets?
- Are targets excluded from important social networks by coworkers as a result of IPV disclosure?
- What is the impact of target mental health on disclosure to coworkers?
- What is the effect of severity of IPV on disclosure to coworkers?

Third Order Effects of IPV

While organizational stressors such as interpersonal demands and conflicts, task performance pressures, and role demands can increase an individual's stress level (Mack et al., 1998), IPV also exacts a toll on a target's co-workers. However, very few researchers have investigated this potentially fruitful topic area. Drawing on the extant family and occupational stress literature, social learning theory, and the antisocial behavior literature, we suggest the following avenues for further exploration:

- What are the specific costs to coworkers of IPV targets in terms of productivity (i.e. performance, absence, and lateness)?
- What are the psychological and physical health consequences of working with targets of IPV on coworkers? Do coworkers of IPV targets suffer similar health effects as targets do from suppressing their potential concerns regarding IPV?
- Are coworkers of IPV targets more likely to engage in antisocial behavior at work?
- What predicts the amount of support coworkers are willing to provide targets of IPV?
- How are workplace stressor perceptions influenced by IPV?
- What are the effects of coworker fear about an IPV event at work on target's mental health (e.g. guilt, depression, shame)?
- How does a target's previous performance affect supportive behavior from coworkers?

Fourth Order Effects

Organizational Costs of IPV

As mentioned earlier, research really has only scratched the surface in terms of exploring the outcomes and costs of IPV for an organization. First, many questions persist in terms of the aggregate cost of IPV for organizations. More specifically, future research must more precisely identify the costs associated with IPV on a number of levels. We hope that researchers will apply the ecological framework and think more deeply about the potential antecedents of IPV-related costs to organizations.

Another interesting research question concerns the costs incurred by organizations that employ perpetrators. Very little research, to our knowledge, has examined the nature or level of such costs. However, the potential costs seem significant and might include: tardiness, absenteeism, turnover, health care use, loss of productivity, and the use of company resources to perpetrate IPV. In addition, there may be costs that arise through organizational efforts to monitor or manage employees who have some history of violence (e.g. increased security measures, litigation). Finally, there may be spillover costs for other employees, such as stress related consequences for coworkers who suspect or know that the perpetrator has a history of violent behavior.

Organizational Factors that Encourage Disclosure

Earlier we mentioned the importance of IPV disclosure to coworkers. Another interesting multilevel research issue relates to employees' decisions to report or not report IPV to employers. Before organizations can influence IPV, they must know about it. Therefore, it would be interesting to consider the types of organizational conditions that encourage reporting. Thus we suggest the following questions for future research.

- Is the existence of an IPV policy associated with greater levels of disclosure?
- Does the employee's trust in the organization influence disclosure?
- How does an organizational climate of target stigmatization affect disclosure?
- How does an employer's response to a disclosure affect a target's attachment to the organization (e.g. identification, psychological contract, commitment)?

Multilevel Effects of IPV

We are aware of no research that has examined the multilevel effects of IPV. Given the recent call for multilevel research among management scholars we believe this a promising avenue for researchers interested in the consequences of IPV for occupational stress and well being (Klein & Kozlowski, 2000). Moreover, a multilevel perspective fits well within the ecological framework. IPV is likely to produce spillover effects that influence social networks, group performance, group mood, stress levels, and group member behaviors. In addition, group characteristics such as cohesion, trust, gender composition, or interdependence may yield different effects on how group members react to targets of IPV within their group. Specifically we suggest the following questions may be of interest to IPV researchers.

- What are the effects of IPV on organizational job satisfaction and commitment?
- What is the effect of IPV on communication and friendship networks in organizations?
- Are targets of IPV less embedded in important organizational networks?

- What is the effect of coworker awareness of IPV victimization on work group cohesion?
- What is the effect of coworker awareness of IPV victimization on work group mood?
- What are the effects of coworker awareness of IPV victimization on trust among coworkers?
- What role do organizational factors (e.g. justice climate, communication climate) play in determining the effects of IPV victimization on coworkers?
- What role do occupational characteristics (e.g. gender composition, culture) play in determining coworker reactions to IPV targets?

PRACTICAL IMPLICATIONS

The Role of the Organization in IPV Prevention

We have offered numerous examples of how IPV leads to negative outcomes for organizations and employees. In addition, statistical data provide estimates of the substantial costs that companies incur as a result of IPV. However, many organizations have yet to take formal action aimed at reducing instances of violence and the associated costs. Too often, a serious IPV related situation must occur before organizational leaders realize the need for IPV prevention strategies and unfortunately, then it is too late. Further, IPV situations often occur suddenly and are worsened by employees' lack of knowledge regarding how to appropriately handle the incident.

For instance, in January, 2004, the Fourth Circuit Court of Appeals held a Maryland business liable for "intentional abuse" when a supervisor of this company allowed an ex-boyfriend of a current employee on the premises in an effort to reconcile the relationship. The supervisor was a friend of the ex-boyfriend and, despite the fact that the employee reported the abuse to management and had a restraining order against her ex-boyfriend, the supervisor persisted. Once the ex-boyfriend was allowed on the property, he kidnapped the employee and raped her. The court concluded that the supervisor's behavior was "intentional abuse" and held the company liable for personal injury (although not legally responsible for the assault).

Clearly, the radiating effects of IPV are "alive and well" and pose many detrimental consequences for organizations. Fortunately, there are several actions that businesses can take to reduce the costs and negative implications associated with IPV outcomes in the workplace. Of primary importance is that organizations' top management team recognize and visibly support the establishment of IPV prevention strategies and programs (USDLWB, 1996). This allows for the on-going education of management and employees on IPV prevention, the funding of IPV prevention programs and benefits, as well as the reinforcement of the organization's commitment to this cause. These actions will encourage an organizational culture in which the negative effects of IPV are not tolerated and IPV targets can obtain the assistance needed in order to break the cycle of abuse.

Consequently, with the support of top management, organizations can engage in a number of actions aimed at reducing the radiating effects of IPV. One such element, that is critical to IPV prevention, is to provide the work force with continuing education on this topic (Cossack et al., 2004; U.S. Department of Labor, Women's Bureau, 1996). Minimally, organizations can provide training to its managers on how to deal with IPV related situations, as well as provide the resources needed to address IPV situations. More effective, however, is to provide all employees with training or seminars related to IPV. Liz Claiborne is one company that offers on-going training on IPV for its workforce by utilizing their Employee Assistance Program (EAP) to provide seminars during business hours. In addition, EAPs may offer counseling and referrals for IPV. Therefore, getting the EAP involved in employee education can be an effective means of familiarizing workers with the EAP so that when dealing with IPV-related situations they are comfortable utilizing EAP counselors. In addition to the EAP, companies should make other resources available such as local shelter contact information and hotline phone numbers (Cossack et al., 2004).

Along with continuing education, organizations can institute a number of IPV policies or practices aimed at prevention. For instance, the City of Tacoma, in their campaign against violence, published educational and prevention articles in the company newsletter as well as created a committee of employees tasked with recommending services to IPV targets and their families. Polaroid Corporation, along with many other programs, developed a family violence protocol to help guide and educate their employees during IPV situations. Furthermore, organizations with labor unions can negotiate contract provisions allowing for benefits such as paid time off for medical or legal emergencies as well as for legal assistance (U.S. Department of Labor, Women's Bureau, 1996). Organizations should even consider providing assistance in obtaining restraining or protection orders if necessary (Cossack et al., 2004).

While some companies have initiated internal IPV prevention strategies, others have begun to realize that, to maximize IPV prevention efforts, building community recognition and support of IPV prevention is also crucial. Thus, many organizational actions have been targeted externally as a means of educating the community. Companies such as Polaroid and Marshalls Department Stores have partnered with battered women's shelters by providing financial support and employee volunteers. In exchange, the shelter agrees to establish certain programs or practices desired by the organization. As another example, the Bank of Boston Foundation sponsors a women's shelter financially so that it can provide training to battered women on how to start their own business. Thus, by taking steps to target IPV prevention externally, organizations can reduce IPV in the local community from which they draw many of their employees.

CONCLUSION

From an occupational health and well being standpoint, it is clear that there are substantial reasons for organizations to take an interest in IPV (Reeves et al., 2001). A first step, then, is for organizational decision makers to recognize that IPV poses a serious threat to occupational well being. Interestingly, data from the RoperASW (1994, 2003) studies (cited earlier) suggest that most (66% of) executives already have taken this step. However, the next, and more critical, step is for these executives to recognize that the work-related effects of IPV can be influenced through managerial action. As we have argued here, IPV will have powerful radiating effects on target, coworker, and organizational functioning if these potential effects are not recognized and addressed. This, then, is the challenge: for executives to seek ways to minimize these negative effects, and for organizational researchers to provide information (through a sustained, cogent stream of research) that will assist in such efforts.

REFERENCES

Allcorn, S. (1994). *Anger in the workplace.* Westport, CT: Quorom.
Aldous, J. (1969). Occupational characteristics and males' role performance in the family. *Journal of Marriage and Family, 31,* 707–712.
American Bar Association Commission on Domestic Violence (2003). *Impact of domestic violence on the workplace,* web link: http://www.abanet.org/domviol/workviolence.html.
American Institute on Domestic Violence (2003). *Domestic violence statistics, crime statistics and workplace violence statistics,* web link: http://www.aidv-usa.com/Statistics.htm.
American Management Association 65th Annual Human Resources Conference On-Site Survey, San Francisco, 1994.
Ashforth, B. E. (1997). Petty tyranny in organizations: A preliminary examination of antecedents and consequences. *Canadian Journal of Administrative Sciences, 14,* 126–141.
Barling, J., & Rosenbaum, A. (1986). Work stressors and wife abuse. *Journal of Applied Psychology, 71,* 346–348.
Barnett, O., & Fagan, R. (1993). Alcohol use in male spouse abusers and their female partners. *Journal of Family Violence, 8,* 1–25.

Barnett, O., Fagan, R., & Booker, J. M. (1991). Hostility and stress as mediators of aggression in violent men. *Journal of Family Violence, 6,* 217–241.

Bell, M., Moe, A., & Schweinle, W. (2002). Partner violence and work: Not just a "domestic issue." *Academy of Management Proceedings.*

Bies, R. J. (1987). The predicament of injustice: The management of moral outrage. *Research in Organizational Behavior, 9,* 289–321.

Bies, R. J., & Tripp, T. M. (1998). Revenge in organizations: The good, the bad, and the ugly. In: R. W. Griffin, A. M. O'Leary-Kelly & J. M. Collins (Eds), *Dysfunctional Behavior in Organizations* (pp. 49–68). Stamford, CT: JAI Press.

Bolger, N., DeLongis, A., Kessler, R., & Wethington, E. (1989). The contagion of stress across multiple roles. *Journal of Marriage and the Family, 15,* 175–183.

Brinkerhoff, M., & Lupri, E. (1988). Interspousal violence. *Canadian Journal of Sociology, 13,* 407–434.

Budd, J., Arvey, R., & Lawless, P. (1996). Correlates and consequences of workplace violence. *Journal of Occupational Heath Psychology, 1,* 197–210.

Bureau of Justice Statistics (2001). *Violence in the workplace, 1993–1999* (NCJ Publication No. 190076). Washington, DC: National Institute of Justice.

Burke, R. J., & Greenglass, E. R. (1987). In: C. L. Cooper & I. T. Robertson (Eds), *Work and Family. International Review of Industrial and Organizational Psychology* (pp. 273–320). Sussex, England: Wiley.

Caliguiri, P., Hyland, & Bross, A. (1998). Testing a theoretical model for examining the relationship between family adjustment and expatriates' work adjustment. *Journal of Applied Psychology, 83,* 598–614.

Cano, A., & Vivian, D. (2001). Life stressors and husband-to-wife violence. *Aggression and Violent Behavior, 6,* 450–480.

Chicago National Organization for Women (2004). Combating domestic and sexual violence. Web Link: www.chicagonow.org.

Cicchetti, D., & Lynch, M. (1993). Toward an ecological/transactional model of community violence and child maltreatment: Consequences for children's development. *Psychiatry, 56,* 96–118.

Collela, A. (2001). Coworker distributive fairness judgments of the workplace accommodation of employees with disabilities. *Academy of Management Review, 26,* 100–116.

Cossack, N., Maingault, A., & Lau, S. (2004). Domestic violence, payback time, 'right to work'. *HR Magazine, 49,* 41–43.

Duffy, M. K., Ganster, D. C., & Pagon, M. (2002). Social undermining and social support in the workplace. *Academy of Management Journal, 45,* 331–351.

Duffy, M. K., Shaw, J. D., Scott, K. D., & Tepper, B. J. (2004). The role of self-esteem and neuroticism in responses to group undermining. Paper presented at the Society for Industrial and Organizational Psychology. Chicago.

Eckenrode, J., & Gore, S. (1990). Stress and coping at the boundary of work and family. In: J. Eckenrode & S. Gore (Eds), *Stress Between Work and Family* (pp. 1–16). New York: Plenum.

Edwards, J. R., & Rothbard, N. P. (2000). Mechanisms linking work and family: Clarifying the relationship between work and family constructs. *Academy of Management Review, 25,* 178–199.

Farrington, K. (1986). The application of stress theory to the study of family violence: Principles, problems, and prospects. *Journal of Family Violence, 1,* 131–147.

Farmer, A., & Tiefenthaler, J. (1997). The economics of domestic violence. *Review of Social Economy.*

Farmer, A., & Tiefenthaler, J. (2003a). The employment effects of domestic violence. *Journal of Labor Research.*

Flannery, J. (1995). *Violence in the workplace.* New York: Cross-road.

Frone, M. (2000). Work-family conflict and employee psychiatric disorders: The national comorbidity survey. *Journal of Applied Psychology, 85,* 888–895.

Ganley, A., & Warshaw, C. (1995). *Improving the healthcare responses to domestic violence: A resource manual for health care providers.* San Francisco: Family Violence Prevention Fund.

Gardner, W. (1992). Lessons in organizational dramaturgy: The art of impression management. *Organizational Dynamics, 21,* 33–46.

Goffman, E. (1963). *Stigma, Notes on the management of spoiled identity.* Englewood Cliffs, NJ: Prentice-Hall.

Greenberg, J. (1997). The STEAL motive: Managing the social determinants of employee theft. In: R. Giacalone & J. Greenberg (Eds), *Antisocial Behavior in Organizations* (pp. 85–108). Thousand Oaks, CA: Sage.

Greenfeld, L. (1998). *Violence by intimates.* Bureau of Justice Statistics, U.S. Dept. Of Justice.

Holtzworth-Munroe, A., Bates, L., Smutzler, N., & Sandin, E. (1997). A brief review of the research on husband violence. *Aggression and Violent Behavior, 2,* 65–99.

Hoobler (2004). Working Paper.

Hoobler, J. M. (2003). Abuse, undermining, and restorative justice: When workers kick the dog. *Annual Meetings of the Academy of Management,* Seattle, WA.

Jasinski, J., Asdigian, N., & Kantor, G. (1997). Ethnic adaptations to occupational strain: Work-related stress, drinking, and wife assault among Anglo and Hispanic husbands. *Journal of Interpersonal Violence, 12,* 814–831.

Johnson, P., & Gardner, S. (1999). Domestic violence and the workplace: Developing a company response. *The Journal of Management Development, 18,* 590–597.

Johnson, P., & Indvik, J. (1999). The organizational benefits of assisting domestically abused employees. *Public Personnel Management, 28,* 365–374.

Jones, E. E., Farina, A., Hastorf, A. H., Miller, D. T., Scott, R. A. et al. (1984). *Social stigma: The psychology of marked relationships.* New York: W. H. Freeman.

Kelly, J. (1966). Ecological constraints in mental health services. *American Psychologist, 21,* 535–539.

Kelly, J. (1971). Qualities for the community psychologist. *American Psychologist, 21,* 535–539.

Kilpatrick, D. (1990). Violence as a precursor of women's substance abuse: The rest of the drugs-violence story. Paper presented at the annual meeting of the American Psychological Association, Boston, MA.

Klein, K., & Kozlowski, S. (2000). *Multilevel theory, research, and methods in organizations: Foundations, extensions, and new directions.* Sage.

Laffaye, C., Kennedy, C., & Stein, M. (2003a). Post-traumatic stress disorder and health-related quality of life in female targets of intimate partner violence. *Violence and Victims, 18,* 227–239.

Laffaye, C., Kennedy, C., & Stein, M. B. (2003b). Post-traumatic stress disorder and health-related quality of life in female victims of intimate partner violence. *Violence Victimization, 18,* 227–238.

Laszlo, A. T., & Rinehart, T. A. (2002). Collaborative problem-solving partnerships: Advancing community policing philosophy to domestic violence victim services. *International Review of Victimology, 9,* 197–209.

Leiter, M., & Durup, M. (1996). Work, home, and in-between: A longitudinal study of spillover. *Journal of Applied Behavioral Science, 32,* 29–47.

Lord, V. B. (1998). Characteristics of violence in state government. *Journal of Interpersonal Violence*, *13*, 489–504.

Mack, D. A., Shannon, C., Quick, J. D., & Quick, J. C. (1998). Stress and the preventive management of workplace violence. In: R. W. Griffin, A. M. O'Leary-Kelly & J. M. Collins (Eds), *Dysfunctional Behavior in Organizations* (pp. 119–141). Stamford, CT: JAI Press.

Margolin, G., John, R., & Foo, L. (1998). Interactive and unique risk factors for husbands' emotional and physical abuse of their wives. *Journal of Family Violence*, *13*, 315–344.

McLaughlin, M. E., Bell, M. P., & Stringer, D. Y. (2004). Stigma and acceptance of persons with disabilities: Understudied aspects of workforce diversity. *Group and Organization Management*, *29*, 302–333.

Mitchell, R. E., & Hodson, C. A. (1983). Coping with domestic violence: Social support and psychological health among battered women. *American Journal of Community Psychology*, *11*, 629–654.

National Center for Injury Prevention and Control (2003). *Costs of intimate partner violence against women in the United States*. Atlanta, GA: Centers for Disease Control and Prevention.

National Institute for Occupational Safety and Health (NIOSH) (2004). *Women's safety and health issues at work*. http://www.cdc.gov/niosh/topics/women/.

National Institute of Justice (1995). *National violence against women survey*. Atlanta, GA: Centers for Disease Control and Prevention.

Nevonen, J. (2001). *Interrupting the cycle of violence: Addressing domestic violence through the workplace*. Duluth: Minnesota Center Against Violence and Abuse.

Paetzold. R. (1998). Workplace violence and employer liability: Implications for organizations. In: R. W. Griffin, A. M. O'Leary-Kelly & J. M. Collins (Eds), *Dysfunctional Behavior in Organizations* (pp. 143–164). Stamford, CT: JAI Press.

Partnership for Prevention (2002). *Domestic violence and the workplace*. Washington, DC Founded by the Centers for Disease Control and Prevention.

Pearson, C., & Porath, C. (2004). On incivility, its impact and directions for future research. In: R. Griffin & A. O'Leary-Kelly (Eds), *The Dark Side of Organizational Behavior* (pp. 403–425). San Francisco: Jossey-Bass.

Perilla, J. L., Bakeman, R., & Norris, F. H. (1994). Culture and domestic violence: The ecology of abused Latinas. *Violence and Victims*, *9*(4), 325–339.

Perin, S. (1999). Employers may have to pay when domestic violence goes to work. *Review of Litigation*, *18*, 365–401.

Perrewé, P., Treadway, D., & Hall, A. (2003). The work and family interface: Conflict, family-friendly policies, and employee well being. In: D. Hofmann & L. Tetrick (Eds), *Health and Safety in Organizations* (pp. 285–315). Jossey-Bass.

Popham, A. (1998). Companies learn domestic violence is, in fact, their business. *The News Tribune*, April 5, p. G2.

Pynoos, R., Sorenson, S., & Steinberg, A. (1993). Interpersonal violence and traumatic stress reactions. In: L. Goldberger & S. Breznitz (Eds), *Handbook of Stress, Theoretical and Clinical Aspects* (2nd ed., pp. 573–590). New York: Free Press.

Reeves, C. (2004). When the dark side of families enters the workplace: The case of intimate partner violence. In: R. Griffin & A. O'Leary-Kelly (Eds), *The Dark Side of Organizational Behavior* (pp. 103–127). San Francisco: Jossey-Bass.

Reeves, C., O-Leary-Kelly, A., Farmer, A., Paetzold, R., & Tiefenthaler, J. (2001). *American government and business: Their individual and joint roles in addressing intimate partner violence*. Fayetteville, AR: University of Arkansas.

Riger, S., Raja, S., & Camacho, J. (2002). The radiating impact of intimate partner violence. *Journal of Interpersonal Violence, 17*(2), 184–205.

Rook, K., Dooley, D., & Catalano, R. (1991). Stress transmission: The effects of husbands' job stressors on the emotional health of their wives. *Journal of Marriage and the Family, 53*, 165–177.

RoperASW (2003). *Corporate leaders on domestic violence: Awareness of the problem, how it's affecting their business, and what they're doing to address it.* Roper Number: C205-007498.

Rothman, E. (2002). Batterers in the workplace. Paper presented at the UNH Family Violence Conference, Durham, NH, July.

Ruckelshaus, C. K. (1996). Unemployment compensation for victims of domestic violence: An important link to economic and employment security. *Clearinghouse Review*, Special Issue, 209–221.

Salzinger, S., Feldman, R. S., Stockhammer, T., & Hood, J. (2002). An ecological framework for understanding risk for exposure to community violence and the effects of exposure on children and adolescents. *Aggression and Violent Behavior, 7*, 423–451.

Scalora, M., O'Neil, W. D., Casady, T., & Newell, S. (2003). Nonfatal workplace violence factors: Data from a police contact sample. *Journal of Interpersonal Violence, 18*, 310–327.

Shinn, M. (1996). Ecological assessment: Introduction to the special issue [Special issue]. *American Journal of Community Psychology, 24*, 1–2.

Skarlicki, D., & Folger, R. (1997). Retaliation for perceived unfair treatment: Examining the roles of procedural and interactional injustice. *Journal of Applied Psychology, 82*, 434–443.

Tepper, B. J. (2000). Consequences of Abusive Supervision. *Academy of Management Journal, 43*, 178–190.

Tepper, B., Duffy, M., & Shaw, J. (1998, 2001). Personality moderators of the relationship between abusive supervision and subordinates' resistance. *Journal of Applied Psychology, 86*, 974–983.

Tjaden, P., & Thoennes, N. (2000). *Extent, nature, and consequences of intimate partner violence: Findings from the National Violence Against Women Survey.* National Institute of Justice and Centers for Disease Control and Prevention, July.

U.S. Department of Health and Human Services (1997). *Trends in the well being of America's children and youth.* Washington, DC: U.S. Government Printing Office.

U.S. Department of Labor, Women's Bureau (1996). *Domestic violence: A workplace issue: Facts on working women.* Washington, DC.

Warchol, G. (1998). Workplace violence, 1992–1996. Washington, DC: Bureau of Justice Statistics, U.S. Department of Justice.

Williams, J., & Alliger, M. (1994). Role stressors, mood spillover, and perceptions of work-family conflict: A Sino-US comparison of the effects of work and family demands. *Academy of Management Journal, 43*, 113–123.

Wilson, K. J. (1997). *When violence begins at home.* Salt Lake City, UT: Publishers Press.

Yoshinko, M., Gilbert, L., & Baig-Amin, M. (2003). Social support and disclosure of abuse: Comparing South Asian, African American, and Hispanic battered women. *Journal of Family Violence, 18*, 171–182.

Zachary, M. (2000). Court strikes down one violence remedy, but others abound. *Supervision, 61*, 22–26.

Zedeck, S. (1992). *Work, families, and organizations.* San Francisco, CA: Jossey-Bass.

THE CHANGING NATURE OF JOB STRESS: RISK AND RESOURCES

Mark Tausig, Rudy Fenwick, Steven L. Sauter,
Lawrence R. Murphy and Corina Graif

ABSTRACT

The nature of work has changed in the past 30 years but we do not know what these changes have meant for worker job stress. In this chapter we compare data from three surveys of the quality of work life from 1972 to 2002. At the most general level, work today is less stressful than it was in 1972. Workers report fewer job demands, more decision latitude, less job strain, more job security and greater access to job resources and job support. However, these changes have not affected all workers equally. Women, those with less education, non self-employed workers, blue collar workers and workers in manufacturing industries showed the greatest decreases in job stress although levels of job stress remain higher than for comparison groups (men, college educated, white collar, service workers). Changes were not always linear across time suggesting that some aspects of job strain are sensitive to economic cycles.

INTRODUCTION

The nature of work has changed considerably in the past 30 years. But there are conflicting interpretations of what these changes have meant for worker job

Exploring Interpersonal Dynamics
Research in Occupational Stress and Well Being, Volume 4, 93–126
Copyright © 2005 by Elsevier Ltd.
All rights of reproduction in any form reserved
ISSN: 1479-3555/doi:10.1016/S1479-3555(04)04003-X

stress. Some argue that work in high performance organizations, for example, is characterized by more stimulating work conducted in a context where workers have considerable say over how the work is done and that this increases decision latitude and reduces job stress (National Research Council, 1999). Other analysts have suggested that the growth in the "service economy" would create vast numbers of low-skill low-paying jobs that feature high levels of job demand and low decision latitude, thus increasing job stress (Braverman, 1974).

Hence, while it is clear that the nature of work has changed, it is not clear whether these changes have increased or decreased job stress among workers. Such an assessment requires comparable data from comparable samples across multiple years. The purpose of this chapter is to provide just such a set of comparisons using data from three surveys of the quality of work life that span 30 years. The data files all utilize representative samples of U.S. workers. These data allow us to document the changing nature of work, the changing nature of workers and changes in job stress and to examine how changes in work and workers have affected changes in job stress.

WORK ORGANIZATION AND JOB STRESS

Job stress is a property of job structures such as the combination of high demands and low decision latitude (Karasek, 1989; Radmacher & Sheridan, 1995). Although it is certainly true that personality and psychological characteristics of workers affect stressful reactions to work conditions, it is employers who largely determine the structure and content of work. In particular, Karasek (1979) has argued that two properties of a job, its level of psychological demands and its level of decision latitude jointly determine the stressful nature of a job. Jobs in which demands are high and decision latitude is low are defined as "high strain" jobs. This demand-control model has become the most prominent model for understanding how job structures affect job stress. Substantial research has been conducted using the model with mixed empirical support (de Lange et al., 2003; Van Der Doef & Maes, 1999). It has also been extended to include the effects that co-worker and supervisor support have on job stress. Workers who receive support from others are less likely to report experiencing job strain. Thus, some researchers refer to the demand-control – support model or the "iso-strain" model (Johnson, 1989; Van Der Doef & Maes, 1999). There are, of course, other models as well. We will investigate the changing nature of job stress using the demand-control model, examining these and other dimensions of work over time. We conceptualize these dimensions in terms of structural "risks" and "resources" that affect the stressful nature of jobs.

Risk, Resources and Stress

The demand-control model or iso-strain models can be contrasted with theoretical approaches that incorporate a broader range of organizational risk factors for stress (Sauter & Murphy, 1995). Findings suggest that not only does support from co-workers and supervisors play a role in determining job stress, but that other job conditions such as job security and access to adequate information and equipment also must be considered.

One way to conceptualize all of these conditions is in the broad context of risks and resources. This perspective has been developed within the Medical Sociology literature as a means for understanding the way in which structural context affects health (Link & Phelan, 1995). Structures both place persons (workers) at risk of illness (stress) and provide access to resources that can be used to avoid stress or to deal with its consequences. It seems clear that the demand-control model falls within this conceptualization. However, the conceptualization also lets us bring in those additional job conditions that are part of a broader explanation for job stress. In this broader model, job conditions that increase the risk of job stress, such as a job with high demands and low decision latitude or one with low job security, can be offset by resources such as co-worker and supervisor support or access to resources with which one can complete work tasks. We use this perspective simply to trace the changing nature of work structures and job stress across data collected in 1972, 1977 and 2002.

THE CHANGING NATURE OF WORK

Since the 1970s the nature of work has changed. Major economic, technological, legal, political and other changes have had a substantial effect on the organization of work in the United States (Sauter et al., 2002). Manufacturing jobs have declined, there is more "knowledge" work, organizations have downsized, there is greater competitive pressure in the marketplace, unionization has decreased and self-employment is reported to have increased. As a consequence of these changes, organizations have implemented practices that change work conditions. Many organizations have adopted flatter management structures and lean production technologies that imply a diffusion of decision-making control (greater decision latitude but, perhaps, also increased job demands). Others argue that changes in the economic environment mean that workers are now less protected from changes in labor and product market forces outside of the organization (Cappelli et al., 1997). Employees are, thus, more vulnerable to job-loss through downsizing, plant closings and use of temporary or contingent workers. According to this argument stress from job insecurity now occurs throughout economic cycles and not only during recessionary phases.

The occupational structure in the U.S. has also changed significantly and the changes may have implications for the distribution of job stress among occupations. Blue-collar jobs have been lost and service and professional jobs have increased. The National Research Council (1999) suggests that blue-collar jobs now offer workers more autonomy and control and job complexity that might reduce job stress. At the same time, while the number of service jobs has grown, this same report suggests that service jobs have become more routinized and that service workers have lost some control over their work activities. These characteristics are associated with more job stress and, if more workers are employed in service jobs, it would imply an increase in overall job stress.

Job structures also change because of changes in the status of the economy. During recessions, for example, firms follow two adjustment strategies. They lay off workers and they restructure jobs (Hachen, 1992). Generally this restructuring includes higher demands for productivity and closer supervision-factors that increase job stress. Likewise, in expanding economic periods firms hire new workers and monitor work less closely-factors that decrease job stress. While broad shifts in the occupational and industrial distribution of jobs and other long-term technological and global changes affect job conditions, economic cycles that affect corporate profits and employment levels also affect job conditions.

THE CHANGING NATURE OF WORKERS

Between 1972 and 2002 (but not beginning or ending with these years) the demographic characteristics of workers changed dramatically. Women entered the labor force in sizable numbers and many of these women are mothers. The labor force has also aged. In addition, the educational attainment of workers is much higher than in 1972.

These changes may have implications for the structure of jobs (and job-related stress) and the distribution of jobs with stressful content.

CHANGES IN JOB STRESS

To document changes in job stress over the past 30 years we need to assess various indicators of job stress in the context of changes in the nature of work and worker changes that have occurred over this same period. Since the nature of work and the nature of workers have changed so much, we need to describe the distribution of risks and resources for job stress in terms of these documented changes. We will examine data from three representative samples of American workers collected in 1972, 1977 and 2002.

THE DATA SETS

1972 (Quality of Employment Survey)

A national survey of the quality of employment was conducted in January and February, 1973 by the Survey Research Center of the Institute for Social Research, The University of Michigan. The survey was sponsored by the Employment Standards Administration, U.S. Department of Labor and the National Institute for Occupational Safety and Health, and was intended to provide an overview of working conditions in the American labor force.

There were 1496 respondents. The requirements for respondent eligibility were that they be at least 16 years old and work for pay 20 or more hours per week. People were also interviewed if they worked for pay but were currently not working due to strike, sickness, weather, vacation, or for personal reasons. The sample was, therefore, not representative of the American labor force but was instead a sample of the population of employed workers who met the above sample eligibility requirements. Although households were sampled at a constant rate, designated respondents had variable selection rates according to the number of eligible persons within the household. The data for each respondent are, therefore weighted by the number of eligible persons in the household to make the data representative of all workers.

1977 (Quality of Employment Survey)

This survey was also undertaken in order to provide an overview of working conditions in the American labor force. Like the 1972 survey, this survey utilized a national probability sample of persons 16 years old or older who were working for pay 20 or more hours per week. Although households were sampled at a constant rate, designated respondents had variable selection rates according to the number of eligible persons within a household. Therefore, data for each respondent was weighted by the number of persons in the household.

The 1977 survey was sponsored by the Employee Standards Administration, U.S. Department of Labor. Information was obtained from a sample of 1515 respondents.

2002 (Quality of Work Life)

The Quality of Work Life (QWL) survey was a module of the General Social Survey (GSS) conducted by the National Opinion Research Center (NORC) in 2002. The GSS is a bi-annual representative sample of English-speaking persons 18 years of age and over, living in non-institutional arrangements within the United States. In 2002, a total of 2765 adults were interviewed. The GSS consists of a set of "core" survey items that are asked of all respondents and topical mini-modules of survey items such as the QWL module that are asked of sub-samples of respondents. The QWL module was sponsored by NIOSH. The QWL module was answered by 1777 respondents who indicated that they were employed for pay in the week previous to the survey or temporarily not working because of vacation, illness, etc.

Comparing the Surveys: Methodological Considerations

To compare the survey responses across the different data sets we must first make the characteristics of the samples comparable. The 1972 and 1977 surveys are based on responses from workers 16 years old or older who were working for pay 20 or more hours each week. By contrast, the QWL is based on the responses of workers 18 years old or older and without the requirement to work 20 hours or more. Hence, we specify that, for all data sets, only workers 18 years old or older and who work 20 or more hours per week will be included. These criteria reduce the size of each sample somewhat. In 1972, the weighted number of respondents is 2048, in 1977 the weighted number of respondents is 2226 and, in 2002, the weighted number of respondents is 3010. The data from each survey is weighted by the number of eligible respondents in each interview household to adjust for biases in the selection of household respondents. The weighted data make the samples representative of all eligible workers. In this study, then, the responses we report and the comparison we perform are based on representative samples of American workers who are at least 18 years old and who work 20 or more hours per week.

MEASURES

Each of the surveys contains extensive data on work life. However, in order to compare responses across the surveys, we must limit our analysis to items that are present in all surveys. Indeed, we do not have a separate measure of job stress per se that is available in all three surveys. Rather, we will measure and compare the components of job stress including risk factors and resources that are components of job stress.

In our analysis we will examine the distribution of these job risks and resources across occupation, industry, union membership and self-employment status to represent the changing nature of work and across gender, marital status, age and education to represent the changing nature of workers.

Job Stress-Risks

According to the demand-control model, job demands and job decision latitude are the components of job strain. In the present analysis, *Job demands* is measured as the sum of three items: The job requires me to work fast; I have enough time to get the job done and I am free from conflicting demands. These items were part of the demand measure developed by Karasek (1979). Scores on this index range between 3 and 12 with higher scores indicating higher demands. Job *decision latitude* is measured as the sum of five items: The job requires that I learn new things; the job allows me to use my skills; I do numerous things on my job; I have a lot of freedom to decide how to do my job; and I have a lot to say in my job. These items were also part of the decision latitude measure used by Karasek (1979). Scores on this index range from 5 to 20, with higher scores indicating greater decision latitude. *Job strain* identifies a situation in which job demands are high and decision latitude is low. High levels of job demands are defined as demand levels above one-half of a standard deviation from the mean and low decision latitude is defined as decision latitude levels below one-half standard deviation from the mean (Karasek & Theorell, 1990). The strain variable is dichotomous; workers who report high demands and low decision latitude are given a score of "1" and all other workers are given a score of "0." Finally, *job security* is measured as a single item: the job security is good. Scores range from 1 to 4 and a higher score indicates greater security.

Job Stress-Resources

While there is continuing discussion about how support and other resources affect the experience of job stress, it is clear that access to supportive co-workers and supervisors and access to needed information and equipment are generally associated with less job stress. In some models, support mediates the effects of job strain on job stress in some it buffers strain while in still others support has an independent effect. In the current analysis, however, we are interested only in documenting changes in the perception of or availability of resources as characteristics of jobs over time and not in the exact manner in which those resources affect job stress.

Job support is measured as the sum of three items that assess co-worker and supervisor support: my co-workers take a personal interest in me; my supervisor is concerned about my welfare; and my supervisor is helpful in getting my job done. Scores on this index range between 3 and 12, with higher scores indicating greater support. Finally, *job resources* is indexed as the sum of two items: I have enough help and equipment to get the job done; and I have enough information to get the job done. Scores on this index range between 2 and 8, with higher scores indicating greater access to job resources.

The Changing Nature of Work

We measure four characteristics of employment that represent the nature of work. These are, *occupation*, collapsed into two categories, white collar and blue collar; *industry* collapsed into two categories, manufacturing and service; *union membership* (member or not) and, *self-employment status*, (self-employed or employed by others). In the tables that follow, we examine the changing distribution of these work contexts and their relationships with job risks and resources.

The Changing Nature of Workers

Similarly, we measure four characteristics of workers that have changed over the past thirty years and that are related to job conditions, as well. We measure *gender* and we measure *education* as a dichotomous variable; no college and some college or greater. We also measure *marital* status in three categories, never married, not married (divorced separated, widowed) and currently married. Finally, we place workers into one of three *age* groups, 18–34, 35–54 or 55 and over. In the tables that follow, we examine the changing relationship between gender, education, marital status and age group and indicators of job risks and resources over time.

ANALYTIC APPROACH

Our purpose in this study is to document changes in job stress between 1972, 1977 and 2002. As such, our analytic approach will first use analysis of variance (ANOVA) to make comparisons of job stress outcomes across years and between categories that represent worker and work characteristics. In making these comparisons our objective is to identify important patterns of change, though these may not all be linear. We will not attempt to compare and discuss every job characteristic or worker characteristic mean score with every other relevant mean score. We also make an attempt to explain the variations that are observed using multivariate statistical models that allow us to consider work and worker characteristics simultaneously.

We will first document changes in the nature of workers and work as they are manifest across surveys. Next, we will examine the changes in job stress across years and then we will present and discuss more detailed tables that document changes in job stress across workers and work characteristics across years.

We will then use multivariate analyses to address the question of how all the changes in both the nature of workers and the nature of work have affected observed changes in job stress. This analysis will first explain how the nature of workers and work affect job stress in 1972 and then in 2002. We will then provide an analysis of how changes in these predictors between 1972 and 2002 have affected job stress.

Two general considerations should be held in mind as these tables are reviewed. First, the numbers examined in this study are averages that are derived from representative samples of American workers 18 years old or older who worked 20 hours or more at the time of the interview. Hence, the conclusions we draw may not apply to specific types of workers in specific industries and occupations. They may also be at variance with other findings that are based on studying specific industries or occupations. The advantage of using representative samples of workers is that the results are true of workers-in-general, but the disadvantage is that the results will not be descriptive of specific workers or work conditions. The data collected in each survey are from different workers so we are not documenting individual changes in job stress. Further, the exact nature of what workers do on their jobs has also changed substantially (e.g. the use of computers). We do not document these changes, but, rather, job characteristics that are independent of the exact work conducted.

Second, we use three "data points" and these are not equally spaced over time. That is, our samples represent workers in 1972, 1977 and 2002-gaps of five years and twenty-five years between surveys. This is fortuitous because it prevents us from assuming that changes observed over two points in time (say 1972 and 2002) represent uninterrupted linear change. Moreover, we need to be aware that the data were collected at different points in general economic cycles and that this may have an effect on reported job stress. The American economy was in a different condition at each survey. In 1972, the U.S. economy was at the crest of a sustained and robust economic expansion. In 1977, the economy was just emerging from the most severe recessionary period since the Great Depression and in 2002 the economy was entering a new recession. Hence, we expect that we will see that not all changes in measured variables are linear and that the broad economic context affects work conditions and job stress as well.

RESULTS

The Changing Nature of Workers and Work

Table 1 documents the changing nature of the American workforce and workplace. The results are in agreement with many previous studies. There has been a linear increase in the percentage of women in the workforce. The percentage increased from 38% in 1972 to almost 50% in 2002. If these women largely entered traditionally "female" jobs, then we might expect an increase in job stress because such jobs tend to be high in job demands and low on decision latitude. On the other hand, there has also been a linear increase in the level of education of workers – those who attended college increased from 36% to almost 61% – that would be related to lower job strain since jobs among educated workers have more decision latitude.

The age composition of the labor force has changed in more complicated ways. There was a slight increase in the proportion of workers 18–24 years old between 1972 and 1977 and then a steep decrease between 1977 and 2002. By contrast, the proportion of workers between 25 and 44 years old decreased slightly between 1972 and 1977 and then increased steeply between 1977 and 2002. There has been a modest increase in the proportion of workers over 45 from 14 to15%. Clearly, the average age of the workforce has increased but most of the observed increase is among workers who were born after 1958 and before 1977 (post-baby boom). The higher average age of workers suggests that job stress may be lower as workers are, on average, more established in their careers or work histories.

The marital status composition of the labor force has also changed substantially. There has been a steady decline in the percent of workers who are married, and increases in the percentages of workers who have never married and who were previously married but are now not married. These changes are partially explained by the general increase in the age of first marriage during this period, the increase in divorce, the increase in female labor force participation and to the decrease in the percentage of younger workers. These patterns would be expected to increase job strain.

In these data self-employment versus working for someone else has not changed. The self-employment rate was 11.7% in 1972 and 12.6% in 2002. The difference is not statistically significant.

Table 1. The Changing Nature of Workers and Work.

	1972	1977	2002	*p*
Worker characteristics				
Gender				
Male	61.9	59.3	50.3	0.000
Female	38.1	40.7	49.7	
Education				
Non-college	63.6	58.7	39.2	0.000
College	36.4	41.3	60.8	
Age				
18–34	46.4	47.3	36.1	0.000
35–54	39.6	38.3	48.9	
55+	14.0	14.4	15.0	
Marital status				
Never married	14.8	19.3	26.1	0.000
Not married	9.5	10.7	17.8	
Married	75.7	70.0	56.1	
Work Characteristics				
Employment type				
Self	11.7	12.1	12.6	0.592 ns
By others	88.3	87.9	87.4	
Occupation				
White collar	52.4	50.9	60.0	0.000
Blue collar	47.6	49.1	40.0	
Industry				
Manfacturing	60.7	59.3	49.5	0.000
Service	39.3	40.7	50.5	
Union member				
Yes	30.0	25.3	15.2	0.000
No	70.0	74.7	84.8	
Weighted *N*	2048	2226	3010	

On the other hand, employment by occupation and industry has changed considerably. Employment in white-collar occupations decreased slightly between 1972 and 1977 but then increased sharply since 1977. The overall pattern of increasing white-collar employment is well known. And employment in white-collar occupations has been found by previous studies to be less stressful. There has also been a linear increase of employment in service industries and a corresponding decrease in manufacturing industry employment. According to previous research this pattern would be expected to increase over-all job stress. Finally, union membership has declined in a linear fashion, cutting in half the proportion of American workers who are members of unions. Because union jobs are often accompanied by strict rules that affect decision latitude, it may be that the decline in union membership would work to decrease the average levels of job strain.

Changes in Job Stress by Year

Table 2 presents mean changes in the indicators of job stress. Two distinct patterns can be observed in these data. First, job demands declined steadily over the period and decision latitude increased steadily over the period. As a consequence, because of the way it is computed, job strain also declined steadily between 1972 and 2002. This pattern suggests that jobs have become "better" over the past thirty years. Moreover, they have improved because of both decreases in the level of job demands and increases in decision latitude.

The second evident pattern applies to the results related to job security, job resources and job support: levels declined significantly from 1972 to 1977, but rebounded significantly by 2002. Indeed, by 2002 job security and job support were significantly higher than in 1972, while job resources were still significantly lower. These changes generally seem to follow the curves of economic cycles. For example, the measure of job security declined by 0.15 points from 1972 (the crest of an economic cycle) to 1977 (toward the end of the mid-1970s recession), but rebounded by one-quarter point by 2002 (as the economic cycle was just beginning to decline). This pattern suggests that some indicators of job stress are sensitive to macro-economic change while others may be related to technical or other factors.

Table 2.   Job Stress Indicators by Year.

	1972	1977	2002	p
Job demands	7.25[a]	7.06	6.80	0.000
Decision latitude	14.96	15.16	16.29	0.000
Job strain	0.23	0.17[a]	0.12	0.000
Job security	3.24	3.09	3.35	0.000
Job resources	6.95	6.62	6.80	0.000
Job support	9.25	8.91	9.80	0.000
Weighted N	2048	2226	3010	

[a]p values for ONEWAY ANOVA.

Table 3.   Job Stress Indicators by Year by Gender.

	1972		1977		2002	
	Male	Female	Male	Female	Male	Female
Job demands	7.20	7.32	7.08	7.04	6.80	6.79[a]
Decision latitude	15.27	14.44	15.51	14.60	16.38	16.21[a,b,c]
Job strain	0.19	0.30	0.14	0.22	0.11	0.14[a,b,c]
Job security	3.28	3.18	3.06	3.14	3.34	3.35[a,c]
Job resources	6.92	7.01	6.52	6.77	6.80	6.79[a,b,c]
Job support	9.16	9.40	8.70	9.20	9.69	9.91[a,b]
Weighted N	1268	780	1321	905	1514	1496

[a] Mean differences by year are significant.
[b] Mean differences by gender are significant.
[c] Mean differences for interaction are significant.

Job Stress by Year by Gender

In Table 3 we observe changes in job stress by gender. Perhaps the most striking result in this table is the apparent "equalization" of job conditions in terms of job stress for women and men. In 1972 women reported higher levels of job demands, less decision latitude, higher job strain and less job security. In 2002 there are no statistical differences between women and men in terms of job demands, job security and job resources (information and equipment availability) and differences in decision latitude and job strain have narrowed and improved. Since we might have expected that the entry of women into the labor force would increase job stress if women entered traditionally female jobs, we could conclude that women are no longer employed in those jobs and/or that traditional "female jobs" have changed. It should also be noted that women have retained better job support (from co-workers and supervisors) but that their advantage in terms of job resources has disappeared.

Job Stress by Year by Education

Table 4 shows changes in job stress indicators by the education level of workers. Overall and over time, workers who have at least attended college report less job strain. Workers who have been to college reported greater job demands, but also much greater decision latitude and less job strain. In 1972 workers who had attended college reported substantially less job strain and, although this continues to 2002, the gap in job strain with workers with less education is reduced somewhat.

Table 4.   Job Stress Indicators by Year by Education

	1972		1977		2002	
	No College	College	No College	College	No College	College
Job demands	7.15	7.42	7.03	7.10	6.53	6.97[a,b,c]
Decision latitude	14.29	16.12	14.51	16.04	15.71	16.67[a,b,c]
Job strain	0.26	0.18	0.20	0.13	0.14	0.11[a,b,c]
Job security	3.21	3.30	3.07	3.12	3.32	3.36[a,b]
Job resources	6.99	6.89	6.66	6.56	6.77	6.81[a]
Job support	9.21	9.34	8.85	9.00	9.69	9.87[a,b]
Weighted N	1280	734	1282	901	1172	1815

[a] Mean differences by year are significant.
[b] Mean differences by education are significant.
[c] Mean differences for interaction are significant.

This would appear to be related to both a decrease in job demands and an increase in decision latitude among workers with less than college education. College educated workers report greater job security and there are no differences by education for reported access to job-related resources. College educated workers report greater amounts of job support across the years.

Job Stress by Year by Age

Table 5 shows changes in job stress indicators by age groups. Between 1972 and 2002 job demands for 18–34 year old workers dropped more substantially than

Table 5.   Job Stress Indicators by Year by Age.

	1972			1977			2002		
	18–34	35–54	55+	18–34	35–54	55+	18–34	35–54	55+
Job demands	7.15	7.13	6.67	7.08	6.94	7.06	6.94	6.79	6.44[a,b,c]
Decision latitude	14.45	15.43	15.29	14.75	15.68	15.04	15.92	16.44	16.82[a,b,c]
Job strain	0.27	0.19	0.16	0.20	0.15	0.15	0.15	0.11	0.08[a,b,c]
Job security	3.18	3.24	3.44	2.99	3.18	3.20	3.31	3.34	3.48[a,b]
Job resources	6.83	7.03	7.14	6.57	6.63	6.79	6.70	6.81	7.00[a,b]
Job support	9.08	9.41	9.55	8.95	8.85	8.98	9.68	9.79	10.19[a,b,c]
Weighted N	950	811	287	1053	852	321	1083	1467	450

[a] Mean differences by year are significant.
[b] Mean differences by age are significant.
[c] Mean differences for interaction are significant.

in any other age group. And, although decision latitude increased for all workers, younger workers have consistently reported the least amount. Hence, job strain is consistently greater among 18–34 year old workers even as the overall proportion of younger workers with high job strain has decreased by almost one-half. Job strain among workers in the 35–54 year old category has declined but not as rapidly as the rate has declined for either younger or older workers.

Job security was lowest among younger workers as would be expected and this has not changed over time. Oldest workers consistently reported the greatest job security as well. Young workers also reported the least access to job resources and the least job support.

The patterns by age group for job stress indicators suggest that entry-level jobs (jobs held by 18–34 year olds) are more stressful than jobs held by older workers. Relatively speaking, these entry levels jobs have become less stressful over time largely because of decreases in the demands made on younger workers and a modest increase in decision latitude. Levels of strain dropped proportionately more for older workers between 1972 and 2002 while also declining substantially for younger workers.

Job Stress by Year by Marital Status

Table 6 shows job stress indicators over time by the marital status of workers. Workers who had never married reported the highest levels of job demand in 1972 but, by 2002 there is no difference between never married workers and other

Table 6. Job Stress Indicators by Year by Marital Status.

	1972			1977			2002		
	Never	Not Married	Married	Never	Not Married	Married	Never	Not Married	Married
Job demands	7.29	7.03	7.27	6.97	7.18	7.07	6.76	6.80	6.81[a]
Decision latitude	13.71	14.65	15.24	14.52	14.94	15.35	15.84	16.07	16.57[a,b,c]
Job strain	0.33	0.25	0.22	0.21	0.22	0.16	0.15	0.15	0.10[a,b]
Job security	3.14	3.08	3.28	3.03	3.04	3.15	3.30	3.33	3.38[a,b]
Job resources	6.90	6.84	6.98	6.76	6.58	6.59	6.71	6.79	6.84[a,c]
Job support	8.86	9.26	9.34	9.33	9.19	8.73	9.73	9.73	9.86[a,c]
Weighted N	297	192	1524	422	234	1526	779	533	1675

[a] Mean differences by year are significant.
[b] Mean differences by marital status are significant.
[c] Mean differences for interaction are significant.

workers. Never married workers, however, had the lowest levels of decision latitude at each time. Although never married workers had the highest level of job strain in 1972, by 1977 there was no difference between the levels of strain recorded for unmarried workers. Married workers consistently reflect lower levels of job strain largely because they consistently report greater decision latitude. While some of these results may be related to age (younger workers were less likely to have ever married), age cannot account for this relationship entirely. There is clearly a "never married-not married" penalty that is persistently faced by such workers. Job strain is 50% higher among never married and unmarried workers compared to married workers across the years.

Married workers also consistently reported the highest levels of job security. Job resources and job support do not vary by marital status.

While some of the differences by marital status of workers may be accounted for by age, it is not clear why married workers would report higher decision latitude, but similar levels of job demand compared to not married workers. This may have been related to greater job stability among married workers since they reported the highest levels of job security. If security is related to job tenure, then married workers may have higher levels of decision latitude for this reason.

Job Stress by Year by Employment Type

Table 7 compares the trends in stress indicators for self-employed respondents with respondents who are employees. Job demands have declined for both the

Table 7. Job Stress Indicators by Year by Employment Type.

	1972		1977		2002	
	Self	Other	Self	Other	Self	Other
Job demands	7.16	7.26	7.11	7.05	6.41	6.85[a,b,c]
Decision latitude	17.75	14.58	17.16	14.86	17.66	16.10[a,b,c]
Job strain	0.01	0.26	0.08	0.19	0.02	0.14[a,b,c]
Job security	3.32	3.23	3.20	3.08	3.47	3.33[a,b]
Job resources	7.28	6.91	6.90	6.59	7.12	6.75[a,b]
Job support	Not asked of self-employed					
Weighted *N*	240	1808	270	1956	378	2630

[a] Mean differences by year are significant.
[b] Mean differences by employment type are significant.
[c] Mean differences for interaction are significant.

self-employed and for employees between 1972 and 2002. The self-employed report significantly fewer job demands than employees. Decision latitude followed a curvilinear pattern among the self-employed – declining and then rebounding. However, non-self employed respondents showed a significant linear increase from 1972 to 1977 and from 1977 to 2002. The self-employed reported higher levels of decision latitude in each survey, but the gap declined significantly between 1977 and 2002. Job strain among self-employed persons increased sharply in 1977 because of a decrease in decision latitude. However job strain decreased substantially by 2002. Job strain remained significantly higher for the non-self employed.

Both job security and job resources showed the same curvilinear trends. They declined for both the self employed and others between 1972 and 1977 and then increased for both to 2002. At each time, the self employed reported significantly higher security and resources, and the gaps have not diminished. Job support is not compared because the questions that make up this indicator were not asked of self-employed respondents.

Job Stress by Year by Occupation

Comparisons between white and blue collar respondents are presented in Table 8.

Blue collar workers reported somewhat lower levels of job demands in 1972 than those in white collar jobs. Demands declined substantially for white collar workers from 1972 to 1977 so that they were lower than those in blue collar occupations. However, this trend reversed between 1977 and 2002: job demands declined for

Table 8. Job Stress Indicators by Year by Occupation.

	1972		1977		2002	
	White	Blue	White	Blue	White	Blue
Job demands	7.33	7.16	7.02	7.10	6.92	6.60[a,b,c]
Decision latitude	16.14	13.66	15.93	14.33	16.74	15.65[a,b,c]
Job strain	0.18	0.30	0.14	0.21	0.11	0.15[a,b,c]
Job security	3.33	3.14	3.18	3.00	3.35	3.35[a,b,c]
Job resources	6.97	6.94	6.67	6.57	6.81	6.78[a]
Job support	9.35	9.18	9.19	8.64	9.98	9.55[a,b,c]
Weighted *N*	1053	957	1111	1072	1783	1189

[a] Mean differences by year are significant.
[b] Mean differences by occupation are significant.
[c] Mean differences for interaction are significant.

both groups, but more steeply for blue collar workers, and by 2002 there was a sizeable gap. Indeed, blue collar respondents reported lower levels of job demands in 2002 than in 1972, while white collar respondents reported only slightly lower levels.

Trends in decision latitude and job strain among white and blue collar jobs are different. Decision latitude follows the same curvilinear pattern for white collar workers, declining then increasing, while among blue collar workers the trend was a linear increase. And, although white collar workers continued to have significantly more decision latitude in 2002 (by 1.09 points), the gap was substantially less than in 1972 (2.48) or 1977 (1.6). Trends in job strain, in contrast, have followed a different pattern. Among white collar workers there was a modest but steady linear decline; for blue collar workers, there was a significant decline between 1972 and 1977, but less change afterwards. As a result, however, the gap in job strain between white collar and blue collar workers that was very large in 1972 is now much narrower.

Curvilinear trends are also apparent in job security, resources and support. Security declined for both groups between 1972 and 1977, then increased, with blue collar workers reporting the greatest increase between 1977 and 2002. As a result, by 2002 white and blue collar workers reported the identical level of security. Resources also declined then increased; however, there was no statistical difference between resources levels at any time. Support declined then increased, but white collar workers always enjoyed higher levels of support and this gap increased, especially between 1972 and 1977.

Job Stress by Year by Industry

Table 9 presents comparisons in job stress levels and trends by industry: manufacturing versus service. Given the occupational make up of these industrial categories (concentration of blue collar job in manufacturing and white collar in service) we would expect the results in Table 9 to be similar to those in Table 8. And, overall, that is what we observe. Trends in job stress measures have generally followed curvilinear patterns (except job demands, decision latitude and job strain), while jobs in service industries, for the most part, have remained less stressful.

Job demands declined among both manufacturing and service industry workers between 1972 and 2002. They declined relatively faster among jobs in manufacturing industries so that in 2002 the job demand level was actually lower than in service industries. However, job demands do not differ statistically between manufacturing and service industries. Decision latitude increased in manufacturing jobs between 1972 and 1977 and between 1977 and 2002. Among

Table 9.   Job Stress Indicators by Year by Industry.

	1972		1977		2002	
	Manuf.	Service	Manuf.	Service	Manuf.	Service
Job demands	7.28	7.19	7.14	6.94	6.75	6.85[a,c]
Decision latitude	14.31	15.92	14.62	15.90	15.86	16.73[a,b,c]
Job strain	0.27	0.18	0.21	0.13	0.14	0.10[a,b,c]
Job security	3.18	3.35	3.02	3.20	3.32	3.39[a,b]
Job resources	6.96	6.96	6.58	6.68	6.77	6.82[a]
Job support	9.14	9.50	8.69	9.23	9.73	9.87[a,b,c]
Weighted *N*	1209	782	1317	905	1475	1503

[a] Mean differences by year are significant.
[b] Mean differences by industry are significant.
[c] Mean differences for interaction are significant.

service industry jobs, there was no significant change between 1972 and 1977, but a significant increase between 1977 and 2002, but the increase was not as great as in manufacturing. In 1972, respondents in manufacturing jobs reported significantly greater levels of job strain (0.27) compared to those in service jobs (0.18), and while strain decreased significantly for both groups by 2002, the decline was greater for those in manufacturing (down to 0.14, versus 0.10 for service).

Job security, resources and support declined in both industries between 1972 and 1977, and then increased through 2002. In all three years, workers in service industries had significantly higher levels of security. They also had significantly higher levels of support in 1972 and 1977, but that gap narrowed by 2002. There were no significant differences by industry in level of resources in any of the three surveys.

Job Stress by Year by Union Membership

Changes in job stress for union members and non-union respondents are compared in Table 10. Job demands were slightly lower for union members in 1972 but became higher than among non-union employees in 1977 and 2002. Job demands declined faster among non-union members than among union members. Decision latitude increased between 1972 and 1977 and again between 1977 and 2002 for both union members and non-members. In both 1972 and 1977, non-union respondents reported significantly more decision latitude (1.07 and 0.91 scale points, respectively), but this difference narrowed substantially by 2002 (0.19). Job strain declined for both groups, especially between 1972 and 1977, but the

Table 10.   Job Stress Indicators by Year by Union Membership.

	1972		1977		2002	
	Union	Non-Union	Union	Non-Union	Union	Non-Union
Job demands	7.20	7.27	7.13	7.04	6.94	6.73[a]
Decision latitude	14.21	15.28	14.46	15.37	16.12	16.31[a,b,c]
Job strain	0.28	0.22	0.23	0.16	0.14	0.12[a,b]
Job security	3.30	3.22	3.09	3.09	3.51	3.33[a,b,c]
Job resources	6.89	6.98	6.34	6.72	6.71	6.80[a,b,c]
Job support	8.94	9.42	8.39	9.16	9.50	9.87[a,b]
Weighted N	602	1408	552	1630	302	1681

[a] Mean differences by year are significant.
[b] Mean differences by union membership are significant.
[c] Mean differences for interaction are significant.

level of strain has remained higher for union members. In 2002 the difference in job strain between union and non-union members is not significant.

Again, we observe general curvilinear trends in job security, resources and support among both union members and non-members: decline and then increase. However, the decline and subsequent increase in security and resources was much greater among union members. In 1972, union members reported greater job security than non-members, but by 1977 there was no difference. However, by 2002, union members again reported greater security than non-members, although both reported more security than in 1972. Indeed the gap was greater in 2002 than in 1972. Union members reported having fewer job resources in 1972 (−0.09) and the gap increased significantly in 1977 (−38). Although this resource gap remained through 2002, it narrowed to what had been reported in 1972. For neither group, however, were reported resources as great as in 1972. Non-union respondents reported significantly higher levels of job support than union members in each of the three surveys, and both groups reported higher levels of support in 2002 than in 1972.

Part Time vs. Fulltime Workers – 2002

There is one more change in the labor market that may be relevant to determining levels of worker job stress. Over the thirty years of these surveys the number of part time employees has increased substantially and some researchers have suggested that part time jobs are more stressful (Tilly, 1991). In the 2002 GSS Quality of Work Life survey we have data for workers who are employed less that 20 hours

Table 11.   Job Stress Indicators by Part-Time, Full-Time Status in 2002.

	Parttime	Fulltime	p
Job demands	5.89	6.83	0.000
Decision latitude	15.66	16.33	0.000
Job strain	0.07	0.13	0.004
Job security	3.38	3.35	0.512 N. S.
Job resources	7.10	6.80	0.000
Job support	10.16	9.78	0.003
Weighted N	334	2887	

Note: p values for ONEWAY ANOVA. Part-time = LESS THAN 20 HOURS/WEEK.

per week. While we cannot make comparisons with previous surveys because they did not collect data on part time workers, we can compare part time and full time workers in 2002.

Table 11 shows job stress indicators for part time and full time workers. The table shows that part time workers had significantly fewer job demands and significantly less decision latitude than full time workers. As a consequence part time workers reported only one-half as much job strain as full time workers. Part time workers also reported higher levels of job resources and job support and no differences in perceptions of job security. These results are somewhat at variance with discussions of the nature of part time work (Tilly, 1996). They suggest that part time work is not uniformly associated with poor working conditions. Although it was not our objective to examine part time employment, it is clear that a more complete contemporary picture of the distribution of job stress must account for the experiences of part time workers.

Multivariate Analyses of Job Stress, 1972 and 2002

In this section we will develop and examine multivariate causal models that predict job stress outcomes from the combination of all worker and work characteristics that have previously been examined individually. By combining all eight of these characteristics into ordinary least square (OLS) regression equations we will be able to determine the relative predictive strengths for each of the six stress outcomes at any given time. We will then use the results of these equations to account for changes in the levels of the job stress outcomes between 1972 and 2002 by using the procedure of "regression standardization" (or "regression decomposition"). The results of these change analyses, along with the explanation of the procedures for obtaining them, will be presented in the following section.

Because of the complexity of the analyses that follow we have made two changes from the previous analyses. First, we analyzed OLS regression equations for 1972 and 2002, only. Second, we combined the age categories of "35–54" and "55+" into a single category of "35+," and combined the marital status categories of "never married" and "not married" into a single "not married" category. We did so in order that all independent variables would be measured in the same "zero-one" format, reflecting the absence (zero) or presence (one) of the particular characteristic. We coded "one" those characteristics which historically have indicated the more "advantaged" statuses: male, older (35+ years of age), college (13+ years of education), married, self-employed, white collar, service industry and union member. Coding all independent variables in the same zero-one format simplifies the interpretation and comparison of the metric (unstandardized) regression coefficients. Each coefficient measures the effect of a respondent being in the more advantaged category versus the less advantaged category; and because all independent variables are comparably measured, their coefficients become directly comparable: those variables with the larger coefficients have the greater effects on job stress outcomes. We retained the previous coding of these job stress measures.[1]

Results for the OLS regression analyses of 1972 job stress outcomes are presented in Table 12. The overall ability of these equations to predict job stress outcomes is indicated by the percentage of explained variance in the outcomes – the R-squares. While these R-squares indicate that the equations explain significant percentages of variance in each of the stress outcomes, the percentages range widely from almost a quarter (0.237) of the variance in decision latitude to just over 1% (0.014) in job resources. In the first equation just over 2% of the variance in job demands is accounted for by the eight worker and job characteristics. Three of these characteristics have significant effects: older workers (35 years and older) and those employed in service industries had significantly fewer demands that did younger workers and those in manufacturing industries, respectively. In contrast, those with more education (college) had significantly more demands.

The measured variables are best at predicting decision latitude in 1972. In addition to explaining almost a quarter of the variance in decision latitude, each characteristic had a significant effect on the level. In 1972, decision latitude was greater among males, older workers, those with higher education, and married workers. The greatest effect was for self-employed workers, followed by white collar workers and those in service industries, all of whom had significantly greater decision latitude than the contrasting categories. Union members had significantly lower decision latitude than those not in unions.

Since job strain is a composite variable of job demands and decision latitude it is not surprising that it is predicted by many of the same characteristics that

Table 12. Ordinary Least Squares Regressions of Job Stress Variables by Characteristics of Workers and Jobs, 1972.

	Job Demands	Decision Latitude	Job Strain	Job Security	Job Resources	Job Support
Male	0.174[a]	0.929***	−0.114***	0.118***	−0.137*	−0.190
	(0.090)	(0.152)	(0.025)	(0.046)	(0.059)	(0.103)
Age (35+)	−0.463***	0.630***	−0.091***	0.074	0.173**	0.323***
	(0.085)	(0.143)	(0.019)	(0.044)	(0.056)	(0.096)
College	0.208*	0.809***	−0.027	−0.010	−0.061	0.111
	(0.097)	(0.162)	(0.021)	(0.050)	(0.063)	(0.110)
Married	0.179	0.709***	−0.029	0.112*	0.084	0.320**
	(0.098)	(0.162)	(0.022)	(0.050)	(0.064)	(0.111)
Self-employed	−0.007	2.363***	−0.185***	0.035	0.300***	−0.172
	(0.132)	(0.223)	(0.029)	(0.068)	(0.087)	(0.150)
White collar	0.142	1.650***	−0.082***	0.171***	−0.013	−0.089
	(0.094)	(0.158)	(0.021)	(0.048)	(0.062)	(0.107)
Service industry	−0.209*	1.052***	−0.086***	0.155***	−0.004	0.232*
	(0.093)	(0.152)	(0.020)	(0.048)	(0.061)	(0.105)
Union	−0.024	−0.436**	0.029	0.108*	−0.062	−0.451***
	(0.092)	(0.155)	(0.020)	(0.047)	(0.060)	(0.105)
Intercept	7.409***	11.801***	0.473***	2.854***	6.895***	9.026***
	(0.116)	(0.195)	(0.025)	(0.059)	(0.076)	(0.132)
R^2	021***	0.237***	0.085***	0.023***	0.014***	0.020***

[a] Metric coefficients (standard errors in parenthesis).
*$p < 0.05$.
**$p < 0.01$.
***$p < 0.001$.

predicted its components. Specifically, 1972 job strain was lower for males, older workers, married workers, the self-employed, white collar workers, and those in service industries.

Among the three remaining job stress outcomes, 1972 job security was greater among males and married workers as well as those in white collar jobs and those in service industries. Women enjoyed more job resources than men, as did older workers and the self-employed. Job support was greater among older and married workers and those working in service industries, but was less among union members.

Of all the worker and job characteristics used in these regression equations, age and being employed in service industries were the most predictive of job stress outcomes in 1972. Each significantly affected job stress in five of the six equations, with older workers and service workers having less stress. Gender had significant effects in four equations, with males having lower levels of job stress in three (decision latitude, job strain and job security) and females having lower levels in one (job resources).

Table 13 presents the regression results for job stress outcomes in 2002. As with 1972, the eight worker and job characteristics combine to account for significant percentages of explained variance in each of the stress outcomes

Table 13. Ordinary Least Squares Regressions of Job Stress Variables by Characteristics of Workers and Jobs, 2002.

	Job Demands	Decision Latitude	Job Strain	Job Security	Job Resources	Job Support
Male	0.068[a]	0.446***	−0.050***	−0.013	0.009	−0.123
	(0.070)	(0.092)	(0.012)	(0.033)	(0.048)	(0.079)
Age (35+)	−0.239***	0.260**	−0.027*	0.038	0.103*	0.139
	(0.072)	(0.096)	(0.013)	(0.034)	(0.049)	(0.081)
College	0.366***	0.488***	−0.001	0.019	0.016	0.050
	(0.074)	(0.098)	(0.013)	(0.035)	(0.050)	(0.053)
Married	0.085	0.389***	−0.031*	0.046	0.050	0.074
	(0.069)	(0.092)	(0.012)	(0.033)	(0.047)	(0.078)
Self-employed	−0.383***	1.379***	−0.109***	0.135**	0.331***	0.104
	(0.102)	(0.135)	(0.018)	(0.048)	(0.070)	(0.115)
White collar	0.232**	0.854***	−0.039*	−0.011	0.013	0.331***
	(0.075)	(0.100)	(0.013)	(0.035)	(0.051)	(0.085)
Service industry	−0.019	0.609***	−0.038*	0.059	0.035	0.020
	(0.071)	(0.095)	(0.013)	(0.035)	(0.049)	(0.081)
Union	0.188	−0.026	0.005	0.059	−0.056	−0.299*
	(0.155)	(0.152)	(0.021)	(0.035)	(0.078)	(0.130)
Intercept	6.537***	14.398***	0.240***	0.179***	6.630***	9.525***
	(0.093)	(0.123)	(0.017)	(0.054)	(0.064)	(0.105)
R^2	0.024***	0.120***	0.028***	0.007***	0.010***	0.012***

[a] Metric coefficients (standard errors in parenthesis).
*$p < 0.05$.
**$p < 0.01$.
***$p < 0.001$.

(*R*-squares). However, in four of the six outcomes the amount of explained variance is dramatically smaller than in 1972: decision latitude, job strain job security and job support. These characteristics do explain slightly more variance in job demands in 2002 than 1972 (0.024 versus 0.021), as shown in the first equation. Also similar to 1972, job demands in 2002 declined with age and increased with education. However, unlike 1972, 2002 job demands were significantly lower among self-employed and white collar workers, while working in service industries made no difference.

Worker and job characteristics were best at explaining variance in decision latitude in 2002, as they were 1972, but the *R*-square was just half that in 1972 (0.120 versus 0.237). All characteristics were again significant predictors of the level of decision latitude in 2002, with the exception of union membership. Decision latitude was greater among males, older, more educated, and married workers, the self-employed, white collar and service industry workers. Conversely, job strain was significantly lower among the same groups, except those with more education (where there was no difference). Together, these characteristics explained just under 3% of the variance in job strain, down from 8.5% in 1972.

The other three job stress outcomes were less well predicted by these characteristics, ranging from 0.7% for job security to 1% for job resources and 1.2% for job support. Job security was greater for the self-employed and for union members. Self-employed workers also had more job resources in 2002, as did older workers. Job support was greater among white collar workers but lower among union members.

Of all characteristics, self-employment was the most important predictor of stress outcomes in 2002: in five of the six equations, self-employed workers had significantly lower levels of job stress. Age continued to be important, with older workers having lower stress in four equations. However, gender and employment in services industries became less important in 2002 than in 1972. Males lost their advantage in job security, while females lost their advantage in job resources. Service industry workers lost their advantages in job demands, job security and job support. In contrast, differences between blue and white collar workers became greater in 2002: white collar workers had more job demands in 2002, but also greater job security and support. Thus, it appears that there has been a shift in an important determinant of job stress – from differences based on service versus manufacturing industry employment in 1972 to differences based on white versus blue collar employment in 2002.

Moreover, there appears to have been a diminishing of the differences in stress outcomes between more and less advantaged groups of workers over this thirty year period. This trend is suggested by the relative sizes of the regression coefficients in 1972 and 2002. Of the forty-eight regression coefficients shown in Table 12 (1972) and 13 (2002), thirty-six are smaller in 2002 than in 1972. Since these coefficients measure the effects of being in the historically more advantaged categories (coded one) versus less advantaged categories (coded zero) for each characteristic, their diminishing sizes indicate lessening of the gaps between these categories. We explore these changes below in developing an analysis that explicitly accounts for changes in job stress between 1972 and 2002.

Accounting for Changes in Job Stress, 1972–2002

Accounting for changes in job stress requires a procedure that allows for the measured differences in job stress outcomes in 1972 and 2002 to be divided up into components that can be attributed to the various worker and job characteristics. The most widely accepted procedure for decomposing differences in outcomes between two groups or two points in time is through the use of regression standardization (Althauser & Wigler, 1972; Duncan, 1969). While this procedure has primarily been used by economists and sociologists to account for differences in earnings between groups, such as blacks and whites or men and women (Duncan, 1969; Iams & Thornton, 1975), it easily adapts to accounting for differences over time in non-panel longitudinal studies, such as the current study (time 1 is one group; time 2 is a second group) and to any studied outcome, including stress.

In the following analysis, we use regression standardization to decompose the measured differences in the six stress outcomes between 1972 and 2002 into four components. First, we can determine the amount of differences that were due to changes in the composition of worker and job characteristics between 1972 and 2002, for example, the amount of change in a stress outcome that was due to the increasing percentage of college educated workers and/or white collar jobs. Second, we can determine the amount of differences that were due to changes in the sizes of the regression coefficients, or slopes, that measure the rates of difference between the zero and one categories for each of the worker and job characteristics. This assesses the degree to which the overall stress outcome is due to the categories becoming more or less similar in their effects – convergence or divergence. Third, there is an "interaction component" that accounts for the amount of change due to simultaneous changes in composition and changes in regression slopes, or rates. The final component accounts for the amount of change due to changes in the intercept of the regression equation. When added together, the subtotals of differences for these four components are equal (within rounding error) to the mean differences in stress outcomes, as calculated by subtracting the mean of the outcome in 1972 from the mean in 2002.

The formula used here for decomposing differences in job stress outcomes between 1972 and 2002 that were presented in Tables 12 and 13 is:

$$\bar{Y}_{(02)} - \bar{Y}_{(72)} = (a_{(02)} - a_{(72)}) + \sum b_{(72)}(\bar{X}_{(02)} - \bar{X}_{(72)})$$
$$+ \sum \bar{X}_{(72)}(b_{(02)} - b_{(72)}) + \sum (\bar{X}_{(02)} - \bar{X}_{(72)})(b_{(02)} - b_{(72)}).$$

$\bar{Y}_{(02)} - \bar{Y}_{(72)}$ is equal to the computed mean differences in a specified stress outcome between 2002 and 1972 (as presented in Table 2). This mean difference is decomposed into the four components on the right side of the equation: (1) $(a_{(02)} - a_{(72)})$ equals the difference in the stress outcome due to the difference in intercepts; (2) $\Sigma \, b_{(72)} \, (\bar{X}_{(02)} - \bar{X}_{(72)})$ is the composition component, the amount of difference in the stress outcome which is due to differences in the means of the independent variables. This represents the amount of change that is due to changing compositions of worker and job characteristics, such as the increasing percentages of women, highly educated workers and those in white collar jobs. (3) $\Sigma \, \bar{X}_{(72)} \, (b_{(02)} - b_{(72)})$ equals the amount of difference in job stress which is due to differences in the slopes of the regression coefficients. This represents the amount of change that is due to increasing or decreasing regression effects, or in this analysis the rates of differences between the zero (disadvantaged characteristics) and one (advantaged characteristics) categories for each independent variable. (4) $\Sigma \, (\bar{X}_{(02)} - \bar{X}_{(72)})$ $(b_{(02)} - b_{(72)})$ is an interaction term, interpreted as the joint effects of changes in variable means and regression slopes. This formula is calculated separately for each job stress outcome.

Table 14 presents a summary of the results of this regression standardization procedure for each of the six job stress outcomes.[2] The table presents, in the columns from left to right, the mean difference for each outcome between 2002 and 1972, the difference between the regression equation intercept in 2002 and that in 1972, the difference due to changing compositions of worker and job characteristics, the difference due to changing rates between categories of worker and job characteristics, and the change due to the interaction between changing compositions and changing rates. The last three columns are sums of the composition, rate, and interaction differences computed individually for each of the eight worker and job characteristics for each of the stress outcomes.

The mean changes in the far left column of Table 14 are the differences in means in stress outcomes between 1972 and 2002 (as also presented in Table 2). Recalling the discussion of Table 2, all mean changes were significant, and all but the decrease in job resources represents changes toward less stressful job characteristics. From examining the four right hand columns of Table 14 it is clear that by far the largest contributions to the mean changes in stress outcomes are from the changes in

Table 14.   Decomposition of Differences in Job Stress Variables Between 1972
and 2002.

	Differences Accounted for by Changes in				
	Mean Change (2002–1972)	Intercepts (2002–1972)	Composition Rates (2002–1972)	Interaction (2002–1972)	Regression Between Slopes Composition and Rate Change
Job demands	−0.449[a]	−0.872	−0.020	0.398	0.051
Decision latitude	1.221	2.597	0.350	−1.422	−0.149
Job strain	−0.108	−0.233	−0.025	0.124	0.029
Job security	0.110	0.371	0.012	−0.227	−0.018
Job resources	−0.155	−0.265	0.013	0.089	0.005
Job support	0.547	0.499	0.104	−0.051	−0.019

[a] Discrepancies between Mean changes in the first column and the sum of the Differences columns are
due to rounding errors.

intercepts and changes in regression slopes. With the exception of job support, changes in the composition of work and jobs make only trivial contributions to the mean changes, as do the contributions of the interaction component.

Intercept changes are the largest changes found in Table 14, and again with the exception of job support, differences in the intercepts are much larger than the differences in means – from 1.7 to 3.7 times as large. And these changes are in the same direction as the mean change of the job stress outcome. Changes in intercepts reflect the amount of changes among those workers who were coded "zero" on all independent variables: i.e. females, younger, less educated, not married, blue collar, manufacturing, non-union workers who were not self employed; that is, the least advantage workers. In other words, the rates of change among the least advantage workers were from 1.7 to 3.7 greater than the rates of change among workers as a whole. With the exception of job resources, these were changes in the direction of less stressful job characteristics.

Conversely, the amount of change due to changing rates, or regression slopes, is the summation of changes in the regression slopes of each independent variable in the equation. This number reflects the amount in change among workers coded "one" on all independent variables (e.g. male, older, college educated, married, white collar, service, union, and self-employed) – *relative to the changes in the intercept.* While changes in intercepts measure changes among the least advantaged workers, changes in regression slopes measure changes among the most advantage workers. That the directions of rate changes are always in the opposite direction of intercept changes and changes in overall means indicates there has been relatively less change in stress outcomes among the most advantaged workers. However, because the absolute values of the rate changes are smaller than those for intercept changes, changes for both more and less advantaged workers are in the same direction. This again points toward a convergence between more and less advantaged workers toward overall less stressful job characteristics.

Among specific independent variables, rate changes by gender and age contribute the most consistently to the overall rate changes, followed by changing rates between blue and white collar occupations. For job demands, gender (0.150) and age (0.120) contribute over half the overall rate change (0.398). For decision latitude, occupational rate change – white collar versus blue collar – contributes almost as much (−0.415) as the combination of gender (−0.299) and age (−0.199). Together, the three contribute over half of the overall rate change (−1.415). Gender (0.040) and age (0.034) again contribute over half of the total rate change in job strain (0.089). Gender (−0.081) and occupation (−0.083) contributed over half of the total rate change for job security, while one of the few instances of divergence– here between male and female (−0.090) – accounted for all the rate change in job resources (0.089). The other variables contribute only small rate changes in opposite directions. For job support, converging rates between married and not married workers contributes substantially (−0.186) to overall rate change, but this is more than offset by another case of increasing divergence, in this case between blue and white collar workers (0.219). As a result, job support is the only stress outcome in which composition change (0.104) is greater than rate change (−0.051). (Results not shown; they are available upon request.)

Although overall changes in the composition of worker and job characteristics contributed only trivial amounts to changes in stress between 1972 and 2002, there were a few specific contributions that were substantial, in particular for increasing decision latitude: these are the increase number of workers with higher levels of education (13+ years), which contributed over half of the total composition change (0.197), followed by the increasing number of white collar workers (0.132) and workers in service industries (0.118).

Likewise, only a few specific interaction changes provided substantial contributions. The interactions between composition and rate changes for gender and age made large contributions to overall mean changes for job demands (0.142 and 0.116, respectively) and decision latitude (−0.465 and −0.174, respectively). Indeed the contribution of the gender interaction for decision latitude is the single largest contribution of any component to the overall mean change, while its interaction component is almost as large as its rate component in accounting for mean change for job demand. These interaction components for age also contribute almost as much as their rate components to mean changes for job demands and decision latitude. The interpretation of interaction components in regression standardization is that they represent the amount of change due to the dependence of rate changes on changes in composition (Duncan, 1969; Iams & Thornton, 1975). Substantively, this means that a substantial part of gender rate convergence in job demands and decision latitude was dependent upon the increasing proportion of women in the labor force, while the increasingly similar levels of job demand and decision latitude between younger and older workers was in part due to the increasing number of older workers.

SUMMARY

During the last thirty years, what people do at work, how they do it, and who does it have changed significantly. It is difficult, therefore, to make many comparative statements about how all these changes have affected workers' job stress. Yet it is possible to track changing characteristics of workers and jobs over time. The demand-control model and the broader risk and resources model of job stress assess job-related conditions that can be measured regardless of the specific content of one's job or how that job may have changed.

In this study we were able to draw on three separate surveys of representative samples of U.S. workers conducted in 1972, 1977 and 2002 to track these changes and we set these changes in the context of the changing nature of workers, work and the economy.

Are jobs more or less stressful in 2002 than they were in the1970s? At first glance the answer appears to be that they are less stressful. However, the precise meaning of this conclusion and its relevance for judging the way that changes in workers and the workplace have affected worker stress are not always clear. In 2002 workers reported more decision latitude in their jobs and less job strain than in 1972 or in 1977. Generally job demands dropped between 1972 and 2002 also. Changes in job security, job resources and job (co-worker and supervisor) support followed a curvilinear pattern of decline between 1972 and 1977 and an increase between 1977 and 2002. These non-linear changes in job stress indicators suggest that the observed changes are not solely a result of a progressive effort by employers to make work better. Economic cycles, changes in worker characteristics and changes in the industrial and occupational distribution of jobs all affect overall levels of job stress.

The pattern of change that was observed between 1972 and 1977 indicates that job conditions related to worker stress are sensitive to cyclic economic changes, such as the severe recession of 1974–1975. The curvilinear effect that we observed in these data tells us that jobs get restructured with regard to conditions that affect job stress and that levels of job security are also affected by cyclical economic conditions.

We also found that exposure to job stress varies by worker characteristics. Women entered the labor force in significant numbers during this 30 year period. Women now (2002) experience lower levels of job demands and higher decision latitude in their work compared to 1972, and their current levels of job strain are nearly identical to those of male workers. Clearly the quality of work conditions has improved for women.

College education remains an advantage in terms of exposure to stressful work conditions, although the level of job strain for non-college educated workers has also declined. Since many more workers have at least some college education compared to 1972, it is clear that a larger proportion of the labor force works under lower stress.

Changes in the age composition of the work force have also affected the experience of job stress. In 2002, younger workers reported relatively high levels of job stress compared to other age groups. However, the levels of job stress have declined substantially from 1972 and are nearly equal to those found among 25–44 year olds. And, although the proportions of the labor force who are either never married or not currently married has increased substantially, married workers have continued to have less stressful jobs.

Self-employed individuals are much less likely to report job strain mostly because they have considerable decision latitude in their work. Indeed they report more job security and better job resources than employees as well.

Changes in the nature of the industrial and occupational distribution of jobs have also affected job stress. There has been a large shift from blue to white collar employment and from manufacturing to service industries over the last thirty years. White collar jobs have continued to be less stressful, as has service work. Hence, part of the explanation for any decline in job stress has been due to these shifts in occupational and industrial distributions of jobs. The differences in job stress between union and non-union workers have remained, but both reported less stress in 2002 than in 1972. Finally we presented some limited data which show that part-time employees (a much higher percent of all workers in 2002) are exposed to more stressful job conditions.

The nature of work vis-à-vis its stressful characteristics has changed but the changes are uneven. The changes we observed here are complex functions of changes in the economy, the nature of workers and of the types of work.

To sort out the effects of these changes we used multivariate analytic techniques to examine differences in the way that worker and job characteristics explain job stress in 1972 and in 2002 and we then assessed how changes in worker and job characteristics between 1972 and 2002 accounted for the differences we observed.

Perhaps the most interesting result of these analyses was the discovery that worker and work characteristics that were considered disadvantageous in 1972 (i.e. female, low education, younger, blue collar, manufacturing and, non-union member) are less disadvantageous today (i.e. in 2002). There has been an overall trend toward less stressful work since the 1970s, and, the pace of this trend has been more rapid among those workers and jobs that had the highest levels of stress in the 1970s.

These conclusions are at odds with some of the literature on the changing nature of work in the United States since the 1970s (Cappelli et al., 1997; Tilly, 1996). A major theme of that literature has been the disappearance of "good" jobs and the proliferation of "bad" jobs. However, the "good" and "bad" nature of these jobs are mostly characterized by their extrinsic properties, especially earnings, fringe benefits, the full time versus contingent nature of the employment contract, and the presence or absence of career ladders. The analyses and conclusions developed in this chapter are concerned rather with the intrinsic work characteristic of job stress.

It should also be reiterated that changes in job stress could be the partial consequences of cyclical changes in markets as well as changes in technology, globalization, or managerial philosophy. That is what the data from the 1977 QES suggests. Thus, the observed changes may also be explained by the particular points in economic cycles during which the 1972 and 2002 data were obtained. Regardless of the extent to which the documented trends in this chapter are linear or cyclical, 2002 is not the end point in workplace trends so observations in future years would be well-justified.

Finally, while many of the job "risks" that are related to stress – such as job demands and job strain have declined, so have job "resources." Moreover, there has been increasing divergence of these resources, with the least advantaged workers and jobs losing resources at a faster pace than the more advantaged. This is consistent with the theme in the literature on workplace change that management is increasingly making workers responsible for doing their jobs, while withdrawing organizational resources (Cappelli et al., 1997). This is what is often referred to as "lean production," or "doing more with less." The question is, if this trend toward lower and diverging job resources continues, will it reverse the other trend toward decreasing and converging risk of stress?

NOTES

1. While job strain is a 0–1 dependent variable, and thus logistic regression is the appropriate method of analysis, logistic regression coefficients do not work for decomposition, and we found that there are no differences between the regression

coefficients that are significant in OLS and those that are significant in logistic regression analysis.

2. The sums of these columns are, within rounding error, equal to the mean differences. We are presenting only the summary results rather than the decomposition for each individual characteristic because of the amount of space such a detailed presentation would take (there would be twenty-four components for each stress outcome, or 144 for all six). The summary presentation more succinctly illuminates the major points that are revealed through this analysis. The contributions of important individual characteristics will be discussed in narrative. The full decompositions are available upon request.

ACKNOWLEDGMENTS

We thank Christopher Hutchinson and Dana Williams for assistance with the data analysis. This research was supported by contract from the Organizational Science and Human Factors Branch, National Institute of Occupational Safety and Health (NIOSH).

REFERENCES

Althauser, R. P., & Wigler, M. (1972). Standardization and component analysis. *Sociological Methods and Research*, *1*, 97–135.

Braverman, H. (1974). *Labor and monopoly capital; the degradation of work in the twentieth century.* New York: Monthly Review Press.

Cappelli, P., Bassi, L., Katz, H., Knoke, D., Osterman, P., & Useem, M. (1997). *Change at work.* New York: Oxford University Press.

de Lange, A. H., Toon, T. W., Kompier, M. A. J., Houtman, Irene, L. D., & Bongers, P. M. (2003). The *very* best of the millennium: Longitudinal research and the demand-control-(support) model. *Journal of Occupational Health Psychology*, *8*, 282–305.

Duncan, O. D. (1969). Inheritance of poverty or inheritance of race? In: D. P. Moynihan (Ed.), *On Understanding Poverty: Perspectives from the Social Sciences* (pp. 85–110). New York: Basic Books.

Hachen, D. S., Jr. (1992). Industrial characteristics and job mobility rates. *American Sociological Review*, *57*, 39–55.

Iams, H. M., & Thornton, A. (1975). Decomposition of differences. *Sociological Methods and Research*, *3*, 341–352.

Johnson, J. J. (1989). Control, collectivity and the psychosocial work environment. In: S. L. Sauter, J. J. Hurrell, Jr. & C. Cooper (Eds), *Job Control and Worker Health* (pp. 55–74). New York: Wiley.

Karasek, R. A. (1979). Job demands, job decision latitude and mental strain: Implications for job redesign. *Administrative Science Quarterly*, *24*, 285–307.

Karasek, R. A. (1989). Control in the workplace and its health-related aspects. In: S. L. Sauter, J. J. Hurrell, Jr. & C. Cooper (Eds), *Job Control and Worker Health* (pp. 129–160). New York: Wiley.

Karasek, R. A., & Theorell, T. (1990). *Healthy work: Stress productivity, and the reconstruction of working life*. New York: Basic Books.

Link, B. G., & Phelan, J. (1995). Social conditions as fundamental causes of disease. *Journal of Health and Social Behavior*, Extra Issue, 80–94.

National Research Council (1999). *The changing nature of work: Implications for occupational analysis*. Washington DC: National Academy Press.

Radmacher, S. A., & Sheridan, C. L. (1995). An investigation of the demand-control model of job strain. In: S. L. Sauter & L. R. Murphy (Eds), *Organizational Risk Factors for Job Stress* (pp. 127–138). Washington, DC: American Psychological Association.

Sauter, S. L., Brightwell, W., Colligan, M., et al. (2002). *The changing nature of organization of work and the safety and health of working people*. DHHS (NIOSH) Publication No. 2002-116. Cincinnati, OH: NIOSH (http://www.cdc.gov/niosh/02-116pd.html).

Sauter, S. L., & Murphy, L. R. (1995). The changing face of work and stress. In: S. L. Sauter & L. R. Murphy (Eds), *Organizational Risk Factors for Job Stress* (pp. 1–6). Washington, DC: American Psychological Association.

Tilly, C. (1991). Reasons for the continuing growth of part-time employment. *Monthly Labor Review*, *114*, 10–18.

Tilly, C. (1996). *Half a job: Bad and good part-time jobs in a changing labor market*. Philadelphia: Temple University Press.

Van Der Doef, M., & Maes, S. (1999). The job demand-control (-support) model and psychological. A review of 20 years of empirical research. *Work & Stress*, *13*, 87–114.

JOB CHARACTERISTICS AND LEARNING BEHAVIOR: REVIEW AND PSYCHOLOGICAL MECHANISMS

Toon W. Taris and Michiel A. J. Kompier

ABSTRACT

This chapter examines employee learning behavior as a function of work characteristics. Karasek's Demand-Control (DC) model proposes that high job demands and high job control are conducive to employee learning behavior. A review of 18 studies revealed that whereas most of these supported these predictions, methodological and conceptual shortcomings necessitate further study. Perhaps the most important weakness of the DC-based research on learning is that the conceptual foundations of the DC model regarding employee learning behavior are quite rudimentary, while the role of interpersonal differences in the learning process is largely neglected. The second part of this chapter explores the relationship between work characteristics and learning behavior from the perspective of German Action Theory (AT). AT explicitly discusses how work characteristics affect learning behavior and assigns a role to interpersonal differences. We conclude by presenting a model that integrates action-theoretical insights on learning with DC-based empirical results.

Exploring Interpersonal Dynamics
Research in Occupational Stress and Well Being, Volume 4, 127–166
Copyright © 2005 by Elsevier Ltd.
All rights of reproduction in any form reserved
ISSN: 1479-3555/doi:10.1016/S1479-3555(04)04004-1

He that will not apply new remedies, must expect new evils.

Francis Bacon, *On Innovation*, 1625

INTRODUCTION

Work plays a pivotal role in everyday life. Not taking into account weekends and holidays, many adults spend about half of their non-sleeping time at work. Further, there is ample evidence that work has a major impact on the non-work domain, including family life and leisure time activities (e.g. Geurts & Demerouti, 2003, for a review). Stimulated by the centrality of work in daily life, researchers in social medicine (and especially in occupational and environmental medicine) became interested in the effects of the psychosocial work environment on employee health. Today, journals such as the *Journal of Occupational and Environmental Medicine, Occupational and Environmental Medicine, Social and Preventive Medicine* (Morabia, 2003), and the *Scandinavian Journal of Work, Environment and Health* (Kompier, 2002), provide fora for research addressing the interrelations between work characteristics and worker well being. Other journals, such as the *Journal of Occupational Health Psychology* and *Work and Stress*, specialize in occupational health psychology (OHP), focusing on the psychological mechanisms that account for the associations between work characteristics and worker health and well being.

Many of the studies published in these journals focus on strain and ill-health. In itself this is not surprising, because over the last decade phenomena such as high job pressure, fatigue, and depression have become quite common in the working population (Bond et al., 1998; Merllie & Paoli, 2001). The obvious importance of strain and ill-health as research topics in OHP notwithstanding, we feel that more attention for the possible *positive* consequences of work is desirable. Whereas it is generally acknowledged in work and organizational psychology that working may be fun and that work may well have positive outcomes for the employee, the number of studies in OHP concentrating on positive consequences of the psychosocial work environment is small, especially when compared to the plethora of studies focusing on the possible negative outcomes of work. This is remarkable, because current theorizing holds that the concept of occupational health and well being should also include positive work outcomes such as aspiration (the degree to which workers pursue challenging goals in their jobs; related terms are intrinsic motivation and growth-need strength), efficacy and competence (Nelson & Simmons, 2003; Ryff & Keyes, 1995; Warr, 1994).

One of the potentially most important positive consequences of work is the *acquisition of skills* and the possible outcomes thereof. The necessity to learn new skills is an important feature of many of today's jobs. For example, 90% of the participants in Bond et al.'s (1998) U.S. survey indicated that their jobs required them "to keep learning new things" (this figure was 71% in Merllie and Paoli's, 2001, European survey). Clearly, learning behavior is an important topic in general work and organizational psychology and – to the degree that concepts such as employee learning, competence and efficacy signify worker health and well being – in OHP as well. Unfortunately, whereas learning issues have drawn the attention of psychologists in many fields, researchers in OHP have tended to neglect this topic. Therefore, this chapter deals with current work on learning in the area of OHP by:

(i) investigating a major model in OHP (i.e. Karasek & Theorell's, 1990, Demand-Control model) that (as an exception to the rule) predicts negative outcomes (strain) as well as positive outcomes (learning) as a function of specific combinations of work characteristics;

(ii) discussing a theory (Action Theory, Frese & Zapf, 1994; Hacker, 1998) that explains *why* and *how* work characteristics stimulate learning; and, in the light of these two theories,

(iii) providing a research agenda in order to better understand why and how certain task characteristics may elicit skill development in employees.

In the next section of this chapter we briefly introduce the Demand-Control (DC) model and its conceptualization of and hypothesis with respect to learning. Then we assess the empirical evidence for its learning hypothesis, also discussing the conceptualization of the relation between strain and learning and the amount of support for these predictions. Finally, we investigate whether this theory answers the question with respect to the mechanism(s) that relate a specific combination of work characteristics to the acquisition of new (or the atrophy of old) skills – why and how do work characteristics affect employee learning? We conclude that the Demand-Control Model pays little attention to the etiology of learning. We further argue that the DC model is by nature essentially an environmental and deterministic model that does not provide a satisfying explanation as to why and how employees develop skills at work.

Therefore, the third section of this chapter turns to Action Theory (AT), which is a general theory of work behavior and its cognitive regulation. We argue that AT opens the black box that connects task characteristics to the acquisition of skills. We first briefly characterize this theory and its central concepts. Then we discuss its conceptualization of learning and the learning process – when, why and how does learning take place? Further, we focus on the relation between learning and personality enhancement. Next, the fourth section first compares and, to some extent, integrates these two perspectives on the relation between work characteristics and learning. Further, against the background of these insights this section presents a research agenda for the study of work characteristics and learning. The final section summarizes the main conclusions of this chapter.

JOB CHARACTERISTICS AND LEARNING: THE DEMAND-CONTROL MODEL

At the heart of the present chapter lies the assumption that there is some connection between employee learning behavior and the characteristics of their jobs. The question, then, is: *which* job characteristics promote the acquisition of new skills? Insofar as OHP has addressed this question, the issue has mainly been dealt with within the context of Karasek's well-known Demand-Control (DC) model and its successor, the Demand-Control-Support (DCS) model (Karasek, 1979; Karasek & Theorell, 1990). Below we first discuss the basic DC model and its predictions as regards employee strain and, more relevant to the present chapter, employee learning. Then we deal with the conceptualization of learning within the DC model, after which we address the empirical evidence for the learning-related predictions of the DC model.

The Demand-Control Model: Strain vs. Active Learning

The DC model proposes that a work environment can be described in terms of the combination of two dimensions: the psychological demands of the work situation and the amount of control workers have to meet these demands, usually measured in terms of worker decision latitude (referring to the amount of say workers have over their work, the methods they apply, and the order in which they handle their tasks) and skill discretion (the degree to which workers make full use of their skills). These two dimensions take a central place in many work stress theories, including the Michigan Organization Stress Model (Kahn et al., 1964), the sociotechnical approach (Cherns, 1976), the Effort-Reward Imbalance model (Siegrist, 2000), and the Vitamin model (Warr, 1996) (Kompier, 2003, for a review). In the DC model the dimensions of job control and job demands are crossed, leading to four basic quadrants that each correspond with a particular job type (Fig. 1):

  (i) High levels of strain will occur in *high demands/low control jobs*, because workers in such jobs have insufficient control to respond optimally to the demands of the work situation. Low control implies that workers cannot experiment with different ways of meeting the demands of their jobs, meaning that they have little opportunity for learning and personal growth. High demands/low control jobs are often referred to as "high strain jobs," but this label mistakes the job content (high demands and low control) for one of its presumed outcomes (high strain).

(ii) If *high job demands occur in conjunction with high job control* ("active jobs," again confounding job content with its presumed outcome), workers will be able to deal effectively with these demands, thus protecting themselves from excessive strain. As they possess high levels of control, they can try out different ways of dealing with the demands in their jobs. Learning and feelings of mastery will result.

(iii) Workers in *low demands/low control jobs* (or "passive jobs") will experience low levels of strain, due to the absence of high demands. As incumbents of these jobs have little opportunity to exert control over their work situation, they are assumed to have little opportunity for learning and personal development.

(iv) Finally, in *low demand/high control jobs* ("low strain jobs") low levels of strain are expected because incumbents have ample possibilities of coping with situational demands. As job demands are low, workers in such jobs can explore different ways of dealing with the demands of the job that is conducive to learning (Bandura, 1997).

During the past 25 years, an impressive body of evidence has been generated on the *strain hypothesis* of the JDC model; juxtaposing high demand/low control jobs to low demand/high control jobs (Axis A in Fig. 1). This research usually revealed adverse effects of low levels of job control and high levels of job demands on employee strain and psychological and physical health complaints, usually in the form of main effects of these two concepts (e.g. De Jonge & Kompier, 1997;

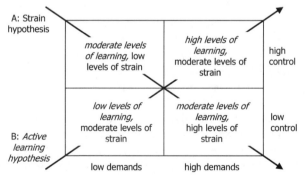

Fig. 1. Job Strain and Learning Behavior as a Function of Job Demands and Job Control (after Karasek, 1998).

De Lange et al., 2003; Jones & Fletcher, 1996; Landsbergis et al., 1995; Schnall et al., 2000; Van der Doef & Maes, 1998, 1999; for overviews).

The DC model not only predicts how strain varies as a function of job characteristics; it also poses that these job characteristics affect levels of *employee learning* (Axis B in Fig. 1, contrasting low control/low demands (or "passive") with high control/high demands ("active") jobs). However, whereas much research using the DC and DCS models focuses on their predictions for strain and ill-health, studies testing their implications for learning are relatively scarce (e.g. Holman & Wall, 2002). This paucity of research addressing the learning-oriented outcomes of the JDC model is remarkable for several reasons. For example, Parker and Sprigg (1999) point out that many popular management philosophies and practices assume that organizations will gain a competitive advantage if they make better use of their human resources. One way of achieving this is to promote the development of self-managing, learning-oriented employees, emphasizing the practical significance of research on the work-related conditions that facilitate or hinder employee learning.

Further, given common antecedents, it is likely that strain and learning are related (Holman & Wall, 2002) – but how are they connected? Karasek and Theorell (1990) argue that the "skill acquisition mechanisms are *independent of* (that is, *orthogonal to*) the residual psychological strain mechanism" (p. 38, italics ours) as well as that the strain and learning mechanisms are related ("strain inhibits learning," and "learning inhibits strain," pp. 100–101). Clearly, both cannot be true. Given that the chances of high levels of strain and high levels of learning both increase with higher levels of job demands and that not all theoretically possible combinations of learning and strain can occur (cf. Fig. 1), it would seem that the DC model proposes that strain and learning are related. Evidence for the *effects of strain on learning* stems from studies conducted from cognitive, clinical and educational perspectives. Experimental work has shown that anxiety (a dimension of strain, Warr, 1990) reduces the effectiveness of information processing, which is crucial in the early stages of skill acquisition. Attending to anxiety provokes nontask activities and inhibits understanding and experimenting with new ideas, thus reducing learning (Warr & Downing, 2000). In line with these findings, Colquitt et al. (2000) reported a negative relationship between anxiety and skill acquisition. Conversely, *learning is assumed to inhibit stress*. Greater knowledge, skill and efficacy should enable the individual to cope more effectively with work demands, thus reducing strain (Lazarus & Folkman, 1984). There is some evidence that individuals with high self-efficacy are less prone to depression and anxiety (Saks, 1994), and feel more able to cope with challenging situations (Ozer & Bandura, 1990). This supports the idea that higher levels of learning produces lower levels of strain. All in all, there is some evidence for the assumption that strain and learning affect each other – making it even more surprising that research on the DC model has largely neglected learning-oriented outcomes.

Employee Learning Behavior in the DC Model

According to Karasek (1998), active learning will occur "when control on the job is high, and psychological demands are also high, but not overwhelming" (p. 34.7). "In such situations, new skills and the motivation to tackle new challenges develop apace" (Karasek & Theorell, 1990, p. 171). Further, "As the individual with decision-making latitude makes a 'choice' as to how to best cope with a new stressor, that new behavior response, if effective, will be incorporated into the individual's repertoire of coping strategies (i.e. it will be 'learned')" (p. 34.7). If this reasoning is correct, the highest levels of active learning should occur among incumbents of high demands/high control jobs, while the lowest levels would be expected for workers in low demands/low control jobs.

One question that must be addressed before reviewing the evidence for the learning hypothesis in the DC model concerns the construct validity of the active learning concept: what do we talk about when we discuss active learning behavior? One obvious way of dealing with this question is to look back into the original sources in an attempt to reconstruct the intended meaning of this concept. Interestingly, Karasek and Theorell (1990) describe the concept of active learning rather broadly, more often referring to its presumed outcomes than to its content. Table 1 provides an overview of the concepts and phenomena mentioned by Karasek and Theorell (1990), distinguishing between descriptions of the active learning concept per se (Section A) and its presumed outcomes (Section B).

As regards the active learning concept (Section A), the descriptions provided in Karasek and Theorell (1990) are grouped on the basis of their similarity. For example, they frequently refer to (the motivation for) learning new skills and behavior patterns (A1–A4 in Table 1), but also to effective problem solving/adaptation to the environment (A5–A8), and work involvement and motivation (A9–A10). Thus, at least three different types of phenomena might be taken to represent the active learning concept. Karasek and Theorell (1990) seem to prefer the first two classes of phenomena. They argue "our model of motivation is that it is an environmentally facilitated, active approach toward *learning new behavior patterns* or *solving new problems*" (p. 170, italics ours). We believe that this definition touches upon the core of active learning behavior. It is also consistent with theoretical approaches that emphasize that learning is "a relatively permanent change in knowledge or skill produced by experience" (Weiss, 1990, p. 173), and that learning should be distinguished from related concepts such as performance or motivation.

Active learning is a theoretical construct that cannot be observed directly; it must be inferred from its outcomes. According to Karasek and Theorell (1990), these outcomes cover a broad range of phenomena, ranging from specific outcomes that are closely related to employee learning to outcomes that may originate from learning processes, but also from a variety of other factors. For example, "skill development" and "additions to competence" (B1 and B2 in Table 1, respectively) are clearly the result of learning new behavior patterns (cf. A1–A4 in Table 1). Skill development may, in turn, increase feelings of mastery and self-efficacy (B3–B5). The other outcomes mentioned in Section B of Table 1 are relatively distant and a-specific outcomes of learning behavior, in the sense that many other processes may affect them or that the link between active learning behavior and these outcomes seems relatively weak. For example, job satisfaction (perhaps the

Table 1. Active Learning Behavior and Related Concepts According to Karasek and Theorell (1990).

A. Descriptions of active learning behavior
    1) "learning motivation to develop new behavior patterns" (p. 32)
    2) "learning new skills at both the individual and the organizational level" (p. 13)
    3) "learning of new patterns of behavior and skills" (p. 51)
    4) "skill acquisition" (p. 38)
    5) "effective problem solving" (p. 36)
    6) "ability to learn solutions to new problems" (p. 100)
    7) "creative adaptations to their environment" (p. 10)
    8) "ability to make successful long-range plans" (p. 13)
    9) "labor motivation" (p. 51)
    10) [absence of] "job-induced passive withdrawal" (p. 13)

B Outcomes of active learning
    1) "skill development" (p. 2)
    2) "incremental additions to competence" (p. 92)
    3) "broadening [of] the range of confrontable challenges" (p. 93)
    4) "feeling of mastery" (p. 99)
    5) "positive personality change" (p. 103), e.g. in terms of locus of control, hardiness and sense of coherence (p. 101)
    6) "high levels of job satisfaction" (p. 35)
    7) "active engagement in the environment" (p. 100)
    8) "more effective performance" (p. 12)
    9) "leisure and political behavior" (p. 51)
    10) "growth" (p. 35)

Note: Page numbers refer to Karasek and Theorell (1990). In later publications (e.g. Karasek, 1998) similar terms are used.

most widely researched concept in organizational psychology) may be the result of active learning behavior, but it would seem at least as plausible that a high wage or even low levels of strain are responsible for high job satisfaction (Judge et al., 2002). These distal, a-specific outcomes of active learning are therefore less suitable for testing the active learning hypothesis than proximal outcomes. With respect to this issue, Karasek and Theorell (1990) state, "the cumulative result of newly learnt behavior patterns is to increase skills and feelings of mastery" (p. 101). Thus, it appears that Karasek and Theorell consider *increases in competence* and *feelings of mastery* as the most important outcomes of active learning.

Demands, Control and Active Learning: The Evidence So Far

Although the active learning hypothesis has been vastly underresearched (especially in comparison to the efforts expended to testing the strain hypothesis), it has not entirely been neglected. Past research using the DC model has with some frequency addressed employee learning, and the results thereof may enhance our insight in the degree to which the learning hypothesis is supported. One issue that must be dealt with before discussing the evidence for the active learning hypothesis is, *which pattern of results supports this hypothesis?* This question has generated some discussion in the past (cf. De Jonge & Kompier, 1997; De Lange et al., 2003; Van der Doef & Maes, 1999). The main issue is whether the DC model is supported in the absence of a significant Demand × Control interaction term; is a statistically significant Demands × Control interaction term required, or do two main effects of demands and control suffice? Karasek argued, "the exact form of the interaction term is not the main issue, since the 'primary' interaction claimed in the model is that two separate sets of outcomes (strain and activity level) are jointly predicted by two different combinations of demands and control" (1989, p. 143). Therefore, we propose that studies support the active learning hypothesis when there are two main effects of job demands and job control *and/or* when there is a multiplicative interaction effect between these two work characteristics, such that incumbents of high demands/high control jobs report the highest and incumbents of low demands/low control jobs the lowest levels of active learning, relative to incumbents of other job types (cf. De Lange et al., 2003).

In order to assess the current evidence with respect to the learning hypothesis, we identified studies addressing the active learning hypothesis through a computer-based search in the Medline and PsycInfo databases, as available in January 2004. Key words used were "demands," "control," "work," "employment," "active," "passive," "activation," "learning," "motivation" and "Karasek," in various combinations. Additionally, publications of experts on the DC model were scrutinized for relevance. Studies were considered possibly relevant if: (i) their abstract revealed that measures of both job demands and job control were included in the study; (ii) the study included at least one outcome variable tapping (aspects of) the phenomena listed in Table 1; and (iii) the results presented in these studies were interpreted in terms of the active learning hypothesis.

Results

Application of these criteria resulted in 18 studies (including 19 statistically independent samples) that provided evidence relating to the active learning hypothesis. Table 2 presents descriptive information on these studies. Twelve of these samples involved incumbents of "contactual" professions (Maslach, 1993), that is, jobs in which contact with other people typically constitutes a major part of the tasks (i.e. nurses/hospital employees, human service workers, teachers, correctional officers, bank employees, insurance agents and call center employees). The four studies employing a longitudinal (i.e. two-wave) design (Cunningham et al., 2002; Holman & Wall, 2002; Taris & Feij, in press; Taris et al., 2003) were published only recently, possibly reflecting the call for high-quality data in OHP (e.g. Kompier, 2002). As regards the outcomes studied, these cover many aspects of the learning-related concepts mentioned in Table 1, including work challenge, work-related efficacy and mastery, organizational and work commitment, and job satisfaction, but also several other types of outcomes (cf. Table 2).

Work challenge. This concept refers to the degree to which workers find their job intrinsically motivating and challenging, conditions that may be construed as antecedents of employee learning (although they are probably neither sufficient nor necessary conditions for learning). Table 2 shows that seven studies measured aspects of this concept (note that Houkes et al., 2001, present data from two independent studies). De Jonge et al. (1996, 1999), Dollard et al. (2000), and Dollard and Winefield (1998) examined "job challenge." Three of these studies supported the active learning hypothesis (i.e. these revealed positive main effects of both job demands and job control). De Jonge et al. (1996) found a main effect for job control; contrary to the active learning hypothesis, job demands were irrelevant. The three remaining studies examined intrinsic motivation. Whereas the active learning hypothesis was supported in Houkes et al.'s (2001) sample of bank employees and in Van Yperen and Hagedoorn (2003), Houkes et al. (2001) found only a main effect of job control in their teacher sample. In sum, job challenge was highest in high demand/high control jobs in five out of seven studies; the two remaining studies reported a main effect of control only.

Table 2. Review of Studies on the Active Learning Hypothesis.

Outcome Variable/Study	Sample	Results	Support for Hypothesis
Work challenge			
De Jonge et al. (1996)	249 nurses and nurses' aids	High job control associated with more job challenge, job demands irrelevant	−
De Jonge et al. (1999)	1489 human service workers	Highest level of challenge in high demand/high control jobs	+
Dollard et al. (2000)	813 human service workers	Highest level of challenge in high demand/high control jobs	+
Dollard & Winefield (1998)	419 correctional officers	Highest level of challenge in high demand/high control jobs	+
Houkes et al. (2001)	245 bank employees	Intrinsic motivation highest among incumbents of high control/high demands jobs	+
Houkes et al. (2001)	362 teachers	Intrinsic motivation highest among incumbents of high control jobs, demands irrelevant	−
Van Yperen & Hagedoorn (2003)	555 nurses	Intrinsic motivation highest in high demand/high control/low social support jobs	+
Motivation for learning			
Van Mierlo et al. (2001)	138 supermarket employees (nine different stores)	Highest levels of motivation for learning reported by participants with high control/high demand jobs	+
Taris et al. (2003)	876 teachers[a]	Higher job demands longitudinally associated with lower learning motivation; higher control positively associated with learning motivation	−
Work related efficacy and mastery			
Dollard et al. (2000)	813 human service workers	Highest level of personal accomplishment in high demand/high control jobs	+
Demerouti et al. (2001)	381 employees of insurance company	Highest level of personal accomplishment in high demand/high control jobs	+
Holman & Wall (2002)	774 call center employees[a]	Job demands irrelevant; efficacy and skill utilization highest in high control jobs	−
Parker & Sprigg (1999)	268 production workers	Self-efficacy highest in high demand/high control jobs; perceived mastery highest in low demand/high control jobs	+ (efficacy), − (mastery)
Taris et al. (2003)	876 teachers[a]	Higher job demands longitudinally associated with lower levels of personal accomplishment; control irrelevant	−

Table 2. (Continued)

Outcome Variable/Study	Sample	Results	Support for Hypothesis
Job satisfaction			
De Jonge et al. (2000)	2485 human service workers	Satisfaction highest in high demand/high control jobs	+
De Jonge et al. (1999)	1489 human service workers	Satisfaction highest in high demand/high control jobs	+
Landsbergis et al. (1992)	297 healthy men, various occupations	Dissatisfaction lowest in low demand/high control jobs	−
Dollard et al. (2000)	813 human service workers	Satisfaction highest in high demand/high control jobs	+
Dollard & Winefield (1998)	419 correctional officers	Dissatisfaction highest in high demand/low control jobs	−
Commitment			
Demerouti et al. (2001)	381 employees of insurance company	High control associated with higher commitment; demands irrelevant	−
De Jonge et al. (1996)	249 nurses and nurses' aids	High control associated with higher commitment; demands irrelevant	−
Landsbergis et al. (1992)	297 healthy men, various occupations	Commitment highest in high demand/high control jobs	+
Other outcomes			
Cotton et al. (2002)	176 students	Students reporting high demands and high control obtained higher grades (i.e. performed better) than others	+
Cunningham et al. (2002)	625 hospital employees (various jobs)[1]	Employees in high demand/high control jobs report active approach to job problem-solving and higher job change self-efficacy	+
Dollard & Winefield (1998)	419 correctional officers	Level of feedback seeking behavior highest in high demand/high control jobs	+
Karasek (1981)	1451 Swedish males	Participation in active leisure behaviors and political activities highest in high demand/high control jobs	+
Meijman et al. (1996)	36 lead-exposed male workers	Levels of lead-in-air lowest for incumbents of active jobs; but levels of lead-in-blood were highest for this group	+ (air), − (blood)
Taris & Feij (in press)	311 newcomers on the labor market[a]	Incumbents of active jobs report higher levels of feedback-seeking behavior, both longitudinally and cross-sectionally	+

Note: "+" = results are fully consistent with the active learning hypothesis; "−" = results not fully consistent with the active learning hypothesis.
[a]This is a longitudinal (two-wave) study.

Motivation for learning. This concept refers to the degree to which workers report that their job motivates them to learn new behavior patterns and skills on their job, or that they have to solve problems at their job. This concept corresponds closely to Karasek and Theorell's (1990) definition of active learning as "an environmentally facilitated, active approach toward learning new behavior patterns or solving new problems" (p. 170). Both studies examining this outcome revealed a positive association between job control and motivation for learning, but whereas Van Mierlo et al. (2001) reported the expected positive association between job demands and learning motivation, the Taris et al. (2003) study found a *negative* association between demands and learning. Both studies reported a positive relationship between job control and learning.

Work-related efficacy and mastery. This cluster of variables refers to feelings of self-confidence, the availability of effective coping strategies, and adequate performance at work and concerns a possible outcome of active learning behavior (Karasek & Theorell, 1990; cf. Table 1). Two of the five studies in this cluster (Demerouti et al., 2001; Dollard et al., 2000) provide full support for the active learning hypothesis. Two other studies (Holman & Wall, 2002; Parker & Sprigg, 1999) found that efficacy and mastery are positively related to job control, but not to job demands. Finally, Taris et al. (2003) reported that control was irrelevant to efficacy and that high job demands had adverse (rather than positive) effects on teacher efficacy. Thus, four out of five studies found that high control was associated with higher levels of efficacy and mastery; two studies reported that high demands were conducive to efficacy/mastery; one study found that high job demands had an adverse impact on efficacy/mastery.

Job satisfaction. Three of the five studies examining job satisfaction found that job satisfaction was highest in high demands/high control jobs (De Jonge et al., 1999, 2000; Dollard et al., 2000). Landsbergis et al. (1992) found that job dissatisfaction was lowest in low demand/high control jobs; Dollard and Winefield (1998) reported that dissatisfaction was highest in high demand/low control jobs. The findings reported in these latter two studies again suggest that having high job control is conducive to high job satisfaction, whereas high demands have adverse effects on satisfaction.

Organizational and work commitment. Three studies examined the association between work characteristics and (affective) commitment to work or the organization. Only one of these (Landsbergis et al., 1992) fully supported the active learning hypothesis. The other two revealed only main effects of control, whereas job demands were irrelevant.

Other outcomes. The six remaining studies employed other outcomes. Two of these deal with *feedback-seeking behavior* (Dollard & Winefield, 1998; Taris & Feij, in press). Receiving feedback constitutes an important element of learning behavior in general. Experimentation with new ways of solving problems is an important way of acquiring new skills. However, without feedback people cannot evaluate the consequences of their behavior, meaning that it is impossible to link the occurrence of a particular outcome to a particular behavior (Bandura, 1998). This implies that without feedback no extension of one's skills is possible. The degree to which workers actively seek feedback (e.g. from their superiors and/or co-workers) is thus an important determinant of the degree to which workers will learn new skills. Both studies investigating feedback-seeking behavior found that incumbents of high demand/high control jobs reported higher levels of feedback seeking.

Two other studies deal with *effective problem-solving at work.* Cunningham et al. (2002) found that workers in high demands/high control jobs reported relatively often that they took an active approach to job problem solving, which is consistent with the active learning hypothesis. Meijman et al. (1996) expected that employees in high demands/high control jobs would have developed ways to deal with the adverse effects of potentially harmful job conditions. Their study among lead-exposed workers revealed that incumbents of high demands/high control jobs worked in environments with the lowest levels of lead dust in ambient air at the workplace (which is consistent with the reasoning that such jobs offer good opportunities for active coping behavior). However, lead levels *in blood* were *highest* among this group. Thus, their study does not unambiguously support the active learning hypothesis.

Karasek (1976, 1981) examined whether incumbents of high demands/high control jobs were also more active regarding their *leisure time activities.* They found some evidence that incumbents of such jobs spent more time on active leisure activities (i.e. community-level participation in recreational and political activities) than others, which is consistent with the predictions of the DC model. (Most interestingly, Karasek tested the learning-related predictions of his model in the non-work domain, thus essentially providing an early test of the spillover hypothesis in research on the work-family interface (cf. Geurts & Demerouti, 2003). Other researchers have ignored this line of research almost completely, focusing on work-related rather than non-work outcomes).

Finally, Cotton et al. (2002) examined students' grades as a function of their subjectively experienced demands and control. This study may be the first that examined objectively recorded *performance* in the context of the active learning hypothesis – albeit not among workers. Consistent with the predictions, students reporting high demands and high control obtained higher grades than others.

Evaluation: What do We Know?

The 18 studies included in this review contributed 19 independent samples. These 19 samples provided in total 30 tests of the effects of job demands and job control (note that within one particular sample these tests are not statistically independent and cannot be taken as cumulative evidence regarding a particular hypothesis). Of these 30 tests, 19 (63.3%) supported the active learning hypothesis, in that there were positive associations between both job control and job demands on the one hand, and the measures of active learning behavior on the other. In the remaining 11 tests usually a positive main effect of job control was found, but no such effect of job demands. Thus, whereas higher levels of job control were virtually always associated with higher levels of active learning behavior or manifestations thereof, the effects of job demands were considerably less unambiguous. Insofar as the active learning hypothesis was not fully supported, this was usually (with the exception of Taris et al., 2003, for efficacy/mastery, cf. Table 2) due to the fact that job demands were either irrelevant or impacted employee learning behavior negatively.

These findings are largely consistent with approaches to learning behavior that emphasize that people must have the opportunity to explore different ways of solving problems (e.g. Bandura, 1997; Weiss, 1990, for an older but still very useful overview of learning theory in the context of work and organizational psychology). They are also consistent with the idea that having control over one's activities is usually healthy; not only is high control associated with the *absence* of stress, strain and health complaints in general (De Lange et al., 2003; Jones & Fletcher, 1996; Van der Doef & Maes, 1999), but also with the *presence* of particular aspects of a broader conceptualization of occupational health – challenge, aspiration, and the will to develop oneself further (Ryff & Keyes, 1995; Warr, 1994).

Is this case closed, then? Frankly, we believe not. Upon closer inspection the results reviewed here are less conclusive than they may seem, due to methodological and conceptual problems. For example, one major shortcoming of previous research on the active learning hypothesis concerns the scarcity of longitudinal research designs; only recently several two-wave studies have been published, providing mixed support for the active learning hypothesis (cf. Table 2; Taris & Kompier, in press, provide a review of methodological shortcomings of earlier studies on the active learning hypothesis). The conceptual problems of research on the active learning hypothesis seem even more important. These concern: (i) the validity of the independent variables; (ii) the validity of the outcome variables; (iii) the nature of the relationship between strain and learning; and (iv) the conceptual foundations of the learning hypothesis itself; which processes are responsible for the effects of work characteristics on learning? The first three shortcomings concern issues that can be addressed within the framework of the

DC model; these issues are discussed below. However, the fourth shortcoming seems to require a reorientation on the processes that account for the effects of work characteristics on active learning. This issue is addressed in a separate section.

(i) *The construct validity of job control and job demands.* The demand-control model construes job control as an amalgamate of worker decision authority (measured in terms of the amount of say workers have over their tasks) and skill discretion (the degree to which workers make full use of their skills). The advantage of combining both aspects is not immediately clear, whereas this strategy has distinct disadvantages, especially in the context of the active learning hypothesis. That is, the concept of skill discretion may operationally overlap with some of the outcomes of active learning such as skill acquisition and development (cf. the outcomes listed in Table 1). One possible venue around this problem is to omit the skill discretion scale from the measurement of job control (cf. De Jonge & Kompier, 1997). "De-skilling" job control operationally solves the overlap between job control and active learning behavior, simultaneously dealing with the conceptual problem of measuring job control as an amalgamate of worker decision latitude and skill discretion. The latter concept does not seem to reflect job control (defined as the amount of say workers have over their job) adequately; previous empirical research has also suggested that this concept be omitted from the measure of job control (Schreurs & Taris, 1998). A similar reservation applies to the practice of measuring job demands in terms of pace and amount of work (e.g. using the respective items of the Job Content Instrument, Karasek, 1985). This seems a too-narrow operationalization of the job demands concept that may also be taken to include emotional and qualitative job demands, high levels of responsibility, and so forth.

In sum, we argue that in much research on the active learning hypothesis (and, indeed, in research on the strain hypothesis as well) there is a gap between the intended concepts (demands, control) and the measurement thereof.

(ii) *The construct validity of the outcome variables.* Much evidence for the active learning hypothesis draws heavily on relatively distant, a-specific outcomes of learning behavior (e.g. self-efficacy, job satisfaction and commitment) rather than on measures of such behavior itself. E.g., the fact that the results of studies examining job satisfaction have provided evidence for both the strain (De Lange et al., 2003, and Van der Doef & Maes, 1999, for reviews) and the active learning hypothesis should make one suspicious: does this variable primarily reflect strain, learning, both, or neither? It is remarkable that the same variable is considered well-suited for testing two rather different hypotheses – and that *both* hypotheses have been confirmed using this variable. This suggests that the results of studies employing distal approximations of learning behavior as outcome variables cannot provide strong evidence for the learning hypothesis. Therefore, future research on the active learning hypothesis should preferably use proximate rather than distal measures of learning behavior.

(iii) *The relationship between job strain and learning.* Although a small body of research has addressed the relationship between job characteristics and employee learning behavior (cf. Table 2), research on the interrelations between job strain and learning is virtually absent. To the best of our knowledge, to date only three studies have explicitly dealt with the relationships between strain and learning. Parker and Sprigg (1999) found that high levels of mastery (a measure capturing work-related efficacy) were associated with low levels of strain. The causal direction of this effect could not be determined due to the cross-sectional nature of this study. In a partly longitudinal study, Holman and Wall (2002) tested various models for the associations between job characteristics, learning and strain. Holman and Wall concluded that their study supported both the "strain inhibits learning" and the "learning inhibits strain" hypotheses, as the effects of job control on learning and strain were mediated through strain and learning, respectively. Finally, a three-wave study by Taris and Feij (in press) revealed lagged negative effects of strain on learning, but failed to support the assumption that learning affects strain. Given these weak and ambiguous findings, perhaps the only conclusion that can be drawn is that – contrary to Karasek and Theorell's (1990, p. 38) suggestion – the strain and learning mechanisms are *not* orthogonal or independent. The exact nature of their interrelation is not clear, however: more research addressing the association between strain and learning is badly needed.

On the Conceptual Foundations of the Active Learning Hypothesis

The three issues discussed above call for qualitatively better research on the active learning hypothesis. On a higher level, we argue that the conceptual foundations of the learning-related predictions of the DC model *itself* are somewhat rudimentary. The reasoning underlying the learning hypothesis can be summarized as: (i) incumbents of a high demand/high control job choose how to cope with a particular stressor, which, if effective; (ii) leads to the development of new behavior patterns (Karasek & Theorell, p. 92). These ideas are intuitively attractive due to their simplicity, while the evidence discussed above speaks admittedly largely in their favor. However, the conceptual simplicity of the demand-control model is also its most important disadvantage. Stripped down to its bones the basic DC model is little more than a stimulus-response model, in which workers are largely considered passive recipients of environmental stimuli: given a particular context (the stimulus), workers (*all* of them) are presumed to display a particular degree of learning behavior (the response). The intrapersonal psychological mechanisms that link various combinations of job demands and job control to learning behavior are not specified, turning this part of the DC model into a black box. Due to this lack of specificity, the model makes it hard to understand *why* and *how* particular combinations of demands and control elicit learning behavior.

We see a second problem as well. As the DC model more or less tends to ignore interpersonal differences, it does not specify why individuals differ regarding their learning behavior. According to Karasek (1998), "one of the challenges behind the development of the Demand/Control model has been to develop an alternative to the [. . .] explanation that the worker's perception or response orientations are primarily responsible for stress" (p. 34.11). With Karasek (1998), one may well find it "hard to accept" that ". . . the majority of stress reactions develop because common personality types habitually misinterpret real world stresses or are oversensitive to them" (p. 34.11), but that would seem an issue that can (and should) be resolved empirically and not a priori. Indeed, previous research on the strain hypothesis found that the adverse effects of high job demands and low job control on burnout complaints were less pronounced for active copers than for others (De Rijk et al., 1998). Similarly, Parker and Sprigg (1999) showed in their cross-sectional study among 268 production workers that incumbents of high demands/low control jobs reported relatively high levels of self-efficacy and mastery, especially if they held a pro-active orientation towards their jobs. Thus, it appears that any model that aims to explain how work characteristics influence work outcomes (including levels of work strain and learning) cannot discard individual-difference variables as being irrelevant or unimportant.

Both problems (the mere neglect of intrapersonal mechanisms and of interpersonal differences) would seem important from a practical as well as from a scientific point of view. Practically, a better understanding of the link between work characteristics, interpersonal differences and learning may be important for job redesign, enhancing our insight in questions such as "will our personnel display a higher level of active learning behavior if their job is redesigned to give them more control over their tasks?" Scientifically, our aim is to enhance our understanding of the factors that promote or hinder active learning behavior. We must therefore specify the mechanisms that regulate learning behavior, i.e. the psychological processes that connect work characteristics to learning as well as the concepts that may influence the strength of this link, including interpersonal differences.

AN ACTION-THEORETICAL PERSPECTIVE ON LEARNING BEHAVIOR

The present section presents a theoretical framework that is not commonly used in OHP (Action Theory, Frese & Zapf, 1994; Hacker, 1998). We believe that Action Theory is capable of enhancing our understanding of employee learning behavior in that it provides both insight in the intrapersonal processes that link work characteristics to learning behavior, and suggests which interpersonal difference variables may be relevant for the acquisition of new skills. Below we discuss: (i) the basic ideas and assumptions of Action Theory; (ii) the conceptualization of employee learning behavior (also termed *personality enhancement*) in action theory, drawing parallels with active learning behavior in the DC model; (iii) the conditions that influence personality enhancement, including job demands, job control, and interpersonal differences; and (iv) the consequences for personality enhancement.

Action Theory: Action as Goal-Directed Behavior

Action Theory (AT) deals with the cognitive regulation of work actions. These actions are taken as *goal-directed* behaviors: the ultimate purpose of work is to produce a product or a service, and without action, there is no change in the work object (Frese & Zapf, 1994; Kompier, 2003). For instance, goals may be teaching a class, writing a research proposal, achieving a professorship, or – relevant to this chapter – mastering new skills to improve one's functioning at work. Action Theory assumes that the process of attaining goals can be subdivided in several stages that follow a particular cycle (i.e. the *feedback cycle*, Volpert, 1971). In each of these stages, actions are regulated by cognitions that differ in the degree to which they require attention and effort. Below we discuss the feedback cycle and the regulation of actions more fully.

The Feedback Cycle
The feedback cycle consists of five phases: (i) goal development; (ii) orientation; (iii) plan generation; (iv) execution and monitoring; and (v) feedback. In the first phase (*goal development*) goals are chosen. The goal concept has both cognitive and motivational aspects. On the one hand, goals constitute a frame of reference against which action outcomes are compared (the cognitive aspect). On the other hand, comparison of action outcomes with the intended goal may have motivational consequences. For example, people may stop trying to attain a goal if it turns out

that this goal is (too) difficult to achieve; conversely, they may increase their efforts if their goal has nearly been reached.

The starting point for work action is the task, defined by the goals that workers must accomplish. This does not imply that workers are merely passive recipients of environmental influences. Rather, they *actively mould* this environment as well. For example, fatigued workers may perceive their – unchanged – tasks as more demanding over time, well-functioning workers may look for new challenges in their jobs or take on a new appointment, and so forth (De Lange et al., 2003, for an overview of possible mechanisms). Such changes may imply that workers either consciously or unconsciously change their goals in time, often in the direction of higher efficiency on the environment (White, 1959).

In the *orientation and prognosis phase*, workers orient themselves towards new stimuli (demands). In dynamic systems such as the workplace, situational characteristics may change rapidly and without interventions by the actors, implying that they must forecast the likelihood of future states (e.g. the likelihood of a higher demand for a particular product, or the probability of changes in legal regulations). In the orientation phase workers actively search for and collect information, and order this information using the knowledge and mental models (e.g. analogies and schemata) they have about the work process. This implies that the actions taken by the worker (including the search for particular types of information) are strongly dependent on their knowledge and models.

Based on this information, workers develop some kind of plan before the action occurs (*plan generation*). Plans may vary in their detail, time frame and consideration of potential problems (Gollwitzer, 1999), and can be more or less consciously represented or automatized. When this plan is put into action, workers must *monitor their progress* in achieving the goals to be attained and take notice of opportunities to attain these goals. Often little time will pass between developing a plan and its execution (for example, going to the kitchen to make a cup of tea). In other cases there may be a long period between developing the plan and attaining the goal, e.g. when striving for an editorship of a prestigious scientific journal. This goal is not dealt with at every point in time, but individuals striving for such a position should note and take advantage of opportunities to bring this goal nearer, such as when meeting an editor from that journal or being asked to review a manuscript for that journal.

Finally, without knowledge of the results of one's actions, learning or performance improvement is impossible (Bandura, 1998; Karasek & Theorell, 1990). Thus, *feedback* is of particular importance, as it allows people to see whether the strategies they applied towards attaining their goals were effective, as well as to see how far they have progressed towards the goal. As noted above, the outcome of this comparison process may lead to changes in the strategies one uses in achieving the goal and the efforts one invests in attaining this goal, but also to changes in the goal itself – including its abandonment and the formulation of new goals. In the latter case the loop is closed as the worker again enters the first phase of the feedback cycle.

Four Levels of Action Regulation

Actions are fueled by cognitions. These differ in the degree to which they require conscious regulation (i.e. cognitive effort). Frese and Zapf (1994) distinguish among four levels of action regulation (cf. Hacker, 1998). The *sensorimotor level* applies to actions that involve largely unconscious, automatic information processing (e.g. walking or writing). Information processing at this level is parallel, rapid, and effortless. Actions at this level vary in the number of movements to be coordinated, their timing, and their accuracy, making some actions more complicated than others. Complicated actions require more exercise before they can be executed flawlessly than simple actions (e.g. the guitar solo in *Hotel California* requires considerably more practice than the three-chord riff in, say, the rock 'n roll classic *Johnny B. Goode*).

The *flexible action patterns level* applies to ready-made, rule-based action programs that are available in memory. These action programs have been established (or *learned*) previously and must be activated and integrated into a chain of actions that applies to a specific situation (Frese & Zapf, 1994). Information processing may be conscious, but this is not always necessary. One example of regulation at this level is braking for a red traffic light.

The *intellectual level of action regulation* involves controlled information processing, requires complex analyses, and finding new solutions for problems that occur. New action programs are designed that comprise all stages of the feedback cycle. Execution on this level is necessarily conscious, slow, laborious, works in a serial mode (it is impossible to regulate two such actions simultaneously), and requires analysis and synthesis of new information. For example, a freshly appointed driver of a courier service may design an optimal route for delivering his parcels, avoiding delays due to slow-moving traffic as much as possible.

The three preceding regulation levels are object-oriented, that is, they are used in the context of a particular, more or less well-defined goal that should be attained and of a relatively concrete environment in which regulation occurs. In the absence of such a goal and environment, abstract heuristics may be used for generating general action plans and strategies. The *heuristic level of action regulation* involves abstract reasoning, consideration of how to go about a certain problem or class of problems in a particular area, testing of logical inconsistencies, and setting of abstract, higher order goals. Researchers may consider the best research strategy for a particular class of problems, e.g. which approach is best suited to tackle particular research questions – should an experimental design, a survey design, or a qualitative design be used in examining, say, the effects of work load on fatigue? On an even higher level, they might consider the type of research strategies and topics that would offer the best chances for publications in top-tier journals.

The likelihood that workers will learn in their work increases when their work offers them the opportunity to regulate their actions at the two higher levels of regulation (i.e. the intellectual and the heuristic level). If workers can only regulate their actions at the lowest regulation levels, it is improbable that they will develop new ways of dealing with old problems, not to mention ways of dealing with new problems. Conversely, if workers can decide about their own goals, opportunities for acquiring new skills emerge; setting new goals means that new action plans must be devised and these may require that workers learn new skills. The next two sections discuss the relationship between work characteristics (i.e. regulation possibilities and regulation requirements) and learning behavior more extensively.

Learning in Action Theory

Action theory promotes completeness of action (Hacker, 1998). That is, work is designed well when it: (i) provides opportunities to the worker to carry out all steps in the action process (goal setting, plan development, et cetera); and (ii) when all levels of regulation are used (cf. Kompier, 2003). If these two requirements are satisfied, the chances of *personality enhancement* are maximized. "Personality" may be defined as "...a set of cognitive and procedural skills developed in work, like problem-solving, social and general meta-cognitive skills," (Frese & Zapf, 1994, p. 294), and personality enhancement thus refers to an increase of cognitive and procedural skills. Two core elements of this definition of personality enhancement are that: (i) skills increase as a function of what one does at work. This would seem tantamount to saying that work should offer opportunities for personal development. Insofar as this involves an increase of skills, personality enhancement is really just a different label for a type of learning that is very similar to Karasek and Theorell's (1990) active learning concept, referring to "skill acquisition," "development of new behavior patterns" and "effective problem solving" (cf. Table 1); and (ii) the skills thus learned transfer from work to other settings, not just the work situation ("spill-over," cf. Geurts & Demerouti, 2003). For example, the skills developed in a complex work situation may generalize to some kind of general use of flexible intellectual functioning. Note that this reasoning meshes very well with the assumptions of Karasek's DC model, in that the active learning hypothesis was first tested using data on political and leisure time activity (Karasek, 1976).

At this point it may be helpful to distinguish between two types of learning that may occur in AT:

(i) One type of learning refers to *finding solutions for new problems* (i.e. the development of new action programs). This requires controlled information processing which takes place in the two highest levels of regulation – the intellectual level and the heuristic level, and may require not only analysis and synthesis of new information and abstract reasoning, but also tests of (parts of) the solutions for their effectiveness. This implies that the feedback cycle must be repeated until an effective action program has been developed.

(ii) Once such a program has been developed, a second type of learning occurs, namely *transferring the actions required for executing these action programs to the two lower levels of regulation* (the sensorimotor and flexible action patterns levels). This type of learning thus refers to the degree of consciousness that is required for regulating a particular action; at these lower levels of regulation, information is processed more or less automatically. While the execution of a new action program may require much attention at first (e.g. writing, learning to ride a bicycle), with practice the skills needed for this program become automatized (*routinization*).

Whereas the first type of learning is directed towards designing effective solutions, the second type of learning is mainly concerned with improving the *feasibility* and *efficiency* of this solution. Indeed, it would seem that in many cases both types of learning must occur before performance improvement follows. Workers may understand the task to be performed and the activities necessary to perform this task, but they may lack the skills needed for executing this program effectively and/or efficiently. Routinization of this program is then necessary before performance improvement occurs.

Interestingly, the active learning concept in the DC approach (Karasek, 1998; Karasek & Theorell, 1990) seems to cover both types of learning. Some of the aliases of active learning behavior presented in Table 1, Section A, mainly concern developing *new* behavior patterns, acquisition of *new* skills, solutions to *new* problems, or *creative* (i.e. new) adaptations to the environment, all suggesting that we are dealing with the development of new action programs. Other paraphrases of learning behavior and the outcomes thereof deal with the routinization of newly developed skills, albeit largely implicitly. For example, learning outcomes such as "incremental additions to competence" and "broadening [of] the range of confrontable challenges" (Table 1, Section B) suggest that workers can use these skills when they desire – how can a challenge be confronted if one knows *how* to confront this challenge, but lacks the skills for actually *dealing* with it? Thus, whereas neither the DC nor the DCS approach explicitly discuss the routinization of skills, it seems fair to conclude that the concept of personality enhancement in AT is roughly equivalent to Karasek's active learning concept, both in terms of its outcomes (development of skills, application thereof in both the work and the non-work domains) and in terms of its components (development of new action programs to cope with problems, as well as routinization of already existing action programs).

Conditions for Personality Enhancement

AT assumes that the likelihood of personality enhancement (learning) increases when: (i) workers can complete the feedback cycle in their work; and (ii) their jobs contain all four levels of regulation. The degree to which these two conditions are met depends on several sets of parameters, including: (i) regulation requirements (e.g. the difficulty and complexity of the task to be performed, partly overlapping with the more commonly used term job demands); (ii) regulation possibilities (especially job control); (iii) learning-facilitating aspects (feedback); and (iv) action styles, referring to the way in which workers deal with problems and opportunities that occur in their jobs (i.e. task-related coping behavior, Meijman & Kompier, 1998).

Regulation Requirements: Job Demands
Regulation requirements influence the organization of action. One important regulation requirement concerns the *complexity* of the task to be performed; what are the *decision necessities* of the task in order to be performed well (Frese & Zapf, 1994)? These decision necessities are (among others) a function of the number of different goals and action plans that must be geared to one another, their (dis)similarity and their relationships. Complexity may stimulate learning, as long as the task offers workers sufficient opportunities to regulate their actions. However, these regulation possibilities may be insufficient to deal with the requirements of the task, or the regulation process may be disturbed. Time pressure and quantitative overload (compare Karasek's, 1985, measure of job demands), qualitative overload (the task is too difficult – one's action plans are inadequately developed, skills are lacking), task interruptions (e.g. due to a computer breakdown or colleagues that keep asking for assistance) and a lack of information needed to perform the task all disturb the regulation of one's task, possibly resulting in strain and impeding the acquisition of new skills. For example, workers under time pressure and quantitative overload have little opportunity for setting new goals, developing new action plans, and tend to revert back to prior automatized skills (Frese & Zapf, 1994; Pomaki et al., 2004). Alternatively, regulation problems may

make it difficult, if not impossible, to complete the feedback cycle; the job simply never gets done. As workers learn from the results of their actions, the absence of such results (i.e. feedback) makes it difficult for them to acquire new skills.

Regulation Possibilities: Job Control

A second important variable in AT is the amount of *job control* workers have. As in the DC model, AT defines control in terms of the amount of say workers have with regard to what should be done (i.e. what goals should be achieved?), and when and how that should be done (i.e. which action plan should be used?). Having high control implies that one can choose between various goals and various action plans for achieving a particular goal: without acceptable alternatives, workers have no freedom in deciding which goal to attain or how that goal should be attained. Thus, similar to job demands as a set of decision necessities, job control can be defined as the range of *decision* (or *regulation*) *possibilities* workers have.

High job control may facilitate learning in several ways. Having high job control implies that workers can largely set their own goals. To obtain their goals, they may need to develop new action programs and learn to master the skills needed to attain these goals. Thus, insofar as workers can decide about their own goals, they can influence their own development (a basic principle of AT, Frese & Zapf, 1994). A further link between high job control and learning is that workers with high job control can decide upon the action programs they want to use to achieve existing goals. For example, they may decide to develop a new action program, meaning that they may need to acquire new skills. Alternatively, if they stick to an already available plan, they may try to attain the intended goal more efficiently by routinizing it. Thus, if high-control workers use the opportunities offered by their job for setting new goals and develop new action programs, it would seem unlikely that they would *not* display active learning behavior and/or personality enhancement (cf. Pomaki et al., 2004).

Feedback

Receiving feedback is a *conditio sine qua non* for learning. Feedback serves several goals in the learning process: (i) without knowledge of the results, employees cannot evaluate the consequences of their behavior as it is impossible to link a particular outcome to a particular behavior (Bandura, 1998); (ii) feedback informs an employee as to how far s/he has progressed towards achieving the intended goal, and whether the action plan that is currently executed is effective; and (iii), positive feedback (i.e. realization of the intended goal) informs them which skills they master; negative feedback (i.e. errors – things do not work out as planned) makes workers aware of skills they lack. Errors serve as signals that a particular action program is not (always) effective in attaining the desired goal and needs to be improved, that one does not sufficiently master the skills required to execute this program, that one has set oneself goals that cannot be attained, and so forth. Frese and Zapf (1994) and Heimbeck et al. (2003) show that people who are allowed to make errors (e.g. by giving them tasks that were too difficult to be completed successfully) were more effective learners than those who received precise instructions how to go about a certain task, in practice not allowing them to make errors. These findings thus underline the importance of errors (and, more generally, of effective feedback) in the skill acquisition process: there is no learning without errors.

Extension: Goal Orientation and Action Styles
One basic assumption in Action Theory is that workers shape their work environment. It would seem plausible that employees differ in the way they act on that environment, and, accordingly, that given particular task characteristics, some workers may learn more than others. This raises the question which types of interpersonal differences are relevant in the process of acquiring new skills. Although this issue is not central to AT, several action-oriented researchers have dealt with this subject. In principle, interpersonal differences may affect employee learning in two ways: (i) workers may be *motivated* to acquire new skills, that is, one of their goals is to learn from their work and to develop themselves, next to performing well at the job; and (ii) workers may differ in the degree to which they possess the skills and cognitions needed to act effectively upon their environment, usually referred to as worker *action styles*.

Goal orientation/motivation. Workers may differ in the degree to which they are intrinsically motivated to acquire new skills. Achievement goal theorists have made a distinction between mastery goals (reflecting the desire to develop and gain competence, i.e. to learn new skills) and performance goals (i.e. to demonstrate one's competence relative to others) (Harackiewicz & Sansone, 1991). It would seem plausible that especially workers oriented towards attaining mastery goals are motivated to learn and achieve personal growth (Van Yperen, 2003). Unfortunately, research examining the relationship between goal orientation as the motivation for acquiring new skills and learning behavior has not generally supported the assumption that mastery-oriented workers learn more than others. E.g., two studies by Ford and his colleagues (Fisher & Ford, 1998; Ford et al., 1998) showed that mastery-oriented workers did not spend more time on task or practice than others. Further, Heimbeck et al. (2003) found no link between mastery orientation and performance among students who were training for a computer task. Finally, Brown

(2003) reported a *negative* association between mastery orientation and the number of practice activities performed by a sample of computer trainees. In conclusion, there seems no straightforward relationship between goal orientation and learning behavior.

Action styles. Interpersonal differences may affect learning also in a less obvious fashion. One particularly important concept in action theory is *action style*, relating to self-regulatory processes such as: (i) goal orientation and planfulness (Frese et al., 1987); (ii) personal initiative; and (iii) state-action orientation.

(i) *Goal orientation* as an action style (in contrast to goal orientation as the motivation for acquiring new skills, see above) refers to the degree to which workers develop long-range goals in detail, as well as the degree to which they stick to these goals. *Planfulness* concerns the degree to which workers develop detailed long-range plans and the perseverance with which these plans are executed. Both types of action styles are presumed to develop as a function of personality (e.g. static personality aspects such as conscientiousness), but also as a function of task characteristics (regulation requirements and possibilities) and practice (Frese & Zapf, 1994; Frese et al., 1997). This implies that action styles can be learned and may change across time. Thus, not only do action styles affect the course and outcomes of work actions, but these in turn influence the development of particular action styles as well.

(ii) A slightly different concept is *personal initiative* (Frese, 2001; Frese et al., 1997; PI), which is understood as a "behavior syndrome resulting in an individual's taking a self-starting, active, and persistent approach to work" (Frese, 2001, p. 100), incorporating the notions of both goal orientation (i.e. the action style) and planfulness. Taking a *self-starting* approach to work means that the goals of one's actions are not determined by someone else, but rather than one develops one's own goals. Having an *active* approach to work implies that one acts pro-actively, attempts to get feedback on the outcomes of one's actions, tries to detect possible problems timely and develops plans to prevent such problems from occurring. Thus, it would seem likely that workers with a high level of personal initiative will acquire more new skills than others. This reasoning was supported in a study by Parker and Sprigg (1999), who demonstrated that high job demands and high job control were associated with higher levels of self-efficacy, but only for those with a pro-active personality.

(iii) According to Kuhl (1992), people may be in different states when they have formed an intention to attempt to achieve a particular goal. They may either be occupied with orienting themselves towards the task and developing action plans to attain a particular goal (an *action orientation*) or with goal-irrelevant cognitions about the situation or their emotional state, e.g. instead of focusing they may think of the stress that achieving that goal may cost them (a *state orientation*). Kuhl (1982) showed that action orientation mediated the relationship between intention and action, suggesting that intentions will only be turned into actions (and, eventually, in attaining the goal and learning) for action-oriented persons.

In conclusion, whereas theoretically there seems reason to expect that interpersonal differences affect worker learning behavior, empirical research on this issue is either largely absent (with the notable exception of Parker & Sprigg, 1999) or inconsistent with the expectations (cf. the effects of goal orientation/motivation for acquiring new skills on learning). Thus, additional research on this issue is indispensable for gaining insight into the role of interpersonal differences in the learning process. For example, whereas a mastery orientation may lead workers to set learning goals for themselves, these may only be turned into actions by those who develop adequate action plans for achieving these goals. Thus, it appears that the lack of support for the assumptions on the effects of goal orientation (as the motivation for acquiring new skills) on learning may be due to neglect of worker action styles.

THE DEMAND-CONTROL MODEL
VERSUS ACTION THEORY

Earlier on we concluded that Karasek's (1979) Demand-Control model provided little insight in the nature of the effects of work characteristics on employee learning behavior. We argued that German Action Theory (Hacker, 1998) could help us open the black box connecting work characteristics to employee learning behavior. At this point the question arises regarding the compatibility of these two approaches: what are their similarities and dissimilarities? And to which degree does combining these two approaches yield new perspectives and new research questions regarding the effects of work characteristics on learning, their connection with job strain, and, possibly, the effects of learning on the work environment? Below we compare the key concepts and assumptions of the DC model and AT and present an integrated model. The latter is used as a tool to map possible areas for future research, leading to a short research agenda for the relationship among work characteristics and worker well being.

Comparison of Models

In order to facilitate comparison of the demand-control model and action theory, Table 3 provides a summary of their similarities and dissimilarities on a number of different aspects, including their conceptualization of: (i) learning; (ii) work (what are its central characteristics?); (iii) the mechanisms linking work characteristics and learning; and (iv) the worker and his/her interaction with the work environment.

Conceptualization of Learning

Earlier on we discussed the similarities between active learning behavior and personality enhancement, the latter concept referring to acquisition of new skills, but also to personal growth in the sense of changes in action styles. We concluded that the concepts of active learning and of personality enhancement are roughly equivalent. Thus, it appears that the basic concepts that are central to the DC model and AT share a common meaning, with the concepts as defined in AT largely comprising the notions used in the DC model.

Central Work Aspects

The two basic concepts in the DC model are psychological job demands and job control. Although job demands are usually operationally defined in terms of high time pressure and having too much to do (cf. Karasek, 1985), conceptually this notion is broader, encompassing the "objective requirements of a situation" (Karasek & Theorell, 1990, p. 34). The latter definition of job demands resembles the notion of "regulation requirements" in Action Theory, referring to issues such as task complexity, quantitative and qualitative demands, and task interruptions. We conclude that job demands and regulation requirements are two by and large overlapping concepts, with the latter largely encompassing the first. Similarly, job control and regulation possibilities refer to the same underlying concepts, i.e. the amount of say one has over what one does, and when and how that needs to be done.

This conceptual similarity extends to the learning-related hypotheses in both approaches. The DC model proposes that high demands and high control promote active learning behavior in workers; especially the combination of high demands with high control should be conducive to high levels of learning. The combination of low demands with low job control leads to skill atrophy, i.e. workers actually *lose* their skills. AT argues that the acquisition of new skills occurs when: (i) regulation possibilities match the regulation requirements of a situation, with both high regulation possibilities and requirements increasing the chances of learning; and (ii) when workers can complete the feedback cycle (i.e. they can set goals, devise plans for achieving these goals, execute these plans and evaluate results).

Table 3.   Comparison of the Demand-Control Model and Action Theory.

	Demand-Control Model	Action Theory
Conceptualization of learning	*Active learning behavior:* finding new solutions for problems, acquisition of new skills, routinization of old skills	*Personality enhancement:* development of new action programs, acquisition of new skills, routinization of action programs
Central work aspects	*Job demands:* high (but not "overwhelming") job demands increase learning	*Regulation requirements:* requirements provide challenges to overcome, but if these requirements are too high, *regulation problems* occur
	Job control: high control increases learning	*Regulation possibilities:* more regulation possibilities (i.e. high job control) facilitate learning
	• *High demands/high control* facilitates learning; low demands/low control leads to de-learning of skills ("skill atrophy")	Personality enhancement occurs particularly when regulation requirements are high and are matched with a high amount of regulation possibilities; completeness of action
Mechanisms linking work characteristics and learning	Particular demand/control combinations elicit learning behavior through *exploration behavior*; *interpersonal differences* not considered. Strain inhibits learning, learning inhibits strain.	*Self-regulatory processes:* goal setting, development of action plans and feedback; *interpersonal differences* (action styles) may influence these processes. Learning may lead to change of goals and task content, and vice versa.
Conceptualization of the worker in interaction with the work environment	Largely a *stimulus-response model:* worker as passive recipient of environmental influences. Learning may lead to different perception of demands and control, and higher efficacy.	Worker as *active moulder* of his/her environment. Workers may choose own goals, possibly leading to the acquisition of new skills. This may lead to different perceptions of work characteristics, but also to changes in the task. Learning leads to higher efficacy and changes in action styles. These, in turn, affect learning.

Operationally, both approaches hypothesize that the combination of high demands with high control promotes learning.

Mechanisms for Learning
The DC model poses that the combination of high demands and high control leads workers to choose how to deal with their job demands. It is not entirely clear what this actually entails. Workers may display blind trial-and-error behavior as well as carefully planned experiments with alternative ways of dealing with new problems (and, of course, everything in between). Interpersonal differences are not considered; basically, all workers are presumed to react in a similar fashion to exposure to a particular combination of job demands and job control. In contrast, Action Theory focuses on the role of *self-regulatory processes* in learning. AT focuses on the role of goal setting in acquiring new skills. Setting oneself new and challenging goals implies that one must acquire new skills to achieve that particular goal. Feedback is of particular importance here; without knowledge of the results of one's actions, learning cannot occur. Interpersonal differences may affect learning behavior, either because some workers have a stronger motivation to learn than others, or because workers differ in the degree to which they possess the skills and cognitions needed to act effectively upon their environment.

Further, both approaches presume that learning affects the work environment as well. The DC model states that learning may reduce strain, leading to a different perception of the work characteristics (cf. De Lange et al., in press). AT assumes that learning may lead workers to set themselves new goals, simultaneously changing the characteristics of their tasks. By routinizing particular action programs, less conscious regulation (effort) is needed for executing this program; this decreases the degree to which this action program is demanding.

The Worker and His/Her Interaction with the Work Environment
In its earliest formulation, the DC model resembles a stimulus-response model; particular work characteristics "elicit" learning behavior, independently from worker characteristics. In contrast, AT acknowledges that workers may actively intervene with their work environment. For example, they may set themselves different work goals or they may change the structure of their task (either through changing perceptions of the regulation requirements of the job, or through factual changes of the content of the job). Later formulations of the DC model (e.g. Karasek & Theorell, 1990) also proposed that learning could lead workers to perceive the characteristics of their jobs differently, but this does not preclude that AT offers considerably more room for interaction between the worker and his/her environment than the DC model. In this sense, AT is more of a *behavioral* model for the effects of work characteristics on learning than the DC model.

Integration of the DC Model and Action Theory:
A Model and a Research Agenda

Our comparison of the ideas and findings underlying the DC model and Action Theory reveals strong similarities between the two. Of course, we are not the first to establish these similarities (e.g. Holman & Wall, 2002). Based on the work of Hacker et al. (1990, pp. 171–173) discuss some implications of Action Theory for their own DC model, focusing on the relation between stress and learning. Karasek and Theorell (1990) acknowledge that two types of learning must be distinguished; open-loop learning, corresponding with developing new solutions for anticipated future problems, and closed-loop learning, referring to the routinization of already developed action plans. Routinization of such action plans means that cognitive resources are made available that allow workers to deal with new challenges. Interestingly, Karasek and Theorell do not seem to realize that Action Theory is potentially broad and flexible enough to encompass all learning-related predictions of their DC model, thereby filling the theoretical void between work characteristics and learning left by the DC model. Indeed, it would appear that it is relatively easy to present a DC-flavored version of Action Theory, that is, a model that draws on action-theoretical concepts to account for the association between job control, job demands and active learning behavior that is proposed in the DC model. Incorporating the notions of goal setting and action styles, such a model simultaneously allows for the incorporation of intrapersonal processes and interpersonal differences (i.e. action styles). Figure 2 presents a first attempt at such an integrated model.

Essentially, the model presented in Fig. 2 is an Action Theory-based model that is specifically designed to account for the relationships among work characteristics, action styles, work actions, and learning behavior itself. This model can be summarized in four basic propositions that are based on the notions discussed earlier in this chapter:

(i) *Regulation requirements (job demands) and regulation possibilities (job control) are positively related to employee learning behavior.* This proposition has largely been confirmed by the evidence presented in Table 2, and matches the active learning hypothesis of the DC model;

(ii) *The effects of regulation requirements and regulation possibilities are mediated through work actions.* That is, we assume that the regulation requirements and possibilities of the task affect the degree to which workers can set themselves goals and attain these by completing the feedback circle.

(iii) *Action styles may influence learning indirectly, through work actions.* Particular action styles (e.g. an action orientation and a high level of personal

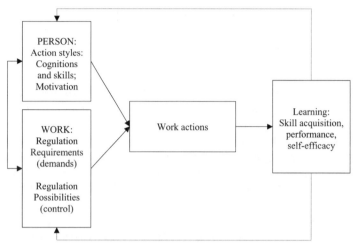

Fig. 2. Heuristic Model for the Relations among Work Characteristics, Learning, and Interpersonal Differences.

initiative) stimulate workers to set themselves new and challenging goals, help them orienting themselves to the task, develop adequate plans for achieving their goals, and execute their plans. Other action styles (e.g. a state orientation) may impede completion of the feedback cycle, thus preventing the acquisition of skills.

(iv) *Learning leads to changes in worker personality and the work environment.* Acquisition of new skills is presumed to lead to personality enhancement. Workers may become increasingly self-efficacious, possibly leading to changes in their action styles and motivations. Further, the acquisition of skills may lead to changes in worker's regulation possibilities and requirements. Increases of their skills may lead workers to set themselves new and challenging goals. These, in turn, affect their regulation requirements; setting challenging goals for oneself may well increase one's work load.

Based on these propositions, an agenda for future research on the relationship between work characteristics and employee learning can be compiled. As regards the *association between work characteristics and learning* (proposition #1), previous – mainly cross-sectional – research has quite convincingly shown that such a relationship exists, at least for job control; the results are somewhat less compelling for job demands. At this moment it would seem important to replicate previous findings using valid measures of the independent (job control) and dependent concepts (learning behavior), preferably using longitudinal designs and, perhaps, examining the possibly reciprocal relationships between employee learning and strain.

Proposition #2 is that *regulation requirements and possibilities affect employee learning indirectly*, through work actions. In order to test this proposition, future research should examine: (a) the link between task characteristics and worker behavior during these actions (e.g. goal setting processes); (b) the link between worker behavior during work actions and employee learning behavior; and (c) the degree to which the association between task characteristics and learning is mediated through these work actions. These issues may be addressed using both survey designs (e.g. Pomaki et al., 2004) and controlled laboratory experiments.

The third proposition is that *action styles may influence learning indirectly*, as they affect the degree to which workers perform at work by completing the feedback cycle. Action-theoretical research has focused on concepts such as Kuhl's (1992) action orientation and Frese's (2001) personal initiative. It would seem important to examine if and how these concepts affect learning behavior, as this type of research may enhance our understanding of the role of interpersonal differences.

Finally, our model suggests that learning will affect both worker personality (i.e. action styles) and the work environment (proposition #4). We propose that workers and their tasks mutually and dynamically influence each other, such that workers actively shape their environment, whereas they are simultaneously being moulded by their tasks. Earlier research on the relationships between employee strain and work characteristics has revealed that these concepts longitudinally influence each other (De Lange et al., 2003, for a review); both Action Theory and – to a much lesser degree – the DC model suggest such reciprocal relationships for learning and work characteristics/worker personality as well. Thus, future research should examine this theoretically interesting proposition, using both longitudinal survey methodology as well as controlled laboratory experiments. For example, Heimbeck et al. (2003) show that the opportunity to make errors promotes employee learning. This paradigm may also be used to examine changes in task-related cognitions and skills (i.e. action styles); participants who have the opportunity to make errors (i.e. to learn) should display greater changes in task-related self-efficacy and set themselves more ambitious goals than participants who have less opportunities to learn.

Finally, it is worth noting that only proposition #1 (work characteristics affect employee learning behavior) can directly be derived from Karasek and Theorell's (1990) DC model, and evidence for this proposition will equally well support the DC model and our AC/DC model. The other three propositions are mainly based on action-theoretical insights, and cannot be derived from the DC framework (with the possible exception of proposition #4, as the DC model holds that "learning inhibits stress"). To the degree that these propositions are scientifically and/or practically interesting and relevant, we believe that our marriage of findings that were based on the Demand-Control model to action-theoretical insights may prove to be rewarding.

CONCLUSIONS

We began this chapter by arguing that job-related well being encompasses not just the absence of illness and strain, but also the presence of possible positive outcomes of work, such as aspiration, feelings of competence and learning (Ryff & Keyes, 1995; Van Horn et al., in press). As learning issues have not attracted great interest from researchers in occupational health psychology, we reviewed the evidence for the learning-related predictions of one of the leading models in OHP: Karasek's (1979) Demand-Control model and its successor, the Demand-Control-Support model (Karasek & Theorell, 1990). Although these predictions were usually supported in empirical studies dealing with learning, we identified several methodological shortcomings of this research, such as the absence of longitudinal designs (implying that the evidence for the presumed causal direction of these processes is largely absent) and low construct validity of both the independent and outcome variables (what is job control? how should learning be measured?).

More importantly, we found that the conceptual basis underlying the DC model was somewhat rudimentary, largely neglecting both the psychological processes that link work characteristics to employee learning behavior and the possible role of interpersonal differences. In order to fill these gaps and to stimulate new areas of research, we presented a theoretical approach that is not typically used in OHP, namely Action Theory. After discussing the similarities and dissimilarities of the DC model and AT, we presented an action theory-based model describing the relationships between work characteristics, worker motivation, cognitive and procedural skills, work actions, and learning behavior. It appears that this model is consistent with all empirical evidence previously gathered in DC-based studies, yet offers new starting points for examining the effects of work characteristics on learning – and vice versa.

The main conclusions of this chapter can be summarized as three empirical and four theoretical issues. As regards these *empirical issues*, the present chapter has shown that:

(i) Job characteristics (i.e. job control, and to some degree job demands as well) are associated with employee learning behavior, such that higher demands and higher control are usually associated with higher levels of learning;

(ii) Due to the absence of longitudinal designs, little can be said about the causal direction of these associations. Further, it appears that the validity of the measures used in research on the relationships between work characteristics and learning is open for improvement;

(iii) Little is known about the effects of interpersonal differences or the structure of the process linking job characteristics to learning; previous research has simply largely failed to address these issues (with the exception of Parker & Sprigg, 1999). Similarly, little is known about the relationships between strain and learning; there are some indications that they are indeed related (e.g. Holman & Wall, 2002; Taris & Feij, in press), but the evidence is scarce and ambiguous.

(iv) The concepts used in Karasek's (1979) Demand-Control model and in Action Theory overlap strongly; the concepts in AT are broader and seem to encompass those used in the DC model, at least on the operational level. Further, the learning-related predictions of both models are the same.

(v) Action Theory assigns an important role to procedural and cognitive skills in the learning process. As such, AT would seem to be able to open the black box that links job characteristics and employee learning behavior. Further, by emphasizing the role of cognitions and skills, AT also assigns a role to interpersonal differences. In this sense, AT is more of a *behavioral* theory on job-related learning than the DC model.

(vi) By introducing additional concepts that may mediate the relationships between job characteristics and learning, AT seems to be able to shed new light on this relation. As such, AT generates fresh hypotheses on relation between work characteristics and learning, potentially taking our understanding of this relationship beyond the simple notion that there *is* such a relationship.

(vii) Finally, the action-theoretical insights on the association between job characteristics and learning can be presented in a relatively simple heuristic model (Fig. 2). We think that this model summarizes the material discussed in the present chapter rather well. Moreover, it would seem to offer new handles for examining the employee learning process.

REFERENCES

Bandura, A. (1997). *Self-efficacy: The exercise of control*. New York: Freeman.

Bond, T., Galinsky, E., & Swanberg, J. E. (1998). *The 1997 national study of the changing workforce*. New York: Families and Work Institute.

Cherns, A. B. (1976). The principles of sociotechnical design. *Human Relations, 29*, 783–792.

Colquitt, J. A., LePine, J. A., & Noe, R. A. (2000). Toward an integrative theory of training motivation: A meta-analytic path analysis of 20 years of research. *Journal of Applied Psychology, 85,* 678–707.

Cotton, S. J., Dollard, M. F., & De Jonge, J. (2002). Stress and student job design: Satisfaction, well being, and performance in university students. *International Journal of Stress Management, 9,* 147–162.

Cunningham, C. E., Woodward, C. A., Shannon, H. S., MacIntosh, J., Lendrum, B., Rosenboom, D., & Brown, J. (2002). Readiness for organizational change: A longitudinal study of workplace, psychological and behavioural correlates. *Journal of Occupational and Organizational Psychology, 75,* 377–392.

De Jonge, J., Dollard, M. F., Dormann, C., Leblanc, P. M., & Houtman, I. L. D. (2000). The demand-control model: Specific demands, specific control, and well-defined groups. *International Journal of Stress Management, 7,* 269–287.

De Jonge, J., Janssen, P. P. M., & Van Breukelen, G. J. P. (1996). Testing the demand-control-support model among health-care professionals: A structural equation model, Work. *Work & Stress, 10,* 209–224.

De Jonge, J., Van Breukelen, G. J. P., Landeweerd, J. A., & Nijhuis, F. J. N. (1999). Comparing group and individual level assessments of job characteristics on testing the job demands-control model: A multilevel approach. *Human Relations, 52,* 95–122.

De Lange, A. H., Taris, T. W., Kompier, M. A. J., Houtman, I. L. D., & Bongers, P. M. (2003). The very best of the millennium: Longitudinal research on the Job demands-control model. *Journal of Occupational Health Psychology, 8,* 282–305.

De Lange, A. H., Taris, T. W., Kompier, M. A. J., Houtman, I. L. D., & Bongers, P. M. (in press). How does mental health affect work characteristics? A longitudinal test of eight mechanisms. *Scandinavian Journal of Work, Environment and Health.*

De Rijk, A. E., Le Blanc, P. M., Schaufeli, W. B., & De Jonge, J. (1998). Active coping and need for control as moderators of the job demand-control model: Effects on burnout. *Journal of Occupational and Organizational Psychology, 71,* 1–18.

Demerouti, E., Bakker, A. B., De Jonge, J., Janssen, P. P. M., & Schaufeli, W. B. (2001). Burnout and engagement at work as a function of demands and control. *Scandinavian Journal of Work, Environment and Health, 27,* 279–286.

Dollard, M. F., & Winefield, A. H. (1998). A test of the demand-control/support model of work stress in correctional officers. *Journal of Occupational Health Psychology, 3,* 243–264.

Dollard, M. F., Winefield, H. R., Winefield, A. H., & De Jonge, J. (2000). Psychosocial job strain and productivity in human service workers: A test of the demand-control-support model. *Journal of Occupational and Organizational Psychology, 73,* 501–510.

Fisher, S. L., & Ford, J. K. (1998). Differential effects of learner effort and goal orientation on two learning outcomes. *Personnel Psychology, 51,* 397–420.

Ford, J. K., Smith, E. M., Weissbein, D. A., Gully, S. M., & Salas, E. (1998). Relationships of goal orientation, metacognitive activity, and practice strategies with learning outcomes and transfer. *Journal of Applied Psychology, 83,* 218–233.

Frese, M. (2001). Personal initiative (PI): The theoretical concept and empirical findings. In: M. Erez, U. Kleinbeck & H. Thierry (Eds), *Work Motivation in the Context of a Globalizing Economy* (pp. 99–110). Mahwah, NJ: Lawrence Erlbaum.

Frese, M., Fay, D., Hilburger, T., & Leng, K. (1997). The concept of personal initiative: Operationalization, reliability and validity of two German samples. *Journal of Occupational and Organizational Psychology, 70,* 139–161.

Frese, M., Stewart, J., & Hannover, B. (1987). Goal orientation and planfulness: Action styles as personality concepts. *Journal of Personality and Social Psychology, 52*, 1182–1194.

Frese, M., & Zapf, D. (1994). Action as the core of work psychology: A German approach. In: H. C. Triandis, M. D. Dunnette & L. M. Hough (Eds), *Handbook of Industrial and Organizational Psychology* (Vol. 4, pp. 271–340). Palo Alto: Consulting Psychologists Press.

Geurts, S. A. E., & Demerouti, E. (2003). Work-nonwork interface: A review of theories and findings. In: M. Schabracq, J. Winnubst & C. Cooper (Eds), *Handbook of Work and Health Psychology* (pp. 279–312). Chichester: Wiley.

Gollwitzer, P. M. (1999). Implementation intentions: Strong effects of simple plans. *American Psychologist, 54*, 493–503.

Hacker, W. (1998). *Allgemeine Arbeitspsychologie: Psychische regulation von Arbeitstätigkeiten*. Bern: Verlag Hans Huber.

Harackiewicz, J. M., & Sansone, C. (1991). Goals and intrinsic motivation: You can get there from here. In: M. L. Maehr & P. R. Pintrich (Eds), *Advances in Motivation and Achievement* (Vol. 7, pp. 21–49). Greenwich, CT: JAI Press.

Heimbeck, D., Frese, M., Sonnentag, S., & Keith, N. (2003). Integrating errors into the training process: The function of error management instructions and the role of goal orientation. *Personnel Psychology, 56*, 333–361.

Holman, D. J., & Wall, T. D. (2002). Work characteristics, learning-related outcomes, and strain: A test of competing direct effects, mediated, and moderated models. *Journal of Occupational Health Psychology, 7*, 283–301.

Houkes, I., Janssen, P. P. M., De Jonge, J., & Nijhuis, F. J. N. (2001). Specific relationships between work characteristics and intrinsic work motivation, burnout and turnover intention: A multi-sample analysis. *European Journal of Work and Organizational Psychology, 10*, 1–23.

Jones, F., & Fletcher, B. C. (1996). Job control and health. In: M. J. Schabracq, J. A. M. Winnubst & C. L. Cooper (Eds), *Handbook of Work and Health Psychology* (pp. 33–50). Chichester: Wiley.

Judge, T. A., Parker, S. K., Colbert, A. E., Heller, D., & Ilies, R. (2002). Job satisfaction: A cross-cultural review. In: N. Anderson, D. S. Ones, H. K. Sinangil & C. Visweswaran (Eds), *Handbook of Industrial, Work and Organizational Psychology, Vol. 2: Organizational psychology* (pp. 25–52). Thousand Oaks: Sage.

Kahn, R. L., Wolfe, D., Quinn, R., Snoek, J., & Rosenthal, R. (1964). *Organizational stress: Studies in role conflict and ambiguity*. New York: Wiley.

Karasek, R. (1998). Demand-Control Model: A social, emotional, and physiological approach to stress risk and active behaviour development. In: J. M. Stellmann (Ed.), *Encyclopaedia of Occupational Health and Safety* (4th ed., pp. 34.6–34.14). Geneva: International Labour Office.

Karasek, R. A. (1976). *The impact of the work environment on life outside the job*. Stockholm: Institutet för Social Forskning.

Karasek, R. A. (1979). Job demands, job decision latitude, and mental strain: Implications for job design. *Administrative Science Quarterly, 24*, 285–308.

Karasek, R. A. (1981). Job socialization and job strain: The implications of two related psychosocial mechanisms for job design. In: B. Gardell & G. Johansson (Eds), *Working Life: A Social Science Contribution to Work Reform* (pp. 75–94). Chichester: Wiley.

Karasek, R. A. (1985). *Job Content Instrument: Questionnaire and user's guide*. Los Angeles: Department of Industrial and Systems Engineering, University of Southern California.

Karasek, R. A. (1989). Control in the workplace and its health-related aspects. In: S. L. Sauter, J. J. Hurrell & C. L. Cooper (Eds), *Job Control and Work Health* (pp. 129–159). New York: Wiley.

Karasek, R. A., & Theorell, T. (1990). *Healthy work: Stress, productivity, and the reconstruction of working life*. New York: Basic Books.

Kompier, M. (2002). The psychosocial work environment and health: What do we know and where should we go? *Scandinavian Journal of Work, Environment and Health, 28*, 1–4.

Kompier, M. A. J. (2003). Job design and well being. In: M. J. Schabracq, J. A. M. Winnubst & C. L. Cooper (Eds), *The Handbook of Work and Health Psychology* (2nd ed., pp. 430–454). Chichester: Wiley.

Kuhl, J. (1992). A theory of self-regulation: Action versus state orientation, self-discrimination, and some applications. *Applied Psychology: An International Review, 41*, 97–129.

Landsbergis, P. A., Schnall, P. L., Deitz, D., Friedman, R., & Pickering, T. (1992). The patterning of psychological job attributes and distress by "job strain" and social support in a sample of working men. *Journal of Behavioral Medicine, 15*, 379–405.

Landsbergis, P. A., Schnall, P. L., Schwartz, J. E., Warren, K., & Pickering, T. G. (1995). Job strain, hypertension, and cardiovascular disease: Empirical evidence, methodological issues, and recommendations for future research. In: S. L. Sauter & L. R. Murphy (Eds), *Organizational Risk Factors for Job Stress* (pp. 97–112). Washington, DC: American Psychological Association.

Lazarus, R. S., & Folkman, S. (1984). *Stress, appraisal, and coping*. New York: Springer.

Maslach, C. (1993). Burnout: A multidimensional perspective. In: W. B. Schaufeli, C. Maslach & T. Marek (Eds), *Professional Burnout: Recent Developments in Theory and Practice* (pp. 19–32). Washington, DC: Taylor & Francis.

Merllie, D., & Paoli, P. (2001). *Ten years of working conditions in the European Union*. Dublin: European Foundation for the Improvement of Living and Working Conditions.

Meijman, T. F., & Kompier, M. A. J. (1998). Bussy business: How urban bus drivers cope with time pressure, passengers, and traffic safety. *Journal of Occupational Health Psychology, 3*, 109–121.

Meijman, T. F., Ulenbelt, P., Lumens, M. E., & Herber, R. F. (1996). Behavioral determinants of occupational exposure to chemical agents. *Journal of Occupational Health Psychology, 1*, 85–91.

Morabia, A. (2003). Work organization: The neglected child of (social) epidemiology. *Social and Preventive Medicine, 48*, 333–335.

Nelson, D. L., & Simmons, B. L. (2003). Health psychology and work stress: A more positive approach. In: J. C. Quick & L. E. Tetrick (Eds), *Handbook of Occupational Health Psychology* (pp. 97–119). Washington, DC: American Psychological Association.

Ozer, E. M., & Bandura, A. (1990). Mechanisms governing empowerment effects: A self-efficacy analysis. *Journal of Personality and Social Psychology, 58*, 472–486.

Parker, S. K., & Sprigg, C. A. (1999). Minimizing strain and maximizing learning: The role of job demands, job control, and proactive personality. *Journal of Applied Psychology, 84*, 925–939.

Pomaki, G., Maes, S., & Ter Doest, L. (2004). Work conditions and employees' self-set goals: Goal processes enhance prediction of psychological distress and well being. *Personality and Social Psychology Bulletin, 30*, 685–694.

Ryff, C. D., & Keyes, C. L. M. (1995). The structure of psychological well being revisited. *Journal of Personality and Social Psychology, 69*, 719–727.

Saks, A. M. (1994). Moderating effects of self-efficacy for the relationship between training method and anxiety and stress reactions of newcomers. *Journal of Organizational Behavior, 15*, 639–654.

Schnall, P. L., Belkic, K., Landsbergis, P., & Baker, D. (2000). The workplace and cardiovascular diseases. *Occupational Medicine: State of the Art Reviews, 15*, 163–188.

Schreurs, P. J. G., & Taris, T. W. (1998). Construct validity of the demand-control model: A double cross-validation approach, Work. *Work & Stress, 12*, 66–84.

Siegrist, J. (2000). A theory of occupational stress. In: J. Dunham (Ed.), *Stress in the Workplace: Past, Present and Future* (pp. 52–66). London: Whurr Publishers.

Taris, T. W., De Lange, A. H., Kompier, M. A. J., Schaufeli, W. B., & Schreurs, P. J. G. (2003). Learning new behavior patterns: A longitudinal test of Karasek's active learning hypothesis among Dutch teachers. *Work & Stress, 17*, 1–20.

Taris, T. W., & Feij, J. A. (in press). Learning and strain among newcomers: A three-wave study on the effects of job demands and job control. *Journal of Psychology*.

Taris, T. W., & Kompier, M. A. J. (in press). *Job demands, job control, strain and learning behavior: Review and research agenda*. In: A. Stamatios Antoniou & C. L. Cooper (Eds), *Research Companion to Organizational Health Psychology*.

Van der Doef, M. P., & Maes, S. (1998). The job demand-control(-support) model and physical health outcomes: A review of the strain and buffer hypotheses. *Psychology and Health, 13*, 909–936.

Van der Doef, M. P., & Maes, S. (1999). The Job Demand-Control(-Support) Model and psychological well being: A review of 20 years of empirical research. *Work & Stress, 13*, 87–114.

Van Horn, J. E., Taris, T. W., Schaufeli, W. B., & Schreurs, P. J. G. (in press). The structure of occupational well being: A study among Dutch teachers. *Journal of Occupational and Organizational Psychology*.

Van Mierlo, H., Rutte, C. G., Seinen, B., & Kompier, M. A. J. (2001). Autonomous teamwork and psychological well being. *European Journal of Work and Organizational Psychology, 10*, 291–301.

Van Yperen, N. W., & Hagedoorn, M. (2003). Do high job demands increase intrinsic motivation or fatigue or both? *Academy of Management Journal, 46*, 339–348.

Volpert, W. (1971). *Sensumotorisches Lernen: Zur Theorie des Trainings in industrie und Sport*. Frankfurt: Limpert.

Warr, P. (1996). Employee well being. In: P. Warr (Ed.), *Psychology at Work* (4th ed., pp. 224–253). Harmondsworth: Penguin.

Warr, P. B. (1990). The measurement of well being and other aspects of mental health. *Journal of Occupational Psychology, 63*, 193–210.

Warr, P. B. (1994). A conceptual framework for the study of work and mental health. *Work and Stress, 8*, 84–97.

Warr, P. B., & Downing, J. (2000). Learning strategies, learning anxiety and knowledge acquisition. *British Journal of Psychology, 91*, 311–333.

Weiss, H. M. (1990). Learning theory and industrial and organizational psychology. In: M. D. Dunnette & L. M. Hough (Eds), *Handbook of Industrial and Organizational Psychology, Vol. 1* (2nd ed., pp. 171–221). Palo Alto: Consulting Psychologists Press.

White, R. W. (1959). Motivation reconsidered: The concept of competence. *Psychological Review, 66*, 297–333.

ORGANIZATIONAL STRESS THROUGH THE LENS OF CONSERVATION OF RESOURCES (COR) THEORY

Mina Westman, Stevan E. Hobfoll, Shoshi Chen, Oranit B. Davidson and Shavit Laski

ABSTRACT

We examined how Conservation of Resources (COR) theory has been applied to work and stress in organizational settings. COR theory has drawn increasing interest in the organizational literature. It is both a stress and motivational theory that outlines how individuals and organizations are likely to be impacted by stressful circumstances, what those stressful circumstances are likely to be, and how individuals and organizations act in order to garner and protect their resources. To date, individual studies and meta-analyses have found COR theory to be a major explanatory model for understanding the stress process at work. Applications of COR theory to burnout, respite, and preventive intervention were detailed. Studies have shown that resource loss is a critical component of the stress process in organizations and that limiting resource loss is a key to successful prevention and post-stress intervention. Applications for future work, moving COR theory to the study of the acquisition, maintenance, fostering, and protection of key resources was discussed.

Exploring Interpersonal Dynamics
Research in Occupational Stress and Well Being, Volume 4, 167–220
Copyright © 2005 by Elsevier Ltd.
All rights of reproduction in any form reserved
ISSN: 1479-3555/doi:10.1016/S1479-3555(04)04005-3

INTRODUCTION

The conceptualization of stress has largely been one of idiographic individual perceptions or appraisals (Lazarus & Folkman, 1984). On one hand, it is hard to argue against stress being in the eye of the beholder. On a clinical level or in the informal kaffee klatsch, who are we to question the individual's report that his or her life is stressful, that the children are a source of strife, that they feel pressured, cornered, exhausted from it all? The problem is that this means that we must wait for the stressors to occur and that we are entirely confounding neurotic processes with environmental factors. Appraisal theory is by its own admission entirely post hoc. Moreover, it agues that stress is only in the eye of the beholder, making predictive inquiry beside the point, or at least beside the theory.

Other theories of stress, such as that of Karasek (1979) turn to particular aspects of the environments. In the case of Karasek's well-researched theory, it is the conditions of high demand and low control that are reasoned to be the basis of stressful conditions. The problem here is the potential confounding of people's resources with their perceptions of control and demand. Secretaries may very well be under stress because of their poor pay and other poor work conditions and not because they lack control. Indeed, most senior executives will argue that they have limited freedom of choice and that their work conditions (boss, board of directors, market considerations) control their choices. Moreover, any theory that speaks to the characteristics of certain environments, such as white-collar business, will have limited applicability to other environments, similar (e.g. teachers, nurses) or dissimilar (Dutch farmers, flood victims in Afghanistan).

Conservation of Resources (COR) theory was offered as an alternative to the individual appraisal or specific environmental approaches to stress (Hobfoll, 1988, 1989). In the current chapter we will review studies that have directly applied COR theory to occupational stress and strain. Before doing so, we will briefly explicate the central tenets and principles of the theory. For more comprehensive theoretical and empirical support of the theory, readers are referred to Hobfoll (1988, 1998a, b, 2001, 2002).

The basic tenet of COR theory constitutes the model as a motivational theory. Specifically, *individuals are seen as motivated to obtain, retain, foster and protect those things they value.* Being social, biological animals these things that are valued fall in the categories of food, shelter, a positive sense of an effective self, and primary social ties. Further, secondary resources are needed to preserve these primary resources. These secondary resources include such things are work, family, insurance, time, credit and other concrete and abstract structures and entities that are part and parcel of the cultural web that all cultures create to support primary resources. Indeed, one definition of culture is the network of institutions and practices that are constituted to preserve resources and insure survival.

From this basic tenet emerge several principles. Again, we must refer the reader to the many writings and empirical tests of the theory that today make it one of the two most well-researched theories of stress.

Principle 1. The Primacy of Resource Loss
The first principle of COR theory is that resource loss is disproportionately more salient than resource gain.

This principle posits that given equal amounts of loss and gain, loss will have significantly greater impact. Moreover, resource gains are seen as acquiring their saliency in light of loss. That is, in the context of resource loss, resource gains become more significant.

Principle 2. Resource Investment
The second principle of COR theory is that people must invest resources in order to protect against resource loss, recover from losses, and gain resources.

These two principles, then lead to 3 major corollaries of COR theory and one critical finding that has emerged from the literature and which follows from these 3 corollaries.

Corollary 1. Those with greater resources are less vulnerable to resource loss and more capable of orchestrating resource gain. Conversely, those with fewer resources are more vulnerable to resource loss and less capable of resource gain.

Corollary 2. Of COR theory states that those who lack resources are not only more vulnerable to resource loss, but that initial loss begets future loss. This is a critical aspect of the theory, because it predicts that loss cycles will occur quickly and powerfully. Further, at each iteration of loss in the sequence, the cycle will gain in strength and momentum.

Corollary 3. Mirrors corollary 2, stating that those who possess resources are more capable of gain, and that initial resource gain begets further gain. However, because loss is more potent than gain, loss cycles will be more impactful and more accelerated than gain cycles.

Finally, it both follows theoretically, due to the lifelong nature of loss and gain cycles across people's lifespans, that resources (or their lack) tend to aggregate in what we have come to call *resource caravans*. Thus, resources aggregate in resource caravans in both an immediate and a life-span sense. Research by Cozzarelli (1993) and by Rini et al. (1999) support the idea suggested in COR theory that having one major resource is typically linked with having others, and likewise lacking major resources is linked to lacking others (Hobfoll, 1998a, b). In this way, although individual resources such as self-efficacy, sense of control, social support, and social status are important in their own right and have their own kinds of influence on mental health and functional performance, they are seldom found singly. Rather, they run in herds, such that they attract each other, form building blocks one for the other, and indeed may vanish in aggregate.

In the coming pages we will review theoretical and empirical developments in the occupational literature based on COR theory and describe other studies in progress which are being conducted to further expand the reaches of the theory.

APPLYING COR THEORY TO OCCUPATIONAL STRESS

The initial presentation of COR theory (Hobfoll, 1989) focused on its unique scientific assertion in the area of human behavior, while supplying a preeminent theory for stress. The primary introduction of the theory displayed resources as the single unit for the understanding of psychological stress. This first introduction concentrated on its inclusive nature, its distinctiveness and basic principles but, did not specifically relate to any particular setting. The theory's recent elaboration (Hobfoll, 2001), however, was more integrative and incorporated exemplifications within the organizational setting, accompanied by empirical evidence. Theoretical expansions focused on various COR ramifications, including the presentation of burnout as stress sequelae. A comprehensive model of COR theory was supplied and further applications were discussed, referring to the organizational context. This recent revision of COR theory (Hobfoll, 2001) unfolded its development, focusing on the individual within the context of work as one of the most significant arenas.

This chapter focuses on the evolution of COR theory and discloses four domains in which investigators have used COR theory as the basis for their research: burnout, the work-family interface, respite and COR based interventions in the work-place. Table 1 A–D presents an overview of the research based on COR theory in the organizational behavior domain.

Integration of Burnout Research in COR Theory

The conceptualization of burnout and the evolution of COR theory have been intertwined. While COR theory has had a major contribution to the understanding of burnout, the latter has been the theory's preliminary foothold in the realm

Table 1. Summary of Characteristics and Findings of Studies Applying (a) COR Model to Burnout Research, (b) COR Model to Work and Family Interface, (c) COR Model to Respite Research, (d) COR Model to Organizational Interventions.

Study/Sample	Research Target	Demands (Conflict Antecedents)	Resources	Design Analysis	Findings
(a) COR model to burnout research					
Cordes et al. (1997) 354 human resource professionals.	To examine the intertemporal sequences of the burnout components and their relations with role overload, non-contingent punishments and contingent rewards.	Quantitative role overload;	Contingent rewards; control.	Cross-sectional.	Support for Maslach's sequential model of burnout (significant paths between EE and D, and between D and PA).
				SEM analysis	Positive relations between: quantitative overload and emotional exhaustion, non-contingent punishment and depersonalization; contingent rewards and personal accomplishment.
Demerouti et al. (2000). 109 German nurses.	To examine the differential effects of job demands and job resources on burnout components.	Workload; time pressure; demanding contacts with patients; environmental conditions and shift work.	Rewards; Participation in decision making; supervisor support; feedback; control; task variety. Job satisfaction.	Cross sectional, SEM analysis.	Strong effects of job demands on exhaustion and job resources on disengagement respectively. Burnout mediates the effect of working conditions (demands and resources) on job satisfaction. Support for the different effects of demands and resources.

Table 1. (Continued)

Study/Sample	Research Target	Demands (Conflict Antecedents)	Resources	Design Analysis	Findings
Janssen et al. (1999), 56 Dutch nurses.	To examine relations between work related and personal demands and resources and the 3 burnout dimensions.	Work overload.	Good quality of work content; social support; career expectations; self esteem.	Cross sectional.	EE was positively related to overload and negatively related to social support and self esteem. EE was found an important correlate of D. Reduced PA was negatively associated with self esteem and with quality of work content; It was positively related to D. Support for COR notion of the value of resource pools and coping.
Lee & Ashforth (1996), A meta-analysis of 61 studies.	To Examine the relationships between demands and resource and the 3 factor burnout components (EE, D, PA)[a]	Job stressors: role ambiguity, role conflict, stressful events, workload and pressure.	Social support, job enhancement opportunities (control, participation in decision making and autonomy), reinforcement contingencies.	Meta-analysis	Demands and resources were more strongly related to EE than to D and PA. EE was more strongly related to demand correlates than resource correlates.

Table 1. (*Continued*)

Study/Sample	Research Target	Demands (Conflict Antecedents)	Resources	Design Analysis	Findings
Taris et al. (2001). 131 Dutch academic staff members	To examine the differential effects of demands and resources.	Interpersonal relationships: research tasks;	Skill discretion; decision authority.	Cross sectional, SEM analysis.	Different effects of demands and resources; time and task related demands were positively related to mental health, psychosomatic complaints and exhaustion; (poor) relationships with colleagues were related to psychological withdrawal from work; strong effect of job stressors related to teaching on perceived job demands.
	To examine antecedents of job strain and resultant withdrawal behaviors.	time pressure.			
Wright & Cropanzano (1998). 152 American welfare workers.	To study effects and outcomes of emotional exhaustion		Emotional resources	Partly cross-sectional 1 year interval for repeated measure of turnover.	EE was negatively related to job performance and positively related to voluntary employee turnover.
(b) COR model to work and family interface					
Demerouti et al. (2004), 335 Dutch employees of an employment agency.	To examine the loss spiral hypothesis of work-home interference through a reciprocal model including work pressure, WHI and exhaustion.	Work pressure		Longitudinal, 3 waves, six weeks intervals. SEM Analysis.	A reciprocal model: T1 work pressure and exhaustion predicted T2 and T3 WHI[b] T1 WHI predicted T2 and T3 of WHI exhaustion and work pressure. Work pressure and exhaustion had causal and reversed causal relationships over time. A strong demonstration of loss spirals.

Table 1. (*Continued*)

Study/Sample	Research Target	Demands (Conflict Antecedents)	Resources	Design Analysis	Findings
Grandy & Cropanzano (1999), 132 American university professors.	To Examine work and family stressors, their interplay and their physical, emotional and cognitive outcomes.	role conflict and ambiguity.	Self-esteem.	Longitudinal: two waves, 5 months interval.	Positive relations between work demands and WFC[c] and job distress (associated with life distress, poor health and turnover intentions). WFC was related to work variables; FWC was related to family variables.
Jansed et al. (2003). 12,095 Men and women in different professions, participating in the "Maastricht Cohort Study."	To learn about risk factors and mental health outcomes of WFC.	Representative examples are: Work schedule; overtime work; psychological and emotional demands; Interpersonal Relationships; commuting time; Home responsibility.	Decision latitude; social support;	Longitudinal, two major waves.	WFC predicted elevated need for recovery and prolonged fatigue, especially among omen. Certain work demands were found as risk factors for wfc. Resources were found to be protective.
Joplin et al. (2003), Focus groups in 5 countries.	To examine macro – level effects on micro – level outcomes.	Cultural demands: work and family demands.	Economic, social, technological, legislative and cultural resources.	Cross-cultural studies, qualitative data.	Rates of changes in economic, social technological legal and cultural conditions (macro-level) were positively associated with stress and WFC. Support for COR notion of loss cycles.

Table 1. (Continued)

Study/Sample	Research Target	Demands (Conflict Antecedents)	Resources	Design Analysis	Findings
Rosenbaum & Cohen (1999). 94 Israeli fully employed mothers (in the human services).	To examine the effect of WFC on distress. To examine the effect of resourcefulness and of the social context.		Control skills; spousal support.	Cross-sectional.	Women possessing at least one resource were less distressed than women who had none. Spousal support was related to distress among low resourcefulness women or those ascribing to non equalitarian context. Social and cultural impact on the individual perception.
Shaffer et al. (2001). 324 expatriates in 46 countries.	To examine the impact of work and home dynamics on withdrawal cognitions and the moderating effect of resources.	Family and home demands.	Organizational support; organizational and family commitment.	Cross sectional,	Organizational support was negatively related to withdrawal cognitions. Organizational commitment increased the effect of WIF[d] conflict whereas family commitment affected FWI conflict. Demonstration of the importance of gain within the context of less.

Table 1. (Continued)

Study/Sample	Research Target	Demands (Conflict Antecedents)	Resources	Design Analysis	Findings
(e) COR model to respite research					
The sabbatical promoted accretion of resources and well being, in terms of reduced stress and burnout and improved positive affect and life satisfaction.	Interrupted time-series design: before, during and after sabbatical combined with matched controls.	Gains and losses (COR based questionnaire). Self efficacy, control and social support.	Faculty stressors.	To examine the impact of Sabbatical leave, on well being.	Davidson et al. (research in progress). American, Israeli and New Zealand University faculty members, 168 Sabbatees and 148 matches.
Stress and burnout declined immediately after vacation. And returned to prevacation level 4 weeks after vacation. Burnout ameliorative effect persisted.	Interrupted time-series design:1 before and 2 after vacation, with controls.	Voluntary annual vacation.	Job stressors, e.g. difficult decisions, taxing duties and responsibilities, deadlines and conflicting demands.	To examine respite effect on stress and burnout.	Etzion (2003). 51 Israeli workers and 51 controls (102 participants).
There was a significant crossover of burnout before vacation and no crossover after vacation.	Before-after design; before and after an organized trip abroad.	Vacation abroad.	Job stressors, e.g. difficult decisions, taxing duties and responsibilities, deadlines and conflicting demands.	To examine crossover of burnout before and after vacation.	Etzion & Westman (2001). 25 Israeli couples.

Table 1. (*Continued*)

Study/Sample	Research Target	Demands (Conflict Antecedents)	Resources	Design Analysis	Findings
Travelers used various combinations of proactive and reactive coping strategies with creating and protecting resources.	Qualitative study	Social support, control, time, energy, objects.	Trip demands.	To examine coping strategies and resources utilized during a business trip.	Westman (in press) 35 business travelers from Israel, Sweden and the US).
Stress and burnout declined during the vacation and returned to prerespite levels 3 weeks after returning to work. Gender and respite satisfaction moderated respite effect.	Interrupted time-series design: 2 before the vacation, 1 during the vacation and 2 after the vacation.	Organizational vacation.	Job stressors (e.g. difficult decisions, taxing duties and responsibilities, deadlines and conflicting demands).	To examine the effect of vacation on stress and burnout.	Westman & Eden (1997). 90 Israeli clerks.
(d) COR model to organizational interventions					
The workshop helped to protect both means efficacy and social support among IT users.	Field experiment.	Means efficacy, Social support and control.	New IT implementation.	To examine the effect of increasing psychological resources on anticipated stress and adjustment to new IT.	Chen et al. (Research in Process). 211 IT users, 37 top managers, 33 middle-level managers and 141 subordinates. New IT users.

Table 1. *(Continued)*

Study/Sample	Research Target	Demands (Conflict Antecedents)	Resources	Design Analysis	Findings
The workshop prevented increase in burnout and contributed to the gain of satisfaction from IT among participants. Demonstration of the impact of an intervention on resource loss threat.					
Participants in the dual resource intervention experienced enhancement in social support and mastery compared to the controls. Enhancement of resources increased coping options and reduced psychological distress.	Intervention program.	Social support and mastery.	Interpersonal contact.	To examine the enhancement of resources as means of reducing distress.	Freedy and Hobfoll (1994). 87 American female nurses.

[a]The 3 burnout measures (Maslach, 1982) repeatedly mentioned are abbreviated all along this chart as follows: Emotional Exhaustion: EE; Depersonalization: D; Personal Accomplishment: PA.
[b]WHI: Work–Home Interference.
[c]WFC: Work – Family conflict; FWC: Family – Work conflict.
[d]WIF: Work Interference with Family conflict; FIW: Family interference with Work conflict.

of organizational behavior. A review of abundant literature unfolds an array of definitional approaches to burnout, presented in different classifications.

Schaufeli and Buunk (2002) discriminated between state and dynamic process definitions of burnout. State definitions reflect that burnout is characteristic of "normal individuals" (p. 8) at the work setting, suffering mainly from mental and behavioral symptoms with emotional exhaustion as its core component. Instances of state definitions include that of Maslach and Jackson (1981, 1986), Pines and Aronson (1988) and Brill (1984). The dynamic/process approaches to burnout (e.g. Cherniss, 1980; Edelwich & Brodsky, 1980; Etzion, 1987) focus on the gradual process starting out from a stressful situation, conscious or unnoticed, developing into emotional strain and change of attitude, eventuating in burnout.

Shirom (2003) focused on three main approaches to burnout, proposed by Maslach and her colleagues (Maslach, 1982; Maslach & Leiter, 1997), by Pines and her colleagues (Pines & Aronson, 1988; Pines et al., 1981) and by Shirom and Melamed (Hobfoll & Shirom, 1993, 2000; Melamed et al., 1992; Shirom, 1989). Shirom (2003) indicated that the most empirically prevalent perception of burnout is that of Maslach (Maslach, 1982; Maslach & Jackson, 1981; Maslach & Leiter, 1997), viewing burnout as a three dimensional syndrome composed of emotional exhaustion, depersonalization/cynicism and reduced personal accomplishment/reduced efficacy. A uni-dimensional view of burnout was proposed by Pines (Pines & Aronson, 1988; Pines et al., 1981) referring to burnout as a state of physical, emotional and mental exhaustion, occurring in occupational as well as non – occupational settings.

Clearly, abundant knowledge and competing approaches to burnout have been proposed but, that has only highlighted the quest for an all-inclusive theory that would supply a solid ground for this myriad viewpoints. Therefore, Shirom (2003) argued that a dynamic concept of burnout, based on COR theory, is a most fitting one. Accordingly, he proposed a definition which focused on physical fatigue, emotional exhaustion and cognitive weariness. This definition had a clear discriminant value, thus differentiating burnout from stress appraisals, coping behaviors and outcomes.

Indeed, COR theory provided an integrative foundation for the great diversity of burnout perceptions, its antecedents and outcomes. The theory's motivational ground lent itself to a better understanding of the ongoing resource depletion, which is at the core of the burnout process (Shirom, 1989, 2003). In this manner, the comprehensive, integrative and parsimonious nature of COR theory proposed a common platform for competing viewpoints thus naturally gaining adaptation into the area of stress and burnout.

The inherent application of COR theory to the study of burnout was mainly due to its conceptual constituents such as the primacy of loss and loss cycles and the binding dynamics within those components which lend themselves to burnout. COR theory argues that stress may occur under one or more of three situations: when resources are threatened, actually lost or when there is a lack of resource gain following significant resource investment. COR theory (Hobfoll, 2001) implies that burnout results from a combination of the three stress conditions, in which people are motivated to protect themselves and therefore invest in gaining resources. When this investment fails, the third stress condition occurs. At this stage, burned-out individuals may enter an escalating spiral of losses, when each loss may lead to further depletion of resources needed for the next confrontations with threats of loss. Resource depletion interferes with the potential ability to reverse loss spirals by engaging in gain cycles.

COR Based Burnout: A Literature Review

The first reference of COR theory in the organizational context was made by Shirom (1989). Following Hobfoll's introductory COR presentation, Shirom (1989) proposed embedding the concept of burnout within COR framework and examining its theoretical, empirical and practical implications. Taking the notion of avoiding loss and maximizing gains a step further, Shirom (1989) first explained that individuals experience burnout when they perceive net loss of valuable resources which cannot be replenished. Accordingly, Shirom defined burnout as a chronic state of depleted resources expressed through fatigue and exhaustion in response to environmental and organizational demands.

The most significant imprint in the developmental application of COR to the area of burnout in the organizational setting was marked by Hobfoll and Freedy (1993) who proposed an application of COR theory, as an "overarching framework" (p. 115) to the understanding of human stress and burnout. They suggested that COR theory has a particular proposition for the understanding of how stress leads on to burnout. Presenting the principles of the primacy of loss, they stated that "workers are more sensitive to workplace phenomena that translate to losses for them" (p. 118). In order to reduce loss effects, people engage in coping efforts actively, thus investing further resources. In this process, unless gains are accomplished to offset resource deterioration, inevitable resource depletion is accelerated and intensified as resources are interrelated. The individual enters a loss spiral leading to ultimate resource impoverishment, defined as burnout. Freedy and Hobfoll (1994) emphasized the dynamic aspect of the development and maintenance of burnout, explaining that burnout is inevitable since the rate by which work demands deplete resources is faster than their replenishment.

A similar process of loss was dealt with by Hobfoll and Shirom (2000) and Shirom (2003) who focused on burnout in the work setting in terms of COR theory as loss of energy resources. While differentiating between extrinsic and intrinsic energy resources, the authors explained burnout as the depletion of intrinsic energy resources resulting from experienced stress. A further contribution of Hobfoll and Shirom (2000) was their reference to the concept of organizational burnout caused by the depletion of organizational resources as a result of their overuse (e.g. unrealistic production targets) by managers, ultimately exerting burnout among employees.

Shirom (2003) further focused on the burnout process, relating its antecedents and outcomes exclusively to the work setting. According to COR, Shirom (2003) referred to initial loss as a primary stage of an escalating loss spiral, ultimately leading to burnout. Shirom also suggested that this process is intertwined with coping behaviors. Based on process burnout theories and COR theory he proposed that in the early stages of burnout, direct and active coping efforts are gathered to offset energy depletion. If these endeavors fail to bear positive results, the individual may engage in emotional detachment and defensive behaviors all reflected through the different dimensions related to burnout, such as emotional exhaustion, reduced personal accomplishment and depersonalization/cynicism (Maslach & Jackson, 1981; Maslach & Leiter, 1997). This process is similarly explicated in Shirom and Ezrachi's (2003) study, presenting COR theory as "most befitting" (p. 93) to advance understanding of the view of burnout mainly reflecting emotional exhaustion and physical fatigue as an affective state.

Alongside the examination of burnout components and their interrelations, validation attempts of the construct, its ample definitions and ensuing measurement tools have been practiced. An early instance of such application was the construction of the COR based S-MBM measurement tool, reflecting the COR notion that resources are interrelated and that lacking one may exert lacking the others (see Shirom, 2003). Empirical use of this measure validated the linkage among physical fatigue, emotional exhaustion and cognitive weariness (Melamed et al., 1992). This association was later reinforced in the discriminant validation of burnout (Shirom & Ezrachi, 2003), supporting the components' interrelations by COR theory resource depletion and loss cycles.

An overview of the theoretical development of COR adaptation to burnout within the organizational setting reveals a dual gradual development. Shirom (1989) made the first notion of burnout explained in COR terms, focusing on the burnout process and its dynamics regardless of context. Hobfoll and Freedy (1993) presented a whole model of COR based burnout, concentrating on the process and its mechanisms in general and within the work setting, in particular. Hobfoll and Shirom (2000) displayed a general explanation of COR theory as well as a thorough analysis of its application to the work context. In Shirom's (2003) "job burnout review," he argued that COR "is the most robust theoretical view of stress and burnout relationships" (p. 11) thus, evidently nesting the term of burnout at work within COR theory framework. On this account, we may witness an initial burnout theory building by the COR principles and a following gradual focus on its application to the work context. This gradual development has also been enhanced by empirical research.

Empirical Developments

The growth of theoretical use of COR theory in the field of organizational behavior is accompanied by empirical applications and testing, however, the latter extended at a slower pace. The initial empirical interest focused on the concept of demands, resources and their correlates, applicability to the area of burnout in general and to organizational behavior, in particular. So far, efforts seem to be centered on the exploration of the differential effect patterns of demands versus resources and the outcoming tangled relationships with burnout components. Every such empirical disclosure simultaneously enhances the realization of the burnout process within the work context on the one hand and COR mechanisms accounting for its evolvement, on the other hand.

An initial discriminant consideration of demands against resources and their respective associations with burnout components (Maslach, 1982), was demonstrated by Leiter (1993). The model proposed challenging previous process models and their exclusive focus on service workers, claiming for a "mixed sequential and parallel development model" (p. 244). It delineated differential patterns of developments for emotional exhaustion as opposed to depersonalization and sense of accomplishment. It implies that demands such as workload, or interpersonal conflicts increase exhaustion which in turn, leads to depersonalization. The presence of resources, on the other hand, such as social support or opportunities for skill enhancement, influences personal accomplishment. Thus, job demands are related to emotional exhaustion while resources are associated with depersonalization and reduced personal accomplishment. Based on Hobfoll's (1989) "circular definition of resources and demands" (p. 245). Leiter (1993) proposed that demands and resources are somewhat interdependent so that a demanding environment is also insufficiently resourceful. The author further explained that while emotional exhaustion is an internal process, depersonalization and sense of accomplishment are inherent to the social contexts including provisions of organizational resources and interpersonal relationships. It should be noted that Leiter (1993) referred to COR theory in the sense of resources and demands and their exertion on burnout, however, no further application of COR theory's diverse components was demonstrated.

A closer examination of burnout in terms of COR was displayed by Lee and Ashforth (1996), already associating demands with losses and resources with gains. In a meta-analysis of burnout studies, they differentiated between indicators of demand characteristics of work, that may lead to resource loss and supportive elements potential of resource gains. Their findings demonstrated that most of the loss correlates were strongly related to higher levels of burnout. Emotional exhaustion was strongly associated with demands but more weakly associated with resources. These findings corroborate the COR principle of the primacy of loss, reflected by demands rather than by resources. Moreover, emotional exhaustion and depersonalization were strongly associated with turnover intentions and organizational commitment but weakly associated with control. In line with COR theory, Lee and Ashforth (1996) explained that resources help to overcome the need for defensive coping and that those who have greater resources have a lower need for defensive strategies. These findings were later reinforced by the study of Cordes et al. (1997) among human resource professionals. Positive relations were found between emotional exhaustion and quantitative overload, depersonalization and non contingent punishment as well as between personal accomplishment and contingent rewards. In a similar manner to Lee and Ashforth (1996), likewise supported by Hobfoll and Shirom (2000), burnout phases were referred to as coping behaviors. This means that energy resource depletion arouses coping mechanisms that are enlisted to protect the individual from further loss, eventually leading to depersonalization and resultant diminished feelings of accomplishment.

Wright and Cropanzano (1998), who conducted a longitudinal study among welfare workers, also explained their findings in terms of coping. They found relationships between emotional exhaustion and diminished job performance and voluntary turnover. They posited that the recognition of deteriorating emotional resources, needed to confront interpersonal stressors, encourages the use of selective coping methods. The authors based their further explanation on previous research of Lee and Ashforth (1993a, b), stating that most individuals in these situations selected coping strategies related to withdrawal from the situation, i.e. job dissatisfaction, decreased performance and turnover. Thus, in COR terms, emotional exhaustion is a state of impoverished resources which does not enable further investment in resources and leads to further resource loss, resulting in deteriorated performance and turnover intentions.

Similar relationships were substantiated in several studies, using various demand and resource correlates and thus explicating and invigorating COR principles. In a study conducted by Janssen et al. (1999) among nurses, emotional exhaustion was strongly associated with work overload whereas personal accomplishment and depersonalization were not. Resources of self-esteem and social support were negatively associated with emotional exhaustion, thus enhancing the COR theory notion that those with greater resources are less vulnerable to further resource loss. Likewise, Demerouti et al. (2000) found strong associations between job demands (e.g. physical workload, time pressure and contacts with patients) and exhaustion, as well as between job resources (e.g. performance feedback, rewards and participation in decision making) and disengagement from work. Furthermore, Taris et al. (2001) found that stressors such as time and task related demands were associated with strain (e.g. emotional exhaustion, psychosomatic and mental health complaints) whereas stress stemming from relationships with colleagues was associated with psychological withdrawal (e.g. cynicism, lack of commitment and turnover). The above studies illustrate a course of testing that confirms the distinct routes of effect, characteristic of demands versus resources and their correlates, thus reflecting their associations with burnout components. It should be emphasized that slight changes in the variables studied have enabled each research to enhance a different aspect of COR theory. This cumulative process is evidently reflected through COR principles hereby demonstrated.

To conclude, COR theory supplied a comprehensive theoretical framework for the notion of burnout as a stress resultant progressive and dynamic process associated with resource loss and impoverishment. It provided a common groundwork for various definitions and perspectives. As such, it has consolidated wide theoretical knowledge into an all-encompassing theory. Such a theory has enabled further examination of the concept, its antecedents, process of development and outcomes. Furthermore, the association between process theories of burnout and COR principles resulted in empirical studies, each validating different aspects of burnout, illuminating its dynamics and components.

Most studies focused on relationships between burnout components, job and personal resources and demands (Cordes et al., 1997; Lee & Ashforth, 1996; Leiter, 1993; Wright & Cropanzano, 1998) whereas others stressed the differential impact patterns of resources and demands. (Demerouti et al., 2000; Janssen et al., 1999; Taris et al., 2001). Moreover, COR based practical implications have emerged, stressing the need to diagnose and "augment and replenish workers' resources" (Shirom & Ezrachi, 2003, p. 93) for the sake of organizational health. It should be noted that the combination of COR theory and burnout has not only contributed to the advancement of burnout theory and research, but also further established and embedded COR theory itself lending it external validity. The examination of burnout through COR mechanisms brings further components and dynamics to light such as additional resources and their values, coping strategies and opportunities for organizational interventions, which may be inspected both subjectively and objectively thus gaining more empirical strength. Hence, the notable contribution of COR theory to the field of burnout within the area of organizational behavior is of reciprocal nature, thus simultaneously enhancing theory and research.

THE CONCEPTUALIZATION OF WORK AND FAMILY DYNAMICS WITHIN THE FRAMEWORK OF THE COR THEORY

Work and family relationship is often viewed from the perspective of role theory (Kahn et al., 1964), which laid the foundation for interrole potential conflict between role-senders within a role set or resulting from the individual's experience of conflicting demands, thus evoking stress. However, role theory as well as other theories relating to the work-family conflict were criticized as being too narrow, attending too little to family roles and to moderators of the relationship between work-family conflict (WFC) and outcomes (Demerouti et al., 2004; Grandy & Cropanzano, 1999).

The area of work and family relationship was in quest of a grounding theory which would provide for the intricate dynamics between the individual and his/her close environment. Accordingly, Westman and Piotrokowski (1999) maintained that work-family research is fragmented, thus making it difficult to draw unequivocal conclusions. Furthermore, Zedeck (1992) concluded that theories in the work-family domain are generally post-hoc, derive descriptions of results obtained from studies measuring work and family variables. The major shortcoming of these "theories," he noted, is their atheoretical basis. Consequently, a stable and most comprehensive theory is required to enable better understanding of antecedents and consequences of this interface. COR theory, that bridges between environmental and individual theories (Hobfoll, 1989) and provides explanations for dynamic processes, is the most elaborated theory available to underlie such complex conditions. These characteristics of the theory present the rational for its application to the area of work and family interplay. Work-family conflict poses extreme conditions of threat and loss as the conflicting domains are interdependent; loss of resources in one domain may exacerbate further loss in the other. Moreover, this dual domain situation may bear potential for mobilization of resources from one domain to the other thus enhancing or threatening one or two domains at the same time. Hence, the work-family interface is a genuine area of complex dynamics.

Grandy and Cropanzano (1999) were the first to establish COR theory as a comprehensive explanation of the work-family dynamics. They suggested that it could be useful to view WFC as the interplay between gains and losses in both work and family domains. Conditions and situations such as role conflict and role ambiguity at work, that consume or threaten resources and thus interfere with resource investment in the family, may exacerbate WFC. Likewise, familial conditions that demand resource investment, leave fewer resources for investment at work and thus lead to family role stress and FWC. As for the conflicting situation, the authors claimed that the "process of juggling both work and family roles" (p. 350), thus creating an interrole conflict, imposes resource loss which may lead to stress; if no action is taken, resources may be further depleted and burnout ensues. The more role conflict experienced at work, the less resources are left for family and vice versa.

The literature displays heterogeneous concepts of work and family relationship as is reflected through related terminology. Thus, it is partly referred to as work-family conflict whereas in other cases, it appears as interference. Likewise, the conflict source is sometimes purposely mirrored through the word order (e.g. work-family conflict vs. family-work conflict). The present integration, in terms of the common grounds of COR theory, depicts empirical references by the respective authors' choices and therefore is characterized by diversified terminology, referring to the work and family interface. However, it is noteworthy that the miscellaneous empirical testing in the field of work and family dynamics converge in the sense that it clearly focuses on the COR mechanism of loss/gain cycles and spirals. Most researches concentrate on outcomes of the work and home interplay as a reflection of resource depletion, exacerbated by the simultaneous dual-domain effect.

Research Findings

Grandy and Cropanzano (1999) presented the first empirical application of work and family relations in COR theory terms. According to their COR based proposed model, individual differences are treated as resources. These include demographics such as age, tenure and gender, marital status and number of children at home. When these resources which are connected to other resources are depleted or threatened, due to investment in the other domain's resources, they may lead to work role stress and WFC as well as family role stress and FWC. The latter then deteriorates to affect further cycles of outcomes including job and family distress. Results indicated that job distress was related to outcomes of turnover intentions (aiming at stopping resource potential or actual loss), life distress and poor physical health. As resources, work and family predictors may also reduce stressors, as in the case of marital status, which was negatively related to family role stress or the personal characteristic of self-esteem, which was negatively related to all work and life outcomes. Indeed, the simultaneous manipulation of individual resource gains and losses induces WFC and affects its intensity. Relating to outcomes, the researchers found that when stressors, such as work role conflict and ambiguity increased and work demands interfered with family demands (WFC), more job distress was experienced, associated with life distress and physical and behavioral consequences. Furthermore, family role stress and family interfering with work (FWC) created family distress, which had no further outcomes as in the case of job distress. They found relationship between WFC and work variables and between FWC and family variables. Therefore, the authors suggested that work-related stress "seemed to eclipse the effect of family related stress" (p. 366) on the outcome variables. The authors also suggested that indicators of compartmentalization efforts aiming to avoid the possibility of one domain draining the resources of the other, may underscore the COR corollary by which personal coping techniques act to minimize resource loss.

The application of COR theory to the work and family dynamics was further adopted as a theoretical framework by other researchers, each focusing on different aspects of the conflict as presented below. Research conducted by Rosenbaum and Cohen (1999) empowered the applicability of COR theory principles to work and family exchange. They examined distress outcomes of WFC among working women, shedding light on the role of individual resources and differences within distinct social contexts. More particularly, the effects of individual resources, i.e. self-control skills and spousal support were examined in two gender-role setting concepts: equalitarian versus non-equalitarian marriages. In line with the COR theory ecological orientation, the authors explained that high demands of outside employment may be interpreted differently, depending on the environmental setting. Thus, for women ascribing to non-equalitarian social context, husband's support would be of greater significance, adding to their resource of self-esteem, more than for their equalitarian oriented counterparts. Findings showed that women possessing at least one kind of resource were less distressed than women who had none. Furthermore, spousal support was associated with distress levels only among low resourcefulness women or within non-equalitarian marriage context. Rosenbaum and Cohen concluded that those who possessed resources were more capable of gaining resources since the latter serves as protection against further loss, may increase the benefit of other resources and offer comfort. Hence, these findings support the value of greater resource pools in offsetting loss and of resource lack in raising vulnerability to further loss and generating loss cycles. Additionally, the significance of the cultural context inherent in COR theory was demonstrated.

Most of COR principles were also demonstrated by Shaffer et al. (2001). Their research reiterated previous outcomes of diminished emotional, cognitive and behavioral energy (Hobfoll & Shirom, 2000). Their findings amplified the significant effects of both work interference with family and family interference with work, social support and commitment on withdrawal cognitions among international assignees. These findings demonstrate their COR based assumptions that "excessive demands and/or insufficient resources within a particular role domain or between domains can result in affective and dysfunctional behaviors" (p. 100). Furthermore, the study corroborated previous findings of Grandy and Cropanzano (1999) whereby organizational commitment enhanced the effects of work interference with family conflict whereas family commitment strengthened the effect of family interference with work conflict.

Jansen et al. (2003) further reinforced the primacy of loss and the loss/gain spiral process, by examining potential consequences of WFC such as elevated need for recovery and prolonged fatigue, in a 2-year longitudinal study among employees of different professions. WFC predicted elevated need for recovery and fatigue. These mental health outcomes were more characteristic of women. The authors suggested that multiple-roles performance, characteristic of women, increased their risk for loss of resources so that need for recovery and fatigue take place more prevalently. Various work demands, e.g. conflicts with co-workers for men as well as work overtime for women, were found as risk factors for future WFC. On the other hand, resources such as co-worker/supervisor support and decision latitude for men, as well as domestic help for women had a protective effect against future WFC. They may have interfered with engagement in loss cycles and enhanced gain reserves. On a more practical note, the authors recommended that organizations limit overtime hours. In COR theory terms, decreasing demands/losses and increasing resources/gains in one domain may leave more resources available for the other domain, thus reducing conflict prospects. This research focuses on outcomes of work and family imbalance, while a broader inspection requires examination of both the conflict's antecedents and its outcomes altogether.

This quest for a more comprehensive view generated a reciprocal model of the relationships among stress, strain and work-home Interference (WHI), presented by Demerouti et al. (2004). The authors found reciprocal relationships between work characteristics, WHI and employee well being in a three wave longitudinal study among workers of an employment agency. More particularly, work pressure and exhaustion measured at the first occasion predicted WHI at the second and third occasions, whereas WHI measured at the first occasion predicted exhaustion and work pressure at the second and third measurement occasions. In addition, work pressure and exhaustion had causal and reversed causal relationships over time. The authors explained that the COR notion of loss spirals is reflected through the process by which work pressure, causing potential and actual loss, evokes WHI and consequently, feelings of exhaustion; feelings of chronic fatigue will then give rise to more work pressure and WHI. The authors concluded that those who lack resources "attempt to employ their remaining resources, often producing self-defeating consequences by depleting their resource reserves" (p. 143).

A different observation was proposed by Joplin et al. (2003), who referred to COR concept of loss cycles within a large scope of the individual-environmental exchange. The basic premise of this study is that individuals in more dynamic societies suffer more interrole stress in general and work family stress in particular. Accordingly, they examined the process by which changes in macro-environmental conditions resulted in WFC. The researchers detected economic, social, technological, legal and cultural conditions that influence the individual struggling with work and family conflicting demands. They found that rates of change in macro-environmental domains and strain levels (i.e. poor economy, low competitive ability etc.), were positively related to stress and WFC. More particularly, people in countries that undergo greater changes, deterioration or growth in economic, social, technical and legal aspects may be expected to experience greater demands and greater threat of resource loss. These experiences may exert further impact on their families, as depicted by the COR idea of loss cycles.

Summary and Conclusions

Grandy and Cropanzano (1999) were the first to present COR theory as a comprehensive ground and framework for the research of work and family dynamics, mainly indicating how work stressors interfere with family demands, each draining the resources of the other and consequently leading to psychological and behavioural outcomes. The theory was further applied to examine antecedents of the conflict, such as various job or personal demands (e.g. conflict with coworkers, job insecurity and physical demands). Psychological and behavioural outcomes (e.g. distress, turnover intentions and withdrawal cognitions) have been empirically studied. Empirical testing of these processes is grounded on COR theory principles and corollaries, manifesting the primacy of loss and the process of loss cycles. The dynamics of work and family appear as a conflict or interference, viewed as unidirectional or bidirectional, either case leading to further resource depletion and resulting in various emotional, physical, cognitive and behavioural outcomes. The reciprocal model (Demerouti et al., 2004) manifests a more complete and comprehensive view of work and family interplay in terms of loss cycles and loss primacy elicited from COR theory. The theory was also applied to a multilevel perspective whereby macro-level situations reflect on micro-level occurrences. In addition, COR theory enables exertion of practical organizational recommendations to avoid or reduce individual as well as organizational consequences related to work and family relations, so clearly manifested through the empirical review.

APPLYING COR THEORY TO RESPITE RESEARCH

While referred to variously by different terms (e.g. vacations, leave, time off etc.) respite has become a research theme in the last twenty years. Respite-researchers study the impact of job stressors using repeated-measures designs, when job stressors are intermittently "on" and "off" (Eden, 2001). The "off" event may be an annual vacation (Caplan & Jones, 1975; Eden, 1990; Etzion, 2003; Etzion & Ofek, 1998; Lounsbury & Hoopes, 1986; Strauss-Blasche et al., 2000; Westman & Eden, 1997; Westman & Etzion, 2001), a stint of reserve service (Etzion et al., 1998), a business trip (Westman, 2004a, b; Westman & Etzion, 2002), or just a slack period at work (Eden, 1982; Etzion et al., 2001). The "on" may be defined either as the before and after of the "off" event (respite) or as an acute stress event itself, such are for example end-of-term exams (Glaser et al., 1985).

Respite research has dealt with the impact of respite on psychological (e.g. burnout, satisfaction) and behavioral (e.g. performance, absenteeism) outcomes and the moderating effects of various personality and demographic characteristics on these relationships. However, little has been done in attempt to lend the issue of respite theoretical support. Thus, respite research has been mostly atheoretical with the general hypothesis that vacation is beneficial for the individual's well being. In an effort to fill this gap, it was proposed by Westman and Eden (1997) and Westman (1999) to embed respite research within COR theory of stress. Whereas most stress theories focus on how people react to stressors, Hobfoll's (1989; Hobfoll & Freedy, 1993) COR theory makes novel predictions about what happens in the absence of stress.

According to COR theory, job stress may force individuals to invest more of their resources into the work role for fear of losing their job status. As resources become scarce (e.g. after a heavy overload) individuals try to change their situation or environment in order to protect them. By decreasing their work-role effort, people conserve resources (e.g. time, self-esteem) which might otherwise be lost. In the absence of stress individuals strive to develop resource surpluses, which, in turn, promote well being (e.g. Hobfoll, 1989, 2001).

In spite of the dominant role of resource loss in COR theory, resource gain may help in buffering the aversive effect of resource loss. Resource loss may be prevented, offset, or forestalled through resource gain. Having experienced loss, gain strategies that might shelter the individual on future occasions are learnt and people seek ways to implement them. One of the mechanisms that might offset the vicious cycle of resource loss caused by stressful job demands and start a cycle of resource gain is a respite from work.

Embedding Respite Research in COR Theory

Vacation is a unique situation in which individuals invest resources (time, money, planning) with the intention and hope to gain resources. Thus, this is a form of proactive coping to stop resource loss and to start a spiral of resource gain. Based on the principles of COR theory, respite might have a beneficial effect on well being through several mechanisms:

First, vacation may alleviate stress and burnout by distancing one from the job thus halting the resource loss cycle. To illustrate, one possible benefit of vacation is the compartmentalization it affords between work and family, allowing employees to maintain their resources rather than allow one role to drain the other. Therefore, compartmentalization between domains during vacation may minimize resource loss.

Second, Hobfoll and Shirom (1993) suggested that a relaxation period between stress episodes allows regrouping of resources, replenishing resource reservoirs. During vacation, rest, reflection, and reconnecting with family and friends, individuals replenish depleted physical and emotional resources, enabling more gains. Furthermore, vacations enhance the opportunity to gain resources. Thus, those who have gained resources such as social support or control during a vacation might experience less stress and burnout.

Crossover of resources such as social support and control can also occur between close partners. Westman et al. (1998) found that one spouse's sense of control affected the other's sense of control. This finding corroborates previous work by Westman and Etzion (2001) who found that sense of control of husbands and their wives were interrelated. These findings indicate the ability of individuals to empower their spouses with their own sense of control. This may lead to the conclusion that one person's sense of control is an external resource available to the other person. As people can gain resources while being with others not only during vacation, vacations provide an opportunity for intimacy between family members and friends and an opportunity to gain from others' resources.

A third related issue is that, according to COR, gaining resources creates a gain cycle. Those who possess strong resource pools often experience spirals of resource gain because initial gain begets further gain. The cycle of gain generates its own positive energy because resource accretion means that more resources can be invested in obtaining still further gains. For example, voluntarily taking a vacation implies practicing control. One may practice control by deciding whether to take a vacation and making other decisions concerning the vacation itself such as where to go or what to do during vacation. Practicing control signifies gains in personal competence, which enhances a person's self-esteem. The enhancement of self-esteem by practicing control may strengthen personal coping resources, which in turn may serve to buffer the adverse effects of negative events and chronic stress.

In sum, vacation releases one from potential loss cycles and slows acting drain cycles, where resource loss occurs through a kind of chronic day to day seepage. It also avails time and replenishment of sleep and leisure. This may produce a state necessary for perspective taking. Perspective taking is important because it allows individuals to plan gain strategies for forestalling or ending outright loss cycles. Clearly, one can also reattach with family and friends thus building family and friendship resources. It must be noted that this depends on a solid relationship that may enable these gains. Nevertheless, some vacations may be characterized by negative circumstances, for instance, being by oneself or vacations that are so busy that they are stressful and people cannot reconnect, can sabotage such gains.

COR theory also indicates the limitations of the beneficial impact of a vacation. As Lounsbury and Hoopes (1986) pointed out, vacations are not uniformly positive experiences. They may have built in stressors that can start a spiral of losses. Vacation may expose workers to stressors not encountered on the job, such as arguments over how and where to vacation and conflict with spouse and children. For couples experiencing marital discord, vacation makes spouse evasion and conflict avoidance harder and may exacerbate the strife, causing undermining behavior that might start a spiral of losses. Furthermore, as going on vacation is an action of investment of resources (time, money, planning etc.) if the investment does not lead to further gains, it will cause stress. Additionally, because loss is more potent than gain, if people return to chronically-draining circumstances, the gains they have made will have only a short-term positive effect. Vacations should have a big enough mental and physical effect to create a lasting "afterglow" and decrease in strain. Therefore, the message is that one must be realistic about a vacation. It will not turn around a terrible situation or even one with slow chronic drain, but it will relieve the pressure for a while.

Considering COR theory, respites differ to the extent by which they provide an opportunity for repletion of exhausted psychological resources or gaining new resources. For example, Etzion et al. (1998) have suggested that being detached from the ongoing demands producing chronic job stress, alleviates stress and burnout. In terms of COR theory, being detached during respite from one's work might prevent the loss of resources that results from the work situation. Conversely, engaging in job-related activities or being "in touch" with one's work during respite might continue loss of resources or at least prevent the gains that might result from the respite situation. Another example is satisfaction with one's respite. When people go on respite they make investments. These investments are expected to yield gains (e.g. joy, meeting interesting people, energy). When the respite "fulfills" one's investments, one might be satisfied with one's respite. When such investments do not provide good returns, one might be dissatisfied from one's respite experience. COR model predicts that when investments of resources do not provide a good return, people will experience this as a loss, a loss of the expected or envisioned gain. Such examples show that the respite nature/situation is not uniform. What happens during the respite affects one's resource levels. Respite might promote well being to the extent that the respite includes positive components in terms of resource gain or lack of loss.

Review of COR-Based Respite Research

Hobfoll (2002) noted that COR theory has added an additional emphasis on resource gains. COR theory maintains that resource gain and the accompanying positive emotions become increasingly important in the face of loss. Hobfoll suggests that resource gains in themselves have a modest effect, however, when they follow resource loss the "ability to obtain resources becomes of increasing importance, providing emotional respite and an increased ability to sustain goal pursuit" (p. 312). Therefore, a vacation from work is characterized by resource gain as it usually takes place after a period of chronic resource loss in the job. Thus, we (Etzion & Westman, 2001; Westman, 2004a, b; Westman & Eden, 1997; Westman & Etzion, 2002, 2003) have conducted several studies in order to investigate the impact of vacation on stress and burnout, thus in COR terms to investigate the beneficial effects of stopping resource loss and that of resource gain after a period of resource loss.

Westman and Eden (1997), using a quasi-experiment, examined the relief from job stressors (losses/demands) and burnout afforded by a vacation respite (gains). Seventy-six clerical employees completed measures of perceived job stressors and experienced burnout twice before a 2-week company-wide vacation, once during vacation, and twice after the vacation. Repeated-measures analysis of variance detected substantial declines in burnout during the vacation. The return to work showed gradual fade-out, as burnout returned toward its prevacation level by 3 weeks after the vacation. Thus, as mentioned before, vacation did not turn around a situation with chronic draining, but it relieved the pressure for a while.

Furthermore, moderator analysis detected differences in the amount and pattern of vacation relief among sub-samples. Westman and Eden (1997) found that those who enjoyed their vacation were more burned out on prevacation occasion, supporting the COR prediction regarding the importance of gain in the context of loss. Moreover, they found that those who were satisfied with their vacation reported greater burnout-relief. The respite effect and its complete fade-out were detected among all subgroups analyzed.

In the following study Westman and Etzion (2001) used a similar quasi-experimental design to examine the relief from job stressors, burnout and absenteeism afforded by a vacation respite. Eighty-seven employees in a food manufacturing company completed questionnaires on three occasions: ten days before a company-wide vacation, immediately after vacation and a month after returning to work. Data on absenteeism both for health reasons and other reasons was obtained from personnel files. The findings showed that vacation alleviated perceived job stress and burnout, replicating findings that a respite from work diminishes levels of strain to lower than chronic, on-the-job levels. Burnout declined immediately after vacation and returned to prevacation levels four weeks later. A similar pattern was found with regard to objective absenteeism data both for health and non-health reasons. The findings that absenteeism for non-health reasons decreased after vacation supports Westman's (1999) view that respite research should be embedded in COR theory. When employees lose resources under chronic stress, one of the possibilities to stop the loss cycle and start a gain cycle is to distance themselves from the cause of loss, taking time off, being absent from work. These findings indicate that that taking a vacation can be regarded as a stress management technique.

In a similar vein, Etzion (2003) investigated the impact of an annual voluntary vacation (as opposed to collective or enforced vacation) on perceived job stressors and burnout of industrial workers. She compared 51 workers who took their annual vacation to 51 matched controls in the same company who did not take their vacation during the same period. Participants completed stress and burnout questionnaires shortly before they left work for vacation, after they returned, and three weeks later. In the vacation group both stress and burnout decreased after returning. However, three weeks later, stress had reverted to its initial level, but burnout remained low. The comparison group, however, showed no changes. The finding that the ameliorative effect of a vacation on burnout persists beyond that of job stressors could be discussed on the basis of COR theory. When workers return to their job, the previous stressful demands are still there and they cause losses and threat of further losses, thus increasing job stress. However, resources gained during vacation temporarily prevent the increase in burnout.

Taking a different perspective, Etzion and Westman (2001) have examined the impact of job stress and vacation on the crossover of burnout between partners in a marital relationship. The main objective of this research was to test whether in times of tranquility (opportunity for resource gain) as compared to times of job stress (resource loss), the crossover of stress and strain process (Westman, 2001) in the family decreases. Here Etzion and Westman (2001) went one step further, trying to explore the possibility that resource gain stops the vicious cycle of resource loss of one spouse and this prevents the contagion of strain from the other spouse occurring through a process of crossover. They hypothesized that the crossover of stress and strain from one spouse to the other is more intense during stressful periods than in more tranquil times. The sample consisted of 25 dual-career couples who participated in an organized tour abroad. The effect of such a vacation on perceived job stress and burnout in both spouses using a before-after quasi-experimental design was examined.

Findings demonstrated a significant crossover effect of burnout between husbands and wives before they went on vacation. That is, the additional amount of variance in burnout of one partner was significantly explained by that of his or her spouse on the first occasion, a period of resource loss. However, no such effect was detected after the respite from work, which was a period of resource gain. These findings demonstrate that a vacation from work may stop, at least temporarily, the serious phenomenon of crossover of burnout from one spouse to the other, thus alleviating stress from the family.

Business Travels as a Special Kind of Respite

Rapid growth, globalization and economic forces have eroded national borders, facilitating the transfer of goods and services from one country to another. In this global economy, short business trips have become common. COR theory lends a wide theoretical ground to the area of business travel. Westman and Etzion (2002) proposed to view business trips as a special case of respite, enabling travelers to replenish their resources. By leaving the regular working atmosphere and distancing oneself from the daily job demands, the travelers might not only cease the loss of resources, resulting from job pressure and family demands, but also gain new ones, such as, new friends, increased sense of self-efficacy, new cultural experiences, rest, pleasant experiences etc. Though business travelers are exposed to job demands while away, they are not exposed to the authentic organizational physical characteristics such as boss and peers. Although the same three mechanisms mentioned before, which contribute to the beneficial effect of respite also operate in the case of business trips, the main difference is that while away the travelers are working as well.

Hobfoll and Lilly (1993) demonstrated that gains become important only in the context of a sequence of losses. Business travel may be a source of resource loss for the traveler, starting at the pre-trip phase with trip planning and job demands, through the trip phase posing physical and psychological demands and ending at the post-trip phase which can be characterized by overload. Against these resource losses, the resources gained during the business trip have a strong positive emotional effect on the traveler. In a similar vein, Presser and Hermsen (1996) maintained that business travels may be regarded as a valued resource because of the autonomy and status they entail. During the business trip the traveler acts as a representative of the firm with minimal supervision, allowing for autonomous scheduling of work and meetings. Furthermore, some travels have additional positive consequences such as enhancing job mobility and expanding one's personal horizons. They conclude that the effect of business travel on personal growth is extremely positive.

Westman and Etzion (2002) were the first to study business travels from the angle of respite. They investigated the impact of overseas business trips on job stress and burnout among 57 employees of Israeli high-tech firms whose jobs include overseas travel. Participants completed questionnaires on three occasions, prior to going abroad, during their stay abroad, and one week after returning to their regular workplace. A significant decline in stress was detected immediately after the trip. Similarly, burnout was lower after returning from the trip than it was prior to departure. Both the anticipation of the overseas journey and the mission abroad may have been stressful for these employees. Only upon returning to their routine jobs did the level of burnout decrease. Westman and Etzion concluded that the decrease in job stress and burnout might be evidence for a delayed respite effect. Though these travelers experienced a heavy workload and ambiguity (losses/demands) during the trip, they also enjoyed the physical detachment (gain) from their office and their families. Etzion et al. (1998) have defined detachment from work as the individual's sense of being away from the work situation. In terms of COR theory, such detachment prevents the loss of resources, resulting from the work situation. Furthermore, these travelers had a chance for new experiences in foreign countries which may have been perceived as gains, thus enhancing their feeling of personal accomplishment.

Business Trips – A Conceptual Model

Based on respite and business travel literature, Westman (2004a, b) initiated a project, aiming at the development of a theoretical framework for business travels embedded in COR theory. In the first stage Westman focused on the issue of gains and losses in business travels. Open-ended, in-depth exploratory interviews were conducted with 35 professional employees (from Israel, the U.S. and Sweden) who travel as part of their job. Frequency of traveling varied between 3 and 24 trips per year, and the duration of each trip varied from three days to four weeks. The interviews elicited information on positive and negative travel experiences.

The interview notes were analyzed and each quote from the notes was assigned a descriptive category according to its content (Westman & Shraga, 2003). Based on these interviews and focusing on gains and losses, the following meta-model (see Fig. 1) was proposed for outlining the relationships between the various facets of the business travel process. A basic assumption of the model is that business trips are job events that occur over time, therefore suggesting that each business trip is an unfolding experience consisting of four phases: (1) Pre-trip; (2) Journey (e.g. flight); (3) Stay; (4) Post-trip. This means relating to these trips as events where each phase has its gains and losses. Furthermore, business trips are viewed as a cycle where gains and losses from previous trips impact the experiences and outcomes of the following trips. The model can guide research to determine how experiences and processes in the work and family domain are linked.

Figure 1 distinguishes between nine facets and constructs: job demands, family demands, business trips gains and losses, coping, time, personal characteristics, family status, organizational support and outcomes. The model delineates bi-directional relationship between Box A and B, indicating that job demands and family demands are interrelated. Furthermore, job and family demands may cause

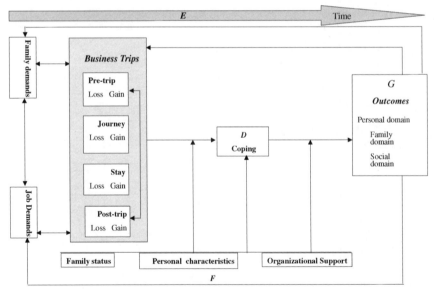

Fig. 1. The Impact of Short Business Travels on the Individual, the Family, and the Organization.

losses and gains at different phases of the trip (Arrow from A & B to C) whereas the gains and losses of the trip affect job and family demands (Arrows from C to A & B). Each phase of the trip (Box C) has unique but also similar negative and positive events, losses and gains. To illustrate, in the Pre-trip phase there is overload, excitement, and expectation to gain. In the second phase good or bad flight conditions; in the third phase while being away there is overload, loneliness, new experiences, detachment, and in the fourth phase overload, success or failure.

The model also indicates the importance of time (Box E), as each phase of trip affects the others and each event unfolds and affects other trips and other facets at different points of time. The loss and gains spirals affect the coping process (Box D) which impacts (Arrow from D to G) the consequences. Box F includes personal characteristics (age, gender, experience, and self esteem), family status (married, children) and organizational support, affect the coping process and moderate the relationship between coping and outcomes.

The dynamics of resource losses and gains in business trips were further elucidated by Westman (in press) who content analyzed interviews of 35 business travelers. The elicited model (see Fig. 2) shows that the demands and experiences including both losses and gains, characteristic of the trip (Box A), bear two main coping strategies (Box B): proactive and reactive. These strategies operate either

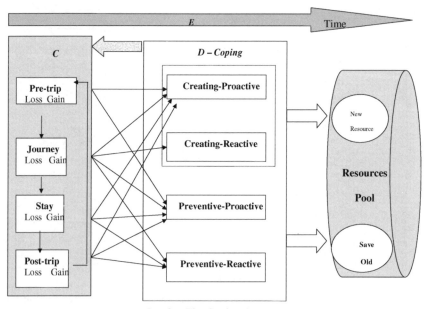

Fig. 2.   The Coping Process.

by the acquisition of new resources and/or the prevention of loss of resources. The various coping strategies are activated and based on the resource pool. A feedback loop describes the reciprocal relations between the coping process and the resource pool under the impact of time (E). Resource and frequency of use differed at each stage of the trip, and across the four exemplified combinations. The coping process affects the size and content of the resource pool. The model treats the business trip as an unfolding experience in which gains and losses can accrue in each of its four phases. Each phase of the trip (Box A) possesses unique negative and positive events, losses and gains. This loss-gain spiral affects the coping process, which in turn impacts the gains and losses of future trips.

The findings showed different combinations of coping strategies and resources used, demonstrating that each phase of the trip was characterized by different resources acquired or saved. Across the whole trip the resources mentioned most frequently were social support, followed by time, relaxation, control, energies, and objects.

This research provides insight into the dynamics of business trip demands, resources and coping behaviors. Of particular interest is the finding that the resources utilized in both proactive and reactive coping were also practiced in the acquiring resources and prevention of loss of resources, thus exemplifying Hobfoll's (2001) argument that proactive and reactive coping often co-occur. These findings augment this assertion by adding that proactive and reactive coping strategies are based on both acquiring new resources and preventing their loss and finally concluding that during business trips, proactive behavior is the primary mechanism of resource acquisition.

Theoretical Implications

Respite research and short business travels research both address the contrast between individuals' well being on their regular job and off it. Thus, these two lines of research could be mutually enriching. However, the main difference between short business trips and other respites is that people on respite (e.g. vacation) can be completely disengaged from their jobs, whereas business travelers can only be detached from the physical job environment. They may experience a change in venue but not in overload and responsibility. One could broaden the scope of respite research by comparing patterns of business travels to learn how different degrees of disengagement (e.g. frequent to no communication with home office, having a spouse join on the trip, having a vacation following the overseas job) relate to indices of stress and strain. This would be a natural extension that would shed light on many of the same issues dealt with by respite research.

Moreover, business travels have disparate effect on different people. While some individuals bloom and find travel exhilarating (gain spiral), others may be almost incapacitated by the same trip (loss spiral). Learning what makes business trips a positive experience for certain people might help us counsel business travelers on how to benefit more from their time away from regular job. However, there are still many moderators to be studied before we know enough to predict who will benefit from what kind of a respite. Research on frequent travelers is timely, given the recent impetus of companies to globalize.

Most of the findings in the respite domain describing the benefits of a respite exemplify resource repletion and are in accord with the adoption of COR as a nomological net to guide such research. However, respites evidently differ in the extent to which they provide an opportunity to replete exhausted psychological resources. An interesting empirical question is to determine what types of vacations actually replenish resources and which ones do not. To cast light on the processes of respite relief, vacation research should include measures of vacation content, participants (e.g. spouse, children, and friends) and vacation stressors. Measures should be devised for acute and chronic family stress, such as economic difficulties and quarrels, which create loss spirals. Whereas respite is conceived of as a time to replenish depleted personal resources, it is also a time when loss spirals may operate. Accordingly, it is advisable to collect repeated measures of resources such as sense of control, freedom from obligations, self-esteem, social support, and satisfaction, during vacation to determine whether the respite does indeed afford the individual a chance to replenish these resources and gain new ones or creates loss spirals. COR theory can thus guide research to what kind of vacation is recommended.

Practical Implications

COR theory proposes intervention guidelines on the individual, group, and system levels. If we focus on respite from work as an intervention to combat job stress, the respite has to be recognized on these three levels. Thus, it is important, for example, that the respite be legitimized and encouraged by the organization and the community and fit the priorities of the individual. Such an intervention should act to prevent or limit loss; that is, individuals should be helped to extricate themselves from a problem situation of the work site. The intervention should also act to create new resources such as mastery, social support, and to facilitate their implementation. The resource systems of other members of the family or the group can and should be utilized.

Furthermore, when dealing with business travels the organization can enhance the traveler's coping ability by providing resources such as cultural preparation and instrumental support to both the travelers and their families. While on the trip, the organization can make sure that the traveler's needs are met so as to minimize resource loss. The organization should also provide more support for maintaining balance between work and home demands. Accordingly, legitimized time off might also help relieve stress by giving travelers more of a sense of control, through providing an option of a day off, whether it is actually taken by the traveler or not. Preventing potential stressors before they occur, counteracting the effects of stressors after they occur and maximizing gains can be facilitated by the traveler and by the organization.

STUDY IN PROGRESS:[1] SABBATICAL LEAVE AS A "TIME OUT" FROM CHRONIC ACADEMIC JOB STRESS – A TEST OF CONSERVATION OF RESOURCES THEORY

COR theory has been used as a framework for recent empirical research in the general field of stress. Some of the studies that have focused on work-related-stressors based on the COR theory did not include the measures or the designs needed to evaluate the fit of the model. Furthermore, most of the studies on COR theory have been conducted among individuals under stressful conditions. Davidson et al. (2004) extended previous research on COR theory by studying a positive life event, namely respite from routine work. This enabled examination of the impact of resource gain or the lack of loss, assumably occurring during times of respite.

As was aforementioned, although accumulated findings have consistently demonstrated that respites bring relief from job stress and strains and respite effects have been documented among different occupations, most respite researchers have not based their predictions on strong conceptual framework. Even though several respite researchers have explained (post-hoc explanations) the ameliorative respite effect they had found in terms of COR theory (e.g. Westman & Eden, 1997; Westman & Etzion, 2002), none of them have measured the main component of the theory, namely resources. Moreover, a test of COR theory implies the need to measure resource levels before, during and after respites. Unfortunately, such measurements have not been part of respite research to date. However, Eden (1982) measured self-esteem (a resource according to COR) repeatedly. Levels of self-esteem declined during a stressful event and rose significantly a month later during a relaxed period (routine occasion at work). Notwithstanding, Eden's predictions and measurements were not based on COR theory; he measured self-esteem but not as one of the resources of COR theory. However, in terms of COR theory, such findings exemplify that even routine (or relaxed) period at work enables accretion of a valued personal resource.

Following Westman's (1999) suggestion, Davidson et al. adapted COR theory to determine the nature and direction of their respite-research. In order to validate COR predictions, they collected repeated measures of resources to test whether the respite does indeed afford the individual a chance to replenish resources and gain new ones and whether such regrouping mitigates burnout. Furthermore, to date, the *beneficial* aspects of respite on well being have mainly been tested in terms of less negative reactions (e.g. burnout) and respite was regarded particularly as a means for *preventing* or *reducing* strain. However, according to COR theory, resource gain during respite may lead to a spiral of resource gain, which, in turn, promotes positive states of being. As Hobfoll (1989) stated, "When people develop resource surpluses, they are likely to experience positive well being" (p. 517). Thus, Davidson et al. have tested positive affect and life satisfaction to reveal whether respite enhances positive well being by promoting the accretion of resources and does not just prevent distress. Based on COR theory, the researchers hypothesized that the absence of job stress (during respite) reduces burnout and enhances positive affect and life satisfaction. This process eventuates in enhanced well being.

Respite researchers have investigated several moderators of the impact of respite on outcomes such as characteristics of the individuals (gender, seniority) and of the respite situation (e.g. detachment from work, respite satisfaction). Gender, vacation satisfaction and detachment from work during respite have been found as moderators of the impact of stress (or the absence of stress) on the individual (e.g. Etzion et al., 1998; Westman & Eden, 1997). COR theory can enhance identification of additional potential moderators of respite effects. In light of COR model, Davidson et al. proposed that individual variables and respite characteristics can be considered as resources. Self-efficacy is an example of a personal characteristic resource that aids stress resistance. Respite characteristics (e.g. respite type, with or without family, detachment from work, quality of respite, control, social support) and demographic characteristics are condition resources. Respite length can be treated as an energy resource that allows one to acquire other resources. The more resources one possesses, the more he or she might enjoy stress and burnout relief while on respite.

Finally, to date, the respite most frequently studied has been vacation, holiday or annual vacations (Aviv, 2000; Caplan & Jones, 1975; Eden, 1990; Etzion, 2003; Etzion & Ofek, 1998; Etzion et al., 2001; Laski, 2002; Lounsbury & Hoopes, 1986; Redian, 1999; Strauss-Blasche et al., 2000; Westman & Eden, 1997; Westman & Etzion, 2001). In the same vein, to the best of our knowledge, the typical length of the respites that were studied ranged from several days to several weeks with the exemption of two months (Eden, 1982; Laski, 2002). Hobfoll (2001) suggested that "long-term resource gain is seen as having greater impact on reversing psychological distress than previously thought" (p. 356). Accordingly, longer respite may provide more time and opportunities for resource gain than short respite. The present study enriches respite research by studying a new type of respite with an appreciably longer time span. Rather than focusing on vacations of few days or weeks, Davidson et al. assessed the extent to which a Sabbatical leave, as experienced by university academic members, enables Sabbatees (individuals on Sabbatical) to replenish their resources, and the conditions under which the replenishment is more successful.

According to Toomey and Connor (1988), sabbaticals historically have been viewed as a way to deal with job stress and burnout, to broaden professional skills and to afford an opportunity for personal growth. The results of sabbaticals are usually new and improved attitudes and perspectives, renewed vigor and intellectual and emotional resources, better physical and emotional health, and such quantifiable outcomes as articles, books and scientific discoveries (e.g. Hendel & Solberg, 1983; Jarecky & Sandifer, 1986; Miller & Kang, 1997; Sorcinelli, 1986). These findings describing the benefits of a sabbatical exemplify resource accumulation and are in accord with the adoption of COR theory to guide the present research.

Taken together and basing on COR theory, it was hypothesized that stress-relief (during Sabbatical) diminishes burnout and increases life satisfaction and positive affect, and otherwise prevents negative states of being and enhances positive well being; and that self efficacy, tenure, rank, gender, age, control, social support, detachment, respite quality, and respite length moderate the impact of stress on well being, predicting that Sabbatees who possess more of such resources would experience a greater improvement in their state of well being while on sabbatical than those reporting lower levels of resources.

A quasi-experiment was conducted among matched pairs of faculty members at ten universities located in Israel, New Zealand and the United States. All faculty members applying for Sabbatical leave during 2000–2001 and 2001–2002 were asked to complete questionnaires before, during, and after their leave. For each individual in the respite sample, matches of the same rank, gender, and academic department, who were not on Sabbatical during the same year, were selected. Due to the matching procedure, there were no significant differences between the two groups on all available demographic indicators (age, degree, rank, discipline) except tenure. Each control respondent was asked to complete questionnaires on the same occasions as his or her colleague in the Sabbatical sample. Whereas a few preceding respite studies measured stress and strain before, *during* and after respite (Eden, 1982, 1990; Westman & Eden, 1997; Westman & Etzion, 2002) and others used a control group (Etzion, 2003; Etzion et al., 1998), no study, to the best of our knowledge, has used both. Thus, a unique contribution of the present research lies in combining the interrupted time-series design with multiple replications (Cook & Campbell, 1979) with the matched-sample design to rigorously test the hypothesis that stress causes strain.

The first occasion was a month before the end of the semester before the Sabbatees began their Sabbatical. The second questionnaire was at the midpoint of their sabbatical, and the third was in the middle of the semester following their return. Self-reported questionnaires measured stress (faculty stress and quantitative workload), well being (burnout, positive affect, and life satisfaction) and resources on all three occasions. Resources were measured using a bipolar gain-loss scale that contained 12 resources, which fall into three categories: *conditions* (e.g. people from whom I can learn), *personal characteristics* (e.g. professional knowledge), and *energies* (e.g. free time, energy). Respondents were asked to indicate how much of each resource they have lost or have gained or neither during the past few months. The resources' index was supplemented with additional measures of control and social support. Thus, changes across three measurement occasions were tracked to compare resource gains and losses and their consequences among Sabbatees and controls. Characteristics of the Sabbatical (e.g. quality of the Sabbatical experience, detachment from work, length of the Sabbatical, control) were measured on the second occasion. Self-efficacy and performance were assessed on the third occasion.

The preliminary findings are based on 168 Sabbatees and 148 matches who completed both the first and the second questionnaires. Commensurate with COR prediction, resources were negatively correlated with each of the stress measures (faculty stressors and overload) at both occasions. A comparison of Sabbatees and control means on perceived stress indexes revealed highly similar levels of stress on pre-respite occasion. Repeated-measures ANOVA of perceived faculty stress and workload revealed significant Occasion X Respite interactions, indicating that the two groups differed in the amount of changes in stress over time. Simple-effect tests of the changes confirmed that faculty stress and workload declined among the Sabbatees and remained unchanged in the comparison group. This is evidence that the Sabbatical provided a practically important respite from stress and validates the on/off-the-job dichotomy as a proxy for the presence or absence of job stressors.

Comparing Sabbatees and control means on resources (gain and loss index and control) across occasions, Davidson at al. found highly similar levels of resources on the pre-respite occasion. Repeated-measures ANOVA revealed significant Occasion X Respite interactions. Those who were on Sabbatical have gained resources as predicted, whereas there was a negligible decline among the controls. Finally, no significant Occasion X Respite effect was detected with regard to social support.

Significant Respite X Occasion effects were found with regard to burnout, positive affect and life satisfaction. Simple-effect tests of the changes indicated that burnout declined among the Sabbatees and remained unchanged in the comparison group. Moreover, while there were no changes in the levels of positive affect and life satisfaction among the control respondents, those who were on Sabbatical experienced significant increases in positive affect and life satisfaction.

Summary and Conclusions

Research showing the ameliorative effects of a short respite from work on job stress and strain was replicated among academics on sabbatical leave. Commensurate with COR theory, the results show that a sabbatical promotes accretion of resources. This process eventuates in enhanced well being in terms of reduced burnout and enhanced positive affect and life satisfaction.

The main contribution of the present research is in embedding it within Hobfoll's COR theory to explain the beneficial but "atheoretical" effects that have been found in previous respite studies. The main differences between the present study and preceding respite research are the present study's broader scope, longer time span, and methodology. The (approximately) year time frame together with the repetitive measurements, afford a better test of the stress-strain-relief process as it unfolds over time. Additionally, the present research expands respite research by measuring resources repeatedly, by studying a unique type of respite and by measuring outcomes and moderators not previously examined with regard to respite. Based on COR theory, along with aversive psychological strains such as burnout, which former respite studies focused on, Davidson et al. examined the beneficial impact of respite on positive states of well being and found that the advantage of respite is not just in preventing (or reducing) aversive states but also in promoting positive well being. Thus, COR theory provides a means for predicting and understanding respite relief and the ensuing attitudinal and emotional outcomes. Finally, the research expands previous COR research by testing it in a novel way among individuals experiencing a positive life event instead of under stressful conditions, which most former COR studies focused on, revealing the impact of resource gain on stress outcomes.

COR THEORY BASED INTERVENTIONS AT THE WORKPLACE

The impact of work-related stress on the individual and organizations is a significant and growing problem. Accordingly, organizations adopt a variety of intervention programs to manage stress at the organization. Stress management programs provide strategies for preventing job stress and strain and channeling job stress into healthy and productive outcomes (Quick et al., 1997). Although stress management interventions have been identified as potentially valuable to organizations there is no consistent body of knowledge indicating how to approach the reduction of work-related stress in the best way. A number of researchers (Arthur, 2000; Coie et al., 1993; Cooper et al., 2003; Murphy, 1996) have pointed out that the links between the theoretical and intervention research literatures are not strong. Thus, it is necessary to use general stress theory, which may offer an appropriate framework for stress management. COR theory with its emphasis on the role of resource investment and resource gain may provide theoretical guide for stress prevention interventions in the workplace. Hobfoll (2001) argued that COR theory has implications for stress interventions and emphasized that "COR theory leads to interventions that change people's resources or their environments" (p. 362). Furthermore, Hobfoll (1998a) described the nature of personal resources and pointed out that personal resources reflect social resources and socioeconomic resources. It means that resources at these levels are interconnected, therefore, according to COR, an intervention has to address the personal level within an ecological context. Otherwise interventions at one level may confront resistance because of the need to maintain resources at another level.

According to the second COR principle (Hobfoll, 2001) "people must invest resources in order to protect against resource loss, recover from losses and gain resources" (p. 349). This means that people should not engage in reactive coping but, act in a proactive way that will help them gain resources and become less vulnerable to the threat of future resource loss or actual loss. The focus on the importance of proactive resource investment creates the implications for stress prevention. Hence, COR theory is a basis for preventive interventions that help increase people's resource pools and might interrupt loss, reduce stress and create a resource gain cycle (Freedy & Hobfoll, 1994; Hobfoll, 1998a, b; Hobfoll & Shirom, 2001). Two interventions have included resource enhancement based on COR theory (Freedy & Hobfoll, 1994; Levine et al., 1993) and only one of them was conducted in the work context (Freedy & Hobfoll, 1994).

Levine et al. (1993) found a significant change in AIDS risk behavior among inner-city women who participated in the intervention aimed at increasing their specific target resources relating to safe sex. The Freedy and Hobfoll (1994) study provided initial evidence of the impact of resource-related intervention during resource loss in the workplace. They found that nurses in an intervention program, aimed at enhancing resources, demonstrated reduced stress outcomes. Participants in the dual resource intervention experienced significant enhancements in social support and mastery compared to participants in the one resource intervention. Freedy and Hobfoll (1994) explained the superior efficacy of a dual-resource intervention over a single-resource intervention in terms of COR model. The multiple resources intervention strengthened the resource pool and increased access to coping resources. By targeting a range of resources, the dual-resource intervention expanded coping options and reduced psychological distress. Thus, work site stress management programs should target more than a single resource. It should also be emphasized that only Levine et al's (1993) study was a field experiment in which the participations were randomly assigned to experimental and control groups. The scarcity of field experiments based on COR theory motivated us to conduct a field experiment based on COR theory, which will lend COR further validation.

STUDY IN PROGRESS:[2] IMPACT OF ENHANCED RESOURCES ON ANTICIPATORY STRESS AND ADJUSTMENT TO NEW INFORMATION TECHNOLOGY: A FIELD EXPERIMENT

Information Technology Implementation and Threat of Resource Loss

COR theory emphasizes that the threat to lose resources can have just as acute consequences as actual loss. However, COR based studies carried out to date have focused on testing actual resource loss in various contexts. No empirical research has yet focused on the threat of resource loss, its role and outcomes. Previous COR studies have focused only on the impact of resource loss and resource gain (Hobfoll, 1998a, b, 2001; Hobfoll & Shirom, 2000). Thus, very little is actually known about the impact of the threat of resource loss on individuals. Lazarus and Folkman (1984) argued that threat differs from loss because it permits anticipatory coping. Kaiser and Ozer (1997) found that emotional stability relates to the experience of reactive stress but not to anticipatory stress. Therefore, the main objective of the present experiment was to investigate the impact of the threat of resource loss on employees and to determine whether it operates in the same way as actual loss. Another objective of the experiment was to strengthen the linkage between COR theory and preventive stress interventions. A common stressful circumstance in the new organizational reality that can be used to target these issues is the implementation of new information technology (IT). Although COR theory has been adopted in the study of various organizational phenomena, no research has yet been done on the threat of resource loss, in general, and during implementation of new IT in the workplace, in particular.

Information Technology Implementation and Stress

Today's workplace is being shaped by substantial changes in technology, especially IT. An organization's success or failure in implementing IT may have a big influence on its effectiveness, profitability and survival. Numerous studies have examined the effects of implementing IT in work organizations and its influence on users, their work and their relations with others within the organization (Sokol, 1994). While the introduction of new IT has the potential for gain of real advantages and anticipation for improvement, it may also cause loss and create threats of loss of resources for both the mangers and the employees (Clegg et al., 1997).

The empirical literature on implementing computerized technologies offers several management strategies that may influence the effectiveness of an implementation process (Klein & Ralls, 1995). Given the importance of job stress in the organizational context, it is surprising that most researchers have not considered preventing users' stress among these strategies. A literature search reveals that relatively few researchers have attempted to explore the relationships between new IT and user stress. Moreover, up until now, studies on the impact of technology in the workplace have reported mixed evidence as to whether new technologies increase (Korunka et al., 1993, 1995, 1996; Korunka & Vitouch, 1999; Stellman et al., 1987), have no effect on (Agervold, 1987; Mullarkey et al., 1997) or decrease stress-related reactions (Kalimo & Leppänen, 1985). Furthermore, very little is actually known about how the encounter with new IT in the workplace increases stress among users. Hence, the psychological process by which new technology causes employee stress remains unclear. Finally, it is apparent that the majority of the studies addressed the question "What was the impact of the new system on its users?" That is, they related to the new IT as the predictor variable and posited stress as the dependent variable. As a result, these studies did not show whether preventing or reducing users' stress might improve IT implementation.

COR Theory and IT Implementation

COR theory principles may enable an insight that has not been discussed in the IT implementation literature. In a review of the consequences of new advanced technology implementation, it has been concluded that IT produces important gains for the organization and its employees (Klein & Sorra, 1996; Wong & Seddon, 2002), but it also increases demands and creates loss (Agervold, 1987, Cooper, 1998; Cooper et al., 2003; Johansson & Aronsson, 1984). Cooper (1998) asserted that new technologies add information overload as well as speed up the pace of work with demands for a greater immediacy of response (e.g. Internet, emails, faxes, etc.), all of which are major sources of loss. Consistent with the idea that loss is more salient than gain, resource loss during IT implementation should have a big impact on new IT users. Consequently, introducing new IT creates uncertainty about aspects of the psychological and physical work environments within an organization. More particularly, the need to become familiar with the new equipment poses a threat to the employees (Cooper et al., 2003). Users may see the new IT as a risk and anticipate that their resources are in danger. Thus, implementation of new IT may lead to a threat of resource loss.

The current field experiment was conducted within a large organization that was planning to implement an advanced IT system, Enterprise Resource Planning – ERP. In testing the impact of the threat of resource loss on the adjustment to the new IT, Chen et al. (2004) examined the effect of enhancing the psychological resource pool by a stress prevention program. The experiment included secondary prevention (Quick et al., 1997), using workshops embedded in the COR theory, applying principles of Stress Inoculation Training (SIT) (Meichenbaum, 1985; Meichenbaum & Deffenbacher, 1988). The workshop was designed to enhance resources before starting work with the new system, hoping that resource gain may improve the adjustment to the new IT. Thus, the aim of the workshop was to increase the users' resource pool. The prediction was that new IT users who participate in the workshop will gain more resources and experience a better IT adjustment than the IT users in the control group.

Based on Freedy and Hobfoll's (1994) finding of a superior efficacy of a dual-resource intervention over a single-resource intervention, three psychological resources were targeted. Resources can be entities that are either centrally valued in their own right (e.g. self-esteem, close attachments, health and inner peace), or a means towards obtaining centrally valued ends (e.g. money, social support and credit) (Hobfoll, 2002). Studies have demonstrated that there are many key resources that relate to stress (Hobfoll, 2001, 2002). Thoits (1994) indicated that key resources are those that might be viewed as management resources. In the present study the focus was on the following resources, which may be related to stress during IT implementation: means efficacy, social support and perceived control. Research has supported the beneficial role of these resources in successful adaptation. However, only a few studies have illustrated that these resources can be imparted by planned training interventions (Eden, 2001; Freedy & Hobfoll, 1994).

The overall project was a pretest-posttest field experiment assigning subunits randomly to experimental and control conditions. All employees participated in a 2–5 days of technical training, conducted by an external body, concerning the new IT (ERP) before the system was installed. The experimental group participated in an additional special 4 hours resources workshop conducted by experienced organizational consultants. The workshop was designed to increase participants' psychological resources pools: (a) to increase participating users' means efficacy, that is, to get them to believe that the new IT is capable of being more useful to their needs; (b) enhance the new users' social support; and (c) to increase the users' control during the IT implementation. The workshop concluded with a self-diagnosis of the resources the employees have, ways to gain them and how to cope with the ERP. The control group participated only in the technical training for ERP.

Participants were asked to fill out self reported questionnaires measuring stress, burnout and satisfaction and resources at three points of time: before the workshop (occasion 1), after they started to work with the new IT (manipulation check – occasion 2) and two months after they started to work with the new IT (occasion 3). Resources (means efficacy, social support and control) were measured on all three occasions whereas stress, satisfaction and burnout were measured only in occasions 1 and 3.

The preliminary findings are based on results of 211 employees, from 23 sub units. Thirty-seven top managers, 33 middle-level managers and 141 subordinates, 57 men and 141 women. Using repeated measures ANOVA, Chen et al., found no differences in levels of means efficacy before workshop (occasion 1). There was a tendency of gain in means efficacy among the participants in the workshop from occasion 1 to 2, and a significant decline among the participants in the control group. Furthermore, there was a tendency of gain in means efficacy among the participants in the workshop from occasion 2 to 3, and a tendency of decline among participants in the control group. There was an increase in social support among participants in the workshop from occasion 1 to 2, and a decline in the control group. No gain of social support was found among the participants in the workshop from occasion 2 to 3, however, there was a decline among the participants in the control group. Finally, no significant Occasion X intervention with regard to control was detected.

The findings concerning the outcomes demonstrating that the amount of before-after change in burnout in the two groups, differed. While there was no change in the level of burnout in the experimental group across occasions, there was a remarkable increase in burnout in the control group. As for satisfaction from the new IT, no change was detected in the experimental group however, there was a decrease in the control group.

Summary and Conclusions

COR theory leads to preventive interventions that help to increase people's resource pools and might interrupt loss, reduce stress and create a resource gain cycle

(Freedy & Hobfoll, 1994; Hobfoll, 1998a, b; Hobfoll & Shirom, 2001). This study included intervention based on COR theory, helping IT users to obtain resources to prevent the threat of resource loss. Because multiple resources intervention ensures a resource pool and increased access to coping resources, the intervention targeted three psychological resources. Means efficacy, social support and perceived control were used because of their contribution to successful IT adaptation.

The findings of this study support previous results of COR- based intervention (Freedy & Hobfoll, 1994; Levine et al., 1993). The resources workshop protected and stopped a loss spiral of both means efficacy and social support among IT users. Furthermore, the resources prevented increase in burnout and contributed to the gain of satisfaction from IT among participants in the intervention. These findings regarding the impact of the intervention on IT users has important implications that may enrich the existing stress literature, especially COR theory. The current and expected changes in the workplace have led to increases in anticipated stress at work. The threat of resource loss stemming from COR theory enhances the comprehension of anticipated stress and its outcomes. The present experiment demonstrates the impact of threat of resource loss manifesting its effects on the control group (less means efficacy, less social support, less satisfaction and more burnout). These findings are important because so far, there has been no research on resource enhancement with regard to the threat of resource loss. The results of the present experiment show that the hypotheses based on COR theory were supported; the enhancement of resources during the threat of resource loss condition minimized actual resource loss, prevented burnout and improved satisfaction from IT. The finding of a significant decrease in means efficacy and social support among those who did not participate in the workshop, indicate that they have lost resources, while the users in the experimental group, anticipating the same "objective" threat, have experienced no resources loss. This suggests that the intervention prevented resource loss or even a loss spiral among those IT users that participated in the workshop. The COR principle of the primacy of loss implies difficulty to prevent loss compared to obtaining gain. Furthermore, the second COR Corollary, "those who lack resources are not only more vulnerable to resource loss but initial loss begets further loss" (Hobfoll, 2001, p. 354), explains the significant increase in burnout among the control users.

In addition, the present experiment is one of few field experiments in stress intervention studies demonstrating preventive means efficacy and social support loss. Following Goldenhar et al.'s (2001) argument that in order to learn why and under what circumstances work intervention may succeed, intervention research needs to be more theory-driven, this intervention was theory driven, based on COR theoretical principles. COR theory received support from these experiment preliminary results as a guide for stress management and stress interventions in the work context. The findings yield knowledge that should help managers understand and prevent some of the problems in IT implementation and how to cope with it in various stages. By preventing anticipated problems and supplying employees with needed resources for coping with technological changes, organizations will save money, prevent unnecessary stress and strain, and enhance employees' satisfaction from the new IT.

CONCLUSIONS AND IMPLICATIONS FOR FURTHER RESEARCH

COR theory should continue to be a helpful heuristic for the study of organizational stress. It allows a complex set of predictions and can be applied across settings, cultures, and circumstances. Its specificity also allows for it wholly or in part to be rejected. While it is not the hope that a theory be summarily rejected, every theory must at some stage be shown to outlast its usefulness. At best, a good theory is incorporated into a greater whole, or a simpler set of laws that have equivalent or better explanatory power. We think that COR theory has only begun to illuminate the stress process, but the point we are making here is that because it is specific, it is given to refinement, testing, and limitations.

Focusing on resource loss and gain, COR theory is unusually applicable across domains and questions. Work demands, work versus home demands, respite, burnout, multiple role demands, and impact of the glass ceiling on women and minorities are but a few of the topics to which COR theory can be applied. We unfortunately are in an age when we must embark on the study of the impact of terrorism on workers, and stress of travel to areas of the world made dangerous by political unrest, disease, and crime. Because COR theory lends itself to catastrophic, major, and minor stress it can be used to bridge these areas and make sense across these quite different levels of stress.

Perhaps one of the most important functions of a chapter such as this is to project to potential new horizons for COR theory. In this regard, we will address several potential areas of application for both research and applied interventions.

One of the key aspects of COR theory is its focus on resources as changing and dynamic. In many areas of stress, resources have been used as predictor variable, with emotions typically considered as outcome variables. For organizational research and applications, it is worthwhile to also consider the reverse of this process, or even resource processes in their own right. Businesses are often in the "business" of acquiring resources. Thus, employees' resources and organizational resources are harnessed with the intention of building further resources. COR theory suggests that this means that resource growth comes out of the intelligent application of available resources. Now, this might appear patently obvious. That is, until we look at the "human resource" practices of many companies. Employees are often treated as if it is merely expected of them to conform without their having input, without regard to their having families to go home to, and with team play only so many words, and little team building. When employees are not allowed input, they lose sense of control, become increasingly alienated, and with these resource and emotional downturns, begin to merely "put in their time," or look for better work opportunities. In a recent consultation, one of the chapter authors (S. E. H.) was told, "by the way, our managers work 62–70 hours a week." This was mentioned almost as an aside, or a statement of the obvious. Equally obvious, there was the message that an intervention designed to decrease those hours was not in the offing – and it came to be known that 70 hours did not include constant evening cell phone calls and late night e-mail checks. COR theory challenges the very assumption of many businesses that people can be used in this way without negative consequences. Employees may not leave if they are not marketable or if the market is in recession. But the better employees will leave when and if they can as businesses are perceived as supporting human resources, rather neutral to human resources, or destructive of human resources. Those who stay will do a poorer job of enhancing business resources, as their own resources are drained.

Another potential area of application for COR theory is in the exchange of resources in organizations through resource flow and interchange. As in the prior case, this moves COR theory away from mental health aspects and closer to questions of direct resource acquisition and performance. Hobfoll (1998a, b) referred to the FALL model in this regard. The acronym standing for Fitting, Accommodation, Limitation and Leniency, but little organizational research or writing has paid attention to this important model within COR theory.

Resource "fit" has long been applied to organizations (French et al., 1982). However, the term fit is static. Instead COR theory suggest that people and organizations put resources in motion, so fitting is a better term than fit. If resources do not fit, people and organizations attempt to reshape, reposition, or acquire resources that do fit. This is an exciting area for future study that would also change the rather static (one moment in time) nature of much organizational research.

Adaptation means that people optimize their resources to meet challenge and demand and if optimization is not enough, they move toward compensation coping (Baltes, 1994). Optimizing is a process of matching one's own or one's organization's resources with demands. This means that individuals and systems having coping choices. If they can cope better in one domain than another, and if they have freedom of choice they will choose that domain. For example, a worker may know that she is better making oral than written presentations. Adaptation includes long-term moves that set her up for more oral than written presentations, and, say, use of a colleague when a written argument is required. If she is trapped into a job where she has to write more, she may choose compensatory moves to increase these resources such as taking a writing course, or perhaps partnering with that writer-colleague on a more ongoing basis, each covering the other's gaps. Again, little work has applied COR theory to study these important processes, but they receive theoretical legs from COR theory.

Next, limitations are important resource processes to consider. Research on stress and organizational processes often implies "a just world model." But, in fact, organizations and individuals often move to thwart successful resource investment. This is apparent in cases of racism and sexism, where individuals may be resource-rich, but limited in the allowance of investing those resources toward further resource gain for themselves or the organization. In the case of office politics, this process can be pernicious and of great detriment to individuals and organizations. How favoritism places limitations on the resources of some and positions others to have greater opportunity for successful applications of resources is a potential focus for COR theory on individual and group levels.

Finally, the last "l" in the FALL model is for leniency. This may be the least studied resource process. Leniency refers to the fact that some individuals are allowed to move ahead, gain bonuses, receive promotions, and let in to favorable financial or other circumstances based on their status. This is the opposite of racism and sexism in a way. If being the member of the right club, graduate of the right school, or congregant of the right church gets you ahead, your resources are made to fit at each juncture where you might otherwise predict failure. This leniency can be personal (e.g. "I like you," or like what you do for me) or may be related to a complex process of trading favors. Despite the fact it's the grease that makes much of the business and organizational world click, it has received little study. These resource exchange processes hold much promise for applying COR theory to research, consultation, and understanding of organizational behavior. We know little about them that we can state with any empirical certainty at this time.

We hope that the current chapter has illustrated the applicability and reach of COR theory. We suspect that given the increasing complexity of the workplace and the increased competition in the marketplace, the topic of resources will continue to be highly salient and germane on both theoretical and practical levels. We especially hope to see interventions using COR theory as illustrated in the work by Freedy and Hobfoll (1994) and as detailed in this chapter in the work of Chen et al. By being theory-based, such interventions are not only likely to bear fruit for the settings in which they are applied, but should be easier to generalize to other settings where the same factors are dominant. In contrast, most stress management work has taken more of the tack of "common sense." Unfortunately, common sense often does not cross settings and without theoretical underpinnings it is difficult to predict how central the intervention's targets and foci will translate to other settings. We finally look forward to research that adopts and contrasts several models of stress in order to examine their viability and strength of specific predictions.

NOTES

1. Davidson, Eden and Westman.
2. Chen, Westman and Eden.

REFERENCES

Agervold, M. (1987). New technology in the office: Attitudes and consequences. *Work and Stress, 1*, 143–153.

Arthur, A. R. (2000). Employee assistance programmers: The emperor's new clothes of stress management? *British Journal of Guidance and Counseling, 28*, 549–559.

Aviv, N. (2000). *The meaning of vacation among women working shifts: The effect of vacation on job stress, burnout and work-home conflict.* Unpublished Manuscript, Faculty of Management, Tel Aviv University.

Brill, P. L. (1984). The need for an operational definition of burnout. *Family and Community Health, 6*, 12–24.

Caplan, R. D., & Jones, K. W. (1975). Effects of work load, role ambiguity, and Type-A personality on anxiety, depression and heart rate. *Journal of Applied Psychology, 60*, 71–719.

Chen, S., Westman, M., & Eden, D. (2004). *Impact of enhanced resources on anticipatory stress and adjustment to new information technology: A field experiment.* Unpublished manuscript.

Cherniss, C. (1980). *Professional burnout in human service organizations.* New York: Praeger.

Clegg, C., Axtell, C., Damodaran, L., Farbey, B., Hull, R., Lloyd-Jones, J. R., Nicholls, J., Sell, R., & Tomlinson, C. (1997). Information technology: A study of performance and the role of human and organizational factors. *Ergonomics, 40*, 851–871.

Coie, J. D., Watt, N., West, S. G., Hawkins, D., Asarnow, J., Markman, H., Ramsey, S., Shure, M., & Long, B. (1993). The science of prevention: A conceptual framework for and some directions for a national research program. *American Psychologist, 48*, 1013–1022.

Cook, D., & Campbell, D. T. (1979). *Quasi-experimentation: Design & analysis issues for field settings.* Chicago: Rand McNally.

Cooper, C. L. (1998). *Theories of organizational stress.* New York: Oxford University Press.

Cooper, C. L., Dewe P. J., & O'Driscoll, M. P. (2003). Employee assistance programs. In: J. C. Quick & L. E. Tetrick (Eds), *Occupational Health Psychology* (pp. 289–304). Washington, DC: American Psychological Association.

Cordes, C. L., Dougherty, T. W., & Blum, M. (1997). Patterns of burnout among managers and professionals: A comparison of models. *Journal of Organizational Behavior, 18*, 685–701.

Cozzarelli, C. (1993). Personality and self-efficacy as predictors of coping with abortion. *Journal of Personality and Social Psychology, 65*, 1224–1236.

Davidson, O. B., Eden, D., & Westman, M. (2004). *Sabbatical leave as a "Time Out" from chronic academic job stress – A test of Conservation of Resources Theory.* Unpublished manuscript.

Demerouti, E., Bakker, A. B., & Bulters, A. (2004). The loss spiral of work pressure, work-home interface and exhaustion: Reciprocal relations in a three-wave study. *Journal of Vocational Behavior, 64*, 131–149.

Demerouti, E., Bakker, A. B., Nachreiner, F., & Schaufeli, W. B. (2000). A model of burnout and life satisfaction amongst nurses. *Journal of Advanced Nursing, 32*(2), 454–464.

Edelwich, J., & Brodsky, A. (1980). Training guidelines. Linking the workshop experience to needs on and off the job. In: W. S. Paine (Ed.), *Job Stress and Burnout Research, Theory and Intervention Perspectives*. Beverly Hills, CA: Sage.

Eden, D. (1982). Critical job events, acute stress, and strain: A multiple interrupted time series. *Organizational Behavior and Human Performance, 30*, 312–329.

Eden, D. (1990). Acute and chronic job stress, strain, and vacation relief. *Organizational Behavior and Human Decision Processes, 45*, 175–193.

Eden, D. (2001). Means efficacy: External sources of general and specific subjective efficacy. In: M. Erez, U. Kleinbeck & H. Thierry (Eds), *Work Motivation in the Context of a Globalizing Economy* (pp. 73–85). Hillsdale, NJ: Lawrence Erlbaum.

Etzion, D. (1987). Burnout: The hidden agenda of human distress. (IIBR Series in Organizational Behavior and Human Resources, Working Paper No. 930/87). Tel Aviv, Israel: The Israel Institute of Business Research, Faculty of Management, Tel Aviv University.

Etzion, D. (2003). Annual vacation: Duration of relief from job stressors and burnout. *Anxiety, Stress and Coping, 16*, 213–226.

Etzion, D., Eden, D., & Lapidot, Y. (1998). Relief from job stressors and burnout: Reserve service as a respite. *Journal of Applied Psychology, 83*, 377–585.

Etzion, D., & Ofek, A. (1998, May). The influence of two types of vacation on perceived job stressors and burnout among social workers. Presented at the 7th International Conference on Social Stress Research, Budapest.

Etzion, D., & Westman, M. (2001). Job stress, vacation and the crossover of strain between spouses-stopping the vicious cycle. *Man and Work, 11*, 106–118.

Etzion, D., Westman, M., & Kremer, F. S (2001). *The impact of vacation and slack work periods on job-stress and burnout among newcomers and veteran Israelis.* Presented at the 22nd conference of the International Society for Stress and Anxiety Research (STAR), Palma de Mallorca, July.

Freedy, J. R., & Hobfoll, S. E. (1994). Stress inculcation for reduction of burnout: A conservation of resources approach. *Anxiety, Stress and Coping, 6*, 311–325.

French, J. R. P., Jr., Caplan, R. D., & Van Harrison, R. V. (1982). *The mechanisms of job stress and strain.* Chichester, UK: Wiley.

Glaser, R., Kiecolt-Glaser, J. K., Speicher, C. E., & Holliday, J. E. (1985). Stress, loneliness, and changes in herpes virus latency. *Journal of Behavioral Medicine, 8*, 249–250.

Goldenhar, L. M., Moran, S. K., & Colligan, M. (2001). Health and safety training in a sample of open-shop construction companies. *Journal of safety Research, 32*, 237–252.

Grandy, A. A., & Cropanzano, R. (1999). The conservation of resources model applied to work-family conflict and strain. *Journal of Vocational Behavior, 54*, 350–370.

Hendel, D. D., & Solberg, J. (1983). Sabbatical and leave experiences of female and male faculty at a large research university. Paper presented at the Annual Meeting of the American Educational Research Association, Montreal, Canada, April.

Hobfoll, S. E. (1988). *The ecology of stress.* Washington, DC: Hemisphere.

Hobfoll, S. E. (1989). Conservation of resources: A new attempt at conceptualizing stress. *American Psychologist, 44*, 513–524.

Hobfoll, S. E. (1998a). *Stress, culture and community: The psychology and philosophy of stress.* New York: Plenum.

Hobfoll, S. E. (1998b). Ecology, Community, and AIDS Prevention. *American Journal of Community Psychology, 26,* 133–144.

Hobfoll, S. E. (2001). The influence of culture, community, and the nested-self in the stress process: Advancing Conservation of Resources Theory. *Applied Psychology: An International Review, 50,* 337–421.

Hobfoll, S. E. (2002). Social and psychological resources and adaptation. *Review of General Psychology, 6,* 307–324.

Hobfoll, S. E., & Freedy, J. (1993). Conservation of resources: A general stress theory applied to burnout. In: W. B. Schaufeli, C. Maslach & T. Marek (Eds), *Professional Burnout: Recent Developments in Theory and Research* (pp. 115–129). Washington, DC: Taylor & Francis.

Hobfoll, S. E., & Lilly, R. S. (1993). Resource conservation as a strategy for community psychology. *Journal of Community Psychology, 21,* 128–148.

Hobfoll, S. E., & Shirom, A. (1993). Stress and burnout in the workplace: Conservation of resources. In: T. Golombiewski (Ed.), *Handbook of Organizational Behavior* (pp. 41–61). New York: Marcel Dekker.

Hobfoll, S. E., & Shirom, A. (2000). Conservation of resources theory: Applications to stress and management in the workplace. In: R. T. Golembiewski (Ed.), *Handbook of Organization Behavior* (pp. 57–81). New York: Dekker.

Jansen, N. W. H., Kant, I. K., Kristensen, T. S., & Nijhuis, F. J. N. (2003). Antecedents and consequences of work – family conflict: A prospective cohort study. *Journal of Occupational and Environmental Medicine, 45*(5), 479–491.

Janssen, P. P. M., Schaufeli, W. B., & Houkes, I. (1999). Work-related and individual determinants of three burnout dimensions. *Work and Stress, 13,* 74–86.

Jarecky, R. K., & Sandifer, M. G. (1986). Faculty members' evaluations of Sabbaticals. *Journal of Medical Education, 61,* 803–807.

Johansson, G., & Aronsson, G. (1984). Stress reactions to computerized administrative work. *Journal of Occupational Behavior, 5,* 159–181.

Joplin, J. R. W., Shaffer, M. A., Francesco, A. M., & Lau, T. (2003). A macro-environment and work-family conflict. *International Journal of Cross Cultural Management, 3*(3), 305–328.

Kahn, R. L., Wolpe, D. M., Quinn, R. P., Snoek, J. D., & Rosenthal, R. A. (1964). *Organizational stress: Studies in role conflict and ambiguity.* New York: Wiley.

Kaiser, R. T., & Ozer, D. J. (1997). Emotional stability and goal related stress. *Personality and Individual Differences, 22,* 371–379.

Kalimo, R., & Leppänen, A. (1985). Feedback from video display terminals, performance control and stress in text preparation in the printing industry. *Journal of Occupational Psychology, 58,* 27–38.

Karasek, R. A. (1979). Job demands, decision latitude, and mental strain: Implication for job redesign. *Administrative Science Quarterly, 24,* 285–307.

Klein, K. J., & Ralls, R. S. (1995). The organizational dynamics of computerized technology implementation: A review of the empirical literature. In: L. R., Gomez-Mejia & M. W. Lawless (Eds), *Implementation Management of High Technology* (pp. 31–79). Greenwich, CT: JAI Press.

Klein, K. J., & Sorra, J. S. (1996). The challenge of innovation implementation. *Academy of Management Review, 21,* 1055–1080.

Korunka, C., Huermer, K. H., Litschauer, B., & Karetta, B. (1996). Working with new technologies: Hormone excretion as an indicator for sustained arousal: A pilot study. *Biological Psychology, 42,* 439–452.

Korunka, C., & Vitouch, O. (1999). Effects of implementation of information technology on employee's strain and job satisfaction: A context-dependent approach. *Work and Stress, 34,* 341–363.

Korunka, C., Weiss, A., Huermer, K. H., & Karetta, B. (1995). The effect of new technologies on job satisfaction and psychosomatic complaints. *Applied Psychology: An International Journal, 44,* 123–142.

Korunka, C., Weiss, A., & Karetta, B. (1993). Effects of new technologies with special regard for implementation process per se. *Journal of Organizational Behavior, 14,* 331–348.

Laski, S. (2002). The effect of summer break activities and personality variables on stress and burnout among high school teachers in Israel. Unpublished Manuscript, Faculty of Management, Tel Aviv University.

Lazarus, R. S., & Folkman, S. (1984) *Stress, appraisal and coping.* New York: Springer.

Lee, R., & Ashforth, B. E. (1996). A meta-analytic examination of the correlates of the three dimensions of job burnout. *Journal of Applied Psychology, 81,* 123–133.

Lee, R. T., & Ashforth, B. E. (1993a). A longitudinal study of burnout among supervisors and managers – Comparisons between the Leiter and Maslach (1988) and Golembiewski et al. (1986) models. *Organizational Behavior and Human Decision Processes, 54,* 369–398.

Lee, R. T., & Ashforth, B. E. (1993b). A further examination of managerial burnout – toward an integrated model. *Journal of Organizational Behavior, 14,* 3–20.

Leiter, M. P. (1993). Burnout as a developmental process: Consideration of models. In: W. B. Schaufeli, C. Maslach & T. Marek (Eds), *Professional Burnout: Recent Developments in Theory and Research* (pp. 115–129). Washington, DC: Taylor & Francis.

Levine, O. H., Britton, P. J., James, T. C., Jackson, A. P., Hobfoll, S. E., & Lavin, J. P. (1993). The empowerment of woman: A key to HIV prevention. *Journal of Community Psychology, 21,* 320–334.

Lounsbury, J. W., & Hoopes, L. L. (1986). A vacation from work: Changes in work and nonwork outcomes. *Journal of Applied Psychology, 71,* 392–401.

Maslach, C. (1982). Understanding burnout: Definitional issues in analyzing a complex phenomenon. In: W. S. Paine (Ed.), *Job Stress and Burnout* (pp. 29–41). Beverly Hills, CA: Sage.

Maslach, C., & Leiter, M. P. (1997). *The truth about burnout.* San Francisco: Jossey-Bass.

Maslach, C., & Jackson, S. (1981). The measurement of experienced burnout. *Journal of Occupational Behavior, 2,* 99–115.

Maslach, C., & Jackson, E. (1986). *MBI: Maslach Burnout inventory; manual research edition.* Palo Alto: CA Consulting Psychologists Press.

Meichenbaum, D. H. (1985). *Stress inoculation training.* New York: Pergamon Press.

Meichenbaum, D. H., & Deffenbacher, J. L. (1988). Stress inoculation training. *The Counseling Psychologist, 16,* 69–90.

Melamed, S., Kushnir, T., & Shirom, A. (1992). Burnout and risk factors for cardiovascular disease. *Behavioral Medicine, 18,* 53–61.

Miller, M. T., & Kang, B. (1997). A Case study of post Sabbatical assessment measure. *Journal of Staff, Program and Organization Development, 15,* 11–16.

Mullarkey, S., Jackson, P. R., Wall, T. D., Wilson, J. R., & Grey-Taylor, S. M. (1997). The impact of technology characteristics and job control on worker mental health. *Journal of Organizational Behavior, 18,* 471–489.

Murphy, L. (1996). Stress management techniques: Secondary prevention of stress. In: M. J. Schabracq, J. A. M. Winnubst & C. L. Cooper (Eds), *Handbook of Work and Health Psychology*. Chichester: Wiley.

Pines, A., & Aronson, E. (1988). *Career burnout – causes and cures*. NY: Free Press.

Pines, A., & Aronson, E., with Kafry, D. (1981). *Burnout – from tedium to personal growth*. NY: Free Press.

Presser, H., & Hermsen, J. (1996). Gender differences in the determinants of work-related overnight travel among employed Americans. *Work and Occupation, 23*, 87–115.

Quick, J. C., Quick, J. P., Nelson, D. L., & Hurrel, J. J. (1997). *Preventive stress management in organizations*. Washington, DC: American Psychological Association.

Redian, R. (1999). The moderating effect of workaholism and Type A on the impact of vacation on job stress and burnout. Unpublished Manuscript, Faculty of Management, Tel Aviv University.

Rini, C. K., Dunkel-Schetter, C., Wadhwa, P. D., & Sandman, C. A. (1999). Psychological adaptation and birth outcomes: The role of personal resources, stress, and sociocultural context in pregnancy. *Health Psychology, 18*, 333–345.

Rosenbaum, M., & Cohen, E. (1999). Equalitarian marriages, spousal support, resourcefulness and psychological distress among Israeli working women. *Journal of vocational behavior, 54*, 102–113.

Schaufeli, W. B., & Buunk, B. P. (2002). Burnout: An overview of 25 years of research and theorizing. In: M. J. Schabracq, J. A. M. Winnubst & C. L. Cooper (Eds), *Handbook of Work and Health Psychology* (pp. 383–425). Chichester: Wiley.

Shaffer, M. A., Harrison, D. A., Gilley, K. M., & Luk, D. M. (2001). Struggling for balance amid turbulence on international assignments: Work-family conflict, support and commitment. *Journal of Management, 27*, 99–121.

Shirom, A. (1989). Burnout in Work Organization. In: C. L. Cooper & I. T. Robetson (Eds), *International Review of Industrial and Organizational Psychology* (pp. 25–48). NY: Wiley.

Shirom, A. (2003). Job-related burnout. In: J. C. Quick & L. E. Tetrick (Eds), *Handbook of Occupational Health Psychology*. Washington, DC: American Psychological Association.

Shirom, A., & Ezrachi, Y. (2003). On the discriminant validity of burnout, depression and anxiety: A re-examination of the burnout measure. *Anxiety Stress and Coping, 16*, 83–97.

Sokol, M. B. (1994). Adaptation to difficult designs: Facilitating use of new technology. *Journal of Business and Psychology, 8*, 277–296.

Sorcinelli, M. D. (1986, April). Sabbaticals and leaves: Critical events in the career of faculty. Paper presented at the Annual Meeting of the American Educational Research Association, San Francisco, California.

Stellman, J. M., Klitzman, S., Gordon, G. C., & Snow, B. R. (1987). Work-environment and the well being of clerical and VDT workers. *Journal of Occupational Behavior, 8*, 95–114.

Strauss-Blasche, G., Ekmekcioglu, C., & Marktl, W. (2000). Does vacation enable recuperation? Changes in well being associated with time away from work. *Occupational Medicine, 50*, 167–172.

Taris, T. W., Schreurs, P. J. G., & Van Iersel-Van Silfhout, I. J. (2001). Job stress, job strain and psychological withdrawal among Dutch university staff: Towards a dual-process model for the effects of occupational stress. *Work and Stress, 15*(4), 283–296.

Thoits, P. (1994). Stressors and problem-solving: The individual as psychological activist. *Journal of Health and Social Behavior, 35*, 135–160.

Toomey, E. L., & Connor, J. M. (1988). Employee sabbaticals: Who benefits and why. *Personnel, 65*, 81–84.

Westman, M. (1999). Gain and loss spirals: Applying Hobfoll's COR theory to respite research. Working Paper No. 29/99. The Israel Institute of Business Research, Tel Aviv University.

Westman, M. (2001). Stress and strain crossover. *Human Relations, 54*, 557–591.

Westman, M. (2004a). The impact of short business travels on the individual, the family and the organization. In: A. Antoniou & C. Cooper (Eds), *Research Companion to Organizational Health Psychology*. New Horizons in Management Series. Cheltenham, England: Edward Elgar Publishing.

Westman, M. (2004b). Strategies for coping with business trips: A qualitative exploratory study. *International Journal of Stress Management, 11*, 167–176.

Westman, M., & Eden, D. (1997). Effects of vacation on job stress and burnout: Relief and fade-out. *Journal of Applied Psychology, 82*, 516–527.

Westman, M., & Etzion, D. (1995). The crossover of stress, strain and resources from one spouse to another. *Journal of Organizational Behavior, 16*, 169–181.

Westman, M., & Etzion, D. (2001). The impact of vacation and job stress on burnout and absenteeism. *Psychology and Health, 16*, 595–606.

Westman, M., & Etzion, D. (2002). The impact of short overseas business trips on job stress and burnout. *Applied Psychology: An International Review, 51*, 582–592.

Westman, M., & Piotrkovski, C. (1999). Work-family research in occupational health psychology. *Journal of Occupational Health Psychology, 4*, 9–16.

Westman, M., & Shraga, O. (2003). Short business trips: Gains and losses to the individual, the family and the organization. HTMS Working Paper No. 4/2003. The Georges Leven High-Tech Management School, Faculty of Management, Tel Aviv University.

Wright, T. A., & Cropanzano, R. (1998). Emotional exhaustion as a predictor of job performance and voluntary turnover. *Journal of Applied Psychology, 83*, 486–493.

Zedeck, S. (1992). Introduction: Exploring the domain of work and family concerns. In: S. Zedeck (Ed.), *Work, Families and Organizations*. San Francisco: Jossey Bass.

THE ROLE OF "HAPPINESS" IN ORGANIZATIONAL RESEARCH: PAST, PRESENT AND FUTURE DIRECTIONS

Thomas A. Wright

ABSTRACT

For many years now, both organizational researchers and practitioners alike have been interested in the role played by employee happiness on a number of workplace outcomes. In particular, many have been fascinated by the happy/productive worker thesis. According to this hypothesis, happy employees exhibit higher levels of job-related performance behaviors than do unhappy employees. However, despite decades of research, support for the happy/productive worker thesis remains equivocal. These inconsistent findings primarily result from the variety of ways in which happiness has been operationalized. Most typically, organizational theorists have operationalized happiness as job satisfaction, as the presence of positive affect, as the absence of negative affect, as the lack of emotional exhaustion, and as psychological well being. I will review this literature using the circumplex framework as the taxonomic guideline. In addition, drawing on the impetus of the "positive psychology" movement, I propose Fredrickson's (1998, 2001, 2003) broaden-and-build theory of positive emotions as one approach especially well-suited for future research to better understand the happy/productive worker thesis.

Exploring Interpersonal Dynamics
Research in Occupational Stress and Well Being, Volume 4, 221–264
Copyright © 2005 by Elsevier Ltd.
All rights of reproduction in any form reserved
ISSN: 1479-3555/doi:10.1016/S1479-3555(04)04006-5

The secret of happiness is this: Let your interests be as wide as possible, and let your reactions
to the things and persons that interest you be as far as possible friendly rather than hostile.
                                              (Bertrand Russell, *The Conquest of Happiness*, 1930, p. 157)

As the quote from Bertrand Russell suggests, the secrets surrounding the conquest
of happiness have long been sought after but remain elusive for many. In
particular, in the applied sciences the role of happiness in the prediction of
performance, i.e. the happy/productive worker thesis, has long been a particularly
vexing question for organizational scientists and practitioners alike (cf. Hoppock,
1935; Pennock, 1930; Wright & Staw, 1999a). According to this "Holy Grail"
of management research, all things being equal, workers who are happy on the
job – however defined – will have higher job performance than those who are less
happy (Landy, 1985; Spector, 1997; Weiss & Cropanzano, 1996). However, for the
past several decades, efforts to test the happy/productive worker thesis have often
met with much skepticism and a certain amount of controversy (see Cropanzano &
Wright, 2001; Davis-Blake & Pfeffer, 1989; Ledford, 1999, for varying perspective
reviews). This uncertainty was highly understandable, given that empirical research
has not consistently demonstrated a link between "happiness" and job performance
ratings (cf. Daniels & Harris, 2000; Fisher, 1980; Podsakoff & Williams, 1986;
Staw, 1986).

Despite these inconsistent findings, the happy/productive worker thesis has
continued to inspire a fair measure of scholarly (as well as practitioner) interest.
In part, this interest seems to be driven by evidence suggesting that happiness
(broadly defined) *should* produce better job performance. In an earlier review,
Cropanzano and Wright (2001) noted that when testing the happy/productive
worker thesis, happiness has primarily been operationalized in four ways:
as job satisfaction (the operationalization of choice for most past research
endeavors), as the profile of positive and negative affectivity (a prominent
present direction), the lack of emotional exhaustion (another prominent present
direction), and as psychological well being (an increasingly prominent present
and proposed future direction). As will be demonstrated, the results of these four
operationalizations are not fully consistent. While some of these measures have
exhibited appreciable associations with job performance, others have not been
as fortunate (Cropanzano & Wright, 2001). To better understand these varied
operationalizations of happiness, I review prior research using the framework
of the circumplex model of emotion as my overview taxonomy. In addition,
drawing on the impetus of the "positive psychology" and Positive Organizational
Behavior/Scholarship (POB/POS) movements (Bernstein, 2003; Buss, 2000;
Diener, 2000; Luthans, 2003; Peterson, 2000; Seligman & Csikszentmihalyi,
2000), I propose Fredrickson's (1998, 2001, 2002, 2003) broaden-and-build model

of positive emotion as one approach especially well-suited to help provide a greater understanding of the role of happiness in the happy/productive worker thesis. Before I examine these tests of the happy/productive worker thesis, it is appropriate to first briefly examine just what it is people are talking about when they discuss being happy.

HAPPINESS DEFINED

Diener (1984) noted that virtually every scientific approach to happiness converges around three distinct, defining phenomena. First, happiness is considered to be a subjective experience (Diener, 1994; Diener et al., 1993; Parducci, 1995). By that I mean people are considered to be happy to the extent that they believe/perceive themselves to be happy. As a result, happiness involves some type of judgment as to the pluses and minuses of one's life (Parducci, 1995). Second, happiness includes both the relative presence of positive emotions and the relative absence of negative emotions (Argyle, 1987; Diener & Larsen, 1993; Michalos, 1985; Warr, 1987, 1990). Third, happiness is a global judgment. It refers to one's life as a whole. As I use the term here, happiness can be best considered as an overall evaluation that exhibits some measure of stability over time (Diener, 1994; Diener et al., 1999; Myers, 1993; Veenhoven, 1988; Wright, 1997, 2002), though it is strongly influenced by environmental events (Pavot et al., 1991; Sandlitz et al., 1993) and responsive to therapeutic interventions (Lykken, 1999; Seligman, 1994, 1995, 2002). Taken together, one can generally conclude that happiness refers to a subjective and global judgment that one is experiencing a good deal of positive and relatively little negative emotions (Cropanzano & Wright, 2001).

The pursuit of happiness, coupled with an avoidance of unhappiness, is considered fundamental to human motivation (Lawler, 1973; Myers, 1993; Russell, 1930). In fact, a belief elemental to many theories of motivation is that humans seek what is pleasurable and avoid what is painful (Sullivan, 1989; Velasquez, 2002). As a result, happiness can be seen as a valuable, though sometimes scarce, resource (Hobfoll, 1998; Myers & Diener, 1997). Hobfoll (1989) defined resources, "as those objects, personal characteristics, conditions, or energies that are valued by the individual or that serve as a means for the attainment of these objects" (p. 516). Regarding the issue of scarcity and happiness, Myers and Diener (1997) suggest that only a minority of Americans can be considered happy. While the adjusted value of after-tax income at least doubled between 1960 and 1990, the percentage of Americans who report themselves as "very happy" remained constant at only 30% (Myers, 1993, pp. 41–42). This inherent value placed on happiness, coupled with its relative scarcity, underscores the importance of conserving, maintaining, or even enhancing one's happiness whenever possible (Hobfoll, 1988, 1989, 1998). More specifically, according to a resource maintenance model, the need to conserve their limited resource supply can lead unhappy people to be poorer performers, while the flexibility afforded by their more generous resource reserve can improve the performance of happy persons (Wright & Cropanzano, 1998).

Prior research provides a number of potential reasons why this may be the case. First, individuals are typically more sensitive to cues that signal a threat to a resource, such as happiness, when it is considered both valuable and scarce (Hobfoll, 1989; Lee & Ashforth, 1996). Individuals can also afford the luxury of less worry when the resource in question, in this case happiness, is more abundant. As a consequence, happy people can be presumed to be more sensitive to positive events, while unhappy people are more sensitive to negative events (Cropanzano & Wright, 2001). Recent empirical research has undertaken to examine this proposition. For example, experimental research by Seidlitz and Diener (1993) and Seidlitz et al. (1997) found that those who were low on well being were more likely to encode an ambiguous event as threatening as compared to their happier counterparts. Likewise, research by Larsen and Ketelaar (1989, 1991) found that unfavorable feedback was more hurtful to those who were prone to negative emotions, and less hurtful to those who were prone to positive emotions. Relatedly, Rusting and Larsen (1997) found that favorable feedback yielded larger benefits for those who were predisposed to positive emotions, while yielding smaller benefits to those predisposed to negative emotions. In addition, these effects appear to persist over time due to the manner in which happy and unhappy people recall events (Cropanzano & Wright, 2001). In particular, happy people tend to remember favorable events, while unhappy people tend to remember unfavorable ones (Seidlitz & Diener, 1993; Seidlitz et al., 1997). In sum, as noted by Cropanzano and Wright (2001), this tendency to emphasize the negative aspects of work life is likely to have deleterious consequences for employee job performance.

Happy people also tend to be more outgoing and extroverted (Diener et al., 1992; Headley & Wearing, 1992; Myers & Diener, 1995). On the other hand, unhappy people tend to be more cautious and protective in social situations, such as a propensity toward extroversion and/or shyness (Argyle, 1987). At times, unhappy people can even become acrimonious (for a further discussion, see Cropanzano & Wright, 2001). In a longitudinal study, Bolger and Schilling (1991) found that people who were prone to negative emotion were apt to use contentious interpersonal tactics, thereby provoking the ire of co-workers. Thus, it is not inconsistent that unhappy people report feeling less co-worker and supervisory support than do their more happy counterparts (Staw et al., 1994).

This [over]emphasis on negative events, coupled with a minimization of social contact, eventually takes its toll. Relative to their happier coworkers, unhappy people are likely to have lower self-esteem (Diener et al., 1999; Myers, 1993). Likewise, unhappy people see themselves as having less control over events in their lives and are less optimistic about the future (Cropanzano & Wright, 2001; Dembers & Brooks, 1989; Seligman, 1991). This sense of demoralization may make unhappy people less proactive (Argyle, 1987) and more prone to stress symptoms (Myers & Diener, 1995). Taken together, these findings suggest that happy people would probably perform better on the wide range of jobs that require significant social interaction (Cropanzano & Wright, 2001).

Using research on the happy/productive worker thesis as my guide, I will now examine the prevailing approaches to operationalizing happiness in organizational research. To that end, I first provide an overview of the long history of organizational research considering happiness as job satisfaction.

HAPPINESS AS JOB SATISFACTION: MORE OR LESS THAN MEETS THE EYE?

Historically, the most common means of testing the happy/productive worker thesis has involved operationalizing happiness as job satisfaction (Smith, 1992). This approach was favored by such early researchers as Brayfield and Crockett (1951); Herzberg et al. (1959); Houser (1927); Kornhauser and Sharp (1932); and Roethlisberger and Dickson (1939). Although a number of contemporary scholars distinguish between satisfaction with a particular job and happiness with life as a whole (e.g. Diener et al., 1999; Judge, 1992; Judge & Locke, 1993), historical convention has typically led the happy/productive worker thesis to be operationalized as the relation between satisfaction with aspects of one's job and job performance. Thus, for many organizational researchers, job satisfaction and happiness have been closely linked together for what seems like an eternity (Wright & Cropanzano, 2000; Wright & Doherty, 1998).

Although there may be nothing inherently wrong with equating a happy worker with a satisfied one, in so doing, one is required to make at least two tacit assumptions (Wright & Cropanzano, 2000). First, because job satisfaction is specific to one's job, it does not include aspects of one's life outside of work (e.g. Smith, 1992; Weitz, 1952). This relatively narrow scope stands in contrast to research on psychological well being in which the happiness component is typically considered as a broader construct than job satisfaction, one that refers to aspects of an individual's life as a whole (Cropanzano & Wright, 2001; Diener, 1984).

The second assumption involves the manner in which job satisfaction has been typically measured in organizational research. Although job satisfaction has been operationalized in many different ways, it usually is considered to be an attitude (Weiss & Cropanzano, 1996). Moreover, as noted by Weiss and Cropanzano (1996), in any investigation of job-related attitudes, it is important to separate the belief, or cognitive, component from the emotional, or affective, component. More specifically, this suggests that job satisfaction is based partially on what one feels and partially on what one thinks. Thus, according to Brief (1998), job satisfaction can best be defined as "an internal state that is expressed by affectively and/or cognitively evaluating an experienced job with some degree of favor or disfavor" (p. 86). However, the most widely used job satisfaction measures (i.e. the Minnesota Satisfaction Questionnaire, the Job Description Index, etc.) contain few, if any, affectively toned scale items (Brief & Roberson, 1989; Wright & Cropanzano, 2000). Alternatively, happiness, as the term is commonly understood, is primarily an affective or emotional experience. In other words, happy individuals feel good in the sense that they experience a good deal of positive emotion and, relatedly, less negative emotion (Diener & Larsen, 1993; Warr, 1987, 1990).

WHY JOB SATISFACTION AS HAPPINESS

As a researcher very interested, and actively engaged, in this topic area, I have always wondered *why* the prominence of job satisfaction as an operationalization of happiness and, relatedly, *why* it took well into the 1930s for job satisfaction to achieve this prominence. After all, the potential importance of any number of worker "attitudes" in the determination of such relevant worker outcomes and behaviors as employee fatigue and monotony, absenteeism, tardiness, turnover and performance was recognized long before the 1930s (Mosso, 1915; Muscio, 1921). For instance, as far back as the late 1800s, Frederick Winslow Taylor noted that the successful implementation of the principles of scientific management involves not only issues of physical strength and dexterity but also a "mental revolution" on the part of both management and employee (Taylor, 1919). According to Locke (1976, p. 1298), underlying Taylor's basic philosophy was the implicit assumption that workers who accepted the basic tenants of scientific management and received the highest possible wages as a result, with the least amount of physical and mental fatigue, would be the most "satisfied and productive."

In like fashion, another leading contemporary of Taylor, the pioneering industrial psychologist Hugo Munsterberg (1913, p. 243), most surely agreed with the importance of employee attitudes when he accurately noted that "Every economic function comes in contact with the mental life of man, first from the fact that the work is produced by the psyche of personalities." Finally, the famous Hawthorne studies began as an investigation of the effects of such factors as rest pauses and incentives on worker fatigue. But the emphasis soon shifted to the study of "attitudes" when the employees failed to react in the "expected" manner to these changes. In short, the Hawthorne researchers "discovered" more definitely what Taylor had observed decades before: that workers have minds, and that the appraisals they make of the work situation affect their reactions to it (Mayo, 1933). As with Taylor, the term attitude, as the Hawthorne researchers used it, referred to more than just job satisfaction. It included the employees' view of their supervisors, their perception of the current economic situation, their perceptions about the goals of the research investigators, and their daily mood (cf. Locke, 1976).

Yet, over the next 80 years, literally thousands of studies have been published which honed in on, often to the exclusion of possible alternative explanations, the supposed connection between job satisfaction and such important organizational outcomes as employee performance. Again, I personally have always been curious *why* this fascination with job satisfaction, especially given the rather dismal findings to date. I suggest here the need to delve deeper than past research has taken us to more fully understand the "sudden" prominence in the 1930s of job satisfaction in applied organizational research. Fortunately, I propose that this "missing link" explanation can be found in two streams of early applied: work on employee susceptibility to various aspects of industrial fatigue and monotony (Bedale, 1924; Crowden, 1932; Dill, 1933; Johnston, 1946; Vernon, 1924) and, work on customer sales and advertising (Nystrom, 1914; Whitehead, 1917).

WORKER FATIGUE, MONOTONY AND JOB SATISFACTION

While interest in worker fatigue and monotony can be traced back to the time of scientific management (Taylor, 1919), the topic became even more prominent as a result of the famous Hawthorne experiments at the Western Electric Company (Mayo, 1933; Roethlisberger & Dickson, 1939) and contemporaneous work in Great Britain by the British Industrial Fatigue and Health Research Boards. Some of the earliest research on worker fatigue and monotony focused on the role of employee intelligence in performance prediction. For instance, the United States Army Alpha testing performed during World War I established that scores on intelligence tests varied according to previous occupation (Blum & Naylor, 1968). It was soon recognized by many applied psychologists that always hiring the most intelligent job candidate might not be the best strategy (Fryer, 1922; Miner, 1921). In particular, Snow (1923) noted the possibility that an employee's intelligence was a factor in establishing his level of satisfaction. According to Snow, while duller individuals demonstrated considerable dissatisfaction when the work was fairly complex in nature, they showed the least dissatisfaction when the work was highly repetitive. The lesson learned was that there were individual differences in experienced employee fatigue and boredom, which affected their performance.

Relatedly, one of the leading lights of applied research on job satisfaction, Patricia Cain Smith, reported that her early research interest in general satisfactions derived from results of the British Industrial Fatigue and Health Research Boards confirming the American findings that there were individual differences in susceptibility to individual monotony (Smith, 1992; Wyatt et al., 1929, 1938). In a fascinating look into how applied research was conducted in the early days, Smith (1992, p. 9) noted that "First I tried to 'validate' workers' reports of boredom by correlating the reports with slumps in output. I watched and made complete records of the behavior of each of a number of machine operators throughout every working day for an entire week." As a result of her efforts, Smith found that production did, indeed, change and that the changes were related to the satisfaction of the employee's self-set goals for the day (Cain, 1942; Smith, 1953). It was observations such as these that led to the proposed importance of job satisfaction. That is, if employee satisfaction is related to employee boredom and employee boredom is related to performance, then maybe employee satisfaction is related to employee job performance! I next examine the second link in my "missing link" explanation, the role of customer sales and advertising.

ADVERTISING, CUSTOMER SALES AND JOB SATISFACTION

By the 1920s, early research on sales and advertising by such well known proponents as Scott (1903, 1908), Hollingworth (1913), Sheldon (1911), Adams (1916) and Eastman (1916) was acknowledged by many contemporaries to be little more than "a jumbled collection of opinions on a great variety of topics" (Strong, 1925, p. 77). Interestingly, while quite significant later on in marketing research, the importance of customer satisfaction was absent from the earliest discussions on proper sales techniques (Strong, 1925). The early marketing objective was primarily focused on securing the particular sale in question. As time evolved, this single objective of making a particular sale became one of not only securing that sale, but one of retaining the customer for future sales. As a result, the often times confusing morass of opinion and conjecture of just what constitutes a proper sale became much more crystallized and actual theoretical models evolved regarding how to influence others to buy (Blanchard, 1921; Charters, 1922; Herrold, 1923; Sloan & Mooney, 1920).

Two of these early theoretical approaches are especially noteworthy in acknowledging the importance of customer satisfaction. According to Strong (1925, p. 75), the first theory was well expressed by the five words: "attention, interest, desire, action, *satisfaction*" (emphasis added). The second theory extended the first and focused primarily on the "creation" of customer wants, hence, the increasing prominence of applied psychology in sales and advertising. Strong (1925, p. 77) succinctly expressed this approach in terms of the action sequence "wants-solution-action-*satisfaction*" (emphasis added). According to Strong (1925, p. 85), ". . . we have a picture of selling where the prospect is very active because he (the customer) has a want to be satisfied and the salesman's job is to aid the prospect in his endeavors to solve his problem." The emphasis became one of what customer need(s) will the product satisfy. In other words, what must be done to enhance customer happiness and satisfaction with the current product to increase the possibility of purchasing another product?

Simple stuff today, but quite a revolutionary concept for the American buying public of the pre World War I era. The role of commercialism rapidly gained momentum after the First World War and sales and advertising philosophy had changed dramatically by the mid 1920s. Customer satisfaction had become extremely important because of the realization that ". . . unless the goods measure up to expectations there will be no repeat orders" (Strong, 1925, p. 86). Surprisingly, to my knowledge, the strong influence of early 1920s sales and advertising research on the role of satisfaction, first for the customer, and later for the employee in organizational research, has never been adequately acknowledged by organizational scholars in reviews of the role of job satisfaction in applied research (Argyris, 1957; Blum & Naylor, 1968; Dalton, 1959; Ghiselli, 1971; Haire, 1956; Homans, 1950; Judge et al., 1998, 2001; Locke, 1969, 1976; Porter & Steers, 1973; Smith, 1992; Smith et al., 1969). Based upon my review of this early research, it is highly apparent that the emphasis on customer satisfaction for increasing repeat sales was not lost on a number of early researchers interested in enhancing employee performance and productivity. In particular, that the interest in sales and advertising was of such importance to our pioneering applied psychologists is well demonstrated by the fact that 22 articles published in the *Journal of Applied Psychology* from 1917 (first year of journal publication) to 1930 had either the words "sales" or "advertising" in the article titles! Now that we have a little better understanding of *where* and *why* satisfaction is important, I will now turn to a review of the literature examining the job satisfaction/performance relation.

THE JOB SATISFACTION/JOB
PERFORMANCE RELATION

Several reviews have provided excellent summaries of the job satisfaction/job performance relation. For example, reviewing the literature to date, Brayfield and Crockett (1955, p. 421) determined that "satisfaction... need not imply strong motivation to outstanding performance." Similar conclusions were reached in a later review by Vroom (1964), who found that the median association between these two variables was a rather modest +0.14. Unfortunately, interpretation of this finding is subject to conjecture as Vroom inappropriately commingled both employee-level and work-group-level studies in his reported results. As a consequence, different conclusions are obtained when one removes the group-based studies from Vroom's analyses (Wright & Cropanzano, 2000). Finally, a highly influential meta-analytic review by Iaffaldano and Muchinsky (1985) obtained a mean corrected correlation of +0.17. It should be noted that this correlation represents the average of the correlations between each of the facet measures of job satisfaction (e.g. pay, co-worker, promotion, supervision, work itself, etc.) and job performance. As a consequence, when one confines the analyses to a measure of overall satisfaction, the corrected correlation is actually 0.29 (Judge et al., 2001). Together, these reviews generated a good deal of doubt regarding the relation between job satisfaction and performance (e.g. Cherrington et al., 1971; Fisher, 1980; Locke, 1976; Podsakoff & Williams, 1986; Staw, 1986). More recently, other research has called these modest conclusions into question.

In contrast to these more modest findings, Petty et al. (1984) place the job satisfaction to job performance relation at +0.31. Certainly correlations in the 0.30 range are large enough to have financial "competitive advantage" consequences for work organizations (cf. Cascio, 1991; Judge et al., 1995). Unfortunately, Organ (1988, Chap. 4) cautioned that Petty et al.'s analysis might have included performance criteria that were contaminated by indexes of citizenship behavior. The most comprehensive qualitative and quantitative analysis of the relation to date was undertaken by Judge et al. (1998, 2001). In their meta-analysis, Judge and his colleagues estimated the association to be roughly +0.30, though they observed some important moderators. For instance, they found some job satisfaction measures were more closely related to performance than others, ranging from an aggregated correlation of +0.06 for research measuring job satisfaction with the GM Faces Scale to an aggregated correlation of +0.51 for research using the Hoppock Job Satisfaction Blank to measure job satisfaction. Judge et al. also reported considerable differences across occupations, with the job satisfaction/job performance correlation being more robust in high-complexity jobs. Finally, their meta-analytic results demonstrated that measures of overall job satisfaction display higher correlations than facet measures of job satisfaction.

Whether or not job satisfaction and job performance are *statistically* significantly related, the *practical* significance appears to be much less consequential in nature. In fact, considered in the aggregate, much prior research indicates that very little of the variation in employee job performance is associated with differences in job satisfaction (typically less than 5%). Or, to look at it from a different perspective, these results imply that typically over 95% of the job performance variation is *not* associated with job satisfaction.

In addition, the positive associations obtained by Judge et al. (2001) and Petty et al. (1984) do not address the issue of causality. There are at least three causal relations between job satisfaction and job performance: (a) job satisfaction may cause job performance; (b) job performance may cause job satisfaction; and (c) both job performance and job satisfaction may be caused by a variety of third variables (Wright & Cropanzano, 2000). During the 1960s and 1970s, several studies investigated these sundry causal paths, and at least nominal evidence was obtained for each causal path (for reviews, see Lawler & Porter, 1967; Nord, 1976; Schwab & Cummings, 1970). Unfortunately, as Judge et al. (1998, 2001) observed, the general skepticism regarding the job satisfaction/job performance relation led to a decline in research. As a consequence, the causal linkage between these two variables, if any, remains a potentially worthwhile topic for future research endeavors.

AFFECTIVE DISPOSITIONAL APPROACHES TO [UN]HAPPINESS

Confusion underlying the term *happiness* stems from the overall structure of dispositional affect. Nowhere is this confusion more evident than in organizational research where [un]happiness has been considered as positive affectivity, negative affectivity, emotional exhaustion and well being. Obviously, a clear "map" of emotion terms would enhance conceptual precision (Cropanzano & Wright, 2001). In fact, starting with Hippocrates, this need to dimensionalize emotional well being has long been recognized (Larsen & Diener, 1992). In the second century, Galen (A.D. 129–c.215) adopted a version of the four-humor theory (e.g. melancholic, choleric, sanguine, and phlegmatic) to describe various differences in emotions. His view, which should resonate with many today, is that an individual's health consists of an appropriate balance of these four bodily constituents. Alternatively, disease results from an imbalance. Much later, Kant expanded on Galen's work in his treatise *Anthropologie*. Still later, Wundt transformed

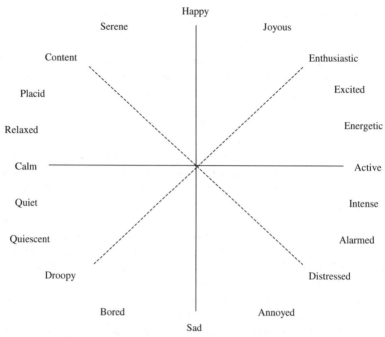

Fig. 1. Note: Adapted from Cropanzano and Wright (2001), this figure represents an idealized representation of the circumplex model of happiness. The solid lines refer to the unrotated factor solution. The dashed lines refer to the rotated solution.

Galen and Kant's work into a pleasantness-unpleasantness interpretation of emotion. More recently, Russell and his colleagues (Russell, 1978, 1979, 1980; Russell et al., 1989), using multidimensional scaling techniques, found that emotions can be organized into a roughly circular structure called a circumplex. An idealized circumplex structure is displayed in Fig. 1. This circumplex structure has been found to be quite robust, as it generalizes to both adults and children (Russell & Ridgeway, 1983) as well as across a variety of cultures (Russell et al., 1989) and different analytic methods (Meyer & Shack, 1989). As a result, the circumplex structure is widely accepted (e.g. Cropanzano & Wright, 2001; Larsen & Diener, 1992; Mayer & Gaschke, 1988), though it is not without problems of its own.

One concern with the circumplex is that it is often impractical to apply. Because the model represents emotions in two-dimensional space, it is not clear how one would use the entire model as a predictor of organizational behaviors (Cropanzano

& Wright, 2001). For this reason, researchers simplify the circumplex model by factor analyzing the emotion terms. Given the circular structure, different factor solutions could potentially provide an equally good fit to the model. For example, consider the solid vertical and horizontal axes in Fig. 1. These two factors result from an unrotated factor model. The vertical factor designates "hedonic tone" or "pleasantness-unpleasantness." It is anchored by such adjectives as "happy" and "joyous" on the high end and "sad" on the low. This dimension is often interpreted as psychological well being (e.g. Cropanzano & Wright, 2001; Myers, 1993). On the other hand, the horizontal axis refers to the level of activation, or "affect intensity," of emotional experience (Larsen & Diener, 1992). In the organizational sciences, this arousal dimension has sometimes been understood as emotional exhaustion (Cropanzano & Wright, 2001). For example, Wright and Bonett (1997a, b) maintained that high emotional exhaustion can be treated as low emotional activation-intensity. This makes sense insofar as exhaustion is defined as a numb state of emotional detachment (Maslach, 1982; Maslach & Leiter, 1997), though I will qualify this observation later on.

When the primary dimensional factors are rotated 45 degrees, two new dimensions emerge: positive and negative affectivity. These are designated in Fig. 1 by the two dashed lines. The positive affectivity (PA) dimension begins in the upper right quadrant of Fig. 1 and runs diagonally to the lower left quadrant. High PAs tend to report experiencing positive emotions, such as "enthusiastic" and "excited." At the low end, PA is best characterized by the absence of positive emotions, such as "droopy" and "bored." In the lower right quadrant of Fig. 1, and running to the upper left quadrant, is the negative affective (NA) dimension. High NAs report emotions that are negative, such as "alarmed" and "distressed." Low NAs tend to endorse the absence of negative emotions. For example, a low NA might indicate a tendency to be "placid" or "relaxed." There is considerable evidence that the NA-PA solution is a potentially useful one (e.g. Brief & Roberson, 1989; Brief et al., 1995; Burke et al., 1989; George, 1996; Watson, 1988; Watson & Clark, 1984; Watson & Tellegen, 1985; Watson et al., 1988; Wright et al., 2004). Moreover, NA and PA show up across cultures (Watson et al., 1984) and when both self- and peer ratings are examined.

As my colleague, Russell Cropanzano and I have previously noted (see Cropanzano & Wright, 2001 for a further review), these are the most widely accepted organizational perspectives on dispositional affect. More important, each of these approaches shares a common origin in the circumplex model. In particular, they result from two different rotational solutions and, as such, are different representations of the same underlying reality. I now turn to a consideration of how each of these perspectives relates to job performance.

THE ROTATED SOLUTION: HAPPINESS AS POSITIVE AND NEGATIVE AFFECTIVITY

According to Diener (1994; Diener et al., 1999), one way to conceptualize happiness is as the presence of dispositional positive affect (PA) and the absence of dispositional negative affect (NA). This approach is also evident in the work of Watson and Clark (1984) and Costa and McCrae (1980). As discussed by George (1992, 1996) and Judge (1992), there is now compelling evidence that PA and NA predict such work attitudes as job satisfaction and organizational commitment (e.g. Cropanzano et al., 1993; Levin & Stokes, 1989; Watson & Slack, 1993). NA also seems to be related to reports of job stress and strain (Brief et al., 1988; Burke et al., 1993; Watson & Pennebaker, 1989). In addition, NA, but not PA, has been positively related to voluntary turnover (Wright & Cropanzano, 1998).

From the perspective of the resource maintenance model discussed earlier (Cropanzano & Wright, 2001), one could expect PA to exhibit a positive association to job performance, whereas NA should exhibit a negative association. However, the evidence is ambiguous. Part of the reason for these disappointing results may have less to do with dispositional affectivity and more to do with the temporal nature of affect. To propose that *enthusiastic*, *inspired*, *upset* or *hostile* individuals are more or less productive says little about whether these feelings are state or trait variables. The temporal distinction appears to be an important one (Wright et al., 2004). For example, while results have failed to support relations among dispositional affect, both NA and PA, and job performance (Cropanzano et al., 1993; Wright & Cropanzano, 1998; Wright & Staw, 1999a), George (1991) found a relation between positive affective mood and one aspect of job performance, prosocial behavior. Expanding upon George's influential earlier work, Wright et al. (2004) recently proposed that these apparent inconsistencies regarding the prediction of performance can be resolved when one distinguishes between NA and PA considered as a dispositional trait versus a state (mood) variable. I now provide the theoretical basis for the proposed relations among negative affective mood, positive affective mood and job performance.

MOOD AND PERFORMANCE

Moods refer to pervasive, generalized affective states (George & Brief, 1992). A state or mood attempts to capture how a person feels at a given point in time (Watson, 1988). Moods are not primarily directed at specific targets. In fact, research suggests that moods are influenced by situational factors (George, 1989).

Isen and her colleagues have induced temporary increases in positive mood state through the presentation of food or a small gift (Isen & Baron, 1991; Isen & Levin, 1972). According to Clark and Isen (1982), moods, both positive and negative, have important effects on cognition and behavior. For instance, Clark and Watson (1988) found the level of negative mood to be related to the incidence of experienced daily irritants and hassles. George and Brief (1996) proposed a model of work motivation providing the theoretical basis for suggesting the possibility that affective mood, both positive and negative, is related to performance.

According to George and Brief's model (1996), moods can influence both distal (i.e. related to behavior choice or effort level) and proximal (i.e. related to the actual task-specific behaviors themselves) aspects of motivation. Regarding distal motivation, moods are seen as influencing the various cognitive mechanisms associated with how one determines the "appropriate" expectancy, instrumentality and valence levels (George, 1996; Wright et al., 2004). For example, positive moods are seen as resulting in higher expectancies due to the effects that they have on such cognitive processes as mood-congruent recall and judgment (George, 1996). Moods, especially positive mood, are also seen as influencing proximal motivation (actual task-specific behaviors) through their ability to stimulate employee self-monitoring behavior. Alternatively, while their potential effects are not as easily observed and are less direct, George and Brief (1996) also noted the motivating potential of negative mood. However, although a solid theoretical basis exists for proposing relations among mood and various organizational outcomes (George, 1996; George & Brief, 1996; Wright & Staw, 1999a), research investigating these relations has been rather limited in scope.

In one of the first studies to undertake to examine the role of mood on organizational behaviors, George (1989) found positive, but not negative mood, to be related to absenteeism. George noted that this finding is intriguing given that one would expect positive and negative moods or states to have ". . . parallel, inverse effects on absenteeism" (p. 321). In addition, while previous research failed to establish a relation between dispositional affect with performance (Cropanzano et al., 1993; Wright & Staw, 1999a), limited support exists for a relation between affective mood and job performance (George, 1991; Wright & Staw, 1999a; Wright et al., 2004). More specifically, George (1991), using a sample of salespeople, established a positive relation between a time-specific measure of positive mood and customer service performance-related behaviors. In this study, George measured PA experienced at work during the *past week* using a subscale of the Job Affect Scale (Burke et al., 1989). She also measured more general or trait levels of PA using the Positive Emotionality Questionnaire (Tellegen, 1982). Consistent with research reviewed above, George found that a trait indicator of PA was unrelated to worker altruism and customer service ratings. Alternatively, the

PA measure of mood experienced at work over the *past week* was correlated with both altruism and customer service.

Wright et al. (2004) found similar results in a more recent study. Although neither positive trait, negative trait, or positive mood measured *today* were related to job performance, negative mood measured *today* was related to job performance. These findings suggest that time- and work-specific measures of NA and PA might prove better predictors of job performance than more general or trait measures. In fact, while general levels of positive and negative emotion are certainly important in their own right, the resource maintenance model (Cropanzano & Wright, 2001; Hobfoll, 1988, 1998) would support the premise that more time-specific measures of emotion or mood at work are the drivers of productive behaviors (for a related argument, see Weiss & Cropanzano, 1996 and Wright et al., 2004). For this reason, the meager findings in studies using general or trait measures of PA and NA do not rule out the possibility that more momentary emotions experienced on the job will predict performance. For this reason, it is premature to close the door to future inquiry, as there are only a few studies that have examined the relation between NA-PA and job performance. I endorse the call for future research on this topic. In addition, there is another reason why inquiry into NA and PA should not be abandoned. There is indirect evidence that NA and PA might be related to performance if we conceptualize the predictors more broadly as either extraversion or emotional stability. It is to this evidence that I now turn.

Extraversion and Emotional Stability

As discussed by George (1996) and Cropanzano and Wright (2001), NA is closely related to the broad personality dimension of emotional stability (also called neuroticism), whereas PA is related to the personality dimension of extraversion (Watson et al., 1992). Given this fact, Costa and McCrae (1980) maintained that a "happy" person can be viewed as one who is high on extraversion and low on neuroticism. In keeping with the happy/productive worker thesis, it therefore follows that extraversion and emotional stability (or neuroticism) could be related to job performance. In fact, meta-analytic evidence suggests that this might indeed be the case (Hough et al., 1990).

Hough et al. (1990) reviewed validity coefficients among a number of military samples and found that emotional stability predicted three dimensions of performance (effort and leadership, personal discipline, and physical fitness and military bearing), but not two other performance dimensions (technical proficiency and general soldiering). Unfortunately, for the present discussion, Hough and her colleagues did not examine a pure extraversion measure that would be certain to include PA. In another meta-analysis, Barrick and Mount (1991) found that emotional stability was not consistently related to performance. However, Barrick and Mount cautioned that these findings might be due to range restriction – those who are very unstable emotionally are quite likely to have left the workforce or, at least, left certain types of jobs. Extraversion was related to performance, though only for those jobs with a strong social interaction component. Salgado (1997) conducted a meta-analysis of personality and performance among studies whose samples were limited to members of the European community. Salgado found that emotional stability was a valid predictor of performance, while the merits of extraversion were limited to occupations with a strong social component. Considered together, these findings lend limited support to the happy/productive worker thesis.

A more controversial meta-analysis was conducted by Tett et al. (1991), who found that extraversion was not an especially useful predictor of job performance (mean corrected validity = 0.16), though emotional stability was. In a critique of this study, Ones et al. (1994) raised concerns about the data analytic technique used by Tett and his colleagues. Fortunately, a more thorough re-analysis conducted by Tett et al. (1994) showed only minimal changes in the results, with no significant changes in the overall conclusions.

Although the meta-analytic literature is not perfectly consistent, it suggests the possibility that NA (via emotional stability) and PA (via extraversion) might be related to job performance. At present, this evidence must be considered as tentative. Although PA is correlated with extraversion and NA with emotional stability (or neuroticism), extraversion and emotional stability are substantially broader constructs than PA and NA. For instance, even though emotional stability or neuroticism is conceptually close to the concept of NA (for evidence, see Watson & Clark, 1984), identifiable differences remain (Costa & McCrae, 1988; McCrae & Costa, 1987). Thus, one cannot be certain whether it is the emotional aspects of extraversion and emotional stability that cause the observed differences in job performance (Cropanzano & Wright, 2001).

Another possible basis for the inconsistent findings involving the role of NA and PA with performance may be related to the type of job examined. To date, the samples examined have been composed of management personnel. Typically, most professional workers are evaluated on some type of subjective, supervisory-based, performance criteria (Wright & Staw, 1999b). Alternatively the activation-based descriptors contained in the PA scale, such as, "alert, active, enthusiastic" might be better suited in job samples, such as sales, where performance is measured more quantitatively. To that end, I recommend continued inquiry into the role of NA and PA, both state and trait, in as wide a range of jobs as possible, incorporating both qualitative and quantitative dimensions of performance.

THE UNROTATED SOLUTION: HAPPINESS AS (THE LACK OF) EMOTIONAL EXHAUSTION

Happiness as Emotional Activation-Intensity: Emotional Exhaustion

Somewhat more supportive findings come when researchers try to predict job performance from the other two dimensions: arousal and well being (Cropanzano & Wright, 2001). I shall begin with the arousal dimension that is represented by the horizontal axis in Fig. 1. As is evident from the figure, this dimension designates the intensity or vigor with which an emotion is felt. This is, of course, without regard to the hedonic tone of the emotion – one can not only feel fervently good or psychologically well (hedonic), but also fervently bad. Although activation-intensity is an important topic in the personality literature (see Larsen & Diener, 1992, for a review), it has typically received minimal attention in the organizational sciences.

One exception to this generalization can be found in research on emotional exhaustion. Emotional exhaustion is a chronic state of physical and emotional depletion that results from excessive job demands and continuous hassles (Shirom, 1989; Zohar, 1997). Emotional exhaustion is widely considered to be a key component of burnout (Cordes & Dougherty, 1993; Shirom, 1989; Wright & Cropanzano, 1998). As a result, emotional exhaustion has gained increasing prominence as a worthwhile topic of interest for organizational researchers, as it has important implications both for the quality of one's work life, as well as for optimal organizational functioning (for reviews, see Cherniss, 1993; Cordes & Dougherty, 1993; Kahill, 1988; Maslach, 1982; Wright & Cropanzano, 1998). Emotional exhaustion typically results when individuals are placed under intensely stressful conditions. As Wright and Bonett (1997b) pointed out, high emotional exhaustion seems to be a manifestation of (very) low emotional arousal. That is, emotionally exhausted employees experience an emotional numbness (Maslach, 1982; Maslach & Leiter, 1997). Thus, emotional exhaustion is different from other conceptualizations of activation because it measures the degree or level of depletion over time of an individual's energetic or activation-based resources (Shirom, 1989; Thayer, 1986; Wright & Bonett, 1997a). Emotional exhaustion has also proven to be a useful predictor of various stress outcomes and work attitudes (Lee & Ashforth, 1996; Leiter & Maslach, 1988; Wolpin et al., 1991). To that end, emotional exhaustion has been related to a host of somatic difficulties, such as colds, gastro-intestinal problems, headaches, and sleep disturbances (Belcastro, 1982; Belcastro & Hays, 1984). Interestingly, until rather recently, the relation between emotional exhaustion and job performance has seldom been investigated.

In one study, Quattrochi-Tubin et al. (1982) found that self-reported emotional exhaustion was related to self-reported performance among social workers. However, this work is limited in that it used self-report measures of both independent and dependent variables: emotional exhaustion and performance. Research by Garden (1991) suggested that burnout shows a higher relation to self-reported performance than to other performance measures. In an extension of previous work, Wright and Bonett (1997a) found that emotional exhaustion was negatively correlated with subsequent supervisory ratings of job performance while controlling for employee age, gender and prior performance. A second study by these authors failed to replicate these findings (Wright & Bonett, 1997b), however. Finally, additional supportive results were obtained by both Jones and Best (1995) and Wright and Cropanzano (1998), who found that emotional exhaustion predicted supervisory ratings of job performance. Wright and Cropanzano further observed that emotional exhaustion scores were associated with employee voluntary turnover as much as one year later. The net result is that emotional exhaustion holds considerable promise as a predictor of job performance. Despite this promise, there are two obvious problems with using emotional exhaustion as an indicator of [un]happiness. One is specific to emotional exhaustion, and the other is a general problem with activation-intensity measures.

Let me begin with the problem specific to emotional exhaustion (for a further discussion, see Cropanzano & Wright, 2001). By definition, emotional exhaustion refers to the emotional numbing that accompanies burnout. Although this would seem to be indicative of low emotional intensity, an examination of the survey items suggests that this might not be the case. The most widely used measure of emotional exhaustion is a subscale from the Maslach Burnout Inventory (Maslach & Jackson, 1986). In this scale, emotional exhaustion is measured by such items as "Working with people all day is really a strain for me," "I feel emotionally drained from my work," "I feel used up at the end of the workday," "I feel frustrated with my job," and "I feel like I'm at the end of my rope." These items could be more indicative of the absence of positive emotion or the presence of negative emotion (or both), rather than the absence of emotion in general (cf. Meyer & Shack, 1989; Watson & Clark, 1984). If so, then this operationalization of emotional exhaustion might suggest low PA, high NA, or low well being, rather than low activation-intensity (Cropanzano & Wright, 2001).

In a test of this possibility, Wright et al. (2002) established moderate to substantial intercorrelations between emotional exhaustion and PA (–0.42) and between emotional exhaustion and NA (0.74). These results provide preliminary evidence that while emotional exhaustion, NA and PA share similar properties, they also appear to be distinct constructs. Further validation of the emotional exhaustion scale, particularly noting its discriminate validity to these other measures of affective disposition, is strongly recommended. Of course, even if emotional exhaustion is shown to be an indicator of NA, PA, or well being, then the findings I have reviewed would still support the happy/productive worker thesis, but they would not be supportive of the notion that activation intensity is related to job performance. It now remains for further research to clarify and refine these various "faces" of happiness in organizational research (Cropanzano & Wright, 2001; Wright et al., 2002).

Regardless of the outcomes of future research, there is a more fundamental problem with using any measure of activation-intensity as an indicator of happiness. With respect to emotion, by definition, an intensity measure does not imply either positive or negative feeling states (Larsen & Diener, 1992). It merely implies that one is experiencing some emotion with vigor; it does not denote whether that emotion is positive or negative (Cropanzano & Wright, 2001, p. 191). By all accounts, a happy person is relatively free of negative emotion, while prone to experience positive emotion (Larsen & Diener, 1992). As a consequence, as my colleague Russell Cropanzano and I have noted elsewhere (Cropanzano & Wright, 2001), activation-intensity can probably be ruled out as a type of happiness, though it will no doubt remain important for other purposes. I now examine happiness considered as psychological well being.

THE OTHER UNROTATED SOLUTION:
HAPPINESS AS PSYCHOLOGICAL WELL BEING

Psychological well being has typically been defined in terms of the overall effectiveness of an individual's psychological functioning (Gechman & Weiner, 1975; Jamal & Mitchell, 1980; Martin, 1984; Sekaran, 1985; Wright & Cropanzano, 2000). The solid vertical line in Fig. 1 captures the construct of psychological or subjective well being. Well being captures both positive and negative emotional states on a single axis. The high pole is anchored by such hedonic or pleasantness-based descriptors as "joyous." The low pole is anchored by "sad" and "annoyed." Thus, to be high on well being is to be simultaneously low on negative emotion and high on positive emotion. For these reasons, various scholars have more or less equated well being with happiness (e.g. Diener, 1984; Myers, 1993; Seligman, 2002).

The role of the hedonic or pleasantness dimension of well being (i.e. happiness vs. sadness or depression) in the determination of various individual outcomes has long been recognized by clinical psychologists (Wright & Cropanzano, 2000). Depressed individuals have very low self-esteem, tend to pessimistic, and exhibit reduced motivation and slowed thought processes (Holmes, 1991;

Wright & Cropanzano, 2000). Unlike job satisfaction, which is centered around the work context, psychological well being is a broader construct. Most typically, psychological well being is considered as a primarily affective-based "context-free" or global construct. Unlike various measures of job satisfaction, psychological well being is not tied to any particular situation (Kornhauser, 1965; Wright & Cropanzano, 2000).

Like our clinical psychology and public health counterparts, organizational theorists have also long recognized the extensive costs, in both human and financial terms, attributable to employee dysfunctional psychological well being (George, 1992; Quick et al., 1997). For instance, depression, loss of self-esteem, hypertension, alcoholism, and drug consumption, have all been shown to be related to work-related dysfunctional psychological well being (Ivancevich & Matteson, 1980). Because these variables have, in turn, been related to declines in work outcomes (Quick et al., 1997), it is possible that psychological well being and employee performance are related (Wright & Cropanzano, 2000; Wright et al., 1993).

RESEARCH ON THE HAPPY/PRODUCTIVE WORKER THESIS

In support of the happy/productive worker thesis, a growing body of empirical research has found significant associations between various measures of well being and measures of job-related performance (Wright & Staw, 1999a). In an experimental study, Staw and Barsade (1993) found that students who were high on well being were superior decision-makers, showed better interpersonal behaviors, and received higher overall performance ratings. Staw and Barsade's study is important for two reasons. First, it used objective, quantifiable indices of performance (e.g. an "in-basket" measure). This argues against the possibility that correlations between well being and job performance are simply misperceptions (Cropanzano & Wright, 2001; Robbins & DeNisi, 1994). Second, Staw and Barsade's experimental data suggest a causal relation, such that performance increases when well being is high. This is consistent with the resource maintenance model, though it is not clear from this evidence alone whether these findings will generalize outside a laboratory setting. These generalizability concerns were addressed in a later field study by Staw et al. (1994). In their longitudinal study, Staw and his colleagues first assessed well being. To do so, the researchers constructed a scale ad hoc out of items indicating the presence of negative emotion (e.g. depression) and the absence of positive emotion. Eighteen months later they measured various criterion variables. To be more specific, when compared with those who were low in well being, workers high in well being had superior performance evaluations and higher pay. Thus, well being predicted both a subjective and an objective indicator of performance.

The work of Staw and his colleagues suggests that well being causes increases in job performance. Also supporting this possibility is a two-year longitudinal study by Wright et al. (1993). Using the 8-item Index of Psychological Well Being developed by Berkman (1971a, b), Wright and his colleagues found that average well being (Time 1 and Time 2 together) was positively related to supervisory performance ratings at Time 3. Similar results were obtained by Cropanzano and Wright (1999) in a five-year longitudinal study. Again using the Index of Psychological Well Being, Cropanzano and Wright found that average well being measured six months apart (Time 1 and Time 2) was positively related to job performance measures at Time 3 (Year 4). Wright and Staw (1999a) conducted additional research to address the possibility of a causal path from well being to performance. To that end, Wright and Staw's two longitudinal studies – incorporating multiple measures of both performance and well being – demonstrated that psychological well being significantly predicted supervisory performance ratings beyond the variance accounted for by prior supervisory performance ratings. Considered together, these findings strongly support the possibility that well being is a cause of job performance.

It is also useful to ascertain the effects of other possible confounding variables. In a longitudinal study by Wright and Bonett (1997b), the authors found that well being was a positive predictor of job performance. Moreover, this relation remained significant even after controlling for the simultaneous effect of emotional exhaustion. Other potentially pernicious third variables are job satisfaction, negative affectivity (NA) and positive affectivity (PA). Given the demonstrated intercorrelations among these variables (e.g. Diener et al., 1999; Judge & Locke, 1993; Wright et al., 2002), it could be that psychological well being and job performance are only associated due to the spurious relations with these other variables. On the basis of the limited evidence to date, this seems to not be the case. In a cross-sectional study, Wright et al. (2002) found that well being was positively related to job performance beyond emotional exhaustion, negative affectivity and positive affectivity. These findings were replicated and extended in a longitudinal follow-up. In this study, Wright et al. (2002) found that well being and job performance (at Time 2) were positively associated even when the effects of job satisfaction, NA, PA, and prior performance (at Time 1) were all taken into account. Finally, Wright and Staw (1999a, Study 2) demonstrated that well being remained significantly related to performance even when controlling for employee age, gender, tenure, educational level and prior performance.

This reference to the ability of a number of studies (e.g. Wright & Staw, 1999a; Wright et al., 2002) to control for prior performance in the prediction of subsequent performance warrants further attention. While interesting, one could argue that the findings reported between psychological well being and performance may well be a function of the type of performance instrument used (Ledford, 1999). Typically, this research has relied on supervisory ratings of employee performance. In critiquing these findings one might posit that these findings are due to halo effects in the dependent variable. Thus, employees who are more psychologically well may be more fun to be around and more likeable (Wright & Cropanzano, 1998). Because people (i.e. supervisors) tend to be more tolerant of those they favor or like, supervisors may provide more positive evaluations for those more psychologically well (Robbins & DeNisi, 1994). In other words, rather than being directly related to changes in performance, psychological well being could serve as a systematic source of halo in performance evaluations.

Though one cannot totally rule out the halo alternative, I offer four basic arguments to the halo option. First, a number of the studies had longitudinal designs affording the opportunity to measure the influence of psychological well being on incremental changes in rated performance over time (Wright & Staw, 1999a; Wright et al., 2002). More specifically, a major strength of the multiple measures of performance over time design is the ability to capture any halo contained in the prior measures of performance (Wright & Staw, 1999b). Second, if halo were driving the results, Staw and Barsade (1993) would not have found significant relations between their measure of well being and objective measures of performance on a laboratory task (Wright & Staw, 1999b). Third, psychological well being has been related to job performance in a number of studies which have also examined a number of possible third variable explanations, including job satisfaction, PA, NA and emotional exhaustion. If rating bias was accounting for the obtained relation between psychological well being and performance, then one could also reasonably expect significant relations between these other variables and performance. As noted in previous research, this has not been the case (Wright & Bonett, 1997b; Wright & Cropanzano, 2000; Wright & Staw, 1999a; Wright et al., 2004, 2002). Fourth, and finally, considered as a worst case scenario, even if halo does play a role in the relation between psychological well being and supervisory ratings of performance, given that many organizations currently emphasize these non-task-specific performance dimensions in their appraisal process (Wright & Cropanzano, 1998), the relation is predictive of "success" from the employees' point of view (Staw et al., 1994; Wright & Staw, 1999b).

The available data point to a common conclusion: When happiness is operationalized as well being, it is positively related to various measures of job performance. In fact, field research has typically found significant bivariate correlations between psychological well being and job performance ratings in the 0.30–0.50 range, far surpassing the typical results obtained for job satisfaction,

NA, PA, and emotional exhaustion (Wright & Cropanzano, 2000; Wright & Staw, 1999a). As a case in point, taking a correlation of 0.50 between psychological well being and job performance indicates that a substantial 25% of the variance in job performance is associated with differences in psychological well being, *several* times greater than that typically explained by job satisfaction in the prediction of job performance. This seems to be the case regardless of whether the criterion variables are objective indices or subjective ratings (Staw & Barsade, 1993; Staw et al., 1994). The effect also holds in experimental, cross-sectional, and longitudinal studies, even after controlling for the effects of possible confounding variables (e.g. Wright & Staw, 1999a; Wright et al., 2002). Despite its value, this literature is in need of extension as, when all is said and done, the work to date has emphasized the main effect relation of well being to performance. In the next section, using theory emanating (cf. Fredrickson, 1998, 2001) from the Positive Psychology/Positive Organizational Behavior movements (Diener, 2000; Luthans, 2002a, b, 2003; Myers, 2000; Seligman & Csikszentmihalyi, 2000; Valliant, 2000), I propose an integration of the most promising (psychological well being) and widely used (job satisfaction) approaches to workplace happiness.

FREDRICKSON'S (1998, 2001, 2002, 2003) BROADEN-AND-BUILD THEORY

As I have documented, psychological well being, and to a lesser degree, job satisfaction, have merit as operationalizations of worker happiness. Despite historical skepticism, both models have recently garnered some measure of research support (Cropanzano & Wright, 2001; Judge et al., 1998, 2001). Despite these encouraging results, these two approaches to operationalizing worker happiness have seldom been considered concomitantly. Moreover, those rare investigations that simultaneously examine job satisfaction and psychological well being usually only consider main effects. As a prime example, consider the two field studies reported by Wright and Cropanzano (2000). In their research, Wright and Cropanzano explored the effects of psychological well being beyond those of job satisfaction. However, the authors did not consider the interaction between the two variables. While main effect studies have their place, ignoring the moderating effect of psychological well being is limiting, since there are good conceptual reasons to think that an interaction might take place.

Drawing on the impetus of the "positive psychology" movement (Diener, 2000; Myers, 2000; Seligman, 1999; Seligman & Csikszentmihalyi, 2000), a number of organizational researchers have noted the need for a more positive-based, proactive approach to organizational research. This approach has been termed Positive Organizational Behavior (POB) (Luthans, 2002a, b) and Positive Organizational Scholarship (Cameron et al., 2003; Peterson & Seligman, 2003; Pratt & Ashforth, 2003; Wrzesniewski, 2003). Luthans (2003, p. 179) defined POB as "...the study and application of positively-oriented human resource strengths and psychological capacities that can be measured, developed, and effectively managed for performance improvement in today's workplace." In a like manner, Cameron et al. (2003, p. 4) define Positive Organizational Scholarship (POS) as being "...concerned primarily with the study of especially positive outcomes, processes, and attributes of organizations and their members. POS does not represent a single theory, but it focuses on dynamics that are typically described by words such as *excellence, thriving, flourishing, abundance, resilience,* or *virtuousness.*" In particular, I suggest Fredrickson's (1998, 2001, 2002, 2003) broaden-and-build model of positive emotions as one approach especially well-suited to help better understand the possible moderating role of psychological well being in the job satisfaction/job performance relation.

Before examining Fredrickson's model, it is appropriate to briefly contrast the burgeoning work on positive emotions, exemplified by Fredrickson and others, with the more typical emphasis of prior work on negative emotions.[1] In the past, the prevailing models of emotion attempted to illustrate the general form and function of emotions (Fredrickson, 2002). To that end, most models were devised around prototypic and negative emotions like anger and fear (Fredrickson, 2003). In other words, the underlying theme of these traditional approaches (cf. Frijda, 1986; Lazarus, 1991; Levenson, 1994) was that emotions, by definition, are associated with specific action tendencies. For example, the negative emotion, fear, is associated with the urge to escape. The negative emotion, anger, is associated with the urge to attack, and so on (Fredrickson, 2003). Thus, according to Fredrickson (2003, p. 165), the key to these traditional, negative-based, models "...is that specific action tendencies are what make emotions evolutionarily adaptive: these are among the actions that worked best in getting our ancestors out of life-or-death situations." Alternatively, the specific action tendencies for positive-based emotions are, by contrast, vague and under-specified (Fredrickson, 2003; Fredrickson & Levenson, 1998). Recognizing this incompatibility of positive emotions with the basic premise of traditional models, Fredrickson developed her broaden-and-build model to help better capture the unique attributes and potential contributions of positive emotion.

According to Fredrickson's (1998, 2001, 2002, 2003) broaden-and-build theory, a number of positive emotions, including the experience of psychological well being, all share the capacity to "broaden" an individual's momentary thought-action repertoires through expanding the obtainable array of potential thoughts and actions that come to mind (Fredrickson & Branigan, 2001). In addition, these positive emotions assist in "building" the individual's enduring personal resources, ranging from physical, psychological, intellectual and social in nature (Wright, 2003). This capacity to experience the positive is proposed to be crucial to one's capacity to thrive, mentally flourish and psychologically grow (Fredrickson, 2001, 2003). In fact, this sense of flourishing appears to make psychologically well or happy people more proactive (cf. Argyle, 1987) and less prone to stress symptoms (Myers & Diener, 1995). For instance, Fredrickson (2001, p. 220) proposed that contented individuals can broaden their array of thought-action repertoires by creating the desire "to savor current life circumstances and integrate these circumstances into new views of self and the world." As a result, a continued focus on these positive feelings expands (broadens) and builds on these urges, creating a potentially moderating "upward spiral" effect, which can further enhance individual character development (Fredrickson & Joiner, 2002; Hobfoll, 1998; Wright, 2003). As a general consequence, this capacity to experience positive feelings is considered to be a fundamental human strength (Fredrickson, 2001; Wright & Wright, 2002).

THE MODERATING ROLE OF PSYCHOLOGICAL WELL BEING

Considered together, the broaden-and-build model suggests the potentially adaptive and interactive nature of positive emotion (Wright, 2003). This possibility of a moderating effect of various positive emotions, such as psychological well being, on the job satisfaction/job performance relation has long been recognized in organizational research (e.g. Fisher & Hanna, 1931; Locke, 1976). However, the theoretical basis for such a disposition-based interaction was always rather tentative and ambiguous (cf. Gerhart, 1987; Staw, 2004; Wright, 2003). The broaden-and-build dimension of Fredrickson's (2001, 2003) theory suggests that the adaptive or moderating nature of psychological well being is potentially more robust for those more psychologically well than for those less psychologically well (cf. Fredrickson, 2001, p. 218). As a result, through the impetus provided by psychological well being, individuals are more easily able to "broaden-and-build" themselves and become more creative, resilient, socially connected, and physically and mentally healthy (Wright, 2003). In addition, as reviewed earlier, these effects would appear to persist over time due, in part, to the differential manner in which happy and unhappy people recall events. Considered together, one can conclude that inducing positive emotion states in people facilitates flexible problem solving, decision making and evaluation of events (e.g. Erez & Isen, 2002; Isen, 2003).

To date, the actual number of empirical studies specifically designed to test an interaction effect has been quite limited (Judge et al., 2001). In fact, my literature review identified only two studies concerned with addressing the moderating effect of affect/emotion on the job satisfaction/job performance relation. In an interesting study, Hochwarter et al. (1999) examined the moderating effects of value attainment and affective disposition on the relation. Hochwarter et al.'s results failed to support a moderating effect of affective disposition. One possible limitation of the Hochwarter et al. study is that their measure of performance consisted entirely of self-report indices. Given the possible tendency to inflate self-ratings of performance, these authors recommended that future research include other, more objective, measures of performance, such as supervisory ratings. Building upon Hochwarter et al.'s (1999) work, Russell Cropanzano and I found that psychological well being moderated the relation between job satisfaction and supervisory ratings of employee performance (Wright & Cropanzano, 2003). In particular, considered individually, both psychological well being and job satisfaction accounted for incremental amounts of variance in job-related performance ratings. In addition, the more positive the psychological well being of the employee, the stronger the observed relation between job satisfaction and job performance.

The broaden-and-build model supports the possibly adaptive and interactive nature of a number of other positive-based emotions and, as a result, should be instrumental in providing greater insight into the happy/productive worker thesis. For instance, joy, exhilaration, optimism and interest all share the potential ability to "broaden" an individual's momentary thought-action experiences and provide valuable assistance in helping to further "build" the individual's personal resource arsenal (Fredrickson, 2001, 2002, 2003). As a consequence, individuals are more easily able to transform themselves and become more creative, hardy, resilient, socially connected, and physically and mentally healthy (Wright, 2003). In my concluding sections, I would like to echo what my colleagues and I have previously proposed as a pivotal research question for future research: What are individuals and organizations to do with these findings?

CAVEATS, CONCERNS, CONUNDRUMS AND CHALLENGES FOR FUTURE RESEARCH ON HAPPINESS

According to Ilgen (1999) and Cropanzano and Wright (1999), psychological interventions at work can take three general forms: composition, training, and situational engineering. *Composition* emphasizes selecting and placing people into appropriate positions, *training* emphasizes assisting workers so that they "fit" their jobs more closely, and *situational engineering* emphasizes changing the work environment so that it more closely fits the needs of people. The happy/productive worker thesis has implications for each approach.

The Composition (or Selection) Approach to Promoting Happiness

As noted there is some measure of stability to self-reported psychological well being or happiness. For instance, Cropanzano and Wright (1999) reported 6-month test-retest correlations of 0.76 ($p = 0.0001$), 4-year test-retest correlations of 0.68 ($p = 0.0001$) and 5-year test-retest correlations of 0.60 ($p = 0.0001$) for the Index of Psychological Well being (Berkman, 1971a, b). These results are consistent with other findings by Wright et al. (1993), Wright and Bonett (1997b) and Wright and Staw (1999a). In particular, Wright and Staw (1999a) reported a 2-year test-retest correlation of 0.74 ($p = 0.0001$, Study 1) and a 1-year test-retest correlation of 0.77 ($p = 0.0001$, Study 2). These findings give clear testimony to the fact that people who report being happy (or unhappy) at one point in time are likely to be happy (or unhappy) at another point in time (Diener et al., 1999) and provide evidence supportive of the notion of the heritability of happiness (Lykken, 1999; Seligman, 2002).

Fascinating research on the possible heritability of happiness (and job satisfaction) has been reported by a number of scholars (Arvey et al., 1989; Bouchard et al., 1990; Lykken, 1999; Lykken et al., 1993; Seligman, 2002; Staw, 2004). While beyond the scope of the present discussion, the possibility of a genetic basis for various employee attitudes and emotions has been highly controversial in organizational research (for varying perspectives, see Davis-Blake & Pfeffer, 1989; House et al., 1996; Schneider, 1987; Staw, 2004; Staw & Ross, 1985). Nevertheless, these findings supportive of a genetic basis do not necessarily imply that stability is entirely due to personal characteristics. Happiness and job satisfaction may be stable because one's life or job circumstances are stable as well. For example, a person may remain at the same job or at a very similar one. For this reason, the "fact" of employee attitudinal [in]stability should not solely be used to argue against the possibility of meaningful training and situational engineering-based interventions.

In theory, denying unhappy individuals jobs should raise the overall, aggregate level of workplace happiness (Cropanzano & Wright, 1999). This approach has some potentially intriguing implications as an increasingly large number of current employees, as well as potential future employees, are reporting that they are becoming increasingly unhappy (Wright & Wright, 2002). Myers and Diener

(1997, p. 5), propose that only a minority of Americans can be considered as truly happy. Beam (2000) reported that 28 million Americans have taken the prescription drug Prozac at some time, with millions more taking other forms of anti-depression medications. Currently, 7 out of the top 10 prescription drugs in the United States are for antidepressant or ulcer medication. These statistics grow even more alarming when one considers that currently there are literally millions of children and adolescents in the United States with serious emotional disturbances (Wright & Wright, 2002). Furthermore, over 6 million children, more than 10% of the school-age population in the United States will be prescribed anti-depressants and stimulants. Of course, the effects of this increasingly prescription-dependent adolescent population (our future employees or employers) are now being felt in the American workforce. Simply stated, the children of today do eventually grow up and many end up getting jobs!

This selection approach raises some serious ethical issues. For example, the failure to select prospective employees on the basis of their lack of psychological well being could depress these individuals further, which in turn could make these job candidates even more unemployable in the future. Obviously, this can engender considerable human and societal costs. As a consequence, careful consideration of these and other related issues is of paramount importance for management personnel, their employing organizations, and practicing consultants, using various measures of psychological well being to select happy workers (Cropanzano & Wright, 2001).

In addition to these ethical reservations, there are a number of other more practical-based issues for those interested in the selection approach to consider. If well being measures become more frequently used for employee selection, and are weighted more heavily in the selection decision process, then it is possible that more and more job applicants will be motivated to consider faking their responses (Cropanzano & Wright, 1999). In particular, research suggests that those who misrepresent have a better chance of receiving offers than those who respond honestly (Douglas et al., 1996; Rosse et al., 1998; Wright & Wright, 2001). Compounding this disturbing finding is the fact that an alarmingly high number of students (up to almost 90%) report that they have cheated, many repeatedly, in high school and college (Whitley & Keith-Spiegel, 2001). Furthermore, students who engage in cheating behavior in college also appear more likely to engage in any number of unethical business practices (e.g. Baldwin et al., 1996; Sims, 1993; Wright, 2004). Obviously, while helping the individual get a job that he/she might not be offered when judged only on their legitimate, actual merits, resume/interview faking is unlikely to maximize the utility of a staffing system from the organization's perspective. These findings must be seriously considered before attempting to systematically hire employees based upon their self-reported well being.

Training

Another option is to change employees by helping them learn to be happier. There is good evidence that various kinds of stress management training can have positive effects on worker well being (for reviews, see Murphy et al., 1995; Quick et al., 1997; Saunders et al., 1996). To that end, a number of strategies exist where individual employees can proactively self-monitor or manage their personal perceptions to enhance positive, and discourage negative, displays of momentary mood and emotion. For example, constructive self-talk is a conscious effort to replace negative with more positive and reinforcing self-talk (Eliot, 1995; Wright et al., 2004). Additionally, Quick et al. (1997) discuss various cognitive restructuring techniques designed to be beneficial in temporarily altering one's current emotional state or providing more permanent or dispositionally-based changes in human behavior. One such trait-oriented approach is learned optimism (Seligman, 1991). Learned optimism is viewed as a developed trait or style emphasizing positive thought patterns (see Quick et al., 1997, for a comprehensive overview of approaches to cognitively restructure one's overall approach to life).

A somewhat different perspective has been taken by Judge and his colleagues (cf. Judge & Bono, 2001; Judge & Larsen, 2001; Judge & Locke, 1993; Judge et al., 2000; Judge et al., 1997, 1998, 2002). These researchers have asked why a person might experience feelings of high or low well being. Judge and his colleagues propose that people make different "core evaluations" regarding their lives and their jobs. On the basis of these core evaluations, individuals experience certain levels of job satisfaction and well being. For example, some workers over-generalize their failures or hold themselves to impossibly high standards. These individuals are apt to experience low job satisfaction and poor well being. Research on core evaluations has practical consequences, since it spurs the development of potentially useful remedial interventions. For example, Beck (1967, 1987) has designed a program of treatment for modifying dysfunctional thought processes. This approach offers useful guidelines for implementing changes in core evaluations to promote enhanced well being and subsequent performance.

Situational Engineering

The third approach to possible intervention involves changing the environment so that it promotes, or at least does not impair, worker well being. Situational engineering would seem to be a promising technique, in that there is evidence that working conditions strongly affect employee well being (Kohn & Schooler, 1982; Wright & Bonett, 1992). As with the selection and training approaches, situational engineering provides a variety of options for organizations to create a more satisfied, happier workforce. Research has documented that something as simple as providing social support can help reduce the negative impact of stressful jobs (Cropanzano & Wright, 1999; Fisher, 1985; George et al., 1993). More generally, employers could manipulate or reengineer any number of organizational factors (i.e. physical, role, task, and/or interpersonal demands) shown to be related to increased displays of employee emotion at work (Quick et al., 1997). For example, work-family conflict seems to diminish life satisfaction (Cropanzano & Wright, 1999); thus, family-friendly polices should increase well being (Grandey & Cropanzano, 1999). Finally, we should not neglect the more obvious change strategies. Maraist et al. (1999) found that equitable pay tends to promote high levels of well being. In short, it should be possible to design human resource techniques so that they induce as much well being as possible.

CONCLUDING THOUGHTS

Applied research's interest in employee happiness has long centered on the happy/productive worker thesis (Houser, 1927; Kornhauser & Sharp, 1932; Mayo, 1933; Roethlisberger, 1941; Roethlisberger & Dickson, 1939; Snow, 1927; Whitehead, 1938). However, for many, the results have sometimes proved disappointing (e.g. Podsakoff & Williams, 1986; Staw, 1986). Fortunately, recent work shows greater promise. It seems that the generations of managers and practitioners alike who believed that a happy worker is a productive worker may well have been correct, especially when the concomitant relation of job satisfaction and psychological well being as predictors of job performance is considered.

Of noteworthy relevance in the "holy grail" pursuit in providing greater insight into the happy/productive worker thesis is the further development of such positive-based approaches as Fredrickson's (1998, 2001, 2002, 2003) broaden-and-build model. In particular, Fredrickson's model provides the necessary theoretical framework to explain the interactive effect of psychological well being on the job satisfaction/job performance relation. Considered individually, psychological well being, and to a lesser extent job satisfaction, have demonstrated statistically significant relations to employee performance. In particular, while job satisfaction/job performance relations typically range from 0.10 to 0.30, the psychological well being/job performance relation is consistently in the 0.30–0.50 range. Preliminary results indicate that consideration of the interactive effects of psychological well being on the job satisfaction/job performance relation may be even more robust (cf. Wright & Cropanzano, 2003). Furthermore, in addition to psychological well being, the broaden-and-build model supports the possible adaptive and interactive nature of a number of other positive-based emotions. For instance, joy, exhilaration, optimism and interest all share the potential ability to "broaden" an individual's momentary thought-action experiences and provide valuable assistance in helping to further "build" the individual's personal resource arsenal (Fredrickson, 2001, 2002, 2003). This means that in addition to studies on happy/productive workers, we may eventually see research on serene/thoughtful workers, caring/helpful workers, joyous/honest workers, and exhilarated/creative workers.

That said, I close by reiterating an important issue previously discussed by my colleagues and myself (cf. Wright & Cropanzano, 2000; Wright & Wright, 2000, 2002). This paper was concerned with the happiness (however measured)/performance relation. However, this should in no way be taken to suggest that performance is the only, or even the most important, reason that "happiness" is important. It seems to me that promoting human happiness is an intrinsic good for which all should work (Wright & Cropanzano, 2000). If happiness promotes better performance, and the present discussion suggests that is the case, then so much the better. Regardless, happiness remains valuable for its own sake. I close by noting that roughly two thousand five hundred years ago, Aristotle posed the question of what constitutes the good life. Similar to Aristotle, I suggest here that the pursuit of happiness (*eudaimonia*) properly defined, is a pivotal step in any attempt designed to address this age-old question.

NOTE

1. While employee emotion is increasingly recognized as playing a significant role in various aspects of organizational behavior, just what is considered an "emotion" has always been somewhat problematic (Fredrickson, 2003; Wright & Doherty, 1998). As an initial step in distinguishing among construct terminology, I take as a given that affect (and its derivative affective) is a super-ordinate term that encompasses all other affect-oriented terminology, including such terms as feelings, emotions, moods, and sentiments (Wright & Doherty, 1998). More specifically, emotions are best considered as multi-component response tendencies that have greater temporal stability than their mood counterparts. According to a number of emotion researchers, the emotion process begins with the person's assessment of the idiosyncratic meaning to themselves of an antecedent event (Fredrickson, 2003; Lazarus, 1991). In fact, Lazarus (1991) termed this adaptational encounter the person-environment relationship. While certainly not isomorphic across all construct dimensions, psychological well being (also termed emotional well being and subjective well being), as typically measured in the research discussed here, exhibits sufficient overlap with a number of consensually agreed upon characteristics of emotion (see Wright & Doherty for a further discussion), to be considered as equivalent for purposes of discussion. That noted,

further work on differentiating such terms as emotion, feeling, mood, sentiment and well being is certainly warranted and encouraged.

REFERENCES

Adams, H. F. (1916). *Advertising and its mental laws.* New York: Macmillan.

Argyle, M. (1987). *The experience of happiness.* London: Methuen.

Argyris, C. (1957). *Personality and organization.* New York: Harper.

Arvey, R. D., Bouchard, T. J., Jr., Segal, N. L., & Abraham, L. M. (1989). Job satisfaction: Environmental and genetic components. *Journal of Applied Psychology, 74,* 187–192.

Baldwin, D. C., Jr., Daugherty, S. R., Rowley, B. D., & Schwartz, M. R. (1996). Cheating in medical school: A survey of second-year students at 31 schools. *Academic Medicine, 71,* 267–273.

Barrick, M. R., & Mount, M. K. (1991). The Big Five personality dimensions and job performance: A meta-analysis. *Personnel Psychology, 44,* 1–26.

Beam, A. (2000, July 12). Listening to Prozac and the backlash. *The Boston Globe,* p. 1C.

Beck, A. T. (1967). *Depression: Causes and treatment.* Philadelphia: University of Pennsylvania Press.

Beck, A. T. (1987). Cognitive models of depression. *Journal of Cognitive Psychotherapy, 1,* 5–37.

Bedale, E. M. (1924). Comparison of the energy expenditure of a woman carrying loads in eight different positions (Report 29). London: Industrial Fatigue Research Board.

Belcastro, P. A. (1982). Burnout and its relationship to teachers' somatic complaints and illnesses. *Psychological Reports, 50,* 1045–1046.

Belcastro, P. A., & Hays, L. C. (1984). Ergophilia . . . ergophobia . . . erg . . . burnout? *Professional Psychology: Research and Practice, 15,* 260–270.

Berkman, P. L. (1971a). Measurement of mental health in a general population survey. *Journal of Epidemiology, 94,* 105–111.

Berkman, P. L. (1971b). Life stress and psychological well being: A replication of Langer's analysis in the midtown Manhattan study. *Journal of Health and Social Behavior, 12,* 35–45.

Bernstein, S. D. (2003). Positive Organizational Scholarship: Meet the movement, an interview with Kim Cameron, Jane Dutton, and Robert Quinn. *Journal of Management Inquiry, 12,* 266–271.

Blanchard, F. L. (1921). *The essentials of advertising.* New York: McGraw-Hill.

Blum, M. L., & Naylor, J. C. (1968). *Industrial Psychology: Its theoretical and social foundations.* New York: Harper & Row.

Bolger, N., & Schilling, E. A. (1991). Personality and problems of everyday life: The role of neuroticism in exposure and reactivity to daily stressors. *Journal of Personality, 59,* 255–286.

Bouchard, T. J., Lykken, D. T., McGue, M., Segal, N., & Tellegen, A. (1990). The sources of human psychological differences: The Minnesota study of twins reared apart. *Science, 250,* 223–228.

Brayfield, A. H., & Crockett, H. F. (1951). An index of job satisfaction. *Journal of Applied Psychology, 35,* 307–311.

Brayfield, A. H., & Crockett, W. H. (1955). Employee attitudes and employee performance. *Psychological Bulletin, 52,* 396–424.

Brief, A. P. (1998). *Attitudes in and around organizations.* Thousand Oaks, CA: Sage.

Brief, A. P., Burke, M. J., George, J. M., Robinson, B., & Webster, J. (1988). Should negative affectivity remain an unmeasured variable in the study of job stress? *Journal of Applied Psychology, 73,* 193–198.

Brief, A. P., Butcher, A. H., & Roberson, L. (1995). Cookies, dispositions, and job attitudes: The effects of positive mood-inducing events and negative affectivity on job satisfaction in a field experiment. *Organizational Behavior and Human Decision Processes, 62*, 55–62.

Brief, A. P., & Roberson, L. (1989). Job attitude organization: An exploratory study. *Journal of Applied Social Psychology, 19*, 717–727.

Burke, M. J., Brief, A. P., & George, J. M. (1993). The role of negative affectivity in understanding relations between self-reports of stressors and strains: A comment on the applied psychology literature. *Journal of Applied Psychology, 78*, 402–412.

Burke, M. J., Brief, A. P., George, J. M., Roberson, L., & Webster, J. (1989). Measuring affect at work: Confirmatory analyses of competing mood structures with conceptual linkages to cortical regulatory systems. *Journal of Personality and Social Psychology, 57*, 402–412.

Buss, D. M. (2000). The evolution of happiness. *American Psychologist, 55*, 15–23.

Cain, P. A. (1942). *Individual differences in susceptibility to monotony.* Unpublished doctoral dissertation. Ithaca, NY: Cornell University.

Cameron, K. S., Dutton, J. E., & Quinn, R. E. (2003). Foundations of positive organizational scholarship. In: K. S. Cameron, J. E. Dutton & R. E. Quinn (Eds), *Positive Organizational Scholarship: Foundations of a New Discipline* (pp. 3–13). San Francisco: Berrett-Koehler.

Cascio, W. F. (1991). *Costing human resources: The financial impact of behavior in organizations* (3rd ed.). Boston: PWS-Kent.

Charters, W. W. (1922). *How to sell at retail.* Boston: Houghton Mifflin.

Cherniss, C. (1993). The role of professional self-efficacy in the etiology and amelioration of burnout. In: W. B. Schaufeli, C. Maslach & T. Marek (Eds), *Professional Burnout: Recent Developments in Theory and Research* (pp. 135–149). Washington, DC: Taylor & Francis.

Cherrington, D. J., Reitz, H. J., & Scott, W. E. (1971). Effects of contingent and non-contingent reward on the relationship between satisfaction and task performance. *Journal of Applied Psychology, 55*, 531–536.

Clark, L. A., & Watson, D. (1988). Mood and the mundane: Relations between daily life events and self-reported mood. *Journal of Personality and Social Psychology, 54*, 296–308.

Clark, M. S., & Isen, A. M. (1982). Toward understanding the relationship between feeling states and social behavior. In: A. H. Hastorf & A. M. Isen (Eds), *Cognitive Social Psychology* (pp. 73–108). New York: Elsevier.

Cordes, C. L., & Dougherty, T. W. (1993). A review and integration of research on job burnout. *Academy of Management Review, 18*, 621–656.

Costa, P. T., & McCrae, R. R. (1980). Influence of extroversion and neuroticism on subjective well being: Happy and unhappy people. *Journal of Personality and Social Psychology, 33*, 668–678.

Costa, P. T., & McCrae, R. R. (1988). From catalog to classification: Murray's needs and the Five-Factor model. *Journal of Personality and Social Psychology, 55*, 258–265.

Cropanzano, R., James, K., & Konovsky, M. A. (1993). Dispositional affectivity as a predictor of work attitudes and job performance. *Journal of Organizational Behavior, 14*, 595–606.

Cropanzano, R., & Wright, T. A. (1999). A five-year study of change in the relationship between well being and job performance. *Consulting Psychology Journal: Practice and Research, 51*, 252–265.

Cropanzano, R., & Wright, T. A. (2001). When a 'happy' worker is really a "productive" worker: A review and further refinement of the happy-productive worker thesis. *Consulting Psychology Journal: Practice and Research, 53*, 182–199.

Crowden, G. P. (1932). *Muscular work, fatigue and recovery.* London: Pitman.

Dalton, M. (1959). *Men who manage*. New York: Wiley.

Daniels, K., & Harris, C. (2000). Work, psychological well being and performance. *Occupational Medicine, 50*, 304–309.

Davis-Blake, A., & Pfeffer, J. (1989). Just a mirage: The search for dispositional effects in organizational research. *Academy of Management Review, 14*, 385–400.

Dembers, W. N., & Brooks, J. (1989). A new instrument for measuring optimism and pessimism: Test-retest reliability and relations with happiness and religious commitment. *Bulletin of the Psychonomic Society, 27*, 366–654.

Diener, E. (1984). Subjective well being. *Psychological Bulletin, 95*, 542–575.

Diener, E. (1994). Assessing subjective well being: Progress and opportunities. *Social Indicators Research, 31*, 103–157.

Diener, E. (2000). Subjective well being: The science of happiness and a proposal for a national index. *American Psychologist, 55*, 34–43.

Diener, E., & Larsen, R. J. (1993). The experience of emotional well being. In: M. Lewis & J. M. Haviland (Eds), *Handbook of Emotions* (pp. 404–415). New York: Guilford Press.

Diener, E., Sandvik, E., Pavot, W., & Fujita, F. (1992). Extraversion and subjective well being in a U.S. national probability sample. *Journal of Research in Personality, 26*, 205–215.

Diener, E., Sandvik, E., Seidlitz, L., & Diener, M. (1993). The relationship between income and subjective well being: Relative or absolute? *Social Indicators Research, 28*, 195–223.

Diener, E., Suh, E. M., Lucas, R. E., & Smith, H. L. (1999). Subjective well being: Three decades of progress. *Psychological Bulletin, 125*, 276–302.

Dill, D. B. (1933). The nature of fatigue. *Personnel, 9*, 113–116.

Douglas, E. F., McDaniel, M. A., & Snell, A. F. (1996, August). The validity of non-cognitive measures decays when applicants fake. Paper presented at the 1996 meeting of the *Academy of Management*, Cincinnati, OH.

Eastman, G. R. (1916). *Psychology of salesmanship*. New York: A. F. Fenno.

Eliot, R. S. (1995). *From stress to strength: How to lighten your load and save your life*. New York: Bantam Books.

Erez, A., & Isen, A. M. (2002). The influence of positive affect on the components of expectancy motivation. *Journal of Applied Psychology, 87*, 1055–1067.

Fisher, C. D. (1980). On the dubious wisdom of expecting job satisfaction to correlate with performance. *Academy of Management Review, 5*, 607–612.

Fisher, C. D. (1985). Social support and adjustment to work: A longitudinal study. *Journal of Management, 11*, 39–59.

Fisher, V. E., & Hanna, J. V. (1931). *The dissatisfied worker*. New York; Macmillan.

Fredrickson, B. L. (1998). What good are positive emotions? *Review of General Psychology, 2*, 300–319.

Fredrickson, B. L. (2001). The role of positive emotions in positive psychology: The broaden-and-build theory of positive emotions. *American Psychologist, 56*, 219–226.

Fredrickson, B. L. (2002). Positive emotions. In: C. R. Snyder & S. J. Lopez (Eds), *Handbook of Positive Psychology* (pp. 120–134). New York: Oxford University Press.

Fredrickson, B. L. (2003). Positive emotions and upward spirals in organizations. In: K. S. Cameron, J. E. Dutton & R. E. Quinn (Eds), *Positive Organizational Scholarship: Foundations of a New Discipline* (pp. 163–175). San Francisco: Berrett-Koehler.

Fredrickson, B. L., & Branigan, C. A. (2001). Positive emotions. In: T. J. Mayne & G. A. Bonnano (Eds), *Emotion: Current Issues and Future Directions* (pp. 123–151). New York: Guilford Press.

Fredrickson, B. L., & Joiner, T. (2002). Positive emotions trigger upward spirals toward emotional well being. *Psychological Science, 13*, 172–175.

Fredrickson, B. L., & Levenson, R. W. (1998). Positive emotions speed recovery from the cardiovascular sequalae of negative emotions. *Cognition and Emotion, 12*, 191–220.

Frijda, N. H. (1986). *The emotions.* Cambridge: Cambridge University Press.

Fryer, D. (1922). Occupational intelligence standards. *School and Sociology, 16*, 273–277.

Garden, A.-H. (1991). Relationship between burnout and performance. *Psychological Reports, 68*, 963–977.

Gechman, A., & Wiener, Y. (1975). Job involvement and satisfaction as related to mental health and personnel time devoted to work. *Journal of Applied Psychology, 60*, 521–523.

George, J. M. (1989). Mood and absence. *Journal of Applied Psychology, 74*, 317–324.

George, J. M. (1991). State or trait: Effects of positive mood on prosocial behaviors at work. *Journal of Applied Psychology, 76*, 299–307.

George, J. M. (1992). The role of personality in organizational life: Issues and evidence. *Journal of Management, 18*, 185–210.

George, J. M. (1996). Trait and state affect. In: L K. M. Murphy (Ed.), *Individual Differences in Behavior in Organizations* (pp. 145–171). San Francisco: Jossey-Bass.

George, J. M., & Brief, A. P. (1992). Feeling good-doing good: A conceptual analysis of the mood at work-organizational spontaneity relationship. *Psychological Bulletin, 112*, 310–329.

George, J. M., & Brief, A. P. (1996). Motivational agendas in the workplace: The effects of feelings on focus of attention and work motivation. In: B. M. Staw & L. L. Cummings (Eds), *Research in Organizational Behavior* (Vol. 18, pp. 75–109). Greenwich, CT: JAI Press.

George, J. M., Reed, T. F., Ballard, K. A., Colin, J., & Fielding, J. (1993). Contact with AIDS patients as a source of work-related distress: Effects of organizational and social support. *Academy of Management Journal, 36*, 157–171.

Gerhart, B. (1987). How important are dispositional factors as determinants of job satisfaction? Implications for job design and other personnel programs. *Journal of Applied Psychology, 72*, 366–373.

Ghiselli, E. E. (1971). *Explorations in managerial talent.* Pacific Palisades, CA: Goodyear.

Grandey, A. A., & Cropanzano, R. (1999). The conservation of resources model applied to work-family conflict and strain. *Journal of Vocational Behavior, 54*, 350–370.

Haire, M. (1956). *Psychology in management.* New York: McGraw Hill.

Headley, B., & Wearing, A. (1992). The sense of relative superiority – central to well being. *Social Indicators Research, 20*, 497–516.

Herrold, L. D. (1923). *Advertising for the retailer.* New York: D. Appleton and Company.

Herzberg, F., Mausner, B., & Snyderman, B. (1959). *The motivation to work* (2nd ed.). New York: Wiley.

Hobfoll, S. E. (1988). *The ecology of stress.* New York: Hemisphere.

Hobfoll, S. E. (1989). Conservation of resources: A new attempt at conceptualizing stress. *American Psychologist, 44*, 513–525.

Hobfoll, S. E. (1998). *Stress, culture, and community: The psychology and philosophy of stress.* New York: Plenum.

Hochwarter, W. A., Perrewe, P. L., Ferris, G. R., & Brymer, R. A. (1999). Job satisfaction and performance: The moderating effects of value attainment and affective disposition. *Journal of Vocational Behavior, 54*, 296–313.

Hollingworth, H. L. (1913). *Advertising and selling.* New York: Garland.

Holmes, D. (1991). *Abnormal psychology.* New York: Harper.

Homans, G. C. (1950). *The human group.* New York: Harcourt, Brace & World.

Hoppock, R. (1935). *Job satisfaction.* New York: Harper.

Hough, L. M., Eaton, N. K., Dunnette, M. M., Kamp, J. D., & McCloy, R. A. (1990). Criterion-related validities of personality constructs and the effect of response distortion on those validities. *Journal of Applied Psychology, 75,* 581–595.

House, R. J., Shane, S. A., & Herold, D. M. (1996). Rumors of the death of dispositional research are vastly exaggerated. *Academy of Management Review, 21,* 203–224.

Houser, J. D. (1927). *What the employee thinks.* Cambridge, MA: Harvard University Press.

Iaffaldano, M. T., & Muchinsky, P. M. (1985). Job satisfaction and job performance: A meta analysis. *Psychological Bulletin, 97,* 366–373.

Ilgen, D. R. (1999). Teams embedded in organizations: Some implications. *American Psychologist, 54,* 129–139.

Isen, A. M. (2003). Positive affect as a source of strength. In: L. G. Aspinwall & U. M. Staudinger (Eds), *A Psychology of Human Strengths: Fundamental Questions and Future Directions for a Positive Psychology* (pp. 179–195). Washington, DC: American Psychological Association.

Isen, A. M., & Baron, R. A. (1991). Positive affect as a factor in organizational behavior. In: B. M. Staw & L. L. Cummings (Eds), *Research in Organizational Behavior* (Vol. 13, pp. 1–54). Greenwich, CT: JAI Press.

Isen, A. M., & Levin, A. F. (1972). Effects of feeling good on helping: Cookies and kindness. *Journal of Personality and Social Psychology, 21,* 384–388.

Ivancevich, J. W., & Matteson, M. T. (1980). *Stress at work: A managerial perspective.* Glenview, IL: Scott, Foresman.

Jamal, M., & Mitchell, V. F. (1980). Work, nonwork, and mental health: A model and a test. *Industrial Relations, 19,* 88–93.

Johnston, H. M. (1946). The detection and treatment of accident-prone drivers. *Psychological Bulletin, 43,* 489–532.

Jones, R. G., & Best, R. G. (1995, August). Further examination of the nature and impact of emotional work requirements. Paper presented at the annual meeting of the Academy of Management, Vancouver, British Columbia, Canada.

Judge, T. A. (1992). The dispositional perspective in human resources management. In: G. R. Ferris & K. M. Rowland (Eds), *Research in Personnel and Human Resources Management* (Vol. 10, pp. 31–72). Greenwich, CT: JAI Press.

Judge, T. A., & Bono, J. E. (2001). Relationship of core evaluations traits – self-esteem, generalized self-efficacy, locus of control, and emotional stability – with job satisfaction and job performance: A meta-analysis. *Journal of Applied Psychology, 86,* 80–92.

Judge, T. A., Bono, J. E., & Locke, E. A. (2000). Personality and job satisfaction: The mediating role of job characteristics. *Journal of Applied Psychology, 85,* 237–249.

Judge, T. A., Hanisch, K. A., & Drankoski, R. D. (1995). Human resources management and employee attitudes. In: G. R. Ferris, S. D. Roden & D. T. Barnum (Eds), *Handbook of Human Resources Management* (pp. 574–596). Oxford, England: Blackwell.

Judge, T. A., Heller, D., & Mount, M. K. (2002). Five-factor model of personality and job satisfaction: A meta-analysis. *Journal of Applied Psychology, 87,* 530–541.

Judge, T. A., & Larsen, R. J. (2001). Dispositional affect and job satisfaction: A review and theoretical extension. *Organization Behavior and Human Decision Processes, 86,* 67–98.

Judge, T. A., & Locke, E. A. (1993). Effects of dysfunctional thought processes on subjective well being and job satisfaction. *Journal of Applied Psychology, 78,* 475–490.

Judge, T. A., Locke, E. A., & Durham, C. C. (1997). The dispositional causes of job satisfaction: A core evaluations approach. In: B. M. Staw & L. L. Cummings (Eds), *Research in Organizational Behavior* (Vol. 17, pp. 151–188). Greenwich, CT: JAI Press.

Judge, T. A., Locke, E. A., Durham, C. C., & Kluger, A. N. (1998). Dispositional effects on job and life satisfaction: The role of core evaluations. *Journal of Applied Psychology*, *83*, 17–34.

Judge, T. A., Thoresen, C. J., Bono, J. E., & Patton, G. K. (1998, August). The job satisfaction-job performance relationship: 1939–1998. Paper presented at the annual meeting of the *Academy of Management*, San Diego, CA.

Judge, T. A., Thoresen, C. J., Bono, J. E., & Patton, G. K. (2001). The job satisfaction-job performance relationship: A qualitative and quantitative review. *Psychological Bulletin*, *127*, 376–407.

Kahill, S. (1988). Symptoms of professional burnout: A review of the empirical evidence. *Canadian Psychology*, *29*, 284–297.

Kohn, M. L., & Schooler, C. (1982). Job conditions and personality: A longitudinal assessment. *American Journal of Sociology*, *87*, 1257–1286.

Kornhauser, A. (1965). *Mental health and the industrial worker: A Detroit study*. New York: Wiley.

Kornhauser, A., & Sharp, A. (1932). Employee attitudes: Suggestions from a study in a factory. *Personnel Journal*, *10*, 393–401.

Landy, F. W. (1985). *The psychology of work behavior* (3rd ed.). Homewood, IL: Dorsey Press.

Larsen, R. J., & Diener, E. (1992). Promises and problems with the Circumplex model of emotion. *Review of Personality and Social Psychology*, *13*, 25–59.

Larsen, R. J., & Ketelaar, T. (1989). Extraversion, neuroticism, and susceptibility to positive and negative mood induction procedures. *Personality and Individual Differences*, *10*, 1221–1228.

Larsen, R. J., & Ketelaar, T. (1991). Personality and susceptibility to positive and negative emotional states. *Journal of Personality and Social Psychology*, *61*, 132–140.

Lawler, E. E., III (1973). *Motivation in work organizations*. Monterey, CA: Brooks/Cole Publishing Company.

Lawler, E. E., & Porter, L. W. (1967). The effects of performance on job satisfaction. *Industrial Relations*, *7*, 20–28.

Lazarus, R. S. (1991). *Emotion and adaptation*. New York: Oxford University Press.

Ledford, G. E., Jr. (1999). Happiness and productivity revisited. *Journal of Organizational Behavior*, *20*, 25–30.

Lee, R. T., & Ashforth, B. E. (1996). A meta-analytic examination of the correlates of the three dimensions of job burnout. *Journal of Applied Psychology*, *81*, 123–133.

Leiter, M. P., & Maslach, C. (1988). The impact of interpersonal environment on burnout and organizational commitment. *Journal of Organizational Behavior*, *9*, 297–308.

Levenson, R. W. (1994). Human emotions: A functional view. In: P. Ekman & R. Davidson (Eds), *The Nature of Emotion: Fundamental Questions* (pp. 123–126). New York: Oxford University Press.

Levin, I., & Stokes, J. P. (1989). Dispositional approach to job satisfaction: Role of negative affectivity. *Journal of Applied Psychology*, *74*, 752–758.

Locke, E. A. (1969). What is job satisfaction? *Organizational Behavior and Human Performance*, *4*, 309–336.

Locke, E. A. (1976). The nature and causes of job satisfaction. In: M. D. Dunnette (Ed.), *Handbook of Industrial and Organizational Psychology* (1st ed., pp. 1297–1349). Chicago: Rand McNally.

Luthans, F. (2002a). Positive organizational behavior: Developing and managing psychological strengths. *Academy of Management Executive*, *16*, 57–72.

Luthans, F. (2002b). The need for and meaning of positive organizational behavior. *Journal of Organizational Behavior, 23*, 695–706.

Luthans, F. (2003). Positive organizational behavior: Implications for leadership and HR development and motivation. In: L. W. Porter, G. A. Bigley & R. M. Steers (Eds), *Motivation and Work Behavior* (pp. 178–195). New York: McGraw-Hill/Irwin.

Lykken, D. (1999). *Happiness*. New York: Golden Books.

Lykken, D., Bouchard, T. F., Jr., McGue, M., & Tellegen, A. (1993). Heritability of interests: A twin study. *Journal of Applied Psychology, 78*, 649–661.

Maraist, C. C., Davison, H. K., Brief, A. P., Dietz, M., & O'Shea, D. P. (1999, April–May). Does pay matter? The effects of work on subjective well being. Paper presented at the annual meeting of the Society for Industrial and Organizational Psychology, Atlanta, Georgia.

Martin, T. N. (1984). Role stress and inability to leave as predictors of mental health. *Human Relations, 37*, 969–983.

Maslach, C. (1982). *Burnout: The cost of caring*. Englewood Cliffs, NJ: Prentice-Hall.

Maslach, C., & Jackson, S. E. (1986). *Maslach Burnout Inventory* (2nd ed.). Palo Alto, CA: Consulting Psychologists Press.

Maslach, C., & Leiter, M. P. (1997). *The truth about burnout: How organizations cause personnel stress and what to do about it*. San Francisco: Jossey-Bass.

Mayer, J. D., & Gaschke, Y. N. (1988). The experience and meta-analysis of mood. *Journal of Personality and Social Psychology, 55*, 102–111.

Mayo, E. (1933). *The human problems of an industrial civilization*. New York: Viking.

McCrae, R. R., & Costa, P. T., Jr. (1987). Validation of the five-factor model of personality across instruments and observers. *Journal of Personality and Social Psychology, 52*, 81–90.

Meyer, G. J., & Shack, J. R. (1989). Structural convergence of mood and personality: Evidence for old and new directions. *The Journal of Personality and Social Psychology, 57*, 691–706.

Michalos, A. C. (1985). Multiple discrepancies theory (MDT). *Social Indicators Research, 16*, 347–413.

Miner, J. B. (1921). Standardizing tests for vocational guidance. *School and Sociology, 13*, 629–633.

Mosso, A. (1915). *Fatigue*. New York: Putnam.

Munsterberg, H. (1913). *Psychology and industrial efficiency*. Boston: Houghton Mifflin.

Murphy, L. R., Hurrell, J. J., Jr., Sauter, S. L., & Keita, G. P. (1995). *Job stress interventions*. Washington, DC: American Psychological Association.

Muscio, B. (1921). Is a fatigue test possible? *British Journal of Psychology, 12*, 31–46.

Myers, D. G. (1993). *The pursuit of happiness*. New York: Avon Books.

Myers, D. G. (2000). The funds, friends, and faith of happy people. *American Psychologist, 55*, 56–67.

Myers, D. G., & Diener, E. (1995). Who is happy? *Psychological Science, 6*, 10–19.

Myers, D. G., & Diener, E. (1997). The new pursuit of happiness. *The Harvard Medical Health Letter, 14*, 4–7.

Nord, W. R. (1976). Attitudes and performance. In: W. R. Nord (Ed.), *Concepts and Controversies in Organizational Behavior* (pp. 518–525). Glenview, IL: Foresman.

Nystrom, P. H. (1914). *Retail selling and store management*. New York: D. Appleton and company.

Ones, D. S., Mount, M. K., Barrick, M. R., & Hunter, J. E. (1994). Personality and job performance: A critique of Tett, Jackson, & Rothstein (1994) meta-analysis. *Personnel Psychology, 47*, 147–171.

Organ, D. W. (1988). *Organizational citizenship behavior: The good soldier syndrome*. Lexington, MA: Lexington Press.

Parducci, A. (1995). *Happiness, pleasure, and judgment: The contextual theory and its applications.* Hillsdale, NJ: Erlbaum.

Pavot, W., Diener, E., Colvin, C. R., & Sandvik, E. (1991). Further validation of the Satisfaction with Life Scale: Evidence for cross-method convergence of well being measures. *Journal of Personality Assessment, 57,* 149–161.

Pennock, G. A. (1930). Industrial research at Hawthorne: An experimental investigation of rest periods, working conditions and other conditions. *Personnel Journal, 8,* 296–313.

Peterson, C. M. (2000). The future of optimism. *American Psychologist, 55,* 44–55.

Peterson, C. M., & Seligman, M. E. P. (2003). Positive organizational studies: Lessons from positive psychology. In: K. S. Cameron, J. E. Dutton & R. E. Quinn (Eds), *Positive Organizational Scholarship: Foundations of a New Discipline* (pp. 14–27). San Francisco: Berrett-Koehler.

Petty, M. M., McGee, G. W., & Cavender, J. W. (1984). A meta-analysis of the relationship between individual job satisfaction and individual performance. *Academy of Management Review, 9,* 712–721.

Podsakoff, P. M., & Williams, L. J. (1986). The relationship between individual job satisfaction and individual performance. In: E. A. Locke (Ed.), *Generalizing from Laboratory to Field Studies* (pp. 207–245). Lexington, MA: Lexington Books.

Porter, L. W., & Steers, R. M. (1973). Organization, work, and personal factors in employee turnover and retention. *Psychological Bulletin, 80,* 151–176.

Pratt, M. G., & Ashforth, B. E. (2003). Fostering positive meaningfulness at work. In: K. S. Cameron, J. E. Dutton & R. E. Quinn (Eds), *Positive Organizational Scholarship: Foundations of a New Discipline* (pp. 309–327).

Quattrochi-Tubin, S., Jones, J. W., & Breedlove, V. (1982). The burnout syndrome in geriatric counselors and service workers. *Activities, Adaptation, and Aging, 3,* 65–76.

Quick, J. C., Quick, J. D., Nelson, D. L., & Hurrell, J. J., Jr. (1997). *Preventive stress management in organizations.* Washington, DC: American Psychological Association.

Robbins, T. L., & DeNisi, A. S. (1994). A closer look at interpersonal affect as a distinct influence on cognitive processing in performance evaluations. *Journal of Applied Psychology, 79,* 341–353.

Roethlisberger, F. J. (1941). *Management and morale.* Cambridge, MA: Harvard University Press.

Roethlisberger, F. J., & Dickson, W. J. (1939). *Management and the worker.* Cambridge, MA: Harvard University Press.

Rosse, J. G., Stecher, M. D., Miller, J. L., & Levin, R. A. (1998). The impact of response distortion on preemployment personality testing and hiring decisions. *Journal of Applied Psychology, 83,* 634–644.

Russell, B. (1930). *The conquest of happiness.* New York: Liveright.

Russell, J. A. (1978). Evidence of convergent validity on the dimensions of affect. *Journal of Personality and Social Psychology, 36,* 1152–1168.

Russell, J. A. (1979). Affective space is bipolar. *Journal of Personality and Social Psychology, 37,* 345–356.

Russell, J. A. (1980). A circumplex model of affect. *Journal of Personality and Social Psychology, 39,* 1161–1178.

Russell, J. A., Lewicka, M., & Nitt, T. (1989). A cross-cultural study of a circumplex model of affect. *Journal of Personality and Social Psychology, 57,* 848–856.

Russell, J. A., & Ridgeway, D. (1983). Dimensions underlying children's emotion concepts. *Developmental Psychology, 19,* 795–804.

Russell, J. A., Weiss, A., & Mendelsohn, G. A. (1989). Affect Grid: A single-item scale of pleasure and arousal. *Journal of Personality and Social Psychology, 57,* 493–502.

Rusting, C. G., & Larsen, R. J. (1997). Extraversion, neuroticism, and susceptibility to positive and negative affect: A test of two theoretical models. *Personality and Individual Differences, 22*, 607–612.

Salgado, J. F. (1997). The five factor model of personality and job performance in the European Community. *Journal of Applied Psychology, 82*, 30–43.

Sandlitz, E., Diener, E., & Seidlitz, L. (1993). Subjective well being: The convergence and stability of self-report measures. *Journal of Personality, 61*, 317–342.

Saunders, T., Driskell, J. E., Johnston, J. H., & Salas, E. (1996). The effects of stress inoculation training on anxiety and performance. *Journal of Occupational Health Psychology, 1*, 170–186.

Schneider, B. (1987). The people make the place. *Personnel Psychology, 40*, 437–453.

Schwab, D. P., & Cummings, L. L. (1970). Theories of performance and satisfaction: A review. *Industrial Relations, 9*, 408–430.

Scott, W. D. (1903). *Theory of advertising*. New York: Garland.

Scott, W. D. (1908). *Psychology of advertising*. Boston; Small, Maynard.

Seidlitz, L., & Diener, E. (1993). Memory for positive versus negative events: Theories for the differences between happy and unhappy persons. *Journal of Personality and Social Psychology, 64*, 654–664.

Seidlitz, L., Wyer, R. S., & Diener, E. (1997). Cognitive correlates of subjective well being: The processing of valanced life events by happy and unhappy persons. *Journal of Research in Personality, 31*, 240–256.

Sekaran, U. (1985). The paths to mental health: An exploratory study of husbands and wives in dual-career families. *Journal of Occupational Psychology, 58*, 129–137.

Seligman, M. E. P. (1991). *Learned optimism*. New York: Random House.

Seligman, M. E. P. (1994). *What you can change and what you can't*. New York: Knopf.

Seligman, M. E. P. (1995). The effectiveness of psychotherapy: The Consumer Report's study. *American Psychologist, 50*, 965–974.

Seligman, M. E. P. (2002). *Authentic happiness*. New York: Free Press.

Seligman, M. E. P., & Csikszentmihalyi, M. (2000). Positive psychology: An introduction. *American Psychologist, 55*, 5–14.

Sheldon, A. F. (1911). *The art of selling*. Chicago: Sheldon School.

Shirom, A. (1989). Burnout in work organizations. In: C. L. Cooper & I. Robertson (Eds), *International Review of Industrial and Organizational Psychology* (pp. 25–48). New York: Wiley.

Sims, R. L. (1993). The relationship between academic dishonesty and unethical business practices. *Journal of Education for Business, 68*, 207–211.

Sloan, C. A., & Mooney, J. D. (1920). *Advertising the technical product*. New York: McGraw-Hill.

Smith, P. C. (1953). The curve of output as a criterion of boredom. *Journal of Applied Psychology, 37*, 69–74.

Smith, P. C. (1992). In pursuit of happiness: Why study general satisfaction? In: C. J. Cranny, P. C. Smith & E. F. Stone (Eds), *Job Satisfaction: How People Feel About Their Jobs and How it Affects Their Performance*. New York: Lexington Books.

Smith, P. C., Kendall, L. M., & Hulin, C. L. (1969). *The measurement of satisfaction in work and retirement*. Chicago: Rand McNally.

Snow, A. J. (1923). Labor turnover and mental alertness test scores. *Journal of Applied Psychology, 7*, 285–290.

Snow, C. E. (1927). Research on industrial illumination: A discussion of the relation of illumination intensity to productivity efficiency. *Tech Engineering News*, *8*, 257, 272, 274, 282.

Spector, P. E. (1997). *Job satisfaction: Application, assessment, causes, and consequences*. Thousand Oaks, CA: Sage.

Staw, B. M. (1986). Organizational psychology and the pursuit of the happy/productive worker. *California Management Review*, *XXVIII*(4), 40–53.

Staw, B. M. (2004). The dispositional approach to job satisfaction: More than a mirage: But not yet an oasis. *Journal of Organizational Behavior* (in press).

Staw, B. M., & Barsade, S. G. (1993). Affect and managerial performance: A test of the sadder-but-wiser vs. happier-and-smarter hypotheses. *Administrative Science Quarterly*, *38*, 304–331.

Staw, B. M., & Ross, J. (1985). Stability in the midst of change: A dispositional approach to job attitudes. *Journal of Applied Psychology*, *70*, 469–480.

Staw, B. M., Sutton, R. I., & Pelled, L. H. (1994). Employee positive emotion and favorable outcomes at the workplace. *Organization Science*, *5*, 71–91.

Strong, E. K., Jr. (1925). Theories of selling. *Journal of Applied Psychology*, *9*, 75–86.

Sullivan, J. J. (1989). Self theories and employee motivation. *Journal of Management*, *15*, 345–363.

Taylor, F. W. (1919). *The principles of scientific management*. New York: Harper & Row.

Tellegen, A. (1982). *Brief manual for the Differential Personality Questionnaire*. Unpublished manuscript, University of Minnesota.

Tett, R. P., Jackson, D. N., & Rothstein, M. (1991). Personality measures as predictors of job performance: A meta-analytic review. *Personnel Psychology*, *44*, 703–742.

Tett, R. P., Jackson, D. N., Rothstein, M., & Reddon, J. R. (1994). Meta-analysis of personality-job performance relations: A reply to Ones, Mount, Barrick, and Hunter (1994). *Personnel Psychology*, *47*, 157–172.

Thayer, R. E. (1986). Activation-deactivation adjective check list: Current overview and structural analysis. *Psychological Reports*, *58*, 607–614.

Valliant, G. E. (2000). Adaptive mental mechanisms: Their role in a positive psychology. *American Psychologist*, *55*, 89–98.

Velasquez, M. G. (2002). *Business ethics: Concepts and cases* (5th ed.). Upper Saddle River, NJ: Prentice-Hall.

Veenhoven, R. (1988). The utility of happiness. *Social Indicators Research*, *20*, 333–354.

Vernon, A. M. (1924). *The influence of rest pauses and changes in posture on the capacity of muscular work* (Report 29). London: Industrial Fatigue Research Board.

Vroom, V. H. (1964). *Work and motivation*. New York: Wiley.

Warr, P. (1987). *Work, employment, and mental health*. New York: Oxford University Press.

Warr, P. (1990). The measurement of well being and other aspects of mental health. *Journal of Occupational Psychology*, *63*, 193–210.

Watson, D. (1988). Intraindividual and interindividual analysis of positive and negative affect: Their relation to health complaints, perceived stress, and daily activities. *Journal of Personality and Social Psychology*, *54*, 1020–1030.

Watson, D., & Clark, L. A. (1984). Negative affectivity: The disposition to experience negative emotional states. *Psychological Bulletin*, *96*, 465–490.

Watson, D., Clark, L. A., McIntyre, C. W., & Hamaker, S. (1992). Affect, personality, and social activity. *Journal of Personality and Social Psychology*, *63*, 1011–1025.

Watson, D., Clark, L. A., & Tellegen, A. (1984). Cross-cultural convergence in the structure of mood: A Japanese replication and a comparison with U.S. findings. *Journal of Personality and Social Psychology*, *47*, 127–144.

Watson, D., Clark, & Tellegen, A. (1988). Development and validation of brief measures of positive and negative affect: The PANAS Scales. *Journal of Personality and Social Psychology, 54,* 1063–1070.

Watson, D., & Pennebaker, J. W. (1989). Health complaints, stress, and distress: Exploring the central role of negative affectivity. *Psychological Review, 96,* 234–254.

Watson, D., & Slack, A. K. (1993). General factors of affective temperament and their relation to job satisfaction over time. *Organizational Behavior and Human Decision Processes, 54,* 181–202.

Watson, D., & Tellegen, A. (1985). Toward the structure of affect. *Psychological Bulletin, 98,* 219–235.

Weiss, H. M., & Cropanzano, R. (1996). An affective events approach to job satisfaction. In: B. M. Staw & L. L. Cummings (Eds), *Research in Organizational Behavior* (Vol. 18, pp. 1–74). Greenwich, CT: JAI Press.

Weitz, J. (1952). A neglected concept in the study of job satisfaction. *Personnel Psychology, 5,* 201–205.

Whitehead, H. (1917). *Principles of salesmanship.* New York: Ronald Press.

Whitehead, T. N. (1938). *The industrial worker* (2 vols). Cambridge, MA: Harvard University Press.

Whitley, B. E., Jr., & Keith-Spiegel, P. (2001). *Academic dishonesty: An educator's guide.* Mahweh, NJ: Lawrence-Erlbaum.

Wolpin, J., Burke, R. J., & Greenglass, E. R. (1991). Is job satisfaction an antecedent or a consequence of psychological burnout? *Human Relations, 44,* 193–209.

Wright, T. A. (1997). Time revisited in organizational research. *Journal of Organizational Behavior, 18,* 201–204.

Wright, T. A. (2002). The importance of time in organizational research. *Academy of Management Review, 27,* 343–345.

Wright, T. A. (2003). Positive organizational behavior: An idea whose time has truly come. *Journal of Organizational Behavior, 24,* 437–442.

Wright, T. A. (2004). When a student blows the whistle [on himself]: A personal experience essay on 'delayed' integrity in a classroom setting. *Journal of Management Inquiry,* in press.

Wright, T. A., & Bonett, D. G. (1992). The effect of turnover on work satisfaction and mental health: Support for a situational perspective. *Journal of Organizational Behavior, 13,* 603–615.

Wright, T. A., & Bonett, D. G. (1997a). The contribution of burnout to work performance. *Journal of Organizational Behavior, 18,* 491–499.

Wright, T. A., & Bonett, D. G. (1997b). The role of pleasantness and activation-based well being in performance prediction. *Journal of Occupational Health Psychology, 2,* 212–219.

Wright, T. A., Bonett, D. G., & Sweeney, D. A. (1993). Mental health and work performance: Results of a longitudinal field study. *Journal of Occupational and Organizational Psychology, 66,* 277–284.

Wright, T. A., & Cropanzano, R. (1998). Emotional exhaustion as a predictor of job performance and voluntary turnover. *Journal of Applied Psychology, 83,* 486–493.

Wright, T. A., & Cropanzano, R. (2000). Psychological well being and job satisfaction as predictors of job performance. *Journal of Occupational Health Psychology, 5,* 84–94.

Wright, T. A., & Cropanzano, R. (2003, April). The role of psychological well being as a moderator of the relation between job satisfaction and Job Performance. Paper presented at the 2003 meeting of the Society for Industrial and Organizational Psychology. Orlando, FL.

Wright, T. A., Cropanzano, R., Denney, P. J., & Moline, G. L. (2002). When a happy worker is a productive worker: A preliminary examination of three models. *Canadian Journal of Behavioural Science, 34,* 146–150.

Wright, T. A., Cropanzano, R., & Meyer, D. G. (2004). State and trait correlates of job performance: A tale of two perspectives. *Journal of Business and Psychology, 18,* 365–383.

Wright, T. A., & Doherty, E. M. (1998). Organizational behavior "rediscovers" the role of emotional well being. *Journal of Organizational Behavior, 19,* 481–485.

Wright, T. A., Larwood, L., & Denney, P. J. (2002). The different 'faces' of happiness-unhappiness in organizational research: Emotional exhaustion, positive affectivity, negative affectivity and psychological well being as correlates of job performance. *Journal of Business and Management, 8,* 109–126.

Wright, T. A., & Staw, B. M. (1999a). Affect and favorable work outcomes: Two longitudinal tests of the happy-productive worker thesis. *Journal of Organizational Behavior, 20,* 1–23.

Wright, T. A., & Staw, B. M. (1999b). Further thoughts on the happy-productive worker thesis. *Journal of Organizational Behavior, 20,* 31–34.

Wright, T. A., & Wright, V. P. (2000). How our 'values' influence the manner in which organizational research is framed and interpreted. *Journal of Organizational Behavior, 21,* 603–607.

Wright, T. A., & Wright, V. P. (2001). The role of [in]civility in organizational research. *Academy of Management Review, 26,* 168–170.

Wright, T. A., & Wright, V. P. (2002). Organizational researcher values, ethical responsibility, and the committed-to-participant research perspective. *Journal of Management Inquiry, 11,* 173–185.

Wrzesniewski, A. (2003). Finding positive meaning in work. In: K. S. Cameron, J. E. Dutton & R. E. Quinn (Eds), *Positive Organizational Scholarship: Foundations of a New Discipline* (pp. 296–308). San Francisco: Berrett-Koehler.

Wyatt, S., Fraser, J. A., & Stock, F. G. L. (1929). The effects of monotony on work (Report 56). London: Industrial Fatigue Research Board.

Wyatt, S., Langdon, J. N., & Stock, F. G. L. (1938). Fatigue and boredom in repetitive work (Report 77). London: Industrial Fatigue Research Board.

Zohar, D. (1997). Predicting burnout with a hassle-based measure of role demands. *Journal of Organizational Behavior, 18,* 101–115.

DISPLAY RULES AND STRAIN IN SERVICE JOBS: WHAT'S FAIRNESS GOT TO DO WITH IT?

Alicia A. Grandey and Glenda M. Fisk

ABSTRACT

The link between emotion display rules and job strain has been well established. This chapter draws upon the organizational justice literature to propose a new individual difference, service emotion rule fairness (SERF), to predict job strain for service workers. We propose that when service workers believe that organizational control of emotional displays is unfair they have poor fit with the job and increased strain. In fact, in the survey and experimental studies presented here, SERF uniquely predicted turnover intentions and emotional exhaustion beyond individual and group characteristics. SERF was rated higher when displays to customers are perceived as a means to gain financial rewards or form relationships with others, supporting a self-interest model of fairness, whereas the extent that display rules made one feel controlled, SERF was lower. We also found evidence that those with more social and organizational power perceived that the requirements were fairer. Practical and research implications are discussed.

Exploring Interpersonal Dynamics
Research in Occupational Stress and Well Being, Volume 4, 265–293
ISSN: 1479-3555/doi:10.1016/S1479-3555(04)04007-7

INTRODUCTION

In 2000, service occupations made up 18% of the U.S. economy, more than any other non-professional occupation, and employment in the service sector is projected to increase by 5000 new jobs in 2010 (www.bls.gov, 2003). As more U.S. workers become service employees, the unique characteristics of this work need to be directly examined in the organizational and psychology research (Offermann & Gowing, 1990). Two unique characteristics of service work are the continual interaction with the public and the requirement to display certain expressions as part of the job (Hochschild, 1983). Service employees work the front lines and act as boundary-spanners – they link the company and the public it serves. In order to manage the public's impressions effectively, service workers are expected to maintain positive expressions, regardless of true feelings. In support of this requirement, the display of positive emotions to customers has been linked with service ratings, customer satisfaction and intentions to return (Pugh, 2001; Tsai, 2001; Tsai & Huang, 2002). In fact, positive displays are often enforced by secret shoppers, supervisors, or customer comment cards, and are an explicit part of employee training programs (Hochschild, 1983; Rafaeli & Sutton, 1987; VanMaanen & Kunda, 1989). Customers enforce these displays as well because they are aware of such expectations, due to marketing "service with a smile." Thus, service employees, as well as others, are likely to agree that service workers are expected to follow emotional "display rules" as part of the job (Ekman & Friesen, 1975; Rafaeli & Sutton, 1987).

Despite the organizational benefits associated with smiling at customers, Hochschild (1983) suggested that treating emotional expression as a commodity, a part of the product for monetary exchange, was inherently unpleasant and dehumanizing to the employee. She argued that unlike social exchanges in private life, those in the service encounter are "ritually sealed and almost inescapable" and the exchange has an inherent inequality between the actors (Hochschild, 1983, p. 19). In support of this view, research has demonstrated that employees who are explicitly aware of display rules have lower job satisfaction and higher burnout and health problems than those who do not perceive such rules (Best et al., 1997; Schaubroeck & Jones, 2000).

Of course, individual differences are likely to moderate the relationship between job-related display rules and the stress that is experienced as a result of those rules (Arvey et al., 1998; Morris & Feldman, 1996). The affective personality of the employee is one type of individual differences that has been examined (Abraham, 1999; Bulan et al., 1997; Diefendorff & Richard, 2003; Diefendorff et al., in press; Morris & Feldman, 1997). In this chapter, we propose a more cognitive type of individual difference: employees' beliefs about the fairness of organizational display rules. That is, to what extent do people believe that it is fair to require that employees smile at customers (no matter what)? What role does perceived fairness of this expectation play in determining job strain? Who is more or less likely to feel this way, and can such attitudes be modified?

In the current chapter, we begin by discussing the links between these emotional requirements and stress. Research on emotion requirements is merged with the organizational justice literature to propose an individual difference for the perceived fairness of display rules, why it should predict job strain, and what the antecedents are. We then provide evidence for this individual difference with a survey study and a laboratory experiment.

EMOTION REQUIREMENTS AND WORK STRESS

The stressful nature of service work has been well documented (Brotheridge & Grandey, 2002; Maslach, 1978; Maslach & Jackson, 1984; Maslach & Pines, 1977; Singh et al., 1994). Front-line service workers often receive low pay and occupy relatively low status positions in the organizational structure. Moreover, these employees typically possess low levels of job autonomy and high demands in terms of the number of customers they are expected to interact with (Grandey & Brauburger, 2002; Hochschild, 1979; Wharton, 1993). Thus, service jobs fit into the "high stress" job category in the "demand-control" model of job strain (Karasek, 1979) as discussed by others (Brotheridge & Grandey, 2002; Pugliesi, 1999).

In addition to these occupational factors, employees who interact with customers or clients are also expected to maintain certain "display rules," or emotional requirements. Though providing service with a smile may seem reasonable, evidence has emerged demonstrating that complying with display rules requires considerable energy and attention. Experimental research has shown that requirements to suppress negative emotions such as disgust or sadness increased physiological arousal compared to people who were permitted to express their true emotions (Gross & Levenson, 1993, 1997). Furthermore, requirements to "hide negative" and "show positive" have been associated with increased levels of strain in field studies (Schaubroeck & Jones, 2000) and in work simulations (Sideman & Grandey, 2003).

Though display requirements themselves may decrease feelings of autonomy and be inherently stressful, more arousal and strain is expected if the display rules are discrepant from employees' emotional state (Hochschild, 1983). In other words, creating "a physical or publicly observable facial and bodily display" (Hochschild, 1983, p. 7) is psychologically taxing when required behavior conflicts with the authentic self (e.g. Ashforth & Humphrey, 1993; Ashforth & Tomiuk, 2000; Hochschild, 1983; Morris & Feldman, 1996). Since most service work display requirements involve hiding negative emotions and/or showing positive emotions, experiencing negative emotions at work would create a discrepancy between the current state and the standard (Diefendorff & Gosserand, 2003). Previous theorists and researchers have proposed the contextual and dispositional factors that may make such a discrepancy more likely and therefore, make display rules more stressful. These factors include: (a) situational factors; and (b) a negative or inexpressive personality style. To these two factors we add a third explanation – (c) perceived fairness of display rule policies. We briefly describe the first two below, then focus on the third.

Situational Factors

Two factors that increase the stress of service work are negative events and low job autonomy (Grandey & Brauburger, 2002). Negative events create a discrepancy between display rules and emotions, and thus create stress during service work. One type of negative event is the extent that the public is rude or aggressive toward service employees (Grandey et al., 2004; Maslach, 1978). In a sample of care workers, frequent interactions with clients led to burnout due, in part, to "hostility directed at the staff person" (Maslach, 1978, p. 112). In a diary study of student workers (Grandey et al., 2002), higher levels of interpersonal conflict (yelling, rudeness) were reported coming from customers as compared to coworkers and supervisors. The power differential between the customer (who is "always right") and the service employee may increase the likelihood that stress occurs (Allan & Gilbert, 2002). Aggression or conflict from customers has been associated with service worker burnout (Grandey et al., 2004).

The extent of job autonomy is another situational factor that has also been proposed to influence the strain of service workers (Grandey & Brauburger, 2002; Spector, 1986). In a study of U.S. and French employees who had contact with the public, Grandey and colleagues found that workers with high levels of job autonomy were less burned out as a result of regulating expressions than were those with low autonomy (Grandey et al., 2004). A sense of control makes work demands less stressful (Karasek, 1979; Wharton, 1993).

Dispositional Factors

Morris and Feldman (1997) proposed that "the greater the conflict between felt and sanctioned expressed emotion the more emotional exhaustion is experienced" (p. 267). Certain dispositional factors may make following display rules more or less demanding (Ashforth & Humphrey, 1993; Morris & Feldman, 1996). Pugh (2001) found that employees who are more emotionally expressive were more likely to smile and make eye contact with customers. Negative affectivity has also been linked to both effortful regulation and burnout (Brotheridge & Grandey, 2002). New research has begun to explore general personality traits as factors predicting the strain of emotional labor (Diefendorff, et al., in press; Tews & Glomb, 2003). This stream of research suggests that people experience strain in service jobs when they lack the predisposition toward, or ability to naturally show, expressions that are congruent with display rules.

FAIRNESS BELIEFS ABOUT SERVICE EMPLOYEE EMOTION DISPLAY RULES

Another explanation for the strain of service worker, beyond the situational factors and the ability to express required emotions, is the willingness or motivation to comply with interpersonal demands. Given the stressful nature of service work, as well as the fact that such jobs are typically characterized by low pay and low status, it is understandable that employees may perceive display rules as an unfair expectation inducing a sense of conflict and strain. Hochschild (1983) suggested that making emotions into a sold commodity is itself untenable. Customers treat an employee's expressions as their personal property, such as the customer who asks the hotel clerk "What, no smile this morning?" (Terkel, 1972, p. 247), and such external controls of expression may seem unfair. These controls are often quite explicit: in one grocery store, management insisted that employees smile, provide a greeting and 3-seconds of eye contact with customers and undercover shoppers enforced the policy. Said one clerk: "I really don't think it should be required. I'm going to treat people nice regardless. I don't like it that they watch you and listen to you and that you could get fired" (Cabanatuan, 1998, p. A19). A recent legal case brought to light suggests that display rules may be interpreted and reciprocated by some customers in an inappropriate manner (e.g. flirting), leading to sexual harassment claims from employees (Curtis, 1998). Thus, the negative events and lack of autonomy that may inspire stress may also inspire a sense of injustice regarding the requirement to be friendly to employees, and this fairness perception may be the more proximal predictor of job strain. We explore this possibility and propose the construct Service Emotion Rules Fairness, or SERF.

Service Emotion Rules Fairness (SERF) and Job Strain

Unfair organizational policies have been linked to negative work outcomes (Colquitt et al., 2001). For example, those who believe that policies are unfair (procedural injustice) are more likely to be dissatisfied with their jobs (Mossholder et al., 1998) and intend to quit (Masterson et al., 2000). Research also suggests that injustice resulting from one's work role is stressful (Zohar, 1995) and that perceptions of unfairness can evoke stress emotions such as anger (Mikula et al., 1998; Weiss et al., 1999).

Since previous research has demonstrated links between justice perceptions and well being or strain, we propose that to the extent display requirements are perceived as unjust more job strain will be experienced by those working under such requirements. Believing that emotional display rules are generally unfair for service workers represents a set of beliefs or values about emotional control. When core beliefs are incongruent with required behaviors of the job, role conflict ensues. In fact, it may even be that compromising "core values regarding appropriateness of emotional displays represents such a fundamental attack on the self that the alienation and hostility aroused are more severe than other forms of role conflict" (Abraham, 1999, p. 451). Thus, if people find display rules to be an unfair job requirement for service workers, this should help explain stress outcomes for those who work in these positions.

As discussed above, Hochschild (1983) argued that display rules were stressful because they removed personal autonomy and identity as well as induced emotional dissonance, a state of tension. The perception that these requirements are fair may aid in strengthening our understanding of these relationships. To the extent that display rules are viewed as unfair expectations, job strain will be increased. This fairness perception bespeaks the extent of role conflict between one's authentic and organizational self. Those who believe that modifying expressions for the public is appropriate for service workers will be more willing to follow such demands, while those who find this to be an unfair "extra" demand will be more resistant and in turn, report job strain. Importantly, we expect these factors to exist when controlling for situational factors and affective personality.

Proposition 1. SERF will negatively relate to the extent of job strain for those with customer contact.

Formation of Fairness Perceptions: Process-Content Distinction

To provide validity evidence for SERF and to understand the antecedents of this perception, we draw on the process-content distinction of justice. This speaks to how outcomes are decided (process approach) and the fairness associated with such outcomes (content approach) (Greenberg, 1987). This taxonomy may be used to understand the notion of justice as a "class of motivated behavior" in that individual and contextual circumstances can create a sense of injustice which, in turn, may prompt cognitive and emotional reactions (Cropanzano et al., 2001, p. 166).

Process: Fairness of the Policy
A process approach helps explain why explicit display rules (enforced via selection, training and rewards) may be viewed as an unfair policy. In short, display rules create a loss of voice and personal control. First, display rules stand in stark contrast to the "fair process" or "voice" criteria (Leventhal, 1976). Display rules regard emotional feelings and expressions as separable (Ashforth & Humphrey, 1993; Morris & Feldman, 1996); thus, display rules may be viewed as a loss of voice in terms of one's emotional self-expression. There is also little opportunity for the low status service employee to request exceptions, alterations, or amnesty from display rules, as illustrated by the grocery store case mentioned earlier. Second, the degree of personal control over behavior is a key factor influencing how individuals respond to procedures (Tyler, 1994). Thus, display rules create a social dilemma as they require individuals to devote resources to the organization while simultaneously putting them at "risk of exploitation, rejection and a loss of identity" (Cropanzano et al., 2001, p.169). The extent that display rules are perceived as taking control away from the individual should influence the extent that the policies are viewed as unfair.

Proposition 2. Perceiving that display rules reduce personal control will be negatively related to SERF.

Content: Fairness of the Outcomes of the Policy
Content approaches to justice suggest that the appraisal of outcomes, whether those outcomes are instrumental or relational, contribute to perceptions of fairness (Cropanzano & Ambrose, 2001; Cropanzano et al., 2001; Lind & Tyler, 1988). From an instrumental perspective, display rules should be perceived as fair as long as they ultimately act in the self-interest of the employee (Cropanzano & Ambrose, 2001). One obvious type of outcome is one's wage or tips. Restaurant servers who follow positive display rules gain larger tips (Tidd & Lockard, 1978). However, many employees with display rules are not well-compensated for this type of work – service/front-line jobs are among the lowest paid jobs (Glomb et al., 2004). Thus, service employees may find display rules unfair in that they potentially create distributive inequities. Compared with the lower effort that may seem to be required by employees in different, yet higher paying jobs (e.g. sales, clerical workers, computer maintenance), service employees may feel distributive

injustice in the sense that they must not only perform in a technically proficient manner, but also make the effort to smile at customers. In contrast, if employees believe that they are being compensated for their emotional displays, display rules are likely to be viewed as more fair.

Proposition 3. Instrumental outcomes will have a positive relationship with SERF.

The relational approach to fairness suggests that procedures reflect the status of one's social position and more specifically, provide individuals with a "positive sense of identity and feelings of self-worth and self-respect" (Tyler, 1994, p. 858). From this vantage point, display rules may be perceived as unfair in that front-line employees are subject to rules while individuals higher in the organization may not be (i.e. the rules lack consistency or neutrality) (Cropanzano & Ambrose, 2001). Moreover, display rules are implemented with little concern for employee interests, thereby reinforcing service workers' low status (Cropanzano & Ambrose, 2001; Lind, 1995). Thus, whether or not display rules are viewed as fair depends on the extent to which service workers feel such rules either undermine or strengthen their relational outcomes. For example, Tolich (1993) discussed that cashiers were friendly to customers because they gained enjoyment from the interactions. While both instrumental and relational models inform fairness, Tyler (1994) notes that relational models drive justice perceptions. Indeed, the earliest conceptualizations of justice underscore the social nature of fairness. Thus, we expect that when display rules are viewed as providing positive relational outcomes, they will more strongly predict fairness than when they contribute to instrumental rewards.

Proposition 4. Perceived relational outcomes will have a positive relationship with SERF, beyond instrumental outcomes.

GROUP DIFFERENCES IN THE PERCEIVED FAIRNESS OF DISPLAY RULES

Attitudes toward external controls on emotional expression may not only vary by individual, but also by group membership. Social groups may vary in their norms regarding emotional displays, and thus may vary in their sense of what is "right" about emotional control. Thus, there may be differences in the perceived fairness of display rules in service encounters by gender, race, and job status. Differences in some or all of these factors mean some groups are more at risk for strain when performing emotional labor.

Gender

Women are socialized to handle the challenges of working with and caring for others emotionally and to "be nice" when interacting with others (Wharton, 1993; Wharton & Erickson, 1995). Women tend to be more likely to hold a job where smiling at others is a prerequisite (Hochschild, 1983). Females view being inexpressive in a situation that has display rules to be censurable and that expressing negative emotions is incompatible with being feminine (Haynes et al., 1978; Lerner, 1985). In fact, women are seen as more likable when expressing positive emotions than men are (Fischer, 1993; Shields, 1987). On the other hand, males are more likely to expect negative outcomes for being expressive (Graham et al., 1981), and are more likely to engage in expressions as a social signal than for their value in securing relational or instrumental outcomes (Bugental et al., 1971). Thus, we expect that women are more likely to view positive displays to customers as leading to instrumental and relational rewards than men, and are therefore more likely to view display rules as fair.

Proposition 5a. Women will be more likely to believe in instrumental and relational outcomes from following display rules with the public than men.

Proposition 5b. Women will have higher SERF ratings than men.

Race/Ethnicity

In addition to gender considerations, minority group members may be less likely than majority group members to feel that display rules reflect an equitable work-related demand. We expect that minority members would be more likely to view the policy as unfair because it is seen as removing a personal resource (i.e. emotional control and self-expression) from a group with limited resources and because the display expectations are more difficult to meet for those who are not in the majority group (Clark et al., 1999). Minorities typically have lower social status than the majority members of society and still face negative stereotypes (Clark et al., 1999). Thus, ethnic minorities must control their emotions day-to-day in an effort to handle impression formation with the higher-status majority members (Rosenfeld et al., 1994). In fact, Latinos, Asian American and African American participants are more likely to report suppressing emotions than Caucasians (Gross & John, 2003). Ethnic minorities are more likely to deal with negative interpersonal events (e.g. racism) that make adherence to display rules difficult and stress-inducing (Clark et al., 1999). In one study of service workers and race, Hispanic call center workers reported more verbally hostile customers than other employees (Grandey et al., 2004). Such hostile conditions may lead minority employees to feel as though display rules are less fair than majority members. In fact, in an examination of U.S. racial groups, Matsumoto (1993) noted that Caucasian participants rated displays of emotion as being more appropriate in a variety of settings (e.g. in public, with acquaintances) than members of minority groups (e.g. African, Asian and Hispanic Americans).

Proposition 6a. Minority employees will be more likely to perceive that display rules are controlling than Caucasians.

Proposition 6b. Minority employees will report lower SERF ratings than Caucasians.

Job Status/Power

In general, service work is routine and scripted, with very little autonomy or decision latitude given to the employee. A social situation where employee behavior (such as emotional expression) is determined by external sources reflects a lack of power and autonomy (Brotheridge & Grandey, 2002; Emerson, 1962). In any social setting, the person of higher power typically has more freedom to express true feelings than the lower-power individual (Hecht & LaFrance, 1998; Henley, 1977; LaFrance & Hecht, 1999). Managers and professionals typically have more autonomy or choice about when positive displays should be shown than service personnel (Leidner, 1996). As Goffman (1967) observed, "the superordinate has the right to exercise certain familiarities which the subordinate is not allowed to reciprocate" (p. 64). These claims are corroborated by work showing that although positive affect is positively associated with smiling for high power persons, this relationship does not hold for low power persons (Hecht & LaFrance, 1998). Those who hold higher status jobs should be more likely to view display rules as fair because they still have more latitude in how they follow these rules. Furthermore, those in higher status jobs may believe it is fair for those in lower status positions to control their emotions toward them, as fits social norms for emotional expression.

Proposition 7. People in higher power positions will have higher SERF than employees in lower power positions.

The following sections describe two studies that provide evidence for these initial propositions. Study 1 provides psychometric evidence for a scale of SERF and tests it as a correlate of turnover intentions, one sign of job strain. Study 2 tests SERF as a predictor of subsequent strain after working under display rules.

STUDY 1: CONSTRUCT VALIDITY STUDY

Methods

Participants and Procedures

Six members of a research group recruited participants from different areas of the Eastern U.S. and Canada. In total, one hundred and sixteen individuals were surveyed regarding the affective demands of their work. The criteria for identifying participants was that they needed to be working over 16 hours a week (2 full work days), be non-students, and interact with the public as part of the job. One hundred and four of the respondents met these criteria.

The respondents were mostly (66%) female who were employed full-time (70%) in various organizations. On average, they had worked at their position for about 8 years and were about 40 years old (range = 19–72 years). Participants held jobs in service (16%), caring (15%), sales (15%), manager/professionals (22%), clerical or administrative (17%) and technical/physical (19%). Note again that all interacted with customers. On average, respondents worked 38 hours per week and interacted with 12 customers per hour.

Measures

SERF. Seven items were developed to tap the fairness of display rules for service work (see Table 1 for items). Participants were asked "To what extent do you agree with the following statements about service work (*not necessarily your job, but service work in general*)?" and given a 1 (strongly disagree) to 5 (strongly agree) Likert-type scale. Sample items include: "It seems unfair for service employees to have to smile at customers in addition to everything else" (reversed) and "Smiling at customers even when you are upset seems like a fair request to make of employees." Two items were reverse-coded to minimize the effect of a response bias. Details about psychometric qualities are reported in Table 1.

Perceptions of policy and outcomes. Nine items from Adelmann (1995) followed the stem "to what extent do you agree or disagree that being friendly and smiling at customers during the workday have the following outcomes for you, generally speaking." These items referred to a variety of outcomes (see Table 1) associated with positive displays, including financial, interpersonal, self-expression, and loss of control.

Affective personality. The PANAS (Watson et al., 1988) was used with trait instructions. Subjects were asked "To what extent do you generally feel this way, on

Table 1. Factor Structure of SERF Items and Perceived Outcomes from Positive Displays to Customers.

M (S.D.)	Items	SERF[a]	Instr.[b]	Relat.[b]	Cont.[b]
SERF					
4.33 (0.96)	It seems reasonable for service employees to be told to "smile" as part of their job.	0.69			
4.28 (0.74)	It is fair for any employee to be expected to hide negative feelings from customers	0.66			
4.03 (0.89)	Smiling at customers even when one is upset seems like a fair request to make of employees.	0.71			
4.06 (1.03)	It is fair to expect service employees to smile: that is part of what they are paid to do.	0.76			
3.44 (1.15)	*Reprimanding employees who show their negative emotions to customers is fair treatment of employees.*	*0.34*		*0.57*	
2.53 (1.18)	Service employees shouldn't have to pretend they aren't upset at a customer when they really are (reversed).	0.50			
2.05 (1.07)	It seems unfair for service employees to have to smile at customers in addition to everything else (reversed).	0.57			
Perceived outcomes from positive displays					
4.22 (0.96)	It results in better sales, tips or commissions.[a]		0.79		
4.62 (0.57)	It makes the customers feel good.		0.64		
4.31 (0.84)	*It pleases my supervisor.*		*0.61*		
4.13 (0.81)	It accurately indicates my friendly personality.			0.82	
3.57 (1.08)	It's a true sign of how I really like people.			0.80	
1.80 (0.98)	It makes me feel that I am being used by my employer.				−0.81
1.94 (1.07)	It makes me feel unsure about what I really feel.				−0.85
3.95 (0.91)	*It makes me feel happy.*		*0.51*		*0.44*
3.40 (1.21)	*It helps in getting raises or promotions.*		*0.46*	*−0.36*	*0.40*

[a] Instructions: For the items tapping SERF, participants were asked "To what extent do you agree with the following statements about service work (not necessarily your job, but service work in general)?"
[b] Instructions: For the items tapping the perceived outcomes from positive displays, Instrumental, Relational, and Control, participants were asked "To what extent do you agree that being nice and smiling at customers during the work day have the following outcomes FOR YOU, generally speaking?" Items in italics were not used in the final composites due to cross-loadings or low reliability coefficients.

average, across all situations?" for twenty affective terms (e.g. hostile, excited), and rated each positive and negative term on a scale of one (very slightly or not at all) to five (extremely). Positive affectivity exhibited an alpha of 0.83 and negative affectivity's internal consistency was 0.85. A self-rated measure of expressive ability (i.e. expressive confidence) developed by emotions researchers (Gross & John, 1998) was also included. This scale is primarily comprised of self-monitoring items from the "performing for others" dimension, and taps one's sense that they are comfortable and able to put on a show or act for others in any situation. Thirteen items were used in the current study ($\alpha = 0.87$).

Job strain. Withdrawal is often a behavioral sign of strain or dissatisfaction, and is a critical outcome to understand in high turnover service occupations. Intent to leave the organization was tapped with three items developed by Cropanzano and colleagues (Cropanzano et al., 1993) and had an alpha coefficient of 0.83.

Group membership. Participants were asked to report their gender, their ethnic identity, and their job title (which was converted into six job categories as done previously by Brotheridge & Grandey, 2002).

Results & Discussion

SERF and Perceptions of Outcomes
To ensure that the perceptions of fairness of display rules was distinct from the perception of outcomes from display rules, an exploratory principal component analysis with varimax rotation was performed with the seven SERF items and the nine outcome items. Four components with eigenvalues over 1.00 emerged, and the scree plot supported that there was a drop in variance explained after 4 factors. Three items loaded weakly on the intended dimension and had strong cross-loadings, so were omitted (see Table 1). In general, the factor structure supported that SERF, loss of control, instrumental and relational outcomes were distinct.

The final six items for SERF had an alpha coefficient of 0.80 and the inclusion of one omitted item did not increase this coefficient. Thus, these six items were used to compute a scale of fairness of display rules. The two relational outcomes ($\alpha = 0.71$) and loss of control ($\alpha = 0.73$) had reasonable alpha coefficients. The three instrumental outcomes had a low alpha (0.58) that would be increased to 0.65 by omitting the item "pleases my supervisor." Thus, each of the three perceptions of display rules composites were formed with two items.

Table 2. Bivariate Correlations of Study 1 Variables.

	M	S.D.	1	2	3	4	5	6	7
SERF	4.01	0.70							
Instrumental outcomes	4.37	0.59	0.33						
Relational outcomes	3.86	0.85	0.42	0.25					
Loss of control	1.87	0.93	−0.40	−0.23	−0.23				
Positive affectivity	3.75	0.53	0.22	0.31	0.27	−0.35			
Negative affectivity	1.59	0.52	−0.12	−0.19	−0.25	0.20	−0.36		
Expressive confidence	2.80	0.82	0.08	0.05	0.07	0.04	0.14	−0.12	
Turnover intentions	2.43	1.31	−0.22	−0.19	−0.03	0.13	−0.26	0.30	0.25

Note: Correlations greater than 0.19 are significant ($p < 0.05$). SERFS = Service Emotion Rules Fairness. Responses are on a 5-point scale.

The newly formed composites of SERF, and perceptions of instrumental outcomes, relational outcomes, and control, were correlated with all other variables as an initial test of the propositions. See Table 2 for bivariate correlations.

As proposed by Proposition 1–4, SERF was significantly correlated with turnover intentions, perceptions of control, instrumental outcomes and relational outcomes in the predicted directions. The more employees believed that display rules were fair, the less likely they were to intend to quit the jobs. Furthermore, perceptions that "service with a smile" entailed a loss of control were negatively correlated with fairness perceptions. Lastly, the more employees perceived that display rules were instrumental for job rewards and gave an opportunity to express oneself with customers, display rules were evaluated as fairer.

It is interesting to note that only positive affectivity was associated with SERF and neither negative affectivity nor expressive confidence were significantly related, supporting that SERF is a distinct type of individual difference. However, affective disposition correlated with the perceptions of outcomes from display rules. Perceived instrumental outcomes were significantly related to positive affectivity and marginally associated with negative affectivity. Both positive and negative affectivity were significantly related with perceived relational outcomes.

To examine the group comparisons in Proposition 4 through 8, a series of t-tests were computed. The mean differences in perceptions of SERF are shown in Fig. 1.

Men and women did not significantly differ in their perceptions of display rules or SERF. Thus, no support was found for Propositions 5a and 5b. Support was found for racial group differences: the Caucasian group rated display rules as less controlling ($M = 1.76$) than minority employees ($M = 2.39, p < 0.01$) in support of Proposition 6a, and as more fair overall than the minority group members (see Fig. 1) in support of Proposition 6b. The other perceptions of display rule outcomes

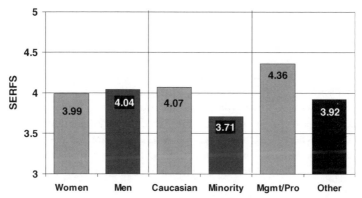

Fig. 1. Group Differences in Service Emotion Rules Fairness Scale (SERFS).

were not significantly different for these two groups. Finally, Proposition 7 was supported in that those who held managerial/professional jobs reported higher SERF values than those in other job categories (see Fig. 1). When examined by individual categories, manager/professionals had significantly higher SERF levels than every other job category. So, men and women were similarly likely to perceive display rules. However, those with higher social status (majority group) or job status (managers/professionals) were more likely to rate display rules as fair than compared to those with lower status.

As a follow-up analysis, paired *t-tests* were performed to determine if the outcomes of display rules were reported at significantly different levels. Instrumental rewards were most likely ($M = 4.37$, S.D. $= 0.59$), followed by relational ($M = 3.86$, S.D. $= 0.84$), and least likely was feeling controlled ($M = 1.87$, S.D. $= 0.93$). All comparisons were significant ($p < 0.001$). This is similar to Adelmann's (1995) finding that there was little support that people were "against" display rules or that they were viewed as controlling, as proposed by Hochschild (1983).

Predicting SERF and Job Strain

To examine the unique prediction of SERF hierarchical regressions were performed. The group membership, affective personality and perceptions of display rules policy and outcomes explained 34% of the variance in SERF.[1] Having a managerial or professional job, beyond all other variables, made one significantly more likely to believe that display rules for service workers were fair ($\beta = 0.23$, $p < 0.05$), while disposition did not significantly add to the variance explained in SERF. The outcomes of display rules contributed 20%

to the variance explained: the perception of relational outcomes ($\beta = 0.35$, $p < 0.01$) and loss of control ($\beta = -0.24$, $p < 0.05$) were significant unique predictors. The fact that perception of instrumental outcomes was not significant supports Proposition 4; relational outcomes will have more impact on display rule fairness than instrumental outcomes. Overall, fairness of display rules seems to be determined by the extent that something is gained or lost personally from service with a smile. Managers and professionals have been found to gain an increase in salary when they are expected to do emotion work (Glomb et al., 2004), whereas front-line service workers do not see such an increase. Instead, employees find display rules fair to the extent that they get positive interactions with others and do not feel that those interactions are controlled by the organization.

Together, group membership, affective personality, perceptions of outcomes, and SERF explained 33% of the variance in turnover intentions. Managerial/professional status was a significant predictor ($\beta = -0.21$, $p < 0.05$) that reduced to marginal significance when SERF was entered. Negative affectivity and expressive confidence predicted turnover intentions as well. SERF explained 3% unique variance in this behavioral intention ($p = 0.08$), providing some support that SERF adds to the prediction of job strain and the idea that when policies are viewed as fair, withdrawal is less likely.

The above study was conducted to provide evidence for the construct of fairness of display rules. Fairness of display rules seems to be an individual difference that is unique from positive and negative affectivity and expressive confidence, and is explained by perceptions of gains or losses from display rules. Importantly, we demonstrated a relationship between SERF and job strain. Those persons who found display rules less fair were more likely to intend to quit their jobs, and this was not accounted for by affective personality or group membership. One main limitation of the demonstrated association with intentions to quit is that this is not a direct measure of job strain. Furthermore, all the measures were self-reported at one point in time. Another issue is that these respondents had already self-selected into jobs that involved customer contact, and thus may handle the job requirements better. An experimental study was designed to correct for these issues and further examine the relationship of SERF with job strain.

STUDY 2: SERF AND JOB STRAIN EXPERIMENT

Study 1 provided evidence for the SERF construct. In Study 2, an experimental design was used to examine the effect of SERF on post-measures of strain after engaging in service encounters.

Method

Participants and Procedures

Fifty-one undergraduate students (42% males, 79% Caucasian, mean age 20.96 years old) from a large university in the Northeast participated in a simulated call center study in which they served as a customer-service representative for a fictional office supply store. First, participants completed a short survey assessing their positive affectivity, negative affectivity and perceptions regarding the fairness of display rules. Participants were then given a half-hour training session where instructions for completing customer order forms and the expectations for efficient and accurate work was communicated. In addition to these task-related instructions, participants were randomly assigned to one of three conditions. In one condition, no explicit display rules were given ($N = 17$), while the remaining participants ($N = 34$) were told that following display rules (hide negative or show positive) was part of their role.

The participants then moved to another room where they handled three incoming calls from customers who, in actuality, were experiment confederates. To increase the realism of the simulation, task and emotional requirements were varied – for example, the second caller behaved in a negative manner, and the third asked for a product by name but did not have the identifying code or page number. The participants completed scales about their strain and the perceived fairness of the display expectations in this particular service situation.

Measures

The same original SERF items were included, and again the one item regarding the reprimanding employees needed to be eliminated in order to increase the reliability of the scale. Thus, the same six items as in Study 1 were formed into a composite ($\alpha = 0.71$). The same positive and negative affectivity items were used (PA $\alpha = 0.79$; NA $\alpha = 0.87$). The five-item Job-related Exhaustion scale by Wharton (1993) was revised to refer to the extent of fatigue felt at the end of the simulation ($\alpha = 0.92$). Lastly, the participants were asked to rate the fairness of the requirements of the job they had completed. These items were: "The requirements of this job were fair," "The requirements were consistent with my expectations for this type of work," and "the job expectations were unfairly high" ($\alpha = 0.88$). This was to examine if the general SERF scale, completed prior to the simulation, would predict their fairness of the specific work requirements they were given.

Results & Discussion

In order to ascertain whether SERF predicted job strain (Proposition 1) two approaches were taken. First, SERF should predict job strain when display rules are required, because that is when the person should experience role conflict. SERF should be less likely to predict strain if the individual does not, him- or herself, have to follow display rules. Thus, we first dichotomized SERF (+/– 1 S.D.) and then conducted a 2 (display rules or not) × 2 (SERF high or low) ANOVA on the outcome. As the next step, we performed a hierarchical regression to determine whether SERF predicted strain beyond affective personality for the participants in the display rules condition.

Hypothesis Testing
The 2 × 2 ANOVA predicting job strain revealed a marginally significant interaction for assigned display rules and fairness of display rules for service workers [$F (1, 12) = 4.12, p = 0.065$]. The means were graphed (see Fig. 2.) These results support that fairness of display rules was more likely to predict job strain when display rules were required than when they were not. When positive displays were a requirement of the job, those who had reported that display rules were generally unfair were more exhausted (greater role conflict) in comparison to those who believed display rules were fairer (less role conflict). When positive displays were not a requirement, the SERF did not predict job strain; fairness of an abstract policy makes little difference to an employee's strain. This is supportive of the theoretical ideas behind SERF and a sense of role conflict between beliefs about emotional control and job requirements.

To examine further the role of SERF on job strain, post-simulation exhaustion was regressed onto SERF ratings, gender, and positive and negative affectivity for those participants in the display rule condition ($N = 34$). For those persons who must work under display rules, the extent of their SERF beliefs should predict their

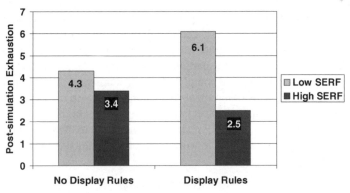

Fig. 2. The Interactive Effect of Display Rules and Service Emotion Rule Fairness (SERF) on Post-Simulation Exhaustion.

job strain while controlling for the situational and individual characteristics. SERF strongly predicted exhaustion ($\beta = -0.60, p < 0.01, \Delta R^2 = 0.43$). As evidence for convergent validity, we regressed the post-simulation fairness items on the pre-simulation SERF and the other predictors. SERF was the significant predictor ($\beta = 0.50, p < 0.01, \Delta R^2 = 0.21$), demonstrating that the general perception of fairness of display rules for service workers was related to fairness of expectations in a job where display rules were required.

The results support the psychometrics of the six-item SERF scale with a different sample, and demonstrate that the level of SERF predicted employee strain for those who work under explicit display rules better than those who do not, as would be expected. Furthermore, SERF was a strong predictor of the extent of exhaustion after performing a service job, beyond gender and affective disposition.

CONCLUSIONS AND FUTURE DIRECTIONS

The purpose of this chapter was to propose a new type of individual difference to understand the job strain experienced by the many employees who work within the service industry. This individual difference was a cognitive belief, rather than an affective disposition or situational event as is normally examined, and represents the extent to which display rules regulating service employee's emotions at work are perceived as fair. We proposed that SERF predicts job strain, and perceptions about the policy and its outcomes and group membership would contribute to the level of SERF. Two studies were presented that provide initial evidence for the validity and utility of SERF in future research on job strain in service.

Are Display Rules Generally Unfair?

Hochschild (1983) proposed that organizational rules that regulate emotional expressions would be viewed as inherently unpleasant. Such requirements remove personal control over a personal aspect of identity – emotional expression – and may be viewed as extraneous and onerous when expected in addition to task performance requirements. The fact that service work is often associated with low pay, low status and rude customers may add insult to injury and make display rules stressful. So, do people believe that display rules that control service workers' emotions are fair or not? Overall, the mean levels of the scale items (SERF = service emotion rules fairness) in Study 1 suggested that most of the participants believed that these rules were fair ($M = 4.01$ on a five point scale). However, all of these respondents were already in jobs that required customer contact. In Study 2, the participants were students who were assigned to working conditions. In that group, the average level of SERF was closer to the midpoint ($M = 4.57$ on a seven point scale). This suggests that there is self-selection into jobs based on this fairness belief, such that the fairness perception is skewed and restricted for those in service jobs. It may also be that individuals convince themselves that the policy is fair, via cognitive dissonance processes, once they hold jobs with display rules.

Does SERF matter? Fairness of Display Rules and Job Strain

Previous research suggests that stress is often induced by external conditions (e.g. job demands such as display rules) which in turn, challenge an individual's status and self-esteem (Hobfoll, 1989). Display rules function as a type of work-related demand and in general may serve as a source of role stress and contribute to burnout and turnover (see Lee & Ashforth, 1996). Furthermore, display rules are a special type of job requirement – they control (inspire?) employee's emotions, generally thought to be an internal and personal aspect of the self. People are likely to vary in the degree to which they believe such requirements are fair or appropriate. We argued that when employees view display rules as unfair, those display rules are more likely to act as a stressor, inducing intentions to quit and exhaustion in the employee. As stated earlier, this is an internal form of role conflict, where the employee's beliefs and job requirements are incompatible.Using two different populations and methods, we identified that SERF is predictive of signs of strain beyond affective personality and when environmental stressors are controlled.

Turnover intentions are a sign of job strain and dissatisfaction, and turnover is a critical issue in the service sector. Employees with customer contact in a wide range of positions who felt that display rules were less fair were more likely to intend to quit their jobs. The bivariate correlation supported this relationship. In addition, SERF explained a unique amount of the variance in turnover intentions; those who felt that emotion display rules were unfair requirements were more likely to desire to quit their customer contact jobs, and this effect existed beyond affective disposition and group membership.

The experimental data also supported that more strain was felt by those who worked under display rules and felt they were unfair. In this case, participants reported their beliefs concerning SERF prior to engaging in the experimental simulation. After performing the tasks and interacting with customers who varied in their interpersonal demeanor, participants recorded their felt exhaustion. SERF beliefs were irrelevant for those who did not receive display rules, thus, SERF does not simply represent a predisposition to job strain. Participants who experienced role conflict – they were assigned to a display rule condition but had reported that they thought display rules were unfair – were more exhausted at the end of the study than those who thought display rules were fair. Moreover, SERF explained exhaustion beyond affectivity and gender among those in the display rule conditions after controlling for situational stressors and environmental factors. This provides evidence for SERF as an explanatory factor for the strain of people work.

What Contributes to the Fairness of Display Rules?

As expected based on the justice literature, when benefits were associated with display rules the policies were seen in a more positive light. Those employees who believed that positive displays served as a means of self-expression and as an opportunity to form relational bonds were less likely to think that display rules were unfair. On the other hand, when display rules were seen as resulting in a loss of control and identity, these rules were reported as being unfair. It should be noted that while instrumental beliefs about smiling at customers were related to fairness of display rules, they did not predict SERF beyond the other (e.g. relational) beliefs. This is consistent with organizational justice theories suggesting that relational aspects of policies drive fairness perceptions beyond the distributions (Tyler, 1994).

In terms of individual differences, the results generally supported that SERF represented a unique individual difference that could not be fully explained by affectivity or confidence in expressive abilities. Positive affectivity (PA) had a significant relationship with SERF, but did not predict fairness beyond more proximal beliefs regarding the outcomes of following display rules. Negative affectivity (NA) and expressive confidence were weakly related to SERF. However, these affective characteristics did relate to beliefs about the *outcomes* of display rules. Those higher in PA were more likely to believe that instrumental and relational outcomes would follow positive displays to customers, and less likely to feel a loss of control from following display rules. In other words, those who are predisposed to feel positively recognize that they are more likely to reap the benefits of display rules. Those high in negative affectivity (NA) were less likely to believe that positive displays resulted in relational or instrumental outcomes and were more likely to endorse the view that display rules are a control mechanism and lead to alienations from real feelings. Since individuals high in NA would likely need to engage in more suppression and faking (i.e. surface acting), it is understandable that they would be less likely to expect positive outcomes. The fact that PA and NA were not strongly related to SERF demonstrates its distinctiveness from these affective personality factors that have typically been examined in the literature on display rules.

There were also some significant differences between groups in the perceived fairness of service display rules. Caucasian respondents were more likely to rate display rules as fair than minority respondents. Interestingly, these two groups did not vary in the extent that they worked under display rules. However, they did vary in their views regarding whether display rules were associated with a loss of personal control. Minority group members were more likely than majority group members to report that smiling at customers made them feel used. We proposed this reaction would be due to a higher likelihood of having to deal with negative/racist events in the work environment and a need to do more impression management to manage stereotypes others hold (Clark et al., 1999). The role of race in determining reactions to display rules within the context of a customer-employee service interaction should be examined further.

Furthermore, people who held managerial or professional positions were significantly more likely to report that such display requirements were fair. It is interesting to note that these employees also reported having to follow display rules at levels similar to service and caring workers (as found by Brotheridge & Grandey, 2002). Thus, the observed difference in fairness is not because managers do not have to worry about such requirements. Instead, the difference may be because higher status jobs have more latitude of expression within display rules, and they are more likely to be compensated for these expressive requirements (Glomb et al., 2004).

Future Research

Future research should examine how people in other culturally distinct countries perceive emotion display rules, specifically display rules in service encounters. Furthermore, combinations of the factors outlined in this paper should be examined. For example, how might someone who is a manager and a minority perceive display rules as compared to a Caucasian lower-status employee? Previous work suggests that low status females would be viewed more negatively for breaking display rules than someone who is male or working in a higher status occupation (Berger et al., 1989). The role of emotional expressions in maintaining power differentials would be an interesting avenue to explore.

In terms of outcomes, future research should test if those who have lower SERF experience have higher physiological arousal when given display rules. Furthermore, comparing the extent of arousal when there is a mismatch between SERF beliefs and the job expectations, to when there is a mismatch between affective disposition and job expectations, would be informative about SERFs predictive validity. Is the extent of role conflict and internal dissonance more stressful when beliefs about emotional control (the willingness to follow display rules) are in contrast with the rules, or when personal affectivity (the ability to follow display rules) is in contrast with the rules? The comparative strength of fairness beliefs over affective disposition was shown here. An interaction between the two may also be possible such that positive affectivity relates to less strain when fairness is high but not when fairness is low (ability × motivation interaction).

Practical Implications

Practically speaking, it may be worthwhile to enhance employees' SERF if they are holding jobs where certain displays are required. Overall, the finding that perceptions regarding the fairness of display rules are independent from individual difference constructs such as affectivity and expressivity suggests that organizations may be able to adopt practices that would serve to improve how their employees view and respond to display rules. The grocery store case did not allow for such personal control or voice, and this unchecked injustice resulted in receiving a lawsuit. Using SERF as part of selection or training may serve as a realistic job preview tool (see Wanous, 1980) and facilitate dialogue about display rules. This may help employees self-select into positions that match their beliefs about emotional control (Schneider, 1987). Managers may also improve SERF by following Leventhal's (1980) procedural justice criteria. For example, employees should be provided with an opportunity to participate in the creation of display rule policies as well as challenge decisions made on the basis of them. Drawing attention to the fairness of display rules may also be beneficial to the extent that it promotes a justice climate. Existing research suggests that when aggregated, perceptions of fairness are associated with improvements in employee performance, decreases in absenteeism and higher levels of customer service (e.g. Colquitt et al., 2002; Simons & Roberson, 2003). Thus, ensuring that employees perceive display rules as fair may have a "trickle-down" or spillover effect on customer satisfaction and the bottom line (Bowen et al., 1999; Masterson, 2001).

Organizations may also be able to enhance SERF in service employees and thereby indirectly decrease conflict and strain. During training and socialization processes, managers should strive to make the link between behavior and rewards explicit (Vroom, 1964) and to explain or justify the rationale behind display policies (Greenberg, 1990, 1994). This may mean discussing research that demonstrates the linkages between displays and rewards such as tips, customer satisfaction, and customer repatronage intentions (Pugh, 2001; Tidd & Lockard, 1978;

Tsai, 2001; Tsai & Huang, 2002). In addition to the importance of highlighting instrumental outcomes, this paper also shows the importance service workers attach to relational considerations. Brotheridge and Lee (2002) note that employee attempts to comply with display rules (via surface acting) could result in resource drain which may be counteracted by establishing meaningful relationships with others. Indeed, the authors maintain that a "lack of rewarding relations affects personal accomplishment through authenticity" which in turn, "fuels the vicious cycle of burnout" (Brotheridge & Lee, 2002, p. 65). Given the characteristics of front-line service work described here (e.g. low status, rude customers) it is rare that service employees will be able to establish meaningful relationships with the people they assist. To counteract poor customer-employee relations, it is important that employees feel that in the event of a problem, the organization will support them and their behavior (Eisenberger et al., 1986).

As one of the fastest growing jobs of the U.S. economy, service employees' strain and turnover is a critical problem. We propose that the perception of fairness of display rules may help predict who will be a poor fit for service work and explain levels of job strain. Nevertheless, the data presented here are preliminary. There are many individual difference variables that predict stress. The value of SERF is that it is specific to this population, but its unique contribution still needs further examination. However, in the minds of these authors, when understanding stress of display rules, we think fairness has something to do with it.

NOTE

1. Regression tables can be obtained from the first author by request.

ACKNOWLEDGMENTS

The authors would like to thank Patricia Barger, Gary Bolling, Matthew Burgard, Erica Chando, Deanna Danski, Jessica Dzieweczynski, Justin Gottlieb, Stephanie Rodrigues, Kathleen Royer, Rima Rynes and Celia Sucheski for their help with data collection and entry.

REFERENCES

Abraham, R. (1999). Negative affectivity: Moderator or confound in emotional dissonance-outcome relationships? *The Journal of Psychology, 133*(1), 61–72.

Adelmann, P. K. (1995). Emotional labor as a potential source of job stress. In: S. L. Sauter & L. R. Murphy (Eds), *Organizational Risk Factors for Job Stress* (pp. 371–381). Washington, DC: American Psychological Association.

Allan, S., & Gilbert, P. (2002). Anger and anger expression in relation to perceptions of social rank, entrapment, and depressive symptoms. *Personality and Individual Differences, 32,* 551–565.

Arvey, R. D., Renz, G. L., & Watson, W. W. (1998). Emotionality and job performance: Implications for personnel selection. *Research in Personnel and Human Resources Management, 16,* 103–147.

Ashforth, B. E., & Humphrey, R. H. (1993). Emotional labor in service roles: The influence of identity. *Academy of Management Review, 18*(1), 88–115.

Ashforth, B. E., & Tomiuk, M. A. (2000). Emotional labor and authenticity: Views from service agents. In: S. Fineman (Ed.), *Emotion in Organizations* (2nd ed., pp. 184–203). Thousand Oaks, CA: Sage.

Berger, J., Fisek, M. H., & Norman, R. Z. (1989). The evolution of status expectations. A theoretical extension. In: J. Berger, J. M. Zelditch & B. Anderson (Eds), *Sociological Theories in Progress.* London: Sage.

Best, R. G., Downey, R. G., & Jones, R. G. (1997). Incumbent perceptions of emotional work requirements. Paper presented at the 12th annual meeting of the Society for Industrial and Organizational Psychology, St. Louis, Missouri, April.

Bowen, D. E., Gilliland, S. W., & Folger, R. (1999). HRM and service fairness: How being fair with employees spills over to customers. *Organizational Dynamics, 27,* 7–23.

Brotheridge, C., & Grandey, A. (2002). Emotional labor and burnout: Comparing two perspectives of "people work". *Journal of Vocational Behavior, 60,* 17–39.

Brotheridge, C. M., & Lee, R. T. (2002). Testing a conservation of resources model of the dynamics of emotional labor. *Journal of Occupational Health Psychology, 7,* 57–67.

Bugental, D. E., Love, L. R., & Gianetto, R. M. (1971). Perfidious feminine faces. *Journal of Personality and Social Psychology, 17,* 314–318.

Bulan, H. F., Erickson, R., & Wharton, A. (1997). Doing for others on the job: The affective requirements of service work, gender, and emotional well being. *Social Problems, 44*(2), 235–256.

Cabanatuan, M. (1998). Let's-be-pals policy turns off some Safeway shoppers. *San Francisco Chronicle,* September 3, p. A19.

Clark, R., Anderson, N. B., Clark, V. R., & Williams, D. R. (1999). Racism as a stressor for African Americans: A biopsychosocial model. *American Psychologist, 54*(10), 805–816.

Colquitt, J. A., Conlon, D. E., Wesson, M. J., Porter, C., & Ng, K. Y. (2001). Justice at the Millennium: A meta-analytic review of 25 years of organizational justice research. *Journal of Applied Psychology, 86*(3), 425–445.

Colquitt, J. A., Noe, R. A., & Jackson, C. L. (2002). Justice in teams: Antecedents and consequences of procedural justice climatem. *Personnel Psychology, 55,* 83–109.

Cropanzano, R., & Ambrose, M. L. (2001). Procedural and distributive justice are more similar than you think: A monistic perspective and a research agenda. In: J. Greenberg & R. Cropanzano (Eds), *Advances in Organizational Justice* (pp. 119–151). Stanford, CA: Stanford University Press.

Cropanzano, R., Byrne, Z. S., Bobocel, D. R., & Rupp, D. E. (2001). Moral virtues, fairness heuristics, social entities, and other denizens of organizational justice. *Journal of Vocational Behavior, 58,* 164–209.

Cropanzano, R., James, K., & Konovsky, M. A. (1993). Dispositional affectivity as a predictor of work attitudes and job performance. *Journal of Organizational Behavior, 14,* 595–600.

Curtis, K. (1998). Smiley face out of place at Safeway, workers say. *The Oregonian*, p. 3.

Diefendorff, J. M., Croyle, M., & Gosserand, R. (in press). The dimensionality and antecedents of emotional labor strategies. *Journal of Vocational Behavior*.

Diefendorff, J. M., & Gosserand, R. H. (2003). Understanding the emotional labor process: A control theory perspective. *Journal of Organizational Behavior*, *24*, 945–959.

Diefendorff, J. M., & Richard, E. (2003). Antecedents and consequences of emotional display rule perceptions. *Journal of Applied Psychology*, *88*(2), 284–294.

Eisenberger, R., Huntington, R., Hutchison, R., & Sowa, D. (1986). Perceived organizational support. *Journal of Applied Psychology*, *71*, 500–507.

Ekman, P., & Friesen, W. V. (1975). *Unmasking the face: A guide to recognizing emotions from facial clues*. Englewood Cliffs, NJ: Prentice-Hall.

Emerson, R. E. (1962). Power dependence relations. *American Sociological Review*, *27*, 31–41.

Fischer, A. (1993). Sex differences in emotionality: Fact or stereotype? *Feminism & Psychology*, *3*, 303–318.

Glomb, T., Kammeyer-Mueller, J., & Rotundo, M. (2004). Emotional labor and compensating wage differentials. *Journal of Applied Psychology*, *89*(4), 700–714.

Goffman, E. (1967). *Interaction ritual: Essays on face-to-face behavior*. Garden City, NY: Anchor Books.

Graham, J. W., Gentry, K. W., & Green, J. (1981). The self-presentational nature of emotional expression: Some evidence. *Personality and Social Psychology Bulletin*, *7*, 467–474.

Grandey, A., & Brauburger, A. (2002). The Emotion regulation behind the customer service smile. In: R. Lord, R. Klimoski & R. Kanfer (Eds), *Emotions in the Workplace: Understanding the Structure and Role of Emotions in Organizational Behavior* (pp. 260–294). San Francisco, CA: Jossey-Bass.

Grandey, A., Dickter, D., & Sin, H.-P. (2004). The customer is *not* always right: Customer verbal aggression toward service employees. *Journal of Organizational Behavior*, *25*(3), 397–418.

Grandey, A., Fisk, G., & Steiner, D. (2004). Investigating French and American service workers' reactions to "service with a smile." Paper presented at the Society of Industrial and Organizational Psychologists, Chicago, IL.

Grandey, A., Tam, A., & Brauburger, A. (2002). Affective states and traits of young workers: A diary study. *Motivation and Emotion*, *26*(1), 31–55.

Greenberg, J. (1987). A taxonomy of organizational justice theories. *Academy of Management Review*, *12*, 9–22.

Greenberg, J. (1990). Employee theft as a reaction to underpayment inequity: The hidden cost of pay cuts. *Journal of Applied Psychology*, *75*(5), 561–568.

Greenberg, J. (1994). Using socially fair treatment to promote acceptance of a work site smoking ban. *Journal of Applied Psychology*, *79*(2), 288–297.

Gross, J., & John, O. P. (1998). Mapping the domain of expressivity: Multimethod evidence for a hierarchical model. *Journal of Personality and Social Psychology*, *74*(1), 170–191.

Gross, J., & John, O. P. (2003). Individual differences in two emotion regulation processes: Implications for affect, relationships, and well being. *Journal of Personality and Social Psychology*, *85*(2), 348–362.

Gross, J., & Levenson, R. (1993). Emotional suppression: Physiology, self-report, and expressive behavior. *Journal of Personality and Social Psychology*, *64*, 970–986.

Gross, J., & Levenson, R. (1997). Hiding feelings: The acute effects of inhibiting negative and positive emotions. *Journal of Abnormal Psychology*, *106*(1), 95–103.

Haynes, S., Levine, S. P., Scotch, N., Feinleib, M., & Kannel, W. B. (1978). The relationship of psychosocial risk factors to coronary heart disease in the Framingham Study. *American Journal of Epidemiology, 107*, 362–383.

Hecht, M. A., & LaFrance, M. (1998). License or obligation to smile: The effects of power and gender on amount and type of smiling. *Personality and Social Psychology Bulletin, 24*, 1332–1342.

Henley, N. M. (1977). Body politics: Power, sex, and nonverbal communication. *Berkeley Review of Sociology, 18*, 1–26.

Hobfoll, S. E. (1989). Conservation of resources: A new attempt at conceptualizing stress. *American Psychologist, 44*, 513–524.

Hochschild, A. R. (1979). Emotion work, feeling rules, and social structure. *American Journal of Sociology, 85*(3), 551–575.

Hochschild, A. R. (1983). *The managed heart: Commercialization of human feeling.* Berkeley, CA: University of California Press.

Karasek, R. A. (1979). Job demands, job decision latitude, and mental strain: Implications for job redesign. *Administrative Science Quarterly, 24*, 285–308.

LaFrance, M., & Hecht, M. A. (1999). Option or obligation to smile: The effects of power and gender on facial expression. In: P. Philippot, R. S. Feldman & E. J. Coats (Eds), *The Social Context of Nonverbal Behavior* (pp. 45–70). New York: Cambridge University Press.

Lee, R. T., & Ashforth, B. E. (1996). A meta-analytic examination of the correlates of the three dimensions of job burnout. *Journal of Applied Psychology, 81*, 123–133.

Leidner, R. (1996). Rethinking questions of control: Lessons from McDonald's. In: C. L. Macdonald & C. Sirianni (Eds), *Working in the Service Society* (pp. 29–49). Philadelphia, PA: Temple University Press.

Lerner, G. (1985). *The dance of anger.* New York: Harper & Row.

Leventhal, G. S. (1976). Fairness in social relationships. In: J. W. Thibault, J. T. Spence & R. C. Carson (Eds), *Contemporary Topics in Social Psychology* (pp. 211–240). Morristown, NJ: General Learning Press.

Leventhal, G. S. (1980). What should be done with equity theory? In: K. J. Gergen, M. S. Greenberg & R. H. Willis (Eds), *Social Exchange: Advances in Theory and Research* (pp. 27–55). New York: Plenum.

Lind, E. A. (1995). Justice and authority in organizations. In: R. Cropanzano & M. K. Kacmar (Eds), *Organizational Politics, Justice and Support: Managing the Social Climate of the Workplace.* Westport, CT: Quorum Books.

Lind, E. A., & Tyler, T. R. (1988). *The social psychology of procedural justice.* New York.: Plenum.

Maslach, C. (1978). The client role in staff burn-out. *Journal of Social Issues, 34*(4), 111–124.

Maslach, C., & Pines, A. (1977). The burn-out syndrome in the day care setting. *Child Care Quarterly, 6*, 100–113.

Maslach, C., & Jackson, S. E. (1984). Patterns of burnout among a national sample of public contact workers. *Journal of Health and Human Resources Administration, 7*, 189–212.

Masterson, S. S. (2001). A trickle-down model of organizational justice: Relating employee customers' perceptions of and reactions to fairness. *Journal of Applied Psychology, 86*(4), 594–604.

Masterson, S. S., Lewis, K., Goldman, B. M., & Taylor, M. S. (2000). Integrating justice and social exchange: The differing effects of fair procedures and treatment on work relationships. *Academy of Management Journal, 43*, 738–748.

Matsumoto, D. (1993). Ethnic differences in affect intensity, emotion judgments, display rule attitudes, and self-reported emotional expression in an American sample. *Motivation and Emotion, 17*(3), 107–123.

Mikula, G., Scherer, K. R., & Athenstaedt, U. (1998). The role of injustice in the elicitation of differential emotional reactions. *Personality and Social Psychology Bulletin, 24*, 769–783.

Morris, J. A., & Feldman, D. C. (1996). The dimensions, antecedents, and consequences of emotional labor. *Academy of Management Review, 21*(4), 986–1010.

Morris, J. A., & Feldman, D. C. (1997). Managing emotions in the workplace. *Journal of Managerial Issues, 9*(3), 257–274.

Mossholder, K. W., Bennett, N., Kemery, E. R., & Wesolowski, M. A. (1998). Relationships between bases of power and work reactions: The mediational role of procedural justice. *Journal of Management, 24*, 533–552.

Offermann, L. R., & Gowing, M. K. (1990). Organizations of the future: Changes and challenges. *American Psychologist, 45*, 95–108.

Pugh, S. D. (2001). Service with a smile: Emotional contagion in the service encounter. *Academy of Management Journal, 44*(5), 1018–1027.

Pugliesi, K. (1999). The consequences of emotional labor: Effects on work stress, job satisfaction, and well being. *Motivation and Emotion, 23*(2), 125–154.

Rafaeli, A., & Sutton, R. I. (1987). Expression of emotion as part of the work role. *Academy of Management Review, 12*(1), 23–37.

Rosenfeld, P., Giacalone, R. A., & Riordan, C. (1994). Impression management theory and diversity: Lessons for organizational behavior. *American Behavioral Scientist, 37*, 601–604.

Schaubroeck, J., & Jones, J. R. (2000). Antecedents of workplace emotional labor dimensions and moderators of their effects on physical symptoms. *Journal of Organizational Behavior, 21*, 163–183.

Schneider, B. (1987). The people make the place. *Personnel Psychology, 40*, 437–453.

Shields, S. (1987). Women, men, and the dilemma of emotion. In: P. Shaver & C. Hendrick (Eds), *Sex and Gender* (pp. 229–250). Newbury Park, CA: Sage.

Sideman, L., & Grandey, A. (2003). Emotion regulation in a simulated call center: A test of the ego depletion model. Paper presented at the Academy of Management, Seattle, WA, August.

Simons, T., & Roberson, Q. (2003). Why managers should care about fairness: The effects of aggregate justice perceptions on organizational outcomes. *Journal of Applied Psychology, 88*, 432–443.

Singh, J., Goolsby, J. R., & Rhoades, G. K. (1994). Behavioral and psychological consequences of boundary spanning burnout for customer service representatives. *Journal of Marketing Research, 16*, 558–569.

Spector, P. E. (1986). Perceived control by employes: A meta-analysis of studies concerning autonomy and participation at work. *Human Relations, 11*, 1005–1016.

Terkel, S. (1972). *Working*. New York: New Press.

Tews, M. J., & Glomb, T. (2003, April). Emotional Labor and the Five-Factor Model of Personality. Paper presented at the Society for Industrial-Organizational Psychologists, Orlando, FL.

Tidd, K. L., & Lockard, J. S. (1978). Monetary significance of the affiliative smile: A case for reciprocal altruism. *Bulletin of the Psychonomic Society, 11*, 344–346.

Tolich, M. B. (1993). Alienating and liberating emotions at work: Supermarket clerks' performance of customer service. *Journal of Contemporary Ethnography, 22*(3), 361–381.

Tsai, W.-C. (2001). Determinants and consequences of employee displayed positive emotions. *Journal of Management, 27*, 497–512.

Tsai, W.-C., & Huang, Y.-M. (2002). Mechanisms linking employee affective delivery and customer behavioral intentions. *Journal of Applied Psychology, 87*(5), 1001–1008.

Tyler, T. R. (1994). Psychological models of the justice motive: Antecedents of distributive and procedural justice. *Journal of Personality and Social Psychology, 67*, 850–863.

VanMaanen, J., & Kunda, G. (1989). Real feelings: Emotional expression and organizational culture. In: *Research in Organizational Behavior* (Vol. 11, pp. 43–103). Greenwich, CT: JAI Press.

Vroom, V. (1964). *Work and motivation.* New York: Wiley.

Wanous, J. P. (1980). *Organizational entry: Recruitment, selection and socialization of newcomers.* Reading, MA: Addison-Wesley.

Watson, D., Clark, L. A., & Tellegen, A. (1988). Development and validation of brief measures of positive and negative affect: The PANAS scales. *Journal of Personality and Social Psychology, 54*(6), 1063–1070.

Weiss, H., Suckow, K., & Cropanzano, R. (1999). Effects of justice conditions on discrete emotions. *Journal of Applied Psychology, 84*(5), 786–794.

Wharton, A. S. (1993). The affective consequences of service work: Managing emotions on the job. *Work and Occupations, 20*(2), 205–232.

Wharton, A. S., & Erickson, R. J. (1995). The consequences of caring: Exploring the links between women's job and family emotion work. *The Sociological Quarterly, 36*(2), 273–296.

Zohar, D. (1995). The justice perspective of job stress. *Journal of Organizational Behavior, 16,* 487–495.

STRESS AND WELL BEING IN THE CONTEXT OF MENTORING PROCESSES: NEW PERSPECTIVES AND DIRECTIONS FOR FUTURE RESEARCH

Angela M. Young

ABSTRACT

Mentoring processes have been researched extensively, but rarely from a perspective that incorporates issues related to stress. In this chapter, a focus is placed on the common themes and connections between these two important literature bases. The first part of the chapter describes the mentoring process, including a description of types of relationships, stages of relationship development, and the mentoring exchange. Stress research is presented along with a presentation of research that explicitly examines stress in relationship to mentoring. Specific stress points related to each aspect of the mentoring process will be described and illusted in a conceptual model. The chapter will conclude with suggestions for future research and methods that will enhance both stress and mentoring research.

INTRODUCTION

There is a growing interest in the impact of stress on the organizational and private lives of individuals. Issues of occupational stress and well being strike a cord with employers and employees who feel the far-reaching health consequences

Exploring Interpersonal Dynamics
Research in Occupational Stress and Well Being, Volume 4, 295–325
© 2005 Published by Elsevier Ltd.
ISSN: 1479-3555/doi:10.1016/S1479-3555(04)04008-9

of poorly managed stress or inadequate attention to well being. Employers are impacted by occupational stress in terms of rising health-care costs (Manning et al., 1996), organizational commitment, and turnover (Jamal, 1990; Sparks et al., 2001). Employees feel the pressures of competing demands at work and home, typically resulting in feelings of inadequacy on both fronts (Westman, 2002).

Mentoring has been researched in relation to positive organizational outcomes such as improved perceptions of fairness and organizational justice (Scandura, 1997) and as a means of social support to abate stress (Kram & Hall, 1989). Individuals in mentoring relationships gain many career-related benefits with mentors reporting greater career revitalization and satsifaction (Allen et al., 1997a; aHunt & Michael, 1983; Kram, 1985; Levinson et al., 1978) and protégés reaping a plethora of benefits from career progress and increased salaries to higher perceived career satisfaction (Bahniuk et al., 1990; Hunt & Michael, 1983; Scandura, 1992; Whitely & Coestier, 1993; Whitely et al., 1992) and job satisfaction (Ragins et al., 2000). Mentorships are not without drawbacks but only a few researchers have attempted to elaborate on the potential dysfunction and negative outcomes associated with unhealthy and unproductive relationships (Eby & Allen, 2002; Scandura, 1998).

Mentoring is above all else, a relationship, and as a relationship it involves a complex interplay of personal and situational variables (Young & Perrewé, 2000a). It is surprising that, given its relevance to organizations and individuals, the important and interesting connection between perceived stress and mentoring have not been explored by many researchers (Kram & Hall, 1989; Nelson & Burke, 2000; Viator, 2001). The purpose of this chapter is to identify and elaborate on potential stress points within the mentoring process. After a brief background on mentoring, stress in the mentoring process will be discussed. A conceptual model will be presented to illustrate the stress points likely to occur in the mentoring process beginning with initiating a relationship, developing and maintaining a relationship, relationship satisfaction, and transforming or terminating the relationship. The chapter will conclude with suggestions for future research and methods that will enhance both stress and mentoring research.

THE MENTORING PROCESS

Mentoring is typically thought of in terms of improving career prospects of a protégé and expanding the mentor's experiences and knowledge through teaching and counseling (Kram, 1985). Both mentors and protégés can benefit from a mentorship although research has typically focused on positive outcomes for protégés with much less attention on mentors (cf. Allen et al., 1997a). Mentoring research has also emphasized empirical investigation over theoretical development (Fagenson-Eland et al., 1997), but there has been some progress toward developing mentoring theory and defining the mentoring process (Young & Perrewé, 2000a). Some basic aspects of mentoring have emerged consistently and repeatedly from research. For example, mentoring occurs in two primary forms, informal and formal. In addition, the mentoring relationship typically progresses through stages and different behaviors are exhibited by mentoring partners across each stage. Next, the types of relationships and stages of relationship development will be explained, and the mentoring exchange process will be presented.

Types of Relationships

Primary forms of mentorship include informal and formal relationships. Informal relationships are spontaneous in nature and have been found to yield greater benefits to the protégé than formal relationships (Chao et al., 1992; Ragins & Cotton, 1999; Ragins et al., 2000; Viator, 2001). Formal relationships are those in which the mentor and protégé are assigned to work together. An interesting study of formal and informal relationships was done by Ragins et al. (2000) who compared job and organizational attitudes among formally, informally, and non-mentored individuals. The authors found that informal relationships yielded the highest levels of positive attitudinal outcomes such as job satisfaction and perceived organizational justice, but only if the informal relationship was perceived to be satisfying. In another study, Ragins and Cotton (1999) found that the degree of formality of the mentorship made a difference in types of support received. Specifically, protégés in informal relationships reported receiving more career-related support and higher salaries than protégés in formal relationships.

Beyond informal and formal mentoring alternative forms of mentorship or substitutes for mentoring have been explored such as peer mentoring, group mentoring, and coworker support (Allen & Finklestein, 2003; Dreher & Dougherty, 1997; Eby, 1997; Kram & Isabella, 1985). These alternative forms of mentoring or substitutes for mentoring are appealing but most researchers note that these alternative forms, while useful in providing support, lack many aspects of a true mentorship. Mentoring relationships, by definition, are meant to challenge us and help us to effectively attain our goals and objectives.

Mentoring Support and Stages

Mentoring in the most traditional sense, takes place when a senior person with experience and expertise provides guidance, expertise, coaching, and other tangible and emotional support to a less experienced person (Hunt & Michael, 1983; Kram, 1985; Noe et al., 2002). Kram provided the first most comprehensive examination of mentoring relationships in organizations, and her work has been relied upon widely by mentoring researchers. Kram interviewed 18 managers who acted in a mentoring role to determine why individuals engage in mentoring and what each partner receives from mentoring, particularly forms of support behaviors received from a mentor. Kram described stages of a mentoring relationship that begin with initiation and end in redefinition of the relationship.

At the initiation stage, mentors and protégés get to know one another and decide whether or not to work together. After relationship initiation, the next stage, cultivation, is dominated by relationship development and productivity. Although the cultivation stage may last an indefinite amount of time, eventually there is a separation stage where one or both partners feels the need to limit participation in the relationship. For a protégé, this may be due to an increased desire to venture out and be more independent in career development. From the mentor's perspective, the separation stage may be entered as a result of a job promotion or work that requires a greater focus. Finally, the last stage in the mentoring process is the redefinition stage when the mentor and protégé transform the mentorship into a new form where mentoring partners have new roles that better reflect their shared experiences, new skills, and career goals.

Throughout the stages of mentoring, career-related and social support is provided to the protégé by the mentor (Kram, 1985). According to Kram, career-related support includes such behaviors as coaching, protection from potentially harmful situations, providing challenging and relevant assignments, and making the protégé visible to influential others. Social support, termed psycho-social support in early mentoring research, includes behaviors such as counseling, befriending, and showing concern for a protégé. Role-modeling was presented by Kram (1985) as a social support behavior but research has indicated that it may be a construct distinct from social support (Scandura & Ragins, 1993). The support behaviors identified by Kram (1985) have been the mainstay of most mentoring research and have been the basis for scale development in mentoring (Noe, 1988; Ragins & McFarlin, 1990; Young & Perrewé, 2000b).

The Mentoring Exchange

Young and Perrewé (2000a) developed a theoretical framework of mentoring based on social exchange theory (Homans, 1958) and posited that mentors and protégés carry out an exchange of distinct but related career and social support behaviors. Moreover, in the course of the mentoring exchange, each partner incurs costs and benefits from participating in the relationship. Costs include time and energy spent with a mentoring partner or risks associated with participating in mentoring. Benefits include the tangible and intangible outcomes of participating in a successful mentorship. For the protégé, benefits may include job advancement (Ragins & Cotton, 1999) and feelings of support and concern from the mentor (Noe et al., 2002), whereas the mentor may experience higher career satisfaction (Hunt & Michael, 1983) and personal satisfaction (Scandura & Ragins, 1994). Examples of costs for a protégé may be time required to participate in the relationship or stress associated with challenging assignments. Costs for mentors could include time taken away from other pressing projects to work with a protégé or perceived responsibility for a protégé's poor performance. From a social exchange perspective, when the perceived benefits of participating in a relationship outweigh the perceived costs, the relationship is likely to continue. Perceptions used to evaluate costs and benefits of mentoring, according to Young and Perrewé (2000a), are based on the support received from a mentoring partner.

While it is granted that the mentor is the more experienced individual with expertise and willingness to be a mentor, Young and Perrewé proposed that the mentoring relationship goes beyond a mentor providing support and includes an exchange of behaviors related to career and social support. Thus both the mentor and the protégé receive and provide behavior related to career and social support. A mentor provides social and career support that will be reacted to by a protégé and a protégé exhibits certain behaviors related to social and career support that can elicit a response from the mentor. Thus for example, while the mentor provides social support in the form of showing concern for the protégé, the protégé reacts to that support behavior and provides the mentor with a reciprocal support behavior such as showing appreciation for the mentor's concern or showing a returned interest in the mentor. Another example involving career related behavior might be a mentor providing a protégé with the opportunity to work on a very challenging project that would be very beneficial to the protégé's career advancement. The protégé may accept the project with enthusiasm, thereby reciprocating the mentor's support behavior with a related behavior such as enthusiastic acceptance of the project. On the other hand, imagine that the protégé does not comprehend the importance of the project, shows little interest in the project and puts forth minimal effort to participate in the project. In this case, the protégé's reciprocal support behavior (i.e. reluctance to participate in the project) may be perceived negatively by the mentor and the mentor's reaction to the protégé will be much different than if the protégé welcomed the opportunity. So, the mentor's support behavior will elicit a response from the protégé and the protégé's reciprocal support behavior will elicit yet another behavior by the mentor. The cycle or exchange of support behaviors will continue and result in an overall evaluation of the success of and satisfaction with the relationship.

When both partners experience positive outcomes, at least to the point where the positive outcomes outweigh the negative outcomes, the relationship is likely to continue. To empirically test a portion of their model, Young and Perrewé (2000b) examined support behaviors received by mentors and protégés and found that mentors valued career related reciprocal support behaviors from protégés (e.g. heeding advise) while protégés valued social support behaviors from the mentor (e.g. showing concern). Satisfaction with levels of support received from a mentoring partner was related to feelings of satisfaction with the relationship. The study adds strength to the idea that mentors and protégés interpret and respond to a partner's actions and that the behavior of both the mentor and protégé impact relationship outcomes.

STRESS AND WELL BEING IN RELATION TO THE MENTORING PROCESS

Despite the interesting connections between stress, well being, and the mentoring process, there has not been much research across these literature bases. Several researchers have noted the importance of mentoring support in relation to positive attitudes and work outcomes (Allen et al., 1997a; Bahniuk et al., 1984; Scandura, 1997), thus alluding to stress-related factors such as social support and its importance to career success. However few researchers have specifically examined the direct connections and relationships between mentoring and stress processes (Kram & Hall, 1989; Viator, 2001).

Approaches and Models

Stress has been defined in many ways but typically involves an imbalance or reaction to perceived or objective demands and one's ability to meet those demands (Edwards & Cooper, 1990; Matteson & Ivancevich, 1987). Just as mentoring research includes aspects of person and environment, stress research acknowledges the importance of person and environment. However, while mentoring research has focused on isolated factors and the relationships among those factors, stress researchers have pondered and tested concepts and relationships from an interactive perspective and a transactional approach (Dewe, 2001). From an interactive perspective, the person and the environment are treated separately and the interaction between the two is of primary importance. The transactional perspective requires viewing the person and his or her environment as one (Lazarus, 1991), thus the weakness of isolating and investigating only the environment or person is acknowledged in stress literature.

Stress research has followed varied paths over the last few decades with a focus on individual and environmental factors ranging from dispositional factors such as self-efficacy to job-related factors such as job demand, support, and perceived control (cf. Xie & Schaubroeck, 2001). As in many disciplines, debate continues over fundamental approaches taken to study relationships among relevant factors in the stress process and terminology used to describe factors in the stress process (Dewe, 2001; Kahn & Byosiere, 1992). Xie and Schaubroeck (2001) provide an overview of stress models and identify relevant components in the stress process. Several relevant factors emerged based on predominant stress models. For example, Karasek's (1979) Job Demands – Control model posits an interaction between job demands and level of perceived discretion in decision making where jobs with high demand and low control are termed high-strain jobs. If levels of demand and control are balanced, less harmful effects and even positive results may occur. The Job-Demands – Control model has been widely used in stress research and aspects of Karasek's model have been used to extend the overall framework of stress (Johnson & Hall, 1988; Murphy, 2002). For example, Murphy (2002) presented an overview of the NIOSH (National Institute for Occupational Safety and Health) model of occupational stress which illustrates an interaction between job stressors and individual factors as well as an interaction between job stressors and non-work factors. Job stressors include job demands, organizational factors such as interpersonal relationships, management styles, and physical condition. Individual factors are identified as factors related to personality and career development, and non-work factors are noted as financial status and family situation. Job stressors are related to acute psychological, physiological, and behavioral reactions, but the relationship between job stressors and stress reactions is mediated by individual and non-work factors as well as by social support and coping. Acute reactions are depicted as leading to illness which in turn relates back to job stressors. From the varied approaches and models of the stress process, several themes and factors relevant to mentoring have emerged.

Common Themes and Factors

Several common themes and factors are present in mentoring and stress literature. For example, social support is a primary form of mentoring behavior. The role of support in stress models has been examined extensively and social support has been tested for main effects on stressors and strains, and mediating and moderating influences between stressors and strains (Beehr & Glazer, 2001). The most common view of social support is that it has buffering effects in the stressor-strain relationship and can minimize strain. Carlson and Perrewé (1999) tested social support in relation to stressors and work-family conflict, finding that social support emerged as an antecedent to strain. When individuals experienced social support, strain was minimized and less stress was perceived.

Social support in stress research includes tangible and intangible forms of support and the term has been used to cover a wide variety of behaviors (Beehr & Glazer, 2001; House, 1981). Mentoring researchers distinguish between types of support and label more emotional forms of support such as listening or befriending as social support and tangible forms of support such as providing useful information or technical advice as career support (i.e. instrumental, informational, or tangible) (Kram, 1985). The comparison of terminology from stress and mentoring literature is shown in Table 1.

Most mentoring research has remained fairly consistent in measuring behaviors related to one or more of Kram's functions (cf. Ragins & McFarlin, 1990). Beehr and Glazer (2001) recently provided an interesting explanation of support terminology in stress literature and delineated structural versus functional support. Whereas structural support is defined as simply belonging to supportive groups such as families, associates, etc., functional support focuses more directly on receiving support from one or more individuals. Within the category of functional support exists both emotional and instrumental support. Emotional support is any type of supportive behavior from another person that increases positive emotions.

Table 1. Support Terminology in Mentoring and Stress Research.

Mentoring (Kram, 1985)	Stress (Beehr & Glazer, 2001)
Career support	Structural support
Sponsorship	Supportive others, groups, associations
Exposure and visibility	
Coaching	Functional support
Protection	Emotional – enhancing emotions
Challenging assignments	Listening
	Paying attention
Social support	Showing concern
Acceptance and confirmation	
Counseling	Instrumental – providing assistance
Frienship	Mental or physical labor
	Financial resources
Role-modeling (Scandura & Ragins, 1993)	Information

Instrumental support more directly addresses stressors and includes tangible assistance in the form of information, financial or other resources, and sharing a workload, for example.

Although definitions of social support differ in stress and mentoring literature, the aspect of providing support to someone to abate stress is prevalent in both literature bases. For the purpose of this chapter, the terms based in mentoring research will be used and social support will refer to the more emotional and intangible types of support behaviors while career support will refer to the tangible, informational, or instrumental forms of support.

Related to social support and referred to as a buffer to stress, coping has been examined in stress literature as a factor that moderates the relationship between stressors and acute stress reactions. Beehr and Glazer (2001) make a clear distinction between support and coping by describing coping as actions taken by an individual while support is something that is provided by another person or group. In terms of coping methods, social networks and relationships were noted by Lazarus and Folkman (1984) as potentially effective problem-focused coping mechanisms. Thus initiating or continuing one or more mentorships in order to receive support would certainly fit the authors' definition of coping.

The authors describe coping as a process that begins with an appraisal of a situation and its potential threat to an individual's well being. Coping takes on two primary forms called problem-focused and emotion-focused coping. Problem-focused coping is indicative of behaviors that directly affect stressors and could be directed outward or inward. Outwardly directed problem-focused coping methods might include actions taken to change the environmental factors related to perceived stress while inwardly directed methods would be changes in thought or feeling. Emotion-focused coping methods include a reappraisal of a situation or event's meaning, thus a person does not change the situation or problem, but decides to change its significance or avoid the thought of it. The coping method depends, in part, upon the person's appraisal of the problem and subsequent perception of what can be done to solve the problem that is the source of distress (Lazarus & Folkman, 1984). Of course, the cognitive appraisal of a situation and consideration of appropriate coping methods would depend upon the person and his or her experiences. Thus whether or not mentoring would be considered as an appropriate coping strategy might depend upon many factors related to the situation and the person.

Personal characteristics are another factor that have been examined in stress and mentoring research. From a stress perspective, personal characteristics have been examined in terms of how people deal with stressors such as job demands (Schaubroeck & Merritt, 1997). From a mentoring perspective, personal characteristics have been used to explain whether or not people initiate or participate in mentoring (Turban & Dougherty, 1994) and the level of expectations formed for a mentoring partner (Young & Perrewé, 2004). There are some personal factors that are common to mentoring and stress research and include internal locus of control, self-esteem and self-efficacy. For example, Newton and Keenan (1990), found a relationship between locus of control and reaction to job demands. In mentoring research it has been shown that individuals with internal locus of control are more likely to initiate mentoring than individuals with external locus of control. Of course, the more often mentoring is initiated, the more often it is received. Self-esteem has also been a common factor across mentoring and stress research and noted by Murphy (2002) as one of the factors depicted in the NIOSH model of occupational stress as a factor moderating the relationship between environmental stressors and psychological, physiological, and behavioral reactions. In mentoring research, Kalbfleisch and Davies (1993) found a relationship between a protégé's communication competence and self-esteem, and a mentor's level of participation in the relationship.

Mentoring researchers have examined a laundry list of personality factors ranging from locus of control, self-esteem, affectivity, need for power, need for achievement, and emotional stability (Fagenson, 1992; Kalbfleisch & Davies, 1993; Noe, 1988; Turban & Dougherty, 1994) and have found these factors to be related to initiation of mentoring and mentoring received. While there are fewer personal variables that have been of specific interest in stress research, one personal factor common to mentoring and stress research that has been shown to play a key role in the relationship between stressors and physiological strain is self-efficacy. Self-efficacy, or the belief in one's ability to succeed at a task, has been posited by Noe (1988) as potentially useful in determining the extent to which individuals will initiate and participate in mentoring. However, the role of self-efficacy in mentoring has not been empirically verified. In stress research, Schaubroeck and Merritt (1997) proposed that self-efficacy interacts with job demands, control and stress outcomes. The authors found that having control decreases stress for individuals high in self-efficacy.

At the heart of stress research is the association between stressors and strain. Perrewé and Ganster (1989) summarized terminology and explained that stressors are related to environmental demands while strain reflects the response to stressors. Typical stressors used in stress research include such factors as conditions of the physical environment, role conflict and amiguity, control, overload, and self-esteem to name a few (cf. Murphy, 2002). Several of these factors also have been addressed by mentoring researchers. For example, mentoring is often loosely referred to as a means by which people can cope with career progression (Burke, 1984) or corporate crises (Kram & Hall, 1989), but few authors focus directly on the relationship between stress and mentoring.

RESEARCH ON STRESS AND MENTORING

Despite the potential for cross-disciplinary research, only two studies focus specifically on mentoring and stress. The most recent study was an examination of informal and formal mentoring in relation to role stress, job performance and turnover (Viator, 2001). The author found that having an informal mentor reduced a protégé's perception of role ambiguity. However, in some cases even though role ambiguity decreased, higher role conflict occurred, thus protégés often traded one stressor for another. The authors also found that individuals with formal mentors experienced fewer benefits than those with informal mentors.

Prior to Viator's work, Kram and Hall (1989) examined the relationship between perceived stress and mentoring, with a focus on whether or not a person's interest in participating in mentoring increased in relation to perceived stress. The authors presented interesting results in that both mentors and protégés had an increased interest in participating in mentoring relationships when jobs were perceived as stressful. Specifically, individuals with low levels of job involvement and challenge had the highest interest in developing mentorships. Despite the limited amount of research on stress and mentoring, there are many conceptual links and relationships that, if understood, would increase our knowledge of mentoring.

STRESS POINTS IN THE MENTORING PROCESS

The conceptual model shown in Fig. 1 illustrates areas for research on stress in mentoring by identifying major phases in the mentoring process and additional

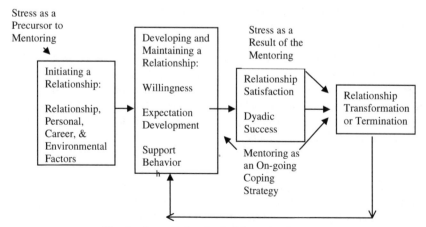

Fig. 1. Stress Points in the Mentoring Process.

components that are influential in each phase of the process. Specific stress points relevant at each phase are illustrated throughout the model and elaborated in the next few sections.

The first phase of relationship development is initiating a relationship and follows the first stress point in the mentoring process: stress as a precursor to mentoring.

Initiating a Relationship

The first step in the mentoring process, as shown in Fig. 1, is initiating a mentoring relationship. As with any relationship, there are several factors that influence whether or not two people become interested enough in each other to develop a relationship. Relationship factors (cf. Young & Perrewé, 2000a), personal traits (cf. Noe, 1988), career factors (cf. Young & Perrewé, 2000a), and environmental factors (cf. Allen et al., 1997a, b) have all been the focus of mentoring researchers and relate to initiating a mentoring relationship. Relationship factors include such issues as attraction, feelings toward mentoring, past mentoring experience, and the ability to thrive in a relationship (Fagenson-Eland et al., 1997; Noe et al., 2002; Young & Perrewé, 2000a). Personal factors have been examined extensively and include personal traits and characteristics such as gender, ethnicity, age, socioeconomic status, locus of control, and self-efficacy (Dreher & Cox, 1996; Noe, 1988; Thomas, 1990; Turban & Dougherty, 1994; Whitely et al., 1991; Young & Perrewé, 2004). Relevant career factors relate to individual progress, experience, and goals (Kram, 1985) and environmental factors deal with opportunities for mentoring, organizational climate (Allen et al., 1997a, b) and reward structures for participating in mentoring (Kram, 1985).

All relationships are dependent upon many factors for success, but mentorships have an added level of complexity in that the relationship must be managed, and the relationship is likely to have a profound affect on the organizational reputation and career progress of each person in the relationship. What draws us together, in any relationship, involves some factors that we can easily understand such as common interests or shared areas of expertise. But there are a multitude of factors that, while we may acknowledge their influence, are undeniably more difficult to measure such as attraction, liking, and respect. Because many of these factors are self-perceived we can ask people whether or not they feel attraction for another person, but it is less likely that we can predict or explain why or how these factors occur. For example, two people with a strong common interest or shared area of expertise would be likely to strike up a conversation and share information for at least a short period of time. Whether or not they would become attracted to one another and decide to develop a relationship is another, less predictable occurrence. Yet, this is precisely what mentoring researchers and mentoring program administrators must do, particularly in formal mentoring programs.

Researchers have explored relationship factors such as issues of attraction and relationship initiation extensively (Allen et al., 1997a; Aryee et al., 1996; Kram, 1985; Whitely et al., 1991). Primary findings indicate that attraction is necessary for two people to develop a successful relationship and that elements of attraction are different depending upon the type of relationship (Berscheid, 1994; Sprecher, 1998). Related to mentoring, attraction has been explored from the mentor's perspective and findings indicate that mentors are attracted to protégés who are perceived by the mentor to be competent and to have a high potential for success (Green & Bauer, 1995). Protégés are more likely to be attracted to mentors that have influence in the organization or are perceived to be powerful individuals (Ragins et al., 1998). From an even deeper psychological basis, Noe et al. (2002) suggested that the sense of security, or lack thereof, formed in childhood greatly influences our interest in and ability to develop healthy relationships.

Personal characteristics are another component of initiating relationships that have been the focus of much research. Perceived similarity based on ethnicity and gender has been found to increase the likelihood that a relationship will be perceived as satisfying (Ensher & Murphy, 1997; Feldman et al., 1999). Other factors such as high socieconomic status (Whitely et al., 1991) and personality characteristics of protégés such as self-esteem and internal locus of control (Turban & Dougherty, 1994) are related to the likelihood that someone will attempt to initiate a mentoring relationship. Gender has been examined as a factor related to relationship development and findings indicate no gender differences in willingness to mentor others (Allen et al., 1997b; Ragins & Cotton, 1993; Ragins & Scandura, 1994).

Career factors have not been as extensively researched as personal characteristics; however, we know that mentors often participate in mentoring to revitalize a career (Hunt & Michael, 1983) and that both mentors and protégés increase participation in mentoring when jobs are perceived as stressful (Kram & Hall, 1989). Likewise, both mentors and protégés have been found to seek out mentoring to increase information exchange (Mullen, 1994). Although given much less attention, environmental factors have been examined in relation to developing mentorships and organizations can create a climate that encourages or hinders heathly mentoring. Opportunities for mentoring, reward structures, and organizational climate have been identified as three variables likely to affect the mentoring exchange (Allen et al., 1997a; Kram, 1985). It is a fairly common belief that mentoring will enhance work and career attitudes and most research supports this belief; however, no mentoring research has been done to examine actual organizational actions taken to ensure that mentoring occurs. Developing an organizational climate in which mentoring is supported by all levels of management and human resource professionals in the organization would certainly provide encouragement to employees interested in mentoring. Further, tangible rewards for participating in mentoring or even bringing interested people together to form mentorships would be likely to increase mentoring support for individuals. As it stands, employees are likely to know that mentoring is important, but without an organization climate and reward structure in place to provide the necessary resources, it is likely that many potential mentorships will not be realized. It is interesting to note that job stressors, many of which are a product of the work environment and include management styles, role clarity, and physical conditions, all of which culminate into highly stressful conditions (Murphy, 2002), might be a stimulus that, once appraised by an individual, will lead to identification of an appropriate coping mechanism. Thus, stress itself may be an antecedent factor in the mentoring process and a partial answer to the question of why mentorships are initiated.

Stress as a Precursor to Mentoring
Stress as a precursor to mentoring is the first stress point illustrated in the model in Fig. 1 and while this stress point has not been examined explicitly, there certainly is reason to propose that perceived stress is a likely antecedent factor to initiating a mentoring relationship. What is typically known of mentors is that they, at the very least, can provide information based on experience and expertise. This would certainly qualify as instrumental support based on stress research and clearly fits the category of career-related support according to mentoring literature. From a protégé's perspective, Noe et al. (2002) suggested that the very existence of a mentoring relationship will abate stress. Using some of the main variables found in stress research such as job demands, control, social support, and self-efficacy, reasoning to consider stress as a precursor to mentoring will be presented.

Becoming a mentor. From the mentor's perspective, it may seem difficult at first glance to link stress to someone becoming a mentor. Why would a successful and busy person spend time and energy helping someone else develop a career? Research has focused primarily on protégés, but some researchers contend that mentors benefit from career revitalization, social recognition from peers and managers (Hunt & Michael, 1983; Kram, 1985), and feelings of personal satisfaction (Scandura & Ragins, 1994). In addition, there is some support for the idea that stress conditions precede participation in mentoring (Kram & Hall, 1989). For example, Kram and Hall (1989) found that during times of organizational uncertainty and stress, interest in participating in mentoring increased for mentors and protégés. This finding would appear to support stress as an antecedent factor in seeking or developing a mentorship; however, it should be noted that Kram and Hall measured attitudes toward mentoring. Using questions such as "I would have liked to receive more mentoring during my career" and "The idea of being of mentor is appealing to me. (pp. 497, 31–32)," the authors accurately assessed interest in mentoring. When perceived job stress increased, attitudes toward mentoring became more favorable.

In a healthy mentoring exchange, there is often a social interaction that takes place between a mentor and protégé and that interaction may be a useful distraction to an otherwise arduous job. Aryee et al. (1996) found that opportunities for interaction was a significant factor related to an individual's motivation to mentor others. Additionally, as any teacher knows, the act of teaching others often serves as a catalyst to learning. Working with a protégé could certainly be a reason to remain interested in learning new issues and skills. The stage of career development also plays a role in likelihood to participate in mentoring (Kram, 1985; Levinson et al., 1978). Although it was originally thought that individuals in mid-career, about the age of 40, would be most likely to initiate and participate in mentoring, Kram and Hall (1989) found that younger individuals in early career stages and older individuals in late career stages were more likely to participate in mentoring. The authors suggested that during mid-career, there is such a strong focus on career development that mentoring someone may not be feasible. The fact that more individuals in a late career stage, or over the age of 50, were more likely to look favorably upon starting a mentorship could be an indicant that once an individual's career is well-established, the thought of working with a protégé is appealing. Moreover, perhaps individuals in a late career stage would perceive more personal benefit than someone in mid-career. Therefore, it is not unreasonable to think that a mentor may seek a protégé to abate stress.

Becoming a protégé. From the protégé's perspective, it is clear that a healthy mentoring relationship would offer career and social support to advance a protégé's career and improve a protégé's ability to deal with challenging or emotional situations. Career benefits of mentoring have been shown by several researchers (Kram, 1985; Ragins & Cotton, 1999; Ragins et al., 2000; Scandura, 1992). Researchers have found that mentoring also is an effective form of social support in organizations (Scandura, 1997). However, social support is only one form of support provided in mentoring relationships and, from a career development view, not the most necessary form of support. In fact, if career progress is a primary reason for participating in mentoring and a person is facing challenges in his or her career, social support may abate negative feelings about a lack of career progress, but it probably will not change career prospects.

Yet, individuals may be inclined to seek more emotional forms of support when under stress. From a stress perspective, depending upon the cognitive appraisal of the situation, a problem-focused or emotion-focused method of coping will be decided upon and associated behaviors will take place (Lazarus & Folkman, 1984). However, one must consider the stimuli present at any given time, including stressors that make the protégé feel overwhelmed or are perceived as harmful such as role amiguity or conflict, career planning, work-family balance demands, group conflicts, work overload or supervisor relations. First, will mentoring be something that is considered as an appropriate coping strategy? In addition, will mentoring actively be sought out or will support of peers, friends or family members be a substitute for more problem-focused coping methods? Finally, given the circumstances of the individual, having someone who provides social support (i.e. emotional) may squelch the need for more career-related support (i.e. instrumental, tangible). Whether or not mentoring will be initiated in reaction to job stress will depend upon the situation, how the situation is interpreted, and individual factors related to the person.

Mentor and protégé self-efficacy. Self-efficacy is the belief one holds in regard to his or her abilities to succeed at a task (Bandura, 1986; Wood & Bandura, 1989). Based on the cognitive appraisal of a situation, an appropriate coping strategy will be enacted. Self-efficacy has been suggested by stress researchers as a relevant component that may, in part, determine the coping strategy enacted and individuals high in self-efficacy may be more inclined to develop coping strategies that increase control (Xie & Schaubroeck, 2001).

Schaubroeck and Merritt (1997) found that depending upon a person's self-efficacy perceived control could have positive or negative effects. For individuals high in self-efficacy, having control decreased stress outcomes, but low levels of control was found to be particularly harmful as individuals had a strong belief that they should be able to impact results. For individuals low in self-efficacy, high demand – high control jobs were related to negative health consequences due to experienced stress. In fact, having control exacerbated stress outcomes for individuals with low self-efficacy. If initiating mentoring were used appropriately as a means to gain perceived control in an otherwise stressful situation, then high self-efficacy mentors and protégés would certainly reap the benefits of participating in mentoring.

The idea that self-efficacy is related to initiating mentoring is suggested in research. Noe (1988) identified self-efficacy as an important predictor of whether or not a person would initiate mentoring, stating that those individuals high in self-efficacy are more likely to seek help in career and job development. Thus self-efficacy may play an important role not only in how a situation is managed but also whether or not mentoring may be initiated by a protégé as a coping strategy to abate stress.

From the mentor's perspective, it would appear that people interested in being a mentor would be higher in self-efficacy than individuals who choose not to be mentors. Mentors are individuals who are expected to have a considerable amount of expertise as well as organizational acumen. Mentors also incur considerable risks in that a protégé's actions reflect upon the mentor (Kram, 1985). Mentoring researchers have stated that traditional mentors are those individuals who have experience and expertise, and organizations would only select people who meet a certain level of success (Hunt & Michael, 1983). Moreover, Green and Bauer (1995) point out that mentors are more attracted to protégés who appear to have a high level of competence and a promising career ahead of them. Given a mentor's responsibilities, it would seem unlikely that a mentor would lack confidence in his or her abilities. To lack such confidence and become a mentor would be like shining a beacon on one's perceived shortcomings.

While the possibility that mentors may have higher self-efficacy than non-mentors seems reasonable in informal mentorships, formal mentoring programs may yield different results. In some formal mentoring programs it may be more difficult to predict self-efficacy of mentors. Formal mentoring programs are typically locked into a curriculum of sorts with a start and end date and, in the worst case, may not use a selection method based on expertise and willingness, but merely a reluctance to refuse to participate in the program.

Developing and Maintaining a Relationship

The initiation phase of the relationship eventually progresses to the cultivation stage where the mentor and protégé focus on productivity (Kram, 1983). This stage can be the most productive and challenging phase of the relationship as the mentor and protégé experience more tangible and challenging events throughout the mentoring exchange.

As shown in Fig. 1, the mentoring relationship is developed into maturity and maintained as long as needed. This stage in the mentoring process is influenced by mentor and protégé willingness to commit to working together, developing expectations for a mentoring partner, and exchanging support behaviors with a mentoring partner. If the mentor and protégé are both willing to develop the relationship, each partner is likely to develop expectations for the relationship and a mentoring partner. It is at this point where an exchange of support behaviors takes place (Young & Perrewé, 2000a). In one study on expectations of mentors and protégés, it was found that among a sample of doctoral students and dissertation advisors, students (i.e. protégés) valued social support behaviors of mentors while chairs (i.e. mentors) valued career-related behaviors of protégés (Young & Perrewé, 2000b). Thus, while protégés found a mentor's shows of concern, liking, and friendship valuable, mentors focused on a protégé's career-related behavior such as accepting challenging assignments and heeding career advice. This division of perspectives sheds light on a deeper problem in any relationship, that is, differing expectations and valuation of the relationship and its outcomes.

Related to stress, if mentors believe that the relationship is for the progress and development of the protégé, but the protégé is waiting for the mentor to engage in more social forms of support, a division of expectations will soon create stress for one or both partners. As the relationship progresses, an evaluation of whether or not the relationship is providing an effective and satisfying means of support may be used to determine whether or not the relationship should continue. However, if the relationship is satisfying to both mentoring partners, support behavior exchanged throughout the relationship may minimize perceived stress. Mentoring as an on-going coping strategy is the next stress point in the mentoring process and is illustrated in the model.

Mentoring as an On-Going Coping Strategy

Career and social support exchanged by a mentor and protégé could certainly deem the relationship valuable enough to consider continuing the relationship. Social support in particular has been noted as a moderator that abates stress (Kram & Hall, 1989) and both career and social support have been linked to many benefits related to general career progression of a protégé. When a mentor or protégé evaluate the relationship and determine whether or not the benefits of the relationship outweigh costs, reduction of strain or reduction of problems causing stress is likely to be a factor of considerable importance. Noe et al. (2002) proposed that the very existence of a mentoring relationship could diminish perceived stress and forms of social support have been shown to reduce perceived stress (Carlson & Perrewé, 1999). Thus, it is possible that mentoring may be used as an on-going coping strategy to minimize perceptions of stress for mentors and protégés. An analysis and understanding of the appraisal processes of mentors and protégés throughout the development of relationships would add much to our understanding of building healthy mentoring exchanges. Further, understanding a mentoring partner's evaluation of exchange behaviors would help us to understand whether or not mentoring is used as an on-going coping strategy.

Relationship Satisfaction

A determining component of whether to continue a relationship is relationship satisfaction, as illustrated in the model in Fig. 1. Underlying relationship satisfaction is the success of the dyad itself, that is the satisfaction perceived by the mentor and protégé. One of the key aspects of having a mentor is the fact that ambiguity and uncertainty in one's job is lessened by the mentor's expertise, power in the organization, and personal concern (Hunt & Michael, 1983; Kram, 1985; Ragins & Scandura, 1994). Similarly, mentors benefit from and value interaction with others (Aryee et al., 1996). Therefore, a mentor or protégé may realize that among the benefits of a healthy mentoring exchange is stress reduction and depending upon the continued career circumstances of both mentoring partners, stress reduction may be viewed as one reason to continue the relationship.

Relationship Transformation or Termination

At some point in the relationship, a separation phase takes place (Kram, 1985) and the mentor and protégé cease working together. The last component of the mentoring process is the step at which a mentor or protégé decides to transform the relationship into something that accommodates one or both mentoring partners' newfound career development and responsibilities or to end the relationship. Of course, the separation stage may not necessarily last for a extended period of time and the transition from separation to transformation may be smooth and natural, even transparent, in some healthy mentoring relationships. However, after one or both mentoring partners decides that working together as mentor and protégé is not the best arrangement, a decision must be made about what form, if any, a new relationship will take. Mentors and protégés who have developed a close personal relationship may continue a friendship or collegial working relationship. If one of the mentoring partners decides to separate before the other wishes, relationship termination may result in bitterness and anger.

A part of the decision to transform or terminate the relationship will depend upon an overall evaluation of relationship satisfaction and the tangible and emotional outcomes of the relationship (Young & Perrewé, 2000a). Some of these outcomes include the extent to which the relationship is necessary and the extent to which the relationship itself has resulted in positive or negative outcomes, including stress, for one or both mentoring partners. The next section deals with the last stress point illustrated in the model: stress as a result of mentoring. Positive and negative stress as a result of mentoring must be considered in deciding to continue, transform, or terminate the relationship.

Stress as a Result of Mentoring
Typically mentoring researchers focus on positive aspects of mentoring for both mentoring partners. While there is no doubt that mentoring has positive benefits, recently there has been some evidence that negative experiences and dysfunctional relationships occur with harmful and costly results in terms of career progress and emotions (Eby & Allen, 2002; Scandura, 1998). Although mentoring may be initiated to alleviate stress, participating in a relationship can expose a mentor or protégé to stressors. Thus, stress may not only be an antecedent factor to initiating mentoring, but also stress may be a result of mentoring.

Oh mentor, my mentor!. Many positive aspects of mentoring have been identified for both mentors and protégés (cf. Kram, 1985; Whitely et al., 1992). Therefore, it isn't difficult to understand why mentoring, in its best sense, could reduce a person's perceived stress in organizational life. Career support such as sponsorship and visibility are clearly needed for career success and social support certainly enhances a protégé's ability to meet stressful job demands. Mentoring has been shown to abate stress, and career and social support is closely linked to types of social support examined in stress literature and related to reducing psychological strain.

Interestingly, however, as a protégé progresses in his or her career and receives mentoring he or she will also be receiving opportunities to take on more challenging and difficult assignments. Therefore, as a protégé receives more mentoring, higher job demands may be placed on him or her. For example, as a mentor provides career support such as visibility in the organization, the protégé must present himself or herself to influential others in the organization and risk having his or competence evaluated. As a mentor provides the protégé with increasingly difficult opportunities, there must be sufficient technical assistance and social support to increase the protégé's self-efficacy to the point where the demands of the new assignment will be outweighed by feelings of mastery and excellent performance.

Additionally, mentoring makes an individual visible in the organization in many respects. Some are obviously good, such as being able to work with others of influence in the organization and vicariously experiencing the benefits of a mentor's network (i.e. structural support in stress research). However, some aspects of visibility may not be as beneficial. For example, having a mentor may appear to be a form of favoritism and will not be interpreted favorably by peers. Thus while protégés may reap the career-related benefits of mentoring, co-worker support or reputation in the organization may be negatively impacted thereby exacerbating stress.

On a slightly more positive note, it could be that a mentor directly creates positive stress for a protégé. In their discussion of executives as creators of positive stress in a work environment, Quick et al. (2004) explained that there may be optimum levels of stress that lead to increased job performance and personal satisfaction. The authors note that appropriate and clear goals, excellent communication, and an openness to explore and learn, to name a few components, create an environment in which a person may experience positive stress. A mentor, for example, who provides social support along with sufficient career support and who can work with the protégé to balance emotions during challenging work assignments could very well create a situation in which the protégé would experience positive performance outcomes and increased personal satisfaction.

Oh mentor, my tormentor!. Unfortunately mentoring relationships do not always yield positive experiences for protégés. Researchers are beginning to uncover aspects and outcomes of dysfunctional relationships and how these unhealthy mentorships impact organizational behavior and have severe negative effects for the organization and mentoring partners (Eby & Allen, 2002; Scandura, 1998). Five primary categories of negative experiences were presented by Eby and Allen (2002) and included a mismatch within the mentoring dyad, distancing behaviors, manipulative behaviors, lack of expertise, and general dysfunctionality. Some of the specific negative effects range from generally mismatched personalities of the mentor and protégé to abuse of power, sabotage, and incompetence. According to the authors, negative experiences incurred in formal relationships had a greater impact on intentions to turnover than did negative experiences of protégés in informal relationships.

A mentor may cause distress by engaging in one or more obviously abusive behaviors such as taking credit for a protégé's work, deceiving the protégé, or generally abusing power. Imagine a protégé's dismay when a relationship that was created with the intention of providing benefits to abate stress becomes instead a focal stressor. To end the relationship would potentially yield additional negative effects, but to continue the relationship would mean continued distress. These negative outcomes clearly could be categorized as stressors and argued to have profoundly negative effects on a protégé's career and health.

A mentor may also create distress for a protégé unintentionally, perhaps by providing insufficient amounts of social support or advising a protégé in a way that the protégé does not understand. For example, asking a protégé to complete assignments of which the protégé does not clearly understand the importance could create distress. In this case, the mentor probably does not intend to cause distress but has done so by providing support that is neither valued nor understood by the protégé. Mentors and protégés have been shown to differ in expectations of support and, often, protégés may value behaviors that do not necessarily lead directly to career attainment (Young & Perrewé, 2000b).

Beyond engaging in obviously abusive behavior or engaging in support behavior that unintentionally causes distress, there may be another form of mentoring behavior that purposefully causes a certain amount of distress but for a positive outcome. Just as emotion and problem-focused coping often work in unison (Lazarus & Folkman, 1984), a mentor may at times, find it necessary to allow the protégé the opportunity to experience some discomfort in the learning process. An important part of creativity is learning and risk-taking, and often learning comes from a state of discomfort or dissatisfaction with the status quo (Csikszentmihalyi, 1996). Thus, at times, the mentor may choose to allow the protégé to feel discomfort, at least to the point where the protégé would be motivated to take action or inquire as to how to resolve a problem, but not to the point where the protégé becomes disheartened. Certainly purposely creating a stressful environment is not what mentoring entails; however, a unique perspective of mentoring, that probably few mentors could fulfill, would be this balance of learning and support that creates, in the long-run, the most positive emotional and tangible outcomes possible.

The mentor's perspective. Research about the mentor's perspective on relationship development or mentoring outcomes has been scant in comparison to the extensive research on proteges (cf. Allen et al., 1997b). From a stress perspective, mentoring could cause stress simply because the mentor is taking responsibility for another person, and the actions of the protégé will reflect positively and negatively on the mentor. While a person with a well-established career may be able to deal with negative impacts of a protégé's failure or lack of performance, it would not be appealing to anyone in a mentoring role to be associated with an unsuccessful protégé. In addition, mentoring others is work and the additional workload from advising one or more protégés may become a burden depending upon a mentor's personal and career goals.

Beyond the most obvious stressors such as a protégé's behavior and work overload, the role of mentor is difficult and challenging. To balance the necessary career support with sufficient amounts of social support is a demanding and challenging task for a mentor, regardless of how much experience and wisdom he or she has accumulated.

Researchers have examined the extent to which mentoring behaviors are enacted (i.e. coaching, protection, visibility, etc.), but little has been done to explore the points in time at which a mentor steps in to provide support or the extent to which a mentor enacts specific support behaviors. It would be beneficial to focus on specific decisions and behaviors enacted by the mentor. Specific interventions in the form of decisions and actions taken need to be understood to begin teaching people how to mentor. A focus on this level of decision making and action puts the mentor in the role of diagnostician, meaning that a mentor must not only know what behaviors to enact but when and to what degree given a specific situation and with a specific protégé. In becoming a diagnostician of sorts, the mentor would be able to create healthier and successful exchanges that are less likely to be a source of stress for either mentoring partner and more likely to yield expected benefits.

DIRECTIONS FOR FUTURE RESEARCH

Directions for future research are open to many possibilities as the relationships between stress and mentoring are relatively unexplored. Despite the many potential relationships and common themes, little is known about stress in relation to the mentoring process. Given the profound impact stress has on individual health and well being and the widespread belief that mentoring is not only beneficial but essential to career development, bridging these two literature bases would enhance our understanding of stress and mentoring processes.

Related Themes in Stress and Mentoring

Exploring through empirical testing, the connections and related themes in mentoring and stress research would broaden our understanding of both processes. Generally speaking, mentoring researchers have focused on mentoring provided to protégés and positive outcomes associated with receipt of mentoring. Within these two aspects of mentoring research, a more thorough examination of protégé behaviors in relation to mentoring received would increase our understanding of the mentoring process. In addition, behavior of mentors has been examined, but only from a broad perspective and typically from the protégé's viewpoint. Given the changing nature of career development and the increased emphasis on alternative forms of mentoring and career development (Allen & Finklestein, 2003; Higgins & Thomas, 2001), it is important to understand specific behaviors related to each form of developmental support.

The first stress point illustrated in the model suggests that stress acts as a precursor to initiating mentoring relationships. For example, from a theoretical perspective, Noe et al. (2002) used attachment theory, that is the extent to which we form a secure base as children influences our ability to develop healthy relationships as adults, to explain why some people might be more attracted than others to mentoring and why some mentors and protégés might be able to develop healthy relationships while others fail. The stress-related implications from the authors' proposition are quite profound. If the theory as applied to mentoring holds true, then developing mentoring relationships would be a likely response to a stressful environment and the very existence of a mentoring relationship would abate perceived stress. Beyond the more psychological basis for why we seek mentoring, other factors related to the relationship, the person, career, and the environment should be clearly identified and examined in terms of stress as a precursor to mentoring.

Both mentors and protégés should be the focus of studies related to why mentoring is initiated and the role of stress in initiating mentoring. Differentiating among the many emerging forms of developmental relationships and perceived stress will be critical to future research. Linking perceived stress to types of mentoring and developmental relationships will provide useful findings for individual career management and managers. For example, human resource managers or mentoring program administrators might plan to use formal mentoring to enhance the organizational climate or reduce perceived job stress, but will that formal mentoring program really deliver the benefits expected? Moreover, will informal traditional mentorships, that is, a more experienced senior person voluntarily paired with a less experience person, be the most effective relationship in terms of tangible and intangible outcomes such as career progress or perceived job and career stress. Finally, will social support or technical advice received from peers or groups of co-workers yield appropriate and sufficient benefits, particularly tangible benefits associated with traditional mentoring? Issues related to stress as an impetus to seek out mentoring or other forms of developmental support have yet to be explored thoroughly, but investigation of such issues will provide valuable insights into stress and mentoring processes.

Using mentoring as an on-going coping strategy, the second stress point illustrated in the model, is another area open to investigation. Stress research could shed light on the mentoring process by delineating support behaviors for mentoring and for other forms of developmental support. Clearly delineating the different aspects of support such as structural, functional-emotional, and functional-instrumental in terms of specific benefits would add much to our understanding of the importance of each form of mentoring. Exchanges of behavior between a mentor and protégé and the related influences on perceived stress are interesting and challenging topics for mentoring and stress researchers. Likewise, the changing levels of perceived stress across the stages of the mentoring process and its effects on the behaviors of mentors and protégés would be fruitful avenues of future research. The challenge for researchers is distinguishing among factors relevant to mentors, protégés, and the dyadic exchange created by the pair. In addition, dyads must be considered within the job and organizational context in which the relationship takes place. For other configurations of support networks such as peer groups, identifying factors relevant to the group dynamic would be important. Further, distinguishing between job-related stress and stress related to the mentoring relationship itself would be required to understand the nature of stress and mentoring, particularly in terms of using stress as an on-going coping strategy.

The last stress point in the model, stress as a result of the relationship, deals with stress created from the relationship itself. Stress could result from outcomes of the relationship (e.g. reactions to the relationship from peers or others in the organization), changing demands or responsibilities on the part of one or both partners, or from the feelings accumulated from working together. Decisions to end or transform the relationship, and the backlash or perceived effects of doing either are potential stressors as well. Even transforming a healthy mentorship into a close friendship could, for some, be perceived as stressful. Examining perceived stress and specific stressors in this stage of the mentoring process would add much to our understanding of mentoring and help individuals interested in participating in mentoring manage associated feelings and the relationship more effectively.

Differentiating Among Effects

Stress research has provided a rigorous examination of the roles of key factors such as social support (cf. Murphy, 2002). Mentoring researchers must delve into not only the factors relevant to the mentoring process but also the specific role each factor plays in the process. For example, the role of social support has been examined from many perspectives including mediating and moderating effects (Beehr & Glazer, 2001; Carlson & Perrewé, 1999). Similar types of analyses would add much to our understanding of existing theoretical models of mentoring. Young and Perrewé (2000a) presented a process model of mentoring and posited several connections related to the relationship, person, career, environment, relationship development process, and willingness to mentor and be mentored. Further, the authors posited that these antecedent factors would influence expectations for support and evaluation of support behaviors. Both mentors and protégés were posited to engage in distinct but related behaviors and the evaluation of the exchange of behaviors would influence the perceptions of relationship success and satisfaction. While some of the relationships posited by Young and Perrewé have been verified, few mentoring researchers focus on forms of influence such as interaction, mediating, or moderating effects of factors related to the mentoring process (Young & Perrewé, 2000b). Examining stress points throughout the mentoring process and their effects would add complexity to the research process, but also would add valuable knowledge and increase our depth of understanding of the mentoring process.

Research Methods

Beyond the factors related to mentoring and stress processes, self-report and survey research has been the mainstay in mentoring and occupational stress research. However, stress researchers have examined far more physiological reactions to job stressors than have mentoring researchers, due to the fact that stress has a direct link to health. In mentoring for example, most research is cross-sectional and often viewed only from the perspective of a mentor or protégé. The interaction between the mentor and protégé and the components relevant to the mentoring dyad such as dyadic success have been examined far less (Eby & Allen, 2002). Examining the mentoring dyad over the long-run is also a necessary step in advancing research. Learning about perceived stress and typical stressors at each stage in the mentoring process throughout the relationship would add depth to our understanding of these unique relationships.

Typically mentor and protégé perceptions are interpreted through surveys on a Likert-type scale to indicate the extent that behavior was enacted or mentoring was received (cf. Ragins & McFarlin, 1990). In some cases, researchers adapted surveys to more specifically define behaviors relevant to a work setting (cf. Noe, 1988). A richer method of study such as an examination of the dyad itself would enhance mentoring research. Again, taking issues from stress research, Lazarus (1991) emphasized the importance of examining the person within the context of his or her environment, thus taking a transactional approach to the study of stress. The same idea could be used in mentoring research to acknowledge that examining a mentor or protégé without understanding each person's environment, past experience, disposition, etc. ignores a potentially important discoveries. Further, examining a mentor's behavior without knowing the protégé and vice versa or studying a mentoring dyad without analyzing the environmental context of the dyad overlooks important aspects of the mentoring process. Perhaps the answer, in part, lies in the process by which we study mentoring. A greater acceptance of qualitative exploration and willingness to commit to longitudinal research would greatly enhance mentoring research.

CONCLUSION

This chapter focuses on specific aspects of stress and well being in the mentoring process. The mentoring process, described as a relationship that progresses through several stages in which an exchange of support behaviors takes place, has within it events and issues that are closely related to stress. Important aspects of stress such as appraisal and coping, support, job stressors, and other factors can clearly be seen in the mentoring process. Stress points at each stage of relationship development have been presented and elaborated including stress as a precursor to mentoring, mentoring as an on-going coping strategy, and stress as a result of mentoring.

Despite the many common themes and factors in stress and mentoring research, few attempts have been made to explicitly examine stress issues in relation to mentoring and vice versa. Developing a broader stream of research that bridges these two literature bases would certainly enhance mentoring research and add a new perspective to stress literature. Although stress and mentoring, separately, have been extensively researched, the association of stress in relation to the mentoring process is relatively unexplored and would yield interesting and useful findings to broaden our understanding of stress and mentoring processes.

ACKNOWLEDGMENTS

The author wishes to acknowledge and express thanks to Dr. Jon S. Bailey, Department of Psychology, Florida State University, for applying the term diagnostitian to mentorship.

REFERENCES

Allen, T. D., & Finklestein, L. M. (2003). Beyond mentoring: Alternative sources and functions of developmental support. *The Career Development Quarterly, 51*(4), 346.

Allen, T. D., Poteet, M. L., & Burroughs, S. M. (1997a). A field study of factors related to supervisors' willingness to mentor others. *Journal of Vocational Behavior, 50*, 1–22.

Allen, T. D., Poteet, M. L., Russell, J. E. A., & Dobbins, G. H. (1997b). The mentor's perspective: A qualitative inquiry and future research agenda. *Journal of Vocational Behavior, 51*, 70–89.

Aryee, S., Chay, Y. W., & Chew, J. (1996). The motivation to mentor among managerial employees: An interactionist approach. *Group and Organization Management, 21*, 261–277.

Bahniuk, M., Dobos, J., & Hill, S. (1990). The impact of mentoring, collegial support, and information adequacy on career success: A replication. Handbook of replication research in the behavioral and social sciences [special issue]. *Journal of Social Behavior and Personality, 5*, 431–451.

Beehr, T. A., & Glazer, S. (2001). A cultural perspective of social support in relation to occupational stress. In: P. L. Perrewé & D.C. Ganster (Eds), *Research in Occupational Stress and Well Being: Exploring Theoretical Mechanisms and Perspectives* (Vol. 1, pp. 97–142). New York: JAI Press, Elsevier.

Berscheid, E. (1994). Interpersonal relationships. *Annual Review of Psychology, 45*, 79–129.

Burke, R. J. (1984). Mentors in organizations. *Group and Organization Studies, 9*(3), 353–372.

Carlson, D. S., & Perrewé, P. L. (1999). The role of social support in the stressor-strain relationship: An examination of work-family conflict. *Journal of Management, 25*, 513–540.

Chao, G. T., Walz, P., & Gardner, P. (1992). Formal and informal mentorships: A comparison on mentoring functions and contrast with nonmentored counterparts. *Personnel Psychology, 45,* 618–636.

Csikszentmihalyi, M. (1996). *Creativity: The flow and the psychology of discovery and invention.* New York: HarperCollins.

Dewe, P. J. (2001). Work stres, coping and well being: Implementing strategies to better understand the relationships. In: P. L. Perrewé & D. C. Ganster (Eds), *Research in Occupational Stress and Well Being: Exploring Theoretical Mechanisms and Perspectives* (Vol. 1, pp. 63–96). New York: JAI Press, Elsevier.

Dreher, G. F., & Cox, T. H. (1996). Race, gender, and opportunity: A study of compensation attainment and the establishment of mentoring relationships. *Journal of Applied Psychology, 81*(3), 297–308.

Dreher, G. F., & Dougherty, T. W. (1997). Substitutes for career mentoring: Promoting equal opportunity through career management and assessment systems. *Journal of Vocational Behavior, 51*(1), 110–124.

Eby, L. T. (1997). Alternative forms of mentoring in changing organizational environments: A conceptual extension of the mentoring literature. *Journal of Vocational Behavior, 51,* 125–144.

Eby, L. T., & Allen, T. D. (2002). Further investigation of protégés' negative mentoring experiences. *Group & Organization Management, 27*(4), 456–479.

Edwards, J. R., & Cooper, C. L. (1990). The person-environment fit approach to stress: Recurring problems and some suggested solutions. *Journal of Organizational Behavior, 11,* 293–307.

Ensher, E. A., & Murphy, S. E. (1997). Effects of race, gender, perceived similarity, and contact on mentor relationships. *Journal of Vocational Behavior, 50*(3), 460–481.

Fagenson-Eland, E. A., Marks, M. A., & Amendola, K. L. (1997). Perceptions of mentoring relationships. *Journal of Vocational Behavior, 51,* 29–42.

Feldman, D. C., Folks, W. R., & Turnley, W. H. (1999). Mentor-protégé diversity and its impact on international internship experiences. *Journal of Organizational Behavior, 20*(5), 597–611.

Green, S. G., & Bauer, T. N. (1995). Supervisory mentoring by advisers: Relationships with doctoral student potential, productivity, and commitment. *Personnel Psychology, 48,* 537–561.

Higgins, M. C., & Thomas, D. A. (2001). Constellations and careers: Toward understanding the effects of multiple developmental relationships. *Journal of Organizational Behavior, 22*(3), 223.

Hunt, D., & Michael, C. (1983). Mentorship: A career training and development tool. *Academy of Management Review, 8,* 475–485.

Homans, G. C. (1958). Social behavior as exchange. *American Journal of Sociology, 63,* 597–606.

House, J. S. (1981). *Work stress and social support.* Reading, MA: Addison-Wesley.

Jamal, M. (1990). Relationship of job stress and Type-A behavior to employees' job satisfaction, organizational commitment, psychosomatic health problems, and turnover motivation. *Human Relations, 43,* 727–738.

Johnson, J. V., & Hall, E. M. (1988). Job strain, workplace social support and cardiovascular disease: A cross-sectional study of a random sample of Swedish working population. *American Journal of Public Health, 78,* 1336–1342.

Kahn, R. L., & Byosiere, P. (1992). Stress in organizations. In: M. D. Dunnette & L. M. Hough (Eds), *Handbook of Industrial/Organizational Psychology* (pp. 571–650). Palo Alto, CA: Consulting Psychologists Press.

Kalbfleisch, P., & Davies, A. (1993). An interpersonal model for participation in mentoring relationships. *Western Journal of Vocational Behavior, 57*, 399–415.

Karasek, R. A. (1979). Job demands, job decision latitude, and mental strain: Implications for job redesign. *Administrative Science Quarterly, 24*, 285–310.

Kram, K. (1983). Phases of the mentor relationship. *Administrative Science Quarterly, 26*, 608–625.

Kram, K. (1985). *Mentoring at work*. Glenview, IL: Scott, Foresman and Company.

Kram, K., & Hall, D. T. (1989). Mentoring as an antidote to stress during corporate trauma. *Human Resource Management, 28*(4), 493–510.

Kram, K., & Isabella, L. A. (1985). Mentoring alternatives: The role of peer relationships in career development. *Academy of Management Journal, 28*, 110–132.

Lazarus, R. S. (1991). Psychological stress in the workplace. In: P. L. Perrewé (Ed.), Handbook on job stress [Special Issue]. *Journal of Social Behavior and Personality, 6*, 1–13.

Lazarus, R. S., & Folkman, S. (1984). *Stress, appraisal and coping*. New York: Springer.

Levinson, D. J., Darrow, C. N., Klein, E. B., Levinson, M. A., & McKee, B. (1978). *Seasons of a man's life*. New York: Knopf.

Manning, M. R., Jackson, C. N., & Fusilier, M. R. (1996). Occupational stress, social support, and the costs of health care. *Academy of Management Journal, 39*, 738–750.

Matteson, M. T., & Ivancevich, J. M. (1987). *Controlling work stress: Effective human resource and management strategies*. San Francisco: Jossey-Bass.

Mullen, E. (1994). Framing the mentoring relationship in an information exchange. *Human Resource Management Review, 4*, 257–281.

Murphy, L. R. (2002). Job stress at NIOSH: 1972–2002. In: P. L. Perrewé & D. C. Ganster (Eds), *Research in Occupational Stress and Well Being: Historical and Current Perspectives on Stress and Health* (Vol. 2, pp. 1–56). New York: JAI Press, Elsevier.

Nelson, D. L., & Burke, R. J. (2000). Women executives: Health, stress, and success. *Academy of Management Executive, 14*(2), 107–121.

Newton, T. J., & Keenan, A. (1990). The moderating effects of the Type A behavior pattern and locus of control upon the relationship between change in job demands and change in psychological strain. *Human Relations, 43*(12), 1229–1255.

Noe, R. A. (1988). An investigation of the determinants of successful assigned mentoring relationships. *Personnel Psychology, 41*, 457–479.

Noe, R. A., Greenberger, D. B., & Wang, S. (2002). Mentoring: What we know and where we might go. In: G. R. Ferris & J. J. Martocchio (Eds), *Research in Personnel and Human Resource Management* (Vol. 21, pp. 129–173). New York: JAI Press, Elsevier.

Perrewé, P. L., & Ganster, D. C. (1989). The impact of job demands and behavioral control on experience job stress. *Journal of Organizational Behavior, 10*, 213–229.

Quick, J. C., Mack, D., Gavin, J., Cooper, C. L., & Quick, J. D. (2004). Executives: Engines for positive stress. In: P. L. Perrewé & D. C. Ganster (Eds), *Emotional and Physiological Processes and Positive Intervention Strategies* (Vol. 3, pp. 359–405). New York: JAI Press, Elsevier.

Ragins, B. R., & Cotton, J. (1993). Gender and willingness to mentor. *Journal of Management, 19*, 97–111.

Ragins, B. R., & Cotton, J. (1999). Mentor functions and outcomes: A comparison of men and women in formal and informal mentoring relationships. *Journal of Applied Psychology, 84*(4), 529–549.

Ragins, B. R., Cotton, J., & Miller, J. S. (2000). Marginal mentoring: The effects of type of mentor, quality of relationship, and program design on work and career attitudes. *Academy of Management Journal, 43*, 1177–1210.

Ragins, B. R., & McFarlin, D. B. (1990). Perceptions of mentor roles in cross-gender mentoring relationships. *Journal of Vocational Behavior, 37*(3), 321–339.

Ragins, B. R., & Scandura, T. (1994). Gender differences in expected outcomes of mentoring relationships. *Academy of Management Journal, 37,* 957–971.

Ragins, B. R., Townsend, B., & Mattis, M. (1998). Gender gap in the executive suite: CEOs and female executives report on breaking the glass ceiling. *Academy of Management Executive, 12*(1), 28–42.

Scandura, T. A. (1992). Mentorship and career mobility: An empirical investigation. *Journal of Organizational Behavior, 13,* 169–174.

Scandura, T. A. (1997). Mentoring and organizational justice: An empirical investigation. *Journal of Vocational Behavior, 51,* 58–69.

Scandura, T. A. (1998). Dysfunctional mentoring relationships and outcomes. *Journal of Management, 24,* 449–467.

Scandura, T. A., & Ragins, B. R. (1993). The effects of sex and gender role orientation on mentorship in male-dominated occupations. *Journal of Vocational Behavior, 43,* 251–265.

Schaubroeck, J., & Merritt, D. E. (1997). Divergent effects of job control on coping with work stressors: The key role of self-efficacy. *Academy of Management Journal, 40*(3), 738–754.

Sparks, K., Faragher, B., & Cooper, C. L. (2001). Well being and occupational health in the 21st century workplace. *Journal of Occupational and Organizational Psychology, 74*(4), 489–509.

Sprecher, S. (1998). Insiders' perspectives on reasons for attraction to a close other. *Social Psychology Quarterly, 61*(4), 287–300.

Thomas, D. A. (1990). The impact of race on managers' experiences of developmental relationships (mentoring and sponsorship): An intra-organizational study. *Journal of Organizational Behavior, 11,* 479–492.

Turban, D., & Dougherty, T. (1994). Role of protégé personality in receipt of mentoring and career success. *Academy of Management Journal, 37,* 688–702.

Viator, R. E. (2001). The association of formal and informal public accounting mentoring with role stress and related job outcomes. *Accounting, Organizations and Society, 26*(1), 73–81.

Westman, M. (2002). Crossover of stress and strain in the family and workplace. In: P. L. Perrewé & D. C. Ganster (Eds), *Research in Occupational Stress and Well Being: Historical and Current Perspectives on Stress and Health* (Vol. 2, pp. 143–181). New York: JAI Press, Elsevier.

Whitely, W., & Coestier, P. (1993). The relationship of career mentoring to early career outcomes. *Organization Studies, 14,* 419–441.

Whitely, W., Dougherty, T., & Dreher, G. (1991). Relationship of career mentoring and socioeconomic origin to managers' and professionals' early career progress. *Academy of Management Journal, 34,* 331–351.

Whitely, W., Dougherty, T., & Dreher, G. (1992). Correlates of career oriented mentoring for early career managers and professionals. *Journal of Organizational Behavior, 13,* 141–154.

Xie, J. L., & Schaubroeck, J. (2001). Bridging approaches and findings across diverse disciplines to improve job stress research. In: P. L. Perrewé & D. C. Ganster (Eds), *Research in Occupational Stress and Well Being: Exploring Theoretical Mechanisms and Perspectives* (Vol. 1, pp. 1–61). New York: JAI Press, Elsevier.

Young, A., & Perrewé, P. (2004). The role of expectations in the mentoring exchange: An analysis of mentor and protégé expectations in relation to perceived support. *Journal of Managerial Issues, XVI*(1), 103–126.

Young, A. M., & Perrewé, P. L. (2000a). An examination of the exchange relationship between mentors and protégés: The development of a framework. *Human Resource Management Review, 10,* 177–209.

Young, A., & Perrewé, P. (2000b). What did you expect? An examination of career-related support and social support among mentors and proteges. *Journal of Management, 26,* 611–632.

ABOUT THE AUTHORS

Peter Y. Chen heads the Occupational Health Psychology Training program within the Industrial/Organizational Psychology program at Colorado State University. His primary research interests are in occupational health, performance evaluation, training, and methodology. He has published a book, numerous book chapters and various empirical articles appearing in the *Journal of Applied Psychology*, *Journal of Business and Psychology*, *Journal of Management*, *Journal of Occupational Health Psychology*, *Journal of Organizational and Occupational Psychology*, *Journal of Organizational Behavior*, *Journal of Personality Assessment*, *Group and Organization Management: An International Journal*.

Shoshi Chen is a Ph.D. Candidate at the Faculty of Management, Tel-Aviv University, Israel (M.Sc., Organizational Behavior). Her current research interests are: work and stress, preventive stress management, and IT implementation.

Oranit B. Davidson is a Ph.D. Candidate at the Faculty of Management, Tel-Aviv University, Israel (M.Sc., Organizational Behavior). Her current research interests are: job stress and strain, respite relief, expectation effects and self-fulfilling prophecy.

Michelle K. Duffy is an Associate Professor and Gatton Endowed Research Professor in the Gatton College of Business and Economics at the University of Kentucky. She received a B.S. in Psychology from Miami University (Ohio), an M.A. in Industrial/Organizational Psychology from Xavier University, and a Ph.D. in Organizational Behavior/Human Resources Management from the University of Arkansas. She previously worked as a Research Psychologist at the National Institute of Occupational Safety and Health (NIOSH). Dr. Duffy teaches courses in the area of Organizational Behavior. Her research interests include employee health and well being, social undermining behaviors and processes, and team composition issues. Her research has appeared or been accepted for publication in journals such as the *Academy of Management Journal*, *Journal of Applied Psychology*, *Journal of Management*, *Research in Personnel and Human*

Resources Management, Group and Organization Management, Small Group Research, and *Security Journal*, among others.

Rudy Fenwick received his Ph.D. in Sociology from Duke University. He is currently Associate Professor of Sociology at the University of Akron. Previously, he taught at the University of South Carolina. His research interests include the effects of markets and organizational structures on jobs characteristics and worker well being, particularly job stress and participation in organizational decision making. His most recent research has appeared in *The American Behavioral Scientist, Journal of Health and Social Behavior*, and *Journal of Family and Economic Issues*. In 2003, he served as guest editor of a special edition of *Sociological Focus* on "Organizations Transforming Work; Work Transforming Organizations."

Glenda M. Fisk is a doctoral student in Industrial/Organizational Psychology at the Pennsylvania State University. She earned her B.A. degree in psychology at the University of Calgary. Her primary research interests include emotions in the workplace and organizational justice.

Corina Graif received her Masters in Sociology from the University of Akron. She is a Ph.D. candidate in the Department of Sociology at Harvard University. Her interests include studying social organizations, institutions, networks, social justice, deviance, gender, and class inequality. She is also interested in the socio-legal mechanisms behind the adoption of social policy programs in the context of comparative social, political, and economic development.

Alicia A. Grandey earned her Ph.D. at Colorado State University and has been an assistant professor in industrial-organizational psychology at Penn State University since 1999. Her research focuses on the experience and expression of emotions and stress in the workplace, particularly within the service industry and as it relates to work-family issues. Her work in these areas has been published in such journals as *Organizational Behavior and Human Decision Processes, Academy of Management Journal, Journal of Vocational Behavior*, and *Journal of Organizational Behavior*, as well as several book chapters. Dr. Grandey is a member of the American Psychological Association, Society for Industrial and Organizational Psychology (APA Div. 14), and Academy of Management.

Paula L. Grubb is a Research Psychologist in the Division of Applied Research and Technology, Organizational Science and Human Factors Branch at the National Institute for Occupational Safety and Health. Dr. Grubb received her doctorate in experimental psychology from the University of Cincinnati. Dr. Grubb's research interests include workplace violence and psychological aggression, racial/ethnic discrimination, traumatic stress, supervisory best practices, organization of work, and job stress. Her current research focuses on developing intervention and evaluation strategies for workplace psychological aggression, as well as examining workplace violence and psychological aggression policies and organizational decision-making.

Stevan Hobfoll has authored and edited 11 books, including *Stress*, *Social Support and Women*, *Traumatic Stress*, *The Ecology of Stress*, and *Stress Culture and Community*. In addition, he has authored over 150 journal articles, book chapters, and technical reports, and has been a frequent workshop leader on stress, war, and terrorism. He has received over $9 million in research grants on stress and health. Dr. Hobfoll is currently Distinguished Professor of Psychology at Kent State University and Director of the Applied Psychology Center and the Summa-KSU Center for the Treatment and Study of Traumatic Stress. Formerly at Tel Aviv and Ben Gurion Universities, he has also been involved with the problem of stress in Israel. Dr. Hobfoll received special commendation for his research on The Psychology of Women and for his AIDS prevention programs with ethnic minority populations, and was cited by the *Encyclopædia Britannica* for his contribution to knowledge and understanding for his *Ecology of Stress* volume. He was co-chair of the American Psychological Association Commission on Stress and War during Operation Desert Storm, helping plan for the prevention of prolonged distress among military personnel and their families, and a member of APA's Task Force on Resilience in Response to Terrorism. He maintains a private practice as a clinical psychologist and organizational consultant.

Michiel A. J. Kompier has a full chair in Work and Organizational Psychology at the University of Nijmegen (The Netherlands). His research area is occupational health psychology. He has published many (inter)national articles, books and book chapters on topics such as work stress, the psychosocial work environment, mental work load, sickness absenteeism, work disability, work and health, productivity, work-home interaction, and working conditions policies. In his studies the emphasis is on prevention and intervention studies in organizations and applied research methodology. Michiel Kompier is chairman of the scientific Committee "Work Organization and Psychosocial Factors" of ICOH (International Commission on Occupational Health), co-editor of the *Scandinavian Journal of Work, Environment and Health*, and member of the editorial boards of *Work and Stress* and the *International Journal of Stress and Health*.

Shavit Laski is a Ph.D. Candidate at the Faculty of Management, Tel-Aviv University, Israel (M.Sc., Organizational Behavior). Her current research interests are: work stress, burnout and work-non-work relationship.

Lawrence R. Murphy, Ph.D. received from DePaul University, Chicago, Illinois and did postdoctoral training at the Institute for Psychosomatic and Psychiatric Research, Michael Reese Medical Center. He joined the Work Organization and Stress Research Section, National Institute for Occupational Safety and Health (NIOSH), as a Research Psychologist in 1977. He has published articles and book chapters on job stress, stress management, and safety climate, and co-edited several books, including *Stress Management in Work Settings* (1989), *Organizational Risk Factors for Job Stress* (1995), and *Healthy and Productive Work: An International Perspective* (2000). He serves on the editorial board of the *Journal of Occupational Health Psychology*, *Work and Stress*, and *Journal of Business and Psychology*. His current research involves identifying characteristics of healthy and productive work organizations, and assessing the quality of work life using a national sample of U.S. workers.

Anne M. O'Leary-Kelly is a Professor in the Department of Management at the University of Arkansas. She received her Ph.D. in Organizational Behavior and Human Resources Management from Michigan State University in 1990 and previously has been on the faculty at Texas A&M University and the University of Dayton. Her research interests include the study of aggressive work behavior (violence, sexual harassment) and individual attachments to work organizations (psychological contracts, identification, cynicism). Her work has appeared in (among others) the *Academy of Management Review*, the *Academy of Management Journal*, the *Journal of Applied Psychology*, the *Journal of Management*, the *Journal of Management Inquiry*, the *Journal of Organizational Behavior*, *Research in Personnel and Human Resources Management*, *Research in Organizational Change and Development*, and the *American Business Law Journal*. She is a member of the Academy of Management and has been co-recipient of the *Outstanding Publication in Organizational Behavior Award* (given by the Organizational Behavior Division) and co-recipient of the *Dorothy Harlow Outstanding Paper Award* (given by the Gender and Diversity in Organizations Division). She currently serves on the Executive Committee of the OB Division of the Academy of Management.

Rashaun K. Roberts is a Research Psychologist in the Division of Applied Research and Technology, Organizational Science and Human Factors Branch at the National Institute for Occupational Safety and Health. Dr. Roberts received her master's and doctorate degrees in Clinical Psychology from Case Western Reserve University. Prior to joining the research team at NIOSH in 2002, Dr. Roberts was a fellow at Duke University Medical Center in the Division of Occupational and Environmental Medicine, where she developed an expertise in occupational mental health. Dr. Roberts' current research at NIOSH focuses on the contributions of structural and psychosocial variables to the emergence of psychological aggression in the workplace and on understanding the implications of psychologically aggressive behaviors for occupational safety and health. As a member of the Federal Interagency Task Force on Workplace Violence Research and Prevention, she is collaborating to develop NIOSH's research agenda in these areas. Dr. Roberts' other research interests include issues related racial/ethnic health disparities, occupational mental health, and women's health.

Steven L. Sauter received his Ph.D. in Industrial Psychology from the University of Wisconsin-Madison and held an appointment in the University of Wisconsin, Department of Preventive Medicine until joining the National Institute for Occupational Safety and Health (NIOSH) in Cincinnati, Ohio in 1985. He currently serves as Chief of the Organizational Science and Human Factors Branch at NIOSH, and leads the NIOSH research program on work organization and health. He also holds an appointment as an Adjunct Professor of Human Factors Engineering at the University of Cincinnati, Department of Industrial Engineering. His research interests focus on work organization and occupational stress. He serves on editorial boards of several scholarly journals – including *Work and Stress* and the *Journal of Occupational Health Psychology*, he has prepared several books and articles on psychosocial aspects of occupational health, and he is one of the senior editors of the 4th Edition of the International Encyclopedia of Occupational Safety and Health.

Kristin L. Scott is a doctoral student in Organizational Behavior/Human Resources Management in the Gatton College of Business and Economics at the University of Kentucky. She received a B.S. in Business Administration from Villanova University and an M.A. in Human Resources from the University of South Carolina. She previously worked as a Human Resources Manager at General Electric Company. Her research interests include employee emotional responses, justice issues, employee antisocial behavior, and compensation and reward systems. Currently, she has manuscripts under review at the *Academy of Management Journal*, *Journal of Applied Psychology*, *Journal of Management and the Leadership Quarterly*.

Lori Anderson Snyder received her Ph.D. in Industrial/Organizational Psychology from Colorado State University. She is now an assistant professor in the psychology department at the University of Oklahoma. Her research interests include workplace aggression, safety, performance errors, multisource feedback, and the Assessment Center method.

Naomi G. Swanson is head of the Work Organization and Stress Research group at the National Institute for Occupational Safety and Health (NIOSH) in the U.S.

She received her Ph.D. from the University of Wisconsin-Madison in 1989. Along with Dr. Steven Sauter, NIOSH, she was involved in some of the initial research in the U.S. examining the relationship of organizational factors to non-fatal workplace violence. She is currently participating in research examining the relationship between workplace stressors and depression, the assessment of work organization interventions designed to improve worker health and well being, and the assessment of workplace violence programs and practices.

Toon W. Taris is an associate professor at the Department of Work and Organizational Psychology of the University of Nijmegen, The Netherlands. He holds a MA degree in Administrative Science (1988) and took his Ph.D. in Psychology in 1994, both from the Free University of Amsterdam. Since 1993 he has been affiliated with various psychology departments of several Dutch universities and also served as a research consultant. His research interests include work motivation, psychosocial work stress models, and longitudinal reearch methods. Taris has published on a wide range of topics in journals such as *Journal of Vocational Behavior, Personnel Psychology, Journal of Organizational and Occupational Psychology*, and *Sociological Methods and Resarch*. Further, he serves on the boards of several journals, including *Work & Stress* and the *Scandinavian Journal of Work, Environment and Health*.

Mark Tausig received his Ph.D. in Sociology from the State University of New York at Albany. He is has been at the University of Akron since 1983 and currently holds the title of Professor of Sociology. His research interests include investigating the relationships between macro-economic conditions, work organization and worker well being. His most recent research has appeared in *The American Behavioral Scientist, Journal of Family and Economic Issues* and, *The Journal of Health and Social Behavior*. He is also co-author of *A Sociology of Mental Illness*.

Mina Westman an associate professor and Researcher, at Faculty of Management, Tel Aviv University, Israel (Ph.D. in Organizational Behavior, Tel Aviv University). Her primary research interests include determinants and consequences of job and life stress, negative and positive crossover between partners and team members, work-family interchange, effects of vacation on psychological and behavioral strain and the impact of short business trips on the individual, the family and the organization. She has authores empirical and conceptual articles that have appeared in such journals as the *Journal of Applied Psychology, Human Relations, Journal of Organizational Behavior, Journal of Occupational Health Psychology, Applied Psychology: An International Journal*, and *Journal of Vocational Psychology*. In addition, she has also contributed to several book chapters and presented numerous scholarly papers at international conferences. She is on the editorial board of *Journal of Organizational Behavior* and *Applied Psychology: An International Journal.*

Thomas A. Wright is a Professor of Organizational Behavior at the University of Nevada, Reno. He received his Ph.D. in organizational behavior and industrial relations from the University of California, Berkeley. Similar to the Claude Rains character from the classic movie, Casablanca, he has published his work in many of the "usual suspects" including the *Academy of Management Review, Journal of Applied Psychology, Psychometrika, Journal of Organizational Behavior, Journal of Occupational Health Psychology, Journal of Management* and the *Journal of Management Inquiry.* He has consulted with a number of organizations over the years on such topics as: optimizing employee performance and organizational productivity, sustaining employee commitment, stimulating employee motivation, developing employee recruitment and retention strategies, and enhancing employee health and well being.

Angela Young is an Associate Professor in the Department of Management at California State University, Los Angeles. Current research interests include mentoring relationships, organizational relationships, equity and fairness in the workplace, and the interview process. Her work has been published in *Journal of Management, Human Resource Management Review, Sex Roles: A Journal of Research,* and other journals. She has presented her research at numerous conferences including National Academy of Management, American Psychological Association, Western Academy of Management, and Society for Industrial/Organizational Psychology.